THE Eternal Grand Adventure

David L. & Susan F. Flotron
Co-Authors
P.O. Box 33, Jeffersonville IN 47131-0033
TheEternalGrandAdventure@reagan.com
TheEternalGrandAdventure.org

THE
Eternal Grand
Adventure

"Deep Down in the Dirt" Dave (because real life can get real messy real quick) and his "Wonder Wife" Susan (because a fabulous wife can be a real blessing through real life)

Dave and Susan Flotron

ISBN 978-1-0980-5795-4 (paperback)
ISBN 978-1-0980-6397-9 (hardcover)
ISBN 978-1-0980-5796-1 (digital)

Christian Faith Publishing, Inc.
832 Park Avenue
Meadville, PA 16335
www.christianfaithpublishing.com

Printed in the United States of America

Our dear Lord and Savior, Jesus Christ, for his honor and glory

Val Thompson Flotron

Our dear sons, David and Gregory

Our dear daughter-in-law, Ira

Our grandsons, Davey Lee and Timothy Wes

The beloved parents and siblings of Dave, Susan, and Val

Kelly Ledbetter, a wonderful true friend

Grace Coulton, another true friend (and "editor in chief")

Rolling Fields Church

Valley Forge Baptist Church

Southeast Christian Church

Voice for Joanie

The Zion Legion of West Chestnut St. Baptist

The Lockhart Family, A team

And, of course, all the other beloved family and *true* friends far too numerous to mention, in addition to the many, many total strangers who came to our assistance and rejoiced with us in love during our times of both trouble and triumph in this life!

Thank you to one and all!

CONTENTS

PREFACE

Dear readers,

Welcome! We are so deeply humbled that you have chosen to read this book!

Every single person, whether they know it or believe it, is currently on an eternal grand adventure that began long, long ago. In some respect, we sense it deep inside, which is why many of us go through most of our earthly lives with very little thought about our inevitable mortality.

We remember how exciting it was for us when we discovered this sometime ago as well as how exciting it is to this day! It is our hope to share with you, through this book, some of our own triumphs and tragedies as we discover and live out our own eternal grand adventure in an effort to assist you in some fashion to discover and live out your own.

Although this book was written from a Christian perspective, because after all "we are who we are," we believe that Christians and non-Christians alike will find helpful information contained within to help them with some of their own life struggles. And most importantly, for those seekers out there who have a deep desire to search for the truth among the prevalent religious quagmire that society has created, we want to extend this invitation of a behind-the-scenes look at how we addressed it in our own quest for the truth.

So come inside the pages of this book and hold our hands as we show you how an introverted lad was presented with the love of his life as a specifically designed gift. See how he came to discover the eternal grand adventure and everything that came with it. See how our little family was chosen so long ago to live out one of the most vexing questions that has plagued humans for centuries. Travel with us on the journey of a little girl who was raised up in a Christian family and beseeched God for decades to grant her the desire of her heart: to have a husband and a family of her own.

We recognize that some of you may well question, "Who are these people and who or what on earth gives them the authority to write a book such as this?" Frankly, our dear readers, you do! Because whether you love us, like us, or leave us, this is an account of our lives that we saw unfold before us. And we've chosen to share with you the innermost thoughts, feelings, decisions, etc. that we had to go through in an effort to assist as many of you as possible.

So sit back, relax, and share our joy, laughter, and tears as you ponder and even possibly record some of your own eternal grand adventure!

May our dear Lord Jesus bless you and watch over each of you!

Sincerely,
Dave and Susan

INTRODUCTION

ANOTHER PHASE BEGINS

It was winter, January 2010 and there we were…

all alone…

holding hands…

just as we had for so many decades. I'll never forget the feel of her lovely, soft, warm little hand nestled securely in mine. And then it came…

from out of nowhere…

the bombshell…

WHAM*!!!*

… and our entire lives and

world exploded…

...never to be the same again. It seemed so surreal, much like a vivid nightmare, and yet it was all too true. But, for your sake, dear reader, we are getting too far ahead of ourselves. For without understanding our background, the rest of our account may not impact your life as it should. So, please allow us now to take you back: way back in time to another century...the mid 1950's...when we were born in the Midwest.

CHAPTER 1

From a Child's Point of View

Dave

I am one of the midfifties baby boomer generation, the firstborn of a midtwenties couple in St. Louis, Missouri. As the only grandson of both sets of grandparents for the first several years of my life, love and attention were lavished upon me. At that time, we lived on the first floor with three large rooms of a two-story flat. Our landlords and their two adopted teenage daughters, who served as "built-in" babysitters for me, lived above us. All my grandparents and uncles lived in the city as well. Life was so very simple then. A few months prior to my fourth birthday, my next brother came along, and about a year later, I had two brothers.

My dad was the youngest of his parents' three boys. Grandpa drove a tractor trailer for a grocery store chain. One of my earliest childhood memories was of riding in Grandpa's truck with him as he drove his route. It was any little boy's dream come to life! Many was the time after that when I would tie my little wagon to the back of my tricycle and play truck driver.

Although our three rooms were quite large, at that point, our family of five was now packed into them rather tight. That, along with the onset of some urban blight, about did it. Mom set out to find us some better living quarters. Dad was a wonderful daddy and a good provider, but Mom was usually the one to make things happen along with Dad's backing. In short order, they purchased a new house in the suburbs in unincorporated Maryland Heights. It was a very small five-room ranch-style house with three bedrooms, a bathroom and a half with a large backyard, and a full basement in a five-house subdivision wrapped around a street corner. Our house held down one end of the subdivision, the third house from the corner up the street on a pretty steep hill. The old farmer who used to own the land lived on the uphill side of us, and there was a Baptist church across the street from us. Many years later, a smaller church purchased the old farmer's remaining property, so we had a church right next to us as well.

What was obviously a reasonable move for our growing little family, as a small boy, this event was quite traumatic for me. I sincerely doubt that my parents ever had even an inkling of just how much of an effect this had on me. And as a wee lad, I did not have the ability to articulate it to them. Suffice it to say though that it continued to impact my life even to this day. To that end, I have pondered many times to what degree such early childhood events play a significant role in all lives well into adulthood. As for me, deep inside my little boy's brain, it was as though we were moving to the other side of the globe, even though the reality of it was that it was only about a half-hour drive out into the county. But I saw it as being dragged possibly forever away from my beloved grandparents and other relatives and, yes, even my babysitters from upstairs. It was horrible, and I believe it was the catalyst to me being deeply troubled anytime any of my beloved family, true friends, great acquaintances, etc. go out of my life as it takes its toll with all its various twists and turns. But alas, move we did!

Mom was a Catholic as was her mom and stepdad, and so my brothers and I were raised attending Catholic Church as well as attending their school, being taught by nuns and lay teachers. On the home front, Mom was relentless in taking every opportunity to teach us about the world around us. We were constantly drilled on multiplication tables, spelling, correct grammar, etc. Although both Mom and Dad told us that they were open-minded and that we could ask them anything and everything, it was well-known that God and religion were forbidden topics around Dad. Even as a child, I found this to be a bit odd, and I certainly wouldn't call it being very open-minded to not even allow for an open, honest discussion about it. To this day, I honestly do not really know Dad's belief about the existence of God, but my perception is that he was probably an atheist, which is so very sad for me. I've often thought that something very traumatic must have happened to him during his childhood to harden him so much on this subject.

As a young child attending Catholic elementary school, I recall the 1961 election of the Catholic Democratic presidential candidate, John F. Kennedy. Although I knew nothing about politics, I couldn't help but notice that all Catholics were quite excited that one of their own was going to be our president. Even though Mom and Dad were usually quite passive about politics in general and perhaps even viewed most politicians with a good dose of contempt, as loyal union Democrats, even they seemed to be quite pleased as well.

In the fall, a couple of years later, not quite nine years following my birth, Mom and Dad probably had a wee bit of a shock as the birth of my third brother was slated for the following summer. As a practicing Catholic, this shouldn't have been a surprise to them as Catholics in those days did not believe in any form of birth control, and as they say, "nature does take its course." So now our completed family of six was once again packed into our little house pretty tight, but we made it work for us.

Our childhood in suburbia actually was quite nice, even though as a youngster I didn't have sense enough to realize it. After all, we had a loving mom and dad and a stable family and life in a home that they owned. We were middle-class, so we certainly didn't have a lot of luxuries. But we did have a roof over our heads, food, a nice neighborhood, and lots of room to play outside as well. In the larger scope of life, we were very blessed indeed.

Mom and Dad raised us with unconditional love and modeled a very good marriage for us. We were brought up to think for ourselves, use logic, and keep an open mind. We were instructed to do good research and to draw our own conclusions. Mom and Dad encouraged us to get a good education, yet they let us know that everyone had different talents, and they assured us that they were indeed happy if we got a C or D on our report cards as long as that *truly was* the very best that we could do. However, heaven help us if we could have gotten a better grade and didn't. Along with that came the very valuable life lesson that it was bad if I lied to Mom or Dad, but much worse if I lied to myself, for that might carry with it very long-lasting and devastating consequences for my future.

Thankfully, our family learned the art of having a great sense of humor, and we never took either ourselves or life too seriously, although we did know and understand the somber moments as well. In addition, though we certainly had some heated disagreements, my brothers and I all managed to escape childhood and love one another unconditionally into adulthood. Once again, it was an art that Mom and Dad modeled wonderfully for us.

Even at our worst, we always knew that we were still loved by our parents. As a child who was hard wired from birth to function on pure logic while in grade school, I had some logistical problems with the Catholic catechism that made no sense to me. Yet from all outward appearances, I was the stereotypical good little Catholic boy. In fact, for a few years, I even performed my duty as an altar boy. Still, it bothered me. I couldn't quite put my finger on it, but it just troubled me.

From my perspective, it certainly did not seem that the good news of the gospel was all that good. For instance, every so often, I would go to confession and tell the priest what sins I could remember. He would give me my penance, which usually equated to saying several prayers such as five Our Fathers and four Hail Marys, which I would race through as I left the church. Furthermore, the thought occurred to me that by the time I got home, I might commit yet another grievous sin and be hit by a bus and end up in purgatory—sort of an eternal Catholic limbo between heaven and hell—to await my fate. Somehow the other devout Catholics left on earth were supposed to persuade God through prayers and petitions to accept me from purgatory and take me into heaven. One of the ways that they could do this would be to pay to light a candle in the church while they knelt and prayed on my behalf. But how would they even know that God had sent me to purgatory? What if I had forgotten to tell the priest a grievous sin? I simply could not comprehend how saying a few prayers could possibly make me okay to a perfectly holy God. In addition, occasionally, I would hear Dad say things like "those Sunday morning church people who drink and curse and live their lives like everyone else the rest of the week." Sadder still, by even my childhood observations, it appeared that Dad was right! Keep in mind that our home had a church both next door to us as well as directly across the street. Something sure seemed out of whack.

Furthermore, I would overhear some people who claimed that all religions eventually lead a person to the same God while others were touting that God was just a man-made idea to keep society in order. There were those who made God out to be so loving that he would *never* send *anyone* to hell—so it did not even exist—while others taught that everyone was destined to hell, except those lucky few who worked hard enough to appease this angry God and so forth and so on. Another problem was that nobody seemed to know *exactly* what you had to do to make God happy enough with you to grant you a place in heaven. Some of the people really irritated me. I couldn't believe the utter audacity of those folks who spoke as if it was an absolute sure thing that they were going to heaven. How arrogant of them, I thought, to claim that they could predict what this apparently capricious God might do with them! Due to this hodgepodge mess, it was no wonder my dad never wanted to talk about it.

One thing was for sure, all of them couldn't possibly be right, as logic dictated that all their basic premises were entirely at odds with one another. Yet it was obvious that all of eternity literally hung in the balance! How on earth could a person possibly tell *who* was correct, if in fact *any* of them was?

I did have a childhood Bible in those days, and I always treasured it, thinking that it must have some sort of special knowledge in it as you always heard it spoken well of in all of society. However, the several times that I set out to actually read it, I quickly became discouraged and quit. It was just too difficult to read, and it didn't make all that much sense to me at that time. Nevertheless, I went on. In those days, a child knew his place!

Back then, Dad worked long hard hours at the factory and spent at least an hour each day driving back and forth, in addition to all his home and car repair work. Mom was the primary disciplinarian, teacher, loving mom, etc. She was predominantly a yeller while Dad could just look at you with disdain and express how disappointed he was in your behavior. Yet it was not beyond either of them to give any of us a swat or two on our fanny to get our attention and get us back on track. Other than the usual childish nonsense, for the most part, all of us were pretty good boys growing up in the sixties.

President Kennedy was a big dreamer, and he set the nation's goal on putting a man on the moon. Sadly, with his assassination in November 1963, he did not get to live to see it become a reality. I was in school on that day when it was announced. Certainly, as a grade school lad, I had no idea of all its ramifications, but I could tell by how much it stunned the adults and the fact that we were shortly dismissed early from school that this was not at all good, and I feared about how it might impact life as I had known it. Our country's escalating cold war with the Russians and now our race to the moon with them along with the possibility of a nuclear engagement frightened me more than a little despite assurances that everything would be all right by Dad and Mom. In that same vain, I remember being quite worried and asking Mom and Dad why both world wars and others were always fought overseas and none took place in our country. Mom comforted me to some degree by telling me, "Oh, honey, don't worry about such things. God has protected us with two large oceans on either side of our country and a strong military. We would know before they got here, and our military would stop them." It was a nice attempt, but still, Pearl Harbor did take place!

Yet life and times continued on, and the John F. Kennedy assassination drifted ever so slowly into history. Amazingly, Mom saw fit to take all of us out of school on Thursday, October 28, 1965. She loaded all of us into our one and only family car after having much earlier gotten up at the crack of dawn to drive Dad to work and return for us. Off we all went into downtown St. Louis to witness firsthand the placement of the final top piece of the St. Louis Gateway to the West Arch monument. Every moment was a teaching moment for Mom to educate her sons, and she saw this as a historic event that she wanted us to witness.

A few years later in July of 1969 while attending a weeklong Boy Scout camp, about midway into earning my final Eagle Scout rank, I was allowed to witness via a black-and-white TV that they set up for us the realization of President Kennedy's dream of our country putting the very first man on the moon. Our entire country was so very proud of our nation's accomplishments, and I felt so very blessed to have been born here.

All through my school years and into my early twenties, I have been somewhat of a shy nerd, particularly in school and around strangers, and have to some degree felt relegated to the status of the odd man out. At home, I was usually a bit older than most of the children, but too young for the adults, although I attempted to gravitate toward them as they allowed since I had spent the first several years of my life around adults. At school since I was shy, I found it difficult to make friends, and in the seventh grade when I switched from parochial school to public school, the other kids had long since formed their little cliques, and that made it difficult for me.

I remember the decade between sixteen and twenty-five (1970–1979) as being one of the most difficult periods of my life. By all outward appearances, I seemed to be the smart, polite Catholic boy. But on the inside, I was a wreck, complete with hormones bouncing around throughout my internal organs.

Due to both God hard wiring me that way as well as my childhood experiences, I am logical to the nth degree while artistically in the negatives. Logic and math? You bet! I'm your guy! Music and art? I have neither a clue nor desire for them, although—thanks to Mom—I do appreciate and respect those who do, as well as the great masters! However, for me to be able to accept anything, much less be passionate about it, I must see that it makes logical sense with respect to the rest of life that I have lived and see all around me.

I recall a lovely day when Mom and Dad herded us into the family car with the promise of an exciting adventure. So off we went, with the four of us no doubt bickering about territory infringement in the back seat or some other really important childhood event. "Mom, he's on my side!" "Are we there yet?" "He's looking at me!" The drive ended at a small airfield where Mom and Dad spent their hard-earned money to show us the excitement of air flight. I'm not sure how long the flight in the little plane lasted, but I vividly remember getting off back at ground level thinking to myself, "Well, *that* will never happen again!" Thus, I developed the second phobia that has plagued me the rest of my life. Little did I know! The first being "white coats"—doctors, nurses, et al. Yep! I was one of the kids that the doctor had to literally chase around the office to get a shot! And I distinctly remember thinking, "Someday I'll be as big as you, pal. Then we'll see what will happen!" Little did I know what life would bring me in my later years!

Please understand as you continue reading on and from time to time I address this topic of my white coat phobia that my fear is literally off the chart. I feel compelled to address this further lest you misunderstand me. As it is mentioned later, it may appear that I have a seething hate and contempt for all medical professionals. That is not the case. Intellectually, I fully well recognize that God gave us those talented people to help us and cure us of some very dreadful diseases. They study long and hard to learn about the very complex bodies that God gave us. However, I write about them throughout the book to attempt to give you a very brief glimpse into what I feel deep inside in the core of my very being any time and every time I am forced to interact with them. I neither like it or want it, but nor have

I been able to rid myself of it, as I certainly would if I could. But it is much like the flip of a light switch deep within me that automatically flips when I am in their presence, and every atom within me wants to immediately run and escape from them.

Even as a child, I was concerned about my mom's health. I always remembered her as a large lady. As a result, I was frequently worried that she might die prematurely as a result. Mom was a prolific photographer and quite good at it, so most of the family pictures did not have her in them. I'll never forget the first time I saw her wedding album and how beautiful, fit, and trim she was in those pictures! It was astounding! But that brought up yet another fear: Why does Dad stay with us? After all, it seemed that all he did was work, work, work. He had a herd of kids around all the time, and his previously very attractive bride was rather, well, fat! So why stay around? And so the years slid by. Little did I know at the time that later in life I would be so very blessed to have two wonderful ladies come into my life.

Val

About ten months after my birth, Val was born in South St. Louis. She was the youngest with two older brothers. All three were born about a year apart. Val's mom was a housewife who did not drive, and her dad drove a tractor trailer for a living all his adult life.

While I had a very good childhood, sadly, from Val's perspective, she did not like her childhood all that much. Among other things, in those days, her family had joined a nondoctrinally sound church. She lamented to me many times that the church forbade them to celebrate any of the typical holidays, such as Christmas. Needless to say, for a wee little girl, this was traumatic!

It should be noted, however, that Val's mom and dad did not have the best of childhoods either, so neither of them really had a very good example to draw upon when they began to forge a family of their own. Val's dad left home when he was very young and enlisted in the US Army while underaged—lying about his age. When he took his young family to live in California for a few years, he had an uncle that continued to challenge him on intellectual things to the point where her dad decided to go to the library to do his own research. Thus, he began quite a library of his own. As a result, he is no doubt one of the best self-educated people that I have ever met. Suffice it to say, I'm sure her parents did the best that they knew how to do.

Val did, however, have two great lifelong friends that she grew up with on her block. Debbe lived at the corner on one end of the block, Val in the middle, and Denise in the house on the other corner of the block—all on the same side of the street.

Susan

My eternal grand adventure began in the midfifties as the firstborn of our family. I began life only about a month after Dave's birth about 750 miles away from him near Philadelphia, Pennsylvania. My dad was from a very large family of nine children. His Polish parents had come over to the United States, and Dad was born here. As a young boy, Dad's mother taught him how to put coal in the furnace in the basement and how to empty the ashes. He was also sent up to the railroad tracks to pick up coal that had fallen off the railroad cars to bring home to heat their house. Grandma or "Babchia"—the Polish name for Grandma and the name I called her—was very affectionate to Dad, but she never learned English. Dad used to tell me that she would often call him "Edju, kochanie," which meant "Edward, honey." Sadly, Grandpa died when Dad was only thirteen years of age.

On the other hand, my mom was the younger sister of only one brother, and she grew up in eastern Pennsylvania. As a young girl, Mom always enjoyed riding the trolley cars into the big city of Philadelphia where she eventually got her first job. Both families were very religious with Dad's family being of Catholic background and Mom's that of the Lutheran faith.

Dad was drafted into the navy just before completing his senior year of high school in World War II. He served in the engine room of the heavy carrier ship named the *USS Wichita* while operating in the Pacific Theater of the war. While in the navy, Dad began reading a book titled *The Robe* by Lloyd C. Douglas. That let him begin to wonder about the existence of God. Mom completed high school but never went onto college. After Dad finished his enlistment in the navy, he met Mom at a dance in the Philadelphia suburb of Upper Darby, Pennsylvania. Mom and Dad dated for about a year. Following their courtship and marriage, Mom and Dad settled down in the Greater Philadelphia area. Several years later, I came along. They later purchased a local hardware store and lived in the town of Crum Lynne, Pennsylvania. As a wee little girl, I certainly enjoyed playing with all the little nuts, bolts, and other cute items Dad had in his hardware store.

One of the most traumatic events of my life occurred when I was too young to have a personal recollection of it, but I learned about it later from my mom. All throughout my life, I have been very curious about the world and how it works. Apparently around the age of two, I was curious about what Mom was cooking on the stove. Even though I was told many times to go out of the kitchen and stay with my grandma in the living room, my curiosity got the best of me and I reached up to grab the handle of the pot and pulled it over to take a look. Unfortunately, the pot contained boiling water which poured all the way down my left side. Yep! I'm a southpaw, a left-handed person.

I was rushed to the hospital with second- and third-degree burns down my left side. I had to spend quite a few days, probably around a week or two, in the hospital to be treated, which included skin grafts. Although healed, I am still left with several scars as a reminder. Fortunately, due to my parents taking me to the Atlantic

Ocean for summer vacation that year, the doctors believe that helped minimize the scars on my face. Little did I know at that time, I was later able to use this experience many times as an object lesson for my students in listening to and obeying their parents.

All during this time, Dad had continued on his cursory search for God. One day, Dad thought he was experiencing heart palpitations. He went to his doctor who examined him and informed him that he did not have a heart problem but what he did have was a "God problem"! And so Dad began a newfound serious search for God and found him on his own while reading his Bible. He enrolled in the Philadelphia College of the Bible for about a year, and then Mom and Dad decided to move to Texas so Dad could study to become a preacher.

Life in rural Texas was quite interesting to this young girl as I had many animal friends: dogs, cats, rabbits, chickens, a rooster, and even some geese. In fact, I even picked up a nice Texas drawl, y'all!

I was quite young in those days, perhaps around four years old. Mom and Dad took me to church every Sunday, and I learned about the core Christian values, such as how sin entered into the world through disobedience and how the love of Jesus for us was shown by his sacrifice on the cross to allow us to have a home with him in heaven for all of eternity. At one point, my dad asked me what I had learned in Sunday school, and I responded that I learned about heaven and wanted to go there. Dad read to me the John 3:16 account that God had given his only Son, Jesus, for the world as a free gift of forgiveness of our sins and salvation. To make sure that I thoroughly understood that verse, Dad had me insert my name into that verse so that it became "God so loved Susan that he gave his only Son, Jesus, as a free gift for the forgiveness of Susan's sins." That very day, in childlike faith—just as the Bible teaches—I accepted Jesus as my personal Savior.

Sadly, my Texas drawl was lost, y'all, when Dad moved us back up to eastern Pennsylvania about three years later to start his own Baptist church. As with most new pastors' families, we had very limited resources in those days, but we did have our faith in our Creator's care for us. Upon arrival in our new town of Harrisburg,

Pennsylvania, Mom asked Dad to stop off at the local post office. Dad asked her, "Why? Nobody knows us here yet, so who would be sending us any mail?" Nevertheless, Mom persisted, so in we went. Lo and behold, awaiting our arrival at the post office were two envelopes, each containing a check for us! One was payment for a couch we had sold, and the other was simply an anonymous gift for us. What an amazing God we have! Of course, Dad and Mom immediately went to work trying to find us a place to live. As it turned out, the low-rent housing that they finally secured was being vacated by a family that also had a young girl about my age, and we became good friends and have remained friends to this day. In addition, the home came complete with a piano that Mom used in that house when Dad started up his new church. Yes, indeed! Our great God surely provided for our little family!

As life went on as a curious only child, I wanted a sister to have as a playmate. Mom was quite content to have just me and told me that I would have to pray for one. And so this little eight-year-old certainly did! Well now, wonder of wonders, along came just that—a sister for me! Then lo and behold, about a year later, another sister was born, and a few years later, my brother was born! God gave me quite a few playmates—more than I ever expected! And that completed our happy family of six! In addition to now having several built-in playmates since I was quite a bit older, Mom also used me as her built-in babysitter from time to time.

My childhood memories, although generally happy ones, do include that my next oldest sister seemed to always be following me around, and the next sister seemed to always be getting into my things, which from her perspective was way better than what she had. Our young brother, on the other hand, was quite the jokester and played many pranks on me through the years. However, on at least one occasion, it backfired on him. It seems that he was hiding in between the pews in the dark auditorium of Dad's church, ready to scare me as I would be coming down the aisle with an armful of books. When he jumped out at me and scared me, I dropped the books, and according to my brother, I jammed his head with my knee into the wooden pew, and blood came gushing out, which resulted in him blaming his innocent sister for being responsible for a poor little five-year-old boy having to go to the hospital to get stitches in his head!

Of course, this older sister is quick to bring up the bygone memory of the time when we were older and I took the same brother to sled near Italian Lake. My brother went down first and was waiting for me at the bottom. In those days, we had the old wooden sleds with metal runners and handlebars for steering. So I lay down on my sled with my hands on the handlebars, and down the hill I went. As I got near my brother, he ever so mischievously kicked my handlebar, causing the sled to veer off course, landing me in a nearby gravel-filled ditch. The gravel ripped through my glove and into my hand and wrist, and once again, off to the hospital we went. This time, I was the bloody one getting sewn up. These little escapades, as well as several others, were events that later on would bring any one of us to stitches during our later years. And as you can see, dearest reader, a pastor's kids aren't always quite as holy as others may think! Still, we did have a happy, loving family!

In our childhood years, my dad had purchased a large three-story house that had previously had a dance school on the lower floor that Dad transitioned into the church auditorium, and we lived on the upper two floors. As a family, we had several dogs and cats for pets. In addition, somehow we always seemed to manage to attract stray female cats ready to birth a cluster of kittens. So over time, we had several "border" cats and kittens that soon became ours to love.

One of our pets was a dog we named Spotty, which looked a lot like a dalmatian but was actually a German shorthaired pointer. One day after a rainstorm, Spotty somehow managed to get up on the roof of the house. We searched and searched the house looking for him and finally found him on the roof. When we called to get him back into the house, Spotty went running toward the fire escape and slid on the slick rooftop and skidded right off the roof, three stories down onto the ground beneath. We thought for sure that we would have to scrape up poor ol' Spotty's dead body off the ground. But thankfully, due to the heavy rain, Spotty was alive and well, leaving only a small crater in the soft ground as a reminder.

Beginning in my elementary school years, math was never my strong suit. Thankfully, in fifth grade, my compassionate teacher, Mrs. Houston, took me under her wing and helped me considerably. I will forever be grateful to her for the extra time she took to coach me along.

CHAPTER 2

Tumultuous Times

Dave

As our family of six grew older, Mom took a job as a part-time school bus driver and also decorated cakes out of our home to help make ends meet. Somewhat of a perfectionist, her cakes were fabulous with elaborate detail. I would help her deliver them. In addition to working at the factory all day, Dad maintained the house and cars and started a small heating and air-conditioning business from home.

Yep! With the advent of the seventies, our family actually had two used cars and a color TV, but still no remote control. Our one phone was hung on the kitchen wall and tethered there by a four-foot cord. People actually still had face-to-face conversations, and wonder of wonders, we all lived through it! Just imagine! A time when churches, gas stations—where they actually pumped the gas for you, washed your windshield, and gave you a free drinking glass for filling up at the unheard-of price of twenty-five cents per gallon—and shops were on each street corner rather than crack houses. It was a time when young ladies and children could safely walk the streets at night and play outside without fear of being abducted or murdered. Suicide bombers, drive-by shootings, and the like never happened. Even criminals had some sense of morals and decency. In world competitions, American students consistently beat students from all other countries. It only made sense that we were the first country to have a man walk on the moon! Yet time rolled on.

As we all got busier and busier, Mom slowly but surely stopped taking us to church on Sundays. As for me, while I never completely closed the door on God altogether, I certainly pushed the door almost shut, leaving it open only a small crack, just in case. During the high school years, I was still the introverted nerd who died a thousand deaths at even the thought of having to do an oral book report in front of the class. As with most folks, I suppose, the high school years bring back many bittersweet memories complete with hormones bouncing off the walls, plenty of activities, falling in lust, etc. It was pretty much an emotional roller-coaster ride! Now that was something totally foreign to my otherwise logical upbringing! I usually had at least an hour or two of homework each day in order to maintain As and Bs on my report card since I was still in the honors' classes. At some point, I recall coming to the realization that I was actually intellectually smarter than Mom and Dad. It was a bit frightening, yet they constantly cheered me on.

Sadly, since I had been an introvert for so many years, I also found that I really had very little use for other people. Quite frankly, at that time, they were little more than an irritation to me. For the most part, most folks seemed to be irrational and illogical. My leisure time was devoted to playing chess—I did need an opponent to move the other pieces—hunting for fossils, playing softball, Boy Scouts, etc. At that time, I aspired to become a geologist, and I was well acquainted with the Darwinian theory of evolution, which certainly seemed plausible, but again, I had some nagging concerns. The first was pretty obvious: If it were true, why do we not see a plethora of living things in various stages of evolution? In addition, decades later, nobody had yet come up with any of the many transition fossils that would have to be necessary to support his theory. Furthermore, the well-known Cambrian explosion in the fossil record was undeniable and certainly shed a very dark outlook for Mr. Darwin's theory. The Cambrian explosion was a relatively short geologic time period in which virtually, on a global scale, most of our current living species suddenly appeared with no known transition fossils. Given this much damning evidence, I found it very bizarre that the public schools taught the theory as pretty much a foregone fact, rather than precisely what it is, merely one person's—rather weak—theory.

One of my personality traits that had plagued me all through childhood and into my early twenties was my lack of patience. I suppose that was one of the reasons I had so little tolerance for most people back in those days. For instance, perhaps I was trying to turn a tight nut on a bolt with a wrench. After some time, it seemed to me as if the nut would almost be taunting me. My response would be "Oh yeah! We'll see about that," and snap, the bolt would break due to my adrenaline-pumping turn of the wrench. This, of course, would cost me a trip to the hardware store to purchase another bolt or possibly a new wrench. Sadly, thickheaded as I was in those days, this went on for many, many years. All of a sudden, one day, a couple of important facts occurred to me: first, this process was costing me a considerable amount of time and money, and second, these were usually inanimate objects which had no brain and therefore could not think, much less purposely taunt me! Obviously, I was my own worst enemy! Now, if we're at all logical and honest with ourselves, we would come to the inevitable same conclusion that I did: as a general rule, whenever things are going wrong or irritating us, the culprit is usually as close as the nearest mirror! *I* needed to change *me*!

Now that I'm considerably older, I have come to realize that the maturing process for adolescent boys is indeed very difficult, and parents need to be critically aware of that and attempt to help and encourage them through it to ensure that they will transition into stable and responsible young men. They need to learn to tame and control their anger and take responsibility for their actions.

During the slow arduous process to do just that, I learned yet another life lesson: bad habits are very, very difficult to break! That being the case, it only stood to reason that our development of good habits in life is the key to relieving ourselves of the long tedious process of having to undo bad ones! Thus, I began to deeply analyze in minute detail every single thing that I did. For example, when taking a shower, I always start by shampooing my hair and working my way down to the feet. It just made sense. To do it any other way is an error. Otherwise, the nasty, dirty, germ-laden rinse water would be going over a part that I just cleaned. It amazed me as I began to change some of the things that I had been doing and watch how others approached various tasks in life. Having observed other people through all these decades later, it still surprises me that an entire huge herd of folks seem to go through most or even all their lives totally oblivious to why or how they approach anything in life. Even worse than that, they spend the entirety of their lives without even beginning an investigation into whether or not eternal life is even a possibility and, if so, how does a person qualify for it? It would seem to be an issue important enough to at least devote a portion of your life to do some thorough investigative research on it. After all, if a person were even to attain the ripe old age of say two hundred years—let's be really generous—that is considerably less than even the tiniest drop in the bucket of all of eternity!

But I have digressed: since none of the school students lived any place near us, I really didn't have much of a chance to associate with them outside of school until I began to drive. Most of the guys that I ended up running around with were pot smokers, but they all knew that I wouldn't stand for it, either in my parents' car or while I was around. Consequently, whenever they wanted to partake of it, they would look at me and say, "We're going to smoke some weed in a few minutes, and you're welcome to join us." I would simply tell them, "No, thanks! I think I'll just be heading back home," and off I'd go. Now please don't misunderstand me. I did have my share of sins and bad habits. My theory at that time was pretty simple: Why do dope, which could potentially get me in some real bad trouble, when alcoholic mixed drinks—which tasted good—were available to me, even though I was underaged? I had my sources, but I did have to be careful about it! Coming home to Mom and Dad in their car plastered would not have worked very well!

The majority of adolescents today both amaze and frustrate me. On the one hand, most of them claim that they want to be their own person, but the reality of it is that if their school buddies do anything, get anything, etc., they go into hysterics to do it or get it as well, even to their own peril! It amazes me that they cannot see the repercussions looming ahead. The long-range effects of drug or alcohol abuse is painfully obvious: potential bodily harm, vehicle collisions possibly injuring or killing innocent people, increased insurance rates, loss of vehicles, jail, or perhaps even death! Any one of those has the very real potential of, at a minimum, making life very difficult going forward, if not totally ruining a young person's life entirely. Is the so-called "enjoyment" of a couple of minutes or even hours *really* worth the risk of those kind of consequences? Think about it! It is flabbergasting and obvious that they have no idea of what a *real* friend is all about, much less *real* life. With "friends" who suck you into that type of life, who needs any enemies? Sadly, those *real* friends are both few and far between, but you have to be willing to be a true friend in order to find a couple of them. And you also have to have the courage not to associate with people who will drag you into a pit of tragedy. It is all about getting rid of the fake nonsense and living a *real* vibrant life! So young folks, *please* think about your long-term future before you act on anything or accept people into your life!

In those days, Frank was our scoutmaster. He was a great guy, and his middle son, Steve, was a scout who was my brother's age. I met Frank when I went to his house to earn a merit badge. He was my counselor, and I liked him so much that I transferred into his troop. One day, when I was a junior in high school, I was working on a project in his basement when it happened. My, oh my! Out of nowhere down his basement steps, she came—Frank's oldest daughter, Carol, who was my age. I couldn't believe my eyes! Kindhearted, long blonde hair, gorgeous beyond my wildest teenage imagination! It was a case of instant lust! Yet what a dilemma! I was still that introvert with three younger brothers, having never given girls much thought, much less date one! Still…there she was!

I was at my wit's end! Finally, many weeks later, I worked up enough nerve to ask her out over the phone. Amazingly, she agreed to go to the junior prom with me!

It was awkward, but off we went in my mom and dad's station wagon. I was a nervous wreck but had a great time. We went on several more dates, but for no apparent reason, she stopped going places with me. My little heart was crushed! And being the introvert, it took me a long, long time to work up the nerve to ask another girl out.

For an introverted Catholic boy going to school during the sixties, the sexual revolution was pretty much a nightmare. Talk about some mixed signals! During my senior year of high school, I distinctly remember sitting in a class and suddenly realizing that I was one of a very, very few students whose parents had never been divorced. From that point on, I often wondered why I was so lucky, and the few times Mom and Dad had a disagreement, I figured this was it, they would get divorced.

With Frank and my parents urging me on, I did manage to earn my Eagle Scout rank. I decided to go with a high school friend to pledge a fraternity at a small-town engineering school about a one hundred miles from my parents' house to get a degree in geology. It was a mistake! In retrospect, I think I would have been much better off staying at Mom and Dad's house and attending the local university. When high school ended and I realized how radically my life would change, how uncertain the future really was, and how *huge* life on earth really is, I was scared to death!

Sadly, throughout my life, I have certainly sinned in almost every category imaginable, but it was never more prevalent in my life than during my late teens and early twenties. I mention this not because I'm at all proud about it but rather to show that even though I might have appeared on the outside to other people as the good little Catholic boy, the reality of it was that I was not. For instance, around our house, I spoke like a gentleman, but around my friends, I cursed like a drunken sailor. Now this was a wee bit of a dangerous practice since the least off-color word in Mom's presence could well get you hit in the back of your head with *Webster's Dictionary* followed immediately by Mom's admonition to pick a better word! As the years progressed, I began to be afraid that I might just accidentally slip in front of the wrong person(s), so I began to clean up my act on my own.

While away at college, I quickly figured out that the frat life was not for me, so I rented a room at the back of a garage at an older couple's house. It wasn't great, but it served its purpose. Sadly, one of the few bad high school teachers that I had was the chemistry teacher. My aspirations to obtain a geology degree quickly went up in flames due in no small part to my lack of knowledge in chemistry. However, I did learn several very important life lessons while away at college.

Due to my mom teaching us to be fiscally responsible, I was always a saver and had some money already saved. Although the two-year experience at college taught me quite a bit, I expended most of my savings and still did not have a degree to show for it and had to move back in with Mom and Dad. Since my parents were still raising my brothers, I worked part-time while I went to college to pay for it.

While at college, I was taking an English literature class which was given by a professor in a huge auditorium with many students. During that class, I became enamored with a young lady sitting not too far from me with long brunette hair, who apparently sat with a friend of hers. Still being the shy fellow, I observed her from afar, and she seemed to be very nice. I thought it would be great to go on a date with her, but I could not get up the nerve to ask her to go on a date with me, not to mention that I did not even know her name.

So I devised a plan to at least learn her name. The next test we had, I finished my paper but held on to it, waiting for her to finish and turn in her paper so I could put mine on top of hers and see her name. It worked! Her name was Dana. Now if only I could get her phone number, but how? In those days, people were more trusting, and if you played your cards right, you could find out things from them much better and easier than you can today. So I called the college and got her phone number. Still, as a shy lad, it took me quite a while to work up the nerve to call her while I pondered what I might say. Finally, one afternoon when I was home all alone, I picked up the phone in our kitchen and dialed the number. A deep male voice answered and said, "Hello." To which I inquired, "May I please speak to Dana?" And he responded back with "This is he." Well now… who knew! As it turns out, Dana can be either a boy's name *or* a girl's name! It also turned out that amazingly they both had the same last name as well. I apologized, and sometime later, I did manage to land a date with the young lady from that class. But although I had a good time, we only went out together just that one time.

Another time, I had my one and only semiblind date. I categorize it as semiblind because of the manner in which it came about. Mom was in the hospital for a female surgery, and she roomed with a fabulous lady who was a few years younger than her. When I went to visit Mom, I always had a great time with the roommate. I thought it was such a shame that she was not in her early twenties as I was; we could have had a wonderful time together. But, alas, she was not only older but also married with children. Well, next thing I know, she suggested that I take her daughter out on a date. I was ecstatic! After all, if she was even one-tenth as good as her mom, it could possibly work out. My, oh my, what a catastrophe! I took her to a nice Chinese restaurant for dinner and sadly told her we would go to a movie afterward. All night long, she had nothing to say but negative comments about virtually every person anywhere near us. I sat there in utter dismay. I couldn't even believe what I was hearing. I mean these were people we didn't even know—total strangers. How on earth could she have that kind of reaction to them? Worse, I wasn't exactly a people person in those days either. But good grief, all I could think about was "How could this sourpuss possibly be the daughter of that fabulous lady in my mom's room? There is no way I'm going to sign up to listen to this for a second date, much less the rest of my life!" And at the end of the night, just like almost every guy on earth, when I took her home, I lied through my teeth and told her that I had a great time and would call her again. Deep inside my head, of course, my brain was thinking, "But not in this lifetime, honey!"

Sometime later, I ended up working as a part-time school bus driver for a huge school bus contracting company. At that time, they were operating 4,900 buses across nine states. Sixty-five buses were assigned to our location. It was the same company where my mom had driven for years. The company operated busing services for many school districts. All their buses were for sale, and they leased buses to other school districts and various groups and offered charters and special events as well. Our particular garage was a large sales' facility, and that was where I met Wayne, the head of bus sales and a member of Mensa. He was a very smart fellow!

Wayne had heard that I was good at math and approached me to do some statistical analysis of the bus sales and the bus contracts. I agreed, and not long after that, I became the assistant garage manager and, a little bit later, the garage manager. As a garage manager in my early twenties, I was blessed to have an assistant in her midfifties who taught me quite a bit about not only the bus business but life as well. During that time, I had gone on a few dates with a young lady who grew up down the street from us. We seemed to have really hit it off, and I thought they were the best dates I had ever been on. We even discussed it in the car after one of the dates, when a scant few days later, out of the blue, she mailed me a "Dear Dave" letter. I couldn't believe it! Total devastation! Once again, my little heart was crushed, so I pretty much resigned from dating yet. I had taken a long hard look at Mom and Dad's lengthy marriage and still really had a deep desire to have what they had. It was a pretty good life!

Still, having your heart torn out of your chest and getting it stomped on was not exactly a barrel of laughs! Oddly, through most of my life, I had always had a lingering premonition that I would end up marrying a broken lady and that I would die young—early to midfifties. All through the tumultuous dating years, I had a pretty solid mental checklist of what I was looking for in a young lady: kind heart, nonsmoker, long straight hair, fun loving, no prior children, capable of loving me unconditionally as I would her, and so on.

It just seemed to make sense. After all, marriage "'til death do us part" is a substantial amount of time, and Mom's stellar advice to me and my brothers of "make sure you pick carefully" rang in my ears. One of her other pieces of sage counsel was "Keep in mind, fellas: women play at sex in an effort to get love while guys play at love in an effort to get sex." Again, truer words were never spoken! And might I add that, in those days, they were rarely spoken. Society as a whole simply would not allow children to be exposed to the constant barrage of sex, sex, sex as they sadly are today. Dad's advice was much more straightforward: "Love 'em all like God does!" Strange words, I thought, from a fellow who doesn't even allow conversation about the Almighty, and it certainly didn't seem like sound advice.

While working at the bus garage, I could not help but notice that our head mechanic always read his Bible during lunch and was always such a nice fellow, in addition to being a championship mechanic. I started asking him about his Bible reading, and he offered to take me to his church with his wife. I accepted, still on the quest for exactly who the *real* God is or even if he existed and, if so, could it be proven or just what. I was initially surprised at the large number of people in attendance. The service was very nice, and all the people seemed very nice as well. However, in the middle of the service, for no apparent reason at all, the minister started just uttering totally unintelligible babble, and not long afterward, the entire congregation joined him. I was stunned. Had the whole lot of them taken total leave of their senses? Several moments later, again for no discernable reason, they just stopped, and the service continued as if nothing ever happened. It was totally weird. I went back a couple of more times just to make sure I wasn't missing something, and sure enough, the same thing happened each time. That was enough for me!

In the meantime, as garage manager, I now had to give safety meetings to the drivers. This, of course, meant standing in front of all of them and talking for about an hour. It was horrible, and I hated it. I decided to have Logical Dave analyze it. After all, if I wanted to keep the job, I had to learn to deal with it. And deal with it I did, and slowly but surely, I made progress with my fear of doing it through self-analysis.

About a year had passed since my last date with the young lady from down our street, and I found myself more or less praying to a God who I was not even sure about and certainly did not know very well. I asked—as best I knew how—if he would help me find a wife. The odds seemed well beyond those of winning the lottery. After all, as big as the entire world was, how on earth could *anyone* find *the* woman of their dreams? Their soul mate or whatever else you wanted to call it! I simply could not fathom it and obviously was no good at finding her on my own! This rejection by the past dates now made me 0 for 6 for success with the number of women I dated!

And *that*, dear reader, was the point I was at when one of the most memorable collisions occurred in my life!

Val

During her high school years and early twenties, Val was gorgeous and ran with the popular crowd. She had a heart of pure gold but was always up and ready for a good prank. However, around unfamiliar people, she was pretty introverted, yet she never lacked having a date. She told me that she dated many guys named Dave and always had a premonition that she would eventually marry a fellow with that name.

In her early twenties, she was engaged to a fellow named John, but they never did set a date to get married. She told me that they quarreled quite a bit during the engagement. One day as she was driving alone, she said it was almost as if a large hand of God slapped her in the face in the car and instructed her to break off the engagement with John. It was so vivid to her that she did just that, but Val also had a deep longing to get married and often prayed for a husband. However, she said that she always had a deep-seated fear that she would end up with a beer-guzzling alcoholic.

Although I'm quite sure that Val's dad loved all his children very much, he did run a pretty tight ship. Consequently, I think Val was always trying to win his approval but never thought she ever got it, which was very difficult for her throughout her life. And *that*, dear reader, was where Val was at exactly the point where the most memorable collision occurred in her life!

Susan

During my middle school and high school days, I walked about a mile to school with a friend. During the high school days, I was well-known for being a Christian girl, and sometimes the other kids even made fun of me. Due in part of this, I did not have much of a dating life. In fact, I believe the young fellows were a bit afraid of my dad being a preacher!

I became active in the school choir and took classes that contained music theory, etc. One of our highlights was singing in the rotunda at the state capitol during Christmastime. On another occasion, I received twenty-five dollars for winning a contest by writing a jingle for the Easter Seal Society. And amazingly, our choir was actually viewed on a TV cable show while singing Christmas carols. Although I never became an accomplished guitarist, my interest in music prompted me to take guitar lessons for about a year, and I did play some very simple tunes for various groups.

Summertimes included attending Christian summer camps at Camp Maranatha in western Pennsylvania where my dad took groups of teenagers from church youth groups. Most summers, I would have to have poison ivy shots as I usually ended up being covered with it while scouting about in the woods. In fact, one year, some of the girls and I were wading in the lake together and had to quickly scamper onto shore to escape a water snake that we had spied. Overall, I had such fun during those times that, after my first year of college, I served as a camp counselor there for the week that the youth of my church attended the camp.

During my senior year of high school, I had already accumulated enough credits to graduate, so I only had to go to school for the first half of the day. As a result, I would leave the school and go home to have lunch with my mom, and afterward, she would take me to my very first job at Woolworth's. As the new kid at their store, I was placed in many different roles to fill slots as they needed me. I served in their jewelry and infant departments as a salesclerk and did several promotional events as well. One of those promotional events had me making and handing out popcorn and cotton candy to the customers. Now that was quite the "sticky" little situation! Yet another memory from those days was when a fellow from that store invited me to go to lunch with him. I accepted his invitation, but nothing further came from it. Nonetheless, I was scared to tell Mom and Dad that their little girl had actually gone to lunch with a guy!

Also during my senior year, I began making plans for college. My heart's desire was to return to Texas, but about that time, I had heard of a new college that had recently been established in Virginia, so my parents and I went to investigate it. Unfortunately, at that time, neither my parents nor I could afford to send me to that college. My God, however, works in mysterious ways and blessed me with having a scholarship to cover the cost of all four years as long as I kept my grades up to standard. I had taken an eye exam at that time and was told that because I was legally blind in my left eye, scholarship money was available to me. How very blessed I was!

During my freshman year, I took general education courses in an effort to determine what would interest me. During my sophomore year, however, I began to take courses to pursue a teaching degree. Ah, the college days! I had so much fun, and they were the best years of my life, up to that point!

I'm sure that my experience of having my fifth grade teacher, Mrs. Houston, coach and encourage me as I struggled with math had a profound influence on me later in college on my decision to devote my career to teaching little elementary students. I simply loved those children and did my very best to invest in their continued education to the very best of my abilities. And my, oh my, has it ever been such a joy to me that so many of them have kept me posted of their life journeys over the decades. It has been fabulous seeing them grow into fine young men and women. Thankfully, years later, as a college student while I was home for the summer, I was given the opportunity to reunite with Mrs. Houston while waiting in line at the local grocery store. This enabled me to thank her for the extra time she spent with me as a much younger student of hers. She was thrilled when I informed her that I was studying to be an elementary teacher as well. In both seeing her joy and later personally experiencing that same joy in my own life of hearing about the lives of my own students, I would highly encourage anyone who had such an extraordinary teacher of their own to go back and tell them how very much it meant to them.

During our childhood years, Dad often took our family camping in or around Cape May, New Jersey, for our vacation. We always had such fun there together! So as a young single college-girl, I felt very blessed to have gotten a summer job at a local Cape May hotel—the Christian Admiral—following my freshman and sophomore years. This was, of course, a dream-come-true job for any college girl! Within a two-block area, I had access to the house the hotel used to house their summer help, my job, and the ocean beach. And once again, I had a job where I could help in several different areas: working the front desk, teaching the Bible to the children during Bible conferences held there, serving ice cream at their internal ice cream shop, etc. And during one of the summers, a young fellow who also worked at the hotel had a pilot's license and took me up in a four-seat plane for my first-ever plane ride to view the ocean from the sky! As an adventuresome young lady, I simply loved it!

However, one of the sad points of my life was that dating was still very limited. While I did have a few dates, nothing ever became very serious. Nevertheless, I always managed to have many guy friends, but they treated me simply as their sister. So I began to pray that God would send me a husband as I watched other friends begin a newfound married life of their own. During my junior year, I did have my first serious dating relationship with a young college fellow. We had a great time on several dates for about three months. At about that time, he wanted to have a more physical relationship than I was comfortable with, so he ended up breaking it off and went back to one of his prior girlfriends.

After graduation, I began my new teaching career at my dad's Christian school as a K first grade teacher. As a young teacher, I was able to display some of my creative talents. I produced yearly Christmas plays for the school while Dad built the backgrounds for us. We even performed one year at our local shopping mall. And time rolled on.

CHAPTER 3

A Collision of a Lifetime

Dave and Val

As I worked at the bus garage, unknown to me, Val's dad was driving his truck down the same street. It was the middle of winter, yet he urged Val to apply there as a bus driver despite the fact that it was easily a thirty-minute drive from their house on a good day. Needless to say, in the school bus business, that is not exactly desirable as you have to make the commute twice each day—once in the morning and once in the afternoon. As a manager, like in most transportation companies, I could never get enough drivers, so we were usually hiring. The first time I ever heard Val's voice was when she called me to ask about a job. I encouraged her to come in to apply and explained the job to her over the phone, just as I had done countless times before for other applicants.

Lo and behold, a day or two later, Val came in dragging her mom behind her. And once again, the first time I saw her, I thought, "Wow! What a cute-looking gal!" With short eyelash-cut dark hair and huge brown eyes, she looked remarkably like Liza Minnelli! While I wouldn't say that I was instantly in lust with her, she certainly got my attention and intrigued me. Still, there were several immediate problems: (1) I was not thrilled to stick my heart out there again and risk getting it crushed and (2) the bus company had a very strict no-dating policy, and she obviously wanted a job, and I needed a bus driver or two. All that notwithstanding, she violated several items on my mental checklist, not the least of which was that I was enamored with long blonde hair while hers was as short as short could be and brunette. Still, there she was—cute as cute could ever be! Needless to say, I hired her and trained her to be a school bus driver.

That first date

As the weeks rolled on, my intrigue with Val increased, and I did my research. Single, check! Ten months younger than me, check! Nonsmoker, check! Sadly, about six weeks after I had hired her, Val resigned. On the one hand, I lost a driver that I would have to replace, *but* on the other hand, this certainly opened up other possibilities! My poor little brain was racing: "Ask her out or get my heart stomped!"

I remember sitting at my desk, holding her final paycheck in my hand, pondering whether or not I should ask her out. Or if I even had the nerve to do so, my poor brain was now in overdrive.

Finally, after working up the nerve, I called her at home in the evening and oh so cleverly asked her if she wanted me to mail her final paycheck to her house or hand deliver it to her on a date. I was amazed when she agreed to go out with me. So she gave me directions to her house, and the date was set. I couldn't believe how far away she lived. The longer I drove, the more I chided myself for even going out with her. "How stupid," I thought, "you're going to drive to the end of the earth, and this gal is going to end up dumping you just like the rest and crush your stupid heart once again! Well, pal, you deserve it!" But then there was a flash of brilliance: "Wait a minute…not if I dump her first!" So the stage was set in my little head. If the least little thing went wrong on this date, I was out of there!

It had snowed a few inches the night prior to our first date despite that I had taken the time to meticulously polish the car for that all-important first impression. I parked on the street and rang her doorbell. Val came out wearing open-toed sandals! "Strike one! I mean, I'm by no means a fashion guru, but sandals in three inches of snow? What on earth did I get myself into now? Somebody, help!"

So I took her by the hand and carefully walked her through the snow to the car.

Off we went to my favorite Mexican restaurant, only to discover that there wasn't a chance on earth that we would get a table in time to make the movie I had planned. "Strike two!" Granted, it was my fault as I did not get a reservation, but poor Val got the called strike, landing her only one more strike before being called out! So we ended up at a different restaurant that was certainly nothing to write home about. In hindsight, I'm surprised I didn't issue her the third strike and call it a night! We ended the date at a movie that I simply hated. You guessed it, strike three! Once again, having practice from the blind date, I took Val back to her house and heard my mouth for the second time utter those infamous words "I had a great time, I'll call you" while my brain was thinking, "But not this lifetime, sweetie!" And off I went scurrying back to the safety of my room in my parents' basement!

The roller-coaster ride takes off

So life went on back at the old bus garage just like normal. I had an assistant at that time who was a woman in her midfifties. She taught me quite a bit: how to negotiate, handle dicey situations, etc. I did not tell anyone about taking Val out on a date. A couple of weeks later, my assistant told me that I had a phone call holding and that it sounded "like that girl, Val." I couldn't believe it! I thought my brain was going to explode as fast as it was racing. I picked up the phone and felt a split second of relief as I heard an older woman's voice on the other end. However, that was quickly shattered when she said, "Hi! I'm Val's mom. I think she would like for you to come over and have dinner with us." I honestly think smoke must have been rolling out of my ears at that moment. Amazingly, this time, my brain was thinking, "Just say no, just say no, just say no" at the speed of light while I heard my mouth spit out okay. I about died right on the spot! "You are an idiot!" my head shouted at me. It turned out that Val had placed the call, but by the time I got to the phone, she had chickened out, but her mom had held the line because Val had told her how great our first date was and how disappointed she was that I had not called for a second one! Sometimes it seems to be very strange how these things end up working out, or is it?

The snowball starts rolling downhill

Nevertheless, off I went for my dinner date at her house. Amazingly, it was great! We had a dish she called "perfect pasta," which is essentially spaghetti with meat sauce. Since I'm pretty much a culinary disaster, with the exception of eating, it was comforting to know that Val could indeed cook! Thoughts drifted back to the days of eating Dad's bologna sandwiches—since he was a great mechanic but wasn't much of a chef, we ate them morning, noon, and night—while Mom was in the hospital giving birth to our last brother. We sat and talked for a while afterward and had a great time. She revealed to me sometime later that her perception of our first date was that it was fantastic and she could not understand why I hadn't called her again. I confessed to my blatant lie. After that dinner, Val and I started dating each other once or twice every two weeks. It didn't take very long for me to realize that she had a very kind and tender heart and that she was introverted, except with family and friends.

Meanwhile, back at the bus garage, my assistant told me that she thought one of our bus drivers was smitten with me. Now *that* was a first! I asked her what made her think that. She then asked me, "Haven't you noticed who is parked outside our gate each morning recently awaiting your arrival and who stays late? Why do you think she does that?" Uh-oh! In fact, I had *not* noticed. But sure enough, not long after that, she approached me and asked me out on a date. I turned her down as gently as I could, telling her that I had recently been dating another young lady, and we had been hitting it off pretty good. But the reality of it was that I wouldn't have gone out with her even if that had not happened as I knew that she was a single mom. In those days, my mindset was firmly set that I would not even consider a lady with a child. I figured that such a gal needed to go back to the fellow with whom she had fun making the child and have him help her raise the child, but I certainly wasn't going to do it.

One day as we were talking, Val told me that she liked me from the moment she met me but never thought that I would ever ask her out as she had categorized me in her head as a Mr. Professor Owl, meaning that she thought that I would think that I was too intellectually superior to take a girl like her out on a date. I told her that I was also attracted to her but thought that she was far too beautiful to go out with a fellow like me. I explained to her why I didn't call her back after the first date, how I had always been the one getting my little heart crushed by the ladies, and how I had determined not to let that happen again. Basically, she got the whole story. Afterward, I asked if she would make a pact with me to tell each other exactly why if we ever decided not to continue to go out with each other. "After all, if you don't like the way I part my hair, I might agree to change it for you, but if you can't stand my face, well, adios!" We further agreed that either of us could date anyone else up to the point that we decided together that we would only date on an exclusive basis. To Logical Dave, that only makes sense. Isn't dating the precursor to an eventual marriage? Why then should either party restrict their search to only one person? If you do, you sure had better pick right!

On one of our dates at her parents' house, we were sitting on the couch watching TV and talking to each other. Suddenly, my attention was drawn to a framed eight-inch-by-ten-inch photograph sitting on the TV set. It was a picture of a simply gorgeous brunette with long straight hair. I looked at it, looked at Val, etc., back and forth between the two, unable to recognize if it was indeed her. Truth be told, I've never been very good at that, which amused the two of us through many of our times together. Finally, unable to figure it out, I asked her, "Who's that in the picture?" I was pleasantly surprised to hear her say that it was of her when she had long hair. I was even more pleasantly surprised when she said that she would be happy to grow it out for me! I have always been highly attracted to ladies with long straight hair. Years later, we would sit on

the couch side by side, and I would wrap her hair around my neck. We nicknamed her hair "husband's delight"! And it was certainly that and much more! From that point on, our courtship was like the proverbial snowball rolling down a steep hill. Looking back on it, I still can't believe it. And wow, what a courtship it was!

The courtship

Our infamous first date was around Valentine's Day. I immediately won points because I cared to send the very best Hallmark, and it was a one-dollar card, which was impressive back in those days. Little did Val realize it at that time that she was on the brink of courtship by the self-proclaimed "King of Romance" and "King of Greeting Cards." All the way through our romance, I did my very best to create wonderful memories for her. The make, model, or price tag of a greeting card has never meant anything to me. I could literally spend hours trying to select exactly the right card for the recipient. Well into our marriage, I'll never forget the first of two times that I opened up her card to me on Christmas and found myself face-to-face with the identical card that I had selected for her. I was dumbfounded and thought, "Uh-oh, how did she do *that*?" It was not unusual for us to pull little love pranks on each other, and I thought she had just upped the ante on me. Nope! It was simply that we had both selected exactly the same card for each other on our own. Talk about an eerie feeling! But back to our whirlwind courtship…

Although I certainly didn't recognize it at the time, in retrospect, having compared "notes" with Val, it was truly remarkable to see how God put the two of us together. Granted, some may look at it as a coincidence, but given the multitude of ways, our marriage never should have happened. I simply find it too overwhelming. At any rate, the longer we dated, the closer and closer the dates became until I quickly found myself driving to be with her at every available moment. Her dad remarked many times that she would breathe in and I would breathe the same breath out. He was right! By now there was no doubt that I was truly in lust with this young lady! Some may find it interesting that I use the word "lust," but that was exactly what it was. Now had you asked me back in those days, I would have said that I had fallen in love with her. But now that I have seen a substantial number of years more of life, I have a much better realization of the difference between lust and *real* love. It is sad to me that our English language affords us only one term for love. For instance, I love my parents, brothers, and many other people. But it is a much different type of love than I had developed with Val as my wife. It is even sadder to me to see the devastation left behind because the vast majority of our single population have bought hook, line, and sinker the Hollywood concept of boy meets girl, go to dinner, hop in the sack together, and call it love. It simply is not! To those who disagree, I say, "Check back with me in ten, twenty, thirty years or just continue reading to the end and then tell me about it!" Val told me much later how refreshing it was during our dating time to go out on a fun date with a guy and come back home later without having to worry about him molesting her. Well now, that being said, I was in quite a perplexing situation with her. Keeping in mind, I was still essentially the introverted nerd who now is in total lust with this cute gal yet with very, very little experience with women—romantic or otherwise. Still, I would like to kiss her at some point! Talk about a lady created just for me! A couple of weeks later, Val asked me why I hadn't tried to kiss her yet. Sensing that she was giving me the green light yet heeding my wise ol' mom's advice, I told her that I certainly wanted to, but I wanted to make sure that she and I could be friends before we got the romantic snowball going too fast with no chance of stopping it. During the next few dates, I was torn apart between the Lust-Filled Dave who desperately wanted to kiss her and the Logical Dave who admitted that Mom had a good point. After all, marriage is a very, very long commitment!

Remember the old original five-flavor Life Savers roll that my grandma used to give me as a wee child? Cherry, orange, lemon, lime, pineapple. As it happens, those Life Savers became very instrumental in me gaining an important insight into championship relationships.

Val and I were driving on one of our first few dates, and I just happened to have a new roll of those in the car. I opened it up and asked if she would like one.

She said sure, so I handed her the red cherry one that was on top. The next one was orange, so I rolled down my window and tossed it out. I thought she was going to have heart failure on me! Turns out, she actually *likes* those nasty old orange ones! And suddenly, it struck me: this could be great! If she likes some of the things I don't and vice versa, how grand would *that* be? Turns out, it's wonderful! So many, many times, we were able to play to each other's strengths and support the other's weaknesses. To name just a few, she was artistic, but I am not. I am logical, and math is a strong suit, but not for her. She would draw things for me, and I was always available to instantly compute the best deal for her when we went shopping together. Sadly, I see so many couples argue over differences that they could choose to use to their advantage. We would often order mixed vegetables at restaurants because we knew in advance which of us was going to eat which vegetables, etc., etc. It was great!

Prior to meeting Val, you might say that my dad's oldest brother—my uncle—and I were a bit fanatical about tennis. It was nothing to meet each other at six o'clock in the morning at the local public park and wait for the park ranger to open the park so we could practice with each other for several hours. In fact, we were so die-hard that we made it a requirement that we each had to carry a push broom, squeegee, and shovel in the wintertime because—sun, rain, or snow—we *were* going to play! Yep! Many was the winter that we played after shoveling the court off! We were very competitive with each other. The bottom line was the other player was simply *not* going to score the next point!

In late March, it was still pretty cold when Val piped up and suggested that the following Saturday we go on a midnight picnic together. She charged me with setting it up and said that she would provide the food. Her suggestion brought back those fond familiar memories of that first date of ours. All I could think of was she must be nuts! Yet once again, my mouth said okay. I couldn't believe that I had agreed to this one! I told her that my uncle and I had indoor tennis court time that evening, so she would have to go watch us, and we could leave on the picnic afterward. It was all true, and she agreed. In retrospect, I honestly believe that a good deal of my lust for her came from some of her off-the-wall moments such as this!

That first kiss

That midnight picnic was the time that Val partially found out just who she had gotten involved with. It took me hours and hours of thought, planning, and finding the exact location that I needed. After our tennis match, I walked Val to the car. Her picnic basket had already been safely stowed in the trunk. The food was bound to be fresh as it was flat freezing that night! I was always an old-fashioned gentleman on all my dates: opening all the doors, making sure that my dates were seated, and so forth. It was quite a pleasant surprise to me on one of our earlier dates when we arrived at our destination and I had honestly forgotten to open the car door for Val. I was several steps past the car and looked back to see why she wasn't holding my hand as she usually did, only to find her still sitting in the car, watching me, and waiting for me to come back and open her door. What a classy lady!

As we sat in the parking lot of the tennis facility, I was on pins and needles wondering how well she would like my plan. I looked at her and said that I wanted to blindfold her at this point so she could not see where we were going. I wasn't sure if she would go for it, but thankfully, she told me to go ahead. So with her blindfolded, off we went into the clear, cold, dark night. Upon arrival several miles later, I told her to just sit in the car and wait while I set up the picnic. It probably took me about five minutes to get it all set up. I came back to get her out of the car and asked her to keep the blindfold on, hold my hand, and follow me. I carefully watched over her and walked her up a pretty steep grassy hill. I sat her on the blanket that I had spread out, gave her our first kiss, and took off the blindfold. From Val's perspective, we were sitting on a candlelit blanket suspended in space with stars all around us, her picnic basket and a red rose sitting in a vase with the candle on the blanket and some extra blankets to keep us warm. It was a hit and a half! What she didn't know was that we were actually in the middle of a baseball field with the lights from an entire large subdivision just below us where I had parked. All she could see was the stars from the night sky and our candlelit picnic area!

Suffice it to say that with that first kiss, our romance was rolling down the hill at a faster and faster pace. Several times in the distant past, I had asked Mom, "How do you *know* that you have found the right girl to marry?" Her answer was always the same: "Honey, you'll just know." That only compounded the issue further for her logical son who was looking for a checklist to find the answer.

On one of our dates, I took Val a pretty good distance to play indoor volleyball with a group that I had played with previously. It was noncompetitive coed with all different skill levels of players. We ended up going there a few times. During one of those dates, I noticed that a fellow who drove a very nice-looking car seemed to be interested in her. Several times, I watched what appeared to be him making advances toward her, although I could not hear what they were saying to each other. Part of me was afraid that I might actually lose her, yet I figured that there was no time like the present to find out where we stood with each other. After the session was over and we were driving back to her house, she looked at me and told me that another fellow tried to get her to allow him to take her home. I feigned surprise and said, "Really? Apparently, that didn't work out too well for him, did it?" She told me that she had told him that I was her date and that, since I took her here, I would be the one taking her home. Not long after that, I started thinking and analyzing, "Uh-oh! This could actually be it! Look at the amount of time we spend together. Look at how much alike we think on the important things and how well we complement each other on the nonessentials. Look at how kindhearted she is, how beautiful she is, etc., etc., etc." By now, even though I was totally consumed with lust for her, I began to look at the situation from a much different perspective. After all, Val could *really* be the girl I had hoped for, prayed for, and dreamed about. So I began turning much of our dating conversation to much more serious topics, like "How many children would you like to have?" "If you were to get married someday, how would you envision it being like?" And the more time we spent together, the more we wanted to be together to the point where we were practically inseparable other than while I worked or when we were each at our respective parents' homes each night. I felt like we were living out the actual *The Patty Duke Show* theme song: "They laugh alike, they talk alike, at times they even walk alike…" Nevertheless, even though I was young, I began to feel like I was wearing pretty thin, "meeting myself coming and going," and I was a wee bit concerned about how long I could keep it up, despite the fact that I was in pretty good shape at that time.

One important item that we discussed and agreed upon was that we both wanted to have two children and that we would make every effort to live off my salary alone in order to allow her to raise our children in our home. We both understood full well that this decision meant that our family would probably have to live in what society would call a lower lifestyle of not being able to buy a brand-new car or eat out every week, but we both felt that raising our own kids was significantly more important than whatever the rest of society thought about us. This being only one of many, many areas in which it is critical to select a spouse who shares your worldview! To do otherwise is pretty much courting an eventual train wreck at some point in the future. It is strange to me how few people that I talk to are even willing to consider it. Often, I will ask either of two people dating each other questions like "Which of you will manage the money and be responsible for it?" "How many children does your dating partner want?" "Where will you live?" Sadly, more often than not, I'm told, "Oh no, we can't discuss *that*! If we did, (s)he might not marry me!" "Really? Great! Maybe today is the time to find out before you have two kids and a mountain of other problems."

All through our courtship, Val's dad and brothers, though cut from a much different cloth than I was, were my biggest fans. I think they all admired me for how I detailed the car to take her out and how much of a gentleman I was to her. One rather warm day, I arrived at Val's house to take her on a date, but she wasn't ready yet. So I found myself standing on the driveway talking to her dad who was seated in a lawn chair. At some point amid the chitchat, he looked right at me and said, "So, young man, what do you think about God?" I couldn't believe it. Was he talking to *me*? Didn't he realize that I was only there because I was in lust with his daughter? Where *was* she anyway? I didn't know quite know what to answer nor exactly how to answer, much less what on earth he was expecting. I managed to mutter something to the effect of "I'm not really sure. I've never seen him or met him or anything, but I suppose there *is* a God." Without missing a beat, he then hit me with "Well then, how would you answer this question: How many animals went on Noah's Ark?" What? He can't be serious! Who is this guy anyway? Where *is* Val? Again, I was at a total loss. I mean, what did he want—a number? Who on earth would even know? As I racked my little brain and attempted to get him to at least give me a clue about what on earth he was driving at, it became apparent that he was serious and no clues would be coming. Then another stroke of brilliance hit me and I answered with "I would presume two of all of them." The words barely left my lips when again he looked straight at me and countered with "What if I told you that you were wrong?" I responded with "I guess I would be shocked as I thought everyone knew that two by two they went on the ark. Are you telling me that I am wrong?" Artfully sidestepping the question, her dad continued, "From whence did you come upon this knowledge?" Though I was somewhat polite, I retorted, "I assumed it was common knowledge among all people, with the possible exception of you." Armed with my grade school Catholic catechism background, I admit that I was a bit arrogant about this line of questioning. Nevertheless, in roughly two point three seconds, he responded with "Yes, in fact, you *are* wrong!" He then went on to advise me to check with God in the Bible and gave me a clue that I might possibly find what I was looking for in Genesis 7:2. Furthermore, he made it clear that he was not going to tell me the answer. *Finally*, Val appeared and we departed on our date. Of *all* days for her to be late! Normally, she was right on time!

Well, my dear reader, how would you have answered his question? No cheating!

Your answer: ____

Not only did he have me intrigued but also given that there was certainly a very high probability that I would see him again in the near future, I thought it might behoove me to actually look up the answer. If nothing else, deep inside of me, I did have high hopes that I would be able to prove him wrong! So look it up I did! Oops! Lo and behold, he was correct, I *was* wrong!

I went back to him as soon as I possibly could and humbly apologized and told him the correct answer so he would know that I did in fact find it. Again, he looked at me intently and said, "Here's a lifetime tip for you, my boy: you will do well if you have any questions about life to go directly to God to get *his* answer. Don't trust me but don't trust anyone else, not your preacher, TV preachers, or anyone else. Go directly to God through his Bible." Ah, if only I hadn't been so hardheaded in those days and had listened to him at that time! Although his advice was never forgotten, sadly, I did not see fit to act upon it as proactively as I should have.

By now it was well into spring, and I was invited to go to my friend Steve's wedding at the other end of the state, which meant I would have to stay overnight. I informed Val, and she was disappointed that we would be apart most of the weekend. I can't really remember how or why, but somehow it came up in front of her dad. To my utter astonishment, he asked me, "Why don't you just take her with you?" I couldn't believe my ears, but I responded with "I would, but I really can't afford to pay for a second motel room." And then he absolutely flabbergasted me with "Well, why don't the two of you shack up in one room then? After all, you're practically married as it is!" Dumbfounded, I managed to stammer out a feeble okay. Talk about a brain full of exploding fireworks!

Nevertheless, let me just say that this decision was a *huge mistake* that I would pay for many times over and that I would *never ever, ever* recommend it to anyone in the future!

It seemed like an eternity, but that Saturday finally came, and off I went to pick up my date for the entire weekend. Now I don't know if any of you have ever driven across Missouri on Interstate 70, but it is pretty flat, straight, and just plain boring. When you couple that with a young lad in total lust with a lovely young lady sitting next to him and raging hormones bouncing all over the place, you have a very interesting situation! And when you interject the fact that this young lad comes from a long line of lead-footed drivers, you have the making of a big, fat speeding citation.

Looking at it in the past, it was funny. There I was with her sitting right next to me, just flat flying low down westbound Interstate 70 early Saturday morning on a sunny spring day with very little traffic on the highway. We're talking pretty much forty to forty-five miles per hour over the speed limit when I did spy on the eastbound side of the highway coming in the opposite direction a county police officer. In a split second, I reasoned, "Well, no need to slow down now. He either had a radar bead on me, or he didn't!" So I kept on rolling! Not long after that, I saw the tiniest black speck in my rear-view mirror get really big really quick! Guess who? It turns out that the good deputy was a bit of a Southern-speaking fellow in about his midfifties. He asked for my license, registration, the usual things and said, "Son, whar's the far?" (Roughly translated: "Where's the fire?") He took me back to his car, and I explained the situation to him. To which he responded, "Wall-ll-ll, ya cudof at leest slowed it down sum when ya seen me a-com, but no ya just had to make me a-chase ya down. Wall-ll-ll, sonny, I'm a-gonna haf to give ya a ticket now." I flat messed up and should have hit the brake the moment I saw him to save him the time and aggravation of coming back to get me. Consequently, he was going to punish me with a big fat speeding ticket. I tried to explain to him that I would have but that I figured it was too late anyway, and I apologized profusely, but to no avail. He wasn't all that happy with me at the moment. Disheartened a bit about the ticket but still with hormones bouncing around the interior of our vehicle, we set off again, but I did trim the speed back to only about ten miles per hour over. Sadly, this was neither my first nor my last covert roadside meeting with traffic enforcement officers of the law! Moreover, since I had high hopes of being able to work at Val's dad's new company in the future, I knew that when we got back, I would have to fess up to him about the citation! Nuts!

With all the excitement of a newlywed couple on their honeymoon, we arrived at our motel a couple of hours later. We got dressed and headed off to the wedding and reception, hardly able to contain ourselves, eagerly awaiting the end of it all! After all, we had things that we needed to investigate!

We arrived at our little nest after the wedding festivities in anxious anticipation. Val was about to discover a couple of tiny, little items that I had not disclosed to her up to this point. Suffice it to say that with my experience level at a solid zero, there were some performance failures on my part. Val was gracious but not too happy about it. Sadly, stupid bonehead that I was, I didn't explain this to her either before or immediately after. On the way home, it got to the point where I parked on the shoulder of the highway to give her all the details. That pretty much did it! She was *very* gracious after that, and it was never an issue in the future. All through our subsequent marriage, many times, Val would introduce me to people as her "virgin husband with two kids." Now while some guys might well cringe at a title like that, I proudly wore it as a badge of honor! I had always heard the saying that "love is blind." It certainly is, and so is lust! I found it pleasantly surprising that some of the very things that teenagers fret over and are mortified by can be the very things that are special and endearing to couples deeply in love with each other. For instance, how many young people are just horrified to wake up the morning of the big date to find a nice juicy zit on their face? I know I was! But interestingly, I have a large area on the upper part of my back that is pockmarked by teenage acne craters. Val's initial response to seeing it for the first time was "Oh my, I guess poor Dave must have fallen into a snake pit and got bitten so much. That must have been very painful for him." Conversely, after we had dated many, many months, she was concerned about what I thought about her huge legs. I hadn't even noticed until she said something about it. Yet bless her heart, she was always self-conscious about them. I simply loved her just for being her and could have cared less. Similarly, the bottom four teeth of hers were very crooked and had large spaces between them. Once I found them, I was totally in love with them and dubbed them my "picket fence." Sadly, it wasn't until many, many years into our marriage that I came to realize and understand just how much they bothered her. I noticed that she had been smiling and talking without exposing them down to a fine art, which explained why I never found them for a while. I about cried the day we went to the dentist to have them extracted and replaced by a nice straight bridge. It literally broke my heart, yet she beamed with delight! I was so very happy for her! I simply loved every teeny, tiny, little atom of her just exactly the way God made her!

Each year in the late spring, after most of the schools closed for the summer, the school bus company had a management meeting in Kansas City for all the garage managers. A few weeks prior to that, I had virtually been running myself ragged and pretty much felt like Val and I were married already. A typical weekday for me was to wake up around five o'clock in the morning to open the bus garage by six o'clock in the morning, wait for the last bus to return around six o'clock in the evening, drive thirty minutes to Val's house, go on a date or simply just be with her, drive another thirty minutes to arrive home around midnight, and replay it all week long. Somewhere in between, I had to eke out some sleep and a shower, etc. I must say it was all purely lust driven. After a date one night, I sat with Val and explained the problem to her and that, unless she wanted to end up with a dead guy, we needed to do something. I suggested that she try to find an apartment for us to live in and to let me know. I told her that the next time I was over at her house, I wanted to ask her dad for permission for this new adventure. She thought it was a horrible idea, but I was able to talk her into it. Little did I know!

Sure enough, the next weekend, I went to her house, and everyone was there. Following our mutual little Kansas City tryst recently promoted by her daddy, I saw no problem with my idea. Oh, boy, was I ever wrong! He went ballistic! We ended up discussing it outside on his driveway. "You're just going to knock up my daughter and leave her with a mess!" he snorted. I countered by telling him that I had only the best intentions and relayed my time dilemma and that we would work on getting married as soon as possible. He came back by suggesting that we pack up and elope to Tennessee or somewhere and get married. He even offered to give me his boat as a gift if I would do it. I declined as the romantic in me wanted my wife to have a fabulous wedding with photos to treasure through the years. Thankfully, her middle brother came to my rescue, and though her dad wasn't happy about it, he accepted it. This part, I did right! My goodness, Val and I looked through that wedding album over and over and over together through the years! She thoroughly enjoyed it!

Sadly, I did my parents a huge disservice at this point in time. I went home and packed my suitcase to go on the mandatory week-long Kansas City trip. I think subconsciously I thought it would break my mom's heart, so I neglected to mention that I would be bypassing their house on the way back to start a new life with Val at the apartment. Sure enough, several days later, Mom tracked me down and called the apartment to inquire. "I guess this means that you won't be coming home." I felt so very ashamed of myself and still do.

Susan

As time rolled on...

After about five years of teaching at Dad's school, enrollment had dropped off to the point that sadly he ended up having to close the school. So I began to look for another position in my teaching career. My search led me to a small Christian school in Morton, Pennsylvania, a suburb of Philadelphia.

I accepted a first and second grade teaching job and moved to a one-room apartment. Dad and Mom helped me move in as it was only about an hour from their home. All my furniture was moved, except my mattress and box springs. Dad put them up on top of my car roof and secured them as tight as possible. There would be someone from the school to help me once I arrived. After saying my goodbyes, I was off on my new adventure with the cargo on top of my roof. The highway entrance was about ten minutes from my mom and dad's house. Once on the highway, I slowly got up to the speed limit, when all of a sudden I heard a loud bang. As I slowed my speed down, I looked in my rearview mirror, and I saw my box spring lying in the middle of the road with a semi barreling down at top speed. I pulled my car over to the side of the highway and watched as the huge semitruck hit the side of my box springs, and it splintered all over the road. My mattress had bounced over the rail and into a ravine. You can only imagine my horror as I watched this all unfold while I stayed safely inside my car. Another car stopped and asked if they could help, but they really couldn't. My mattress and box springs were now gone forever. Since this was before we all had cell phones, the only thing I could do is turn around at the next exit and head home to tell my dad the news. How did it all end? you ask. Well, from what I can remember, I ended up getting a new box springs and mattress at a local place near where I moved, and they delivered it and set it up for me.

I stayed at the school for one year and then accepted a job at another Christian school in Aston, Pennsylvania, teaching second grade. I had a good year at both of these schools, but a friend of mine whose husband was stationed in Norfolk, Virginia, while in the military told me about a Christian school her kids were attending in nearby Virginia Beach, Virginia. Being the adventurous person that I am, I applied and was accepted to teach second grade. Dad and Mom helped moved me again. I stayed with my friend for about a week while I searched for another apartment.

Teaching phonics to Southern second graders was quite the experience for this Pennsylvania girl. I certainly was not prepared to hear these little ones speak with such a pronounced Southern twang. During the year that I was there, I joined the single's class at the church. On one of their activities, we went to a shooting range. I had never before even looked at or held a gun. So it was a bit scary for me, but I went ahead and tried my hand at shooting at the paper dummy. I hated it. The pistol that they provided for me was awkward to hold, and my arm hurt holding it in a certain position. Even though we had all the safety gear on, I didn't like the sound or how I felt after I pulled the trigger. It was quite the experience. In the spring, I joined a women's softball team from the church. I played second base and catcher for our team. Even though I am not experienced playing sports, I did enjoy my time with my teammates. Dating in the early to mideighties was nonexistent, even though I had my eye on a few young men.

And time rolled on…

CHAPTER 4

The Fabulous Marriage That Never Should Have Happened

Dave and Val

And so the die was cast. There we were. Yet another live-in, love-in couple of the eighties. Though it did work for us, statistically, this is still a *huge mistake*. And knowing what I now know through solid research, I would *never* recommend it to anyone! *Please get married first!* And *please* be *totally* committed to it. Divorce is simply *never* an option!

This was an enlightening period for us. In both of our minds, we were truly married already. We were operating totally on pure lust, but also on pure commitment to each other. We were simply going to be "lifers," and that was that. Separation, divorce, none of that was an option for us. We simply forced ourselves to make our relationship work out. In addition to our lust and commitment for each other, we also had whatever meager pieces of furniture that people gave us or that we could afford to buy. For many, many, many months, she slept on a single mattress on the bedroom floor, and I slept next to her on a single box springs on the floor. It was fabulous—and uncomfortable! Her brother gave us an ancient refrigerator, and my mom got us a dining room set that she bought at a yard sale. Val's parents gave us a couch and love seat, and we had a small black-and-white TV that was Val's.

We immediately went into the stereotypical husband-wife roles. She took care of the apartment, packing my brown bag lunch each day and sending me off to work early in the morning. It was a bit of a surprise to me when we had our first disagreement, and in the heat of the battle, out of sheer frustration with me, she winged a bottle of something nearby out the door onto the yard beneath. After we had resolved our differences, I insisted that she go retrieve it and told her that I was not going to live a lifetime with a spouse that would allow a disagreement to escalate to the point where we started calling each other names and throwing pots and pans at each other. That was the start of us learning how to properly resolve our differences and how to graciously engage in battle with each other. It was a great learning incident for both of us, and like all future disagreements, neither of us ever brought it up again.

But of course, we did have disagreements throughout our marriage. Her dad used to point out, and rightly so, that we practically had to make up trivial things to argue about as we were so closely matched on the really important things. He used to chide both of us with "Both of you really need to kiss and make up and put this thing behind you. Stop and think about it. A day or two from now, a week from now, neither of you will even know what this argument was about nor care about the outcome. In the broad scope of your lives, it really doesn't matter at all." And of course, he was right!

As the weeks rolled on, Val began to exert a little bit of pressure on me to get her a ring, set a date, make wedding arrangements, etc. Unfortunately, poor Val was unaware that her romantic roommate had already started the process. Little did she know that prior to my birth, my mom had worked for a downtown jeweler. I had Mom set up an appointment to go see the fellow. What an education that was for me! An appointment? She had to be kidding me! Don't you just walk in the door, pick out your ring, pay, and go home? Nope! In fact, you don't, at least not in Mom's world! The big day came, and off Mom and I went downtown in the big city. To my astonishment, she took me to a door with bars on it that was locked tight as a drum. She pushed a button on an intercom system next to the door, and I heard a male voice inquire, "Who is it?" Mom identified herself and told the man that she had me along with her. The door buzzed. Mom opened it, and in we went. We were in a dark, dimly lit small foyer at the bottom of a dark narrow stairway leading up to the second floor. I must admit I was a bit concerned about exactly what we were getting ourselves into. Up the stairs we went. At the top of the staircase was a nice-looking well-lit room behind a well-marked business door, again with security bars and again locked up tight with another intercom. This time, the middle-aged man behind one of the counters looked up, and upon seeing Mom, the door once again buzzed, and in we went with the door shutting and locking behind us.

I found the room to be quite intriguing for a jewelry store, looking around while Mom and the business owner caught up on old times. It was a pretty quick look. There was literally nothing to see! "Hmmmm," I thought, "nice selection!" At this point, the thought did cross my mind: "What are we doing here?" But Mom had always come through in the past!

This time was no different. When they finally got finished chitchatting, the fellow looked at me and said, "Well, son, what were you looking for, and how much did you plan on spending?" I really didn't know exactly how to answer. After all, I had in mind that I would actually get to look at something, preferably with a price tag! Thankfully, Mom intervened, as is her specialty. The next thing I knew, the man came out from a dark back room with several cases which he opened up on the counter between us. It was stunning! Right there between us must have been literally zillions of dollars' worth of diamonds of all makes, models, sizes, and shapes. The other cases held a countless variety of gold wedding rings and diamond mounts. I couldn't believe it. It turns out that this fellow was a wholesaler to the local area retail jewelers. Mom had hit the jackpot! I got a very unique ring that the three of us literally built right there at a very discounted value. I couldn't wait to surprise Val! I had to wait a few days for him to mount the ring, and then I went back to pick it up and pay him. It was spectacular!

Meanwhile, poor Val! She had not yet been with me long enough to know how much I love to surprise people with nice things. So each morning, we continued the same routine of her dutifully sending me off to work, etc. Now the transportation business can be a tricky creature at times. Sometimes I had time to eat my sack lunch. Sometimes I didn't. Sometimes a few of us ate out, etc. You just never knew. Thankfully, since she had been around truckers all her childhood, she had a basic understanding of the lifestyle. You really did not know what might happen minute to minute. Now as it happened, I figured that if I didn't eat my sack lunch, I should bring it home to her to be recycled for the next day, and I had done just that two days in a row. The third day was the day I had to go back and pick up the surprise engagement and wedding set that Mom and I had selected a few days ago. So I thought it would be a nifty little surprise to put the ring in the sack lunch and take it to her that night since I used my lunchtime to drive downtown to get it. I was so excited driving home to give her the big surprise. I even rang the doorbell, even though I had a key. She came to the door, and with a big grin, I said, "I've got a surprise for you!" And I took the bag from behind my back and handed it to her. *Wham!* Recognizing the same bag for the third day in a row now, she slammed it straight in the wastebasket.

It's amazing how innocently and quickly spousal arguments can flare up, isn't it? I couldn't believe it! My fuse was lit! Actually, it normally takes quite a bit to light it. In fact, Val used to always tell people that I was the most even-tempered person she had ever met. A much smarter fellow than me once said that people get angry with each other when they anticipate another person to react in a certain way and the other person reacts in a much different way. That fellow was certainly correct! I didn't say a word. I was scared to death of what I might say. It was a *very* quiet evening. At bedtime, around ten o'clock in the evening or so on a Friday night, she started up on me again about the engagement ring, marriage issue, etc., climaxing with "You probably never will marry me!" To which I smugly retorted, "I guess not! *You* threw your engagement ring in the trash earlier today!" Trash was flying everywhere that night!

Of course, being who I am, I was forced to dub her wedding ring as her "trash can ring," and poor Val was stuck with it for the rest of our marriage. We both thought it was funny, and it served well as a reminder to both of us not to jump to conclusions about each other and our intentions toward each other. Ironically, many years later, Val told me, "You know…you never did propose to me." Yep! She was right! The trash can episode had short-circuited it. I responded back to her with "Well, I noticed you were still with me, so I figured you must have wanted to marry me!" And so the snowball kept rolling faster and faster downhill at breakneck speed. It was great! Though with meager means, we were so happy and so much in total lust with each other in our happy little apartment!

One day, again on the driveway at Val's parents' house, her dad gave me yet another piece of invaluable worldly advice. He looked at me and said, "Well, son, do you and Val intend to have any children?" I explained to him that we had hoped to have two. He then told me that if it was my intent to have enough money set aside to pay for their births, upbringing, college, and so forth, I could rest assured that I would die childless. Once again, he was correct! A wee bit too late, but correct!

We set a fall wedding date and began to put together plans for our wedding. As it turned out, because a lot of people that I knew at that time were involved in businesses associated with weddings, we were able to put our wedding together for very minimal cost. A major plus for a young couple with very limited resources!

Though in our midtwenties, in so many ways, Val and I were so very naive, happy, and enjoying every second of our time together. Yes, we had our disagreements, but we learned to work our way through them and resolve them or agree just to disagree. On the major really important things, we were both of one mind. We began making the arrangements for our fall wedding. We got Val a one-hundred-dollar JCPenny catalogue dress and purchased some invitations, and that was pretty much it. I'm sure our out-of-pocket expenses were well less than two hundred fifty dollars. Mom made our wedding cake, and since my brothers were all my groomsmen, she rented all of us tuxedos. Mom also found a local church to perform the ceremony. A friend of mine at work was a professional photographer, and he offered to do the wedding album for his cost. My next oldest brother worked at a flower shop and provided all the wedding flowers. We held a brief reception in the church basement for everyone, and after that, we had close family and friends meet in the backyard at my parents' house nearby for a longer celebration. We held our breath that it wouldn't rain. It didn't, and we had a wonderful time.

Just prior to our wedding, her maid of honor, Denise from the corner house on her street, decided to give her a surprise bridal shower at Denise's parents' house. Being the loving romantic that I am, I was up for it and helped her. We decided to solicit my second brother to go on a fake blind double date with Denise, Val, and me. We would go out to eat and then go over to the house where everyone else would have already arrived and would be waiting for us to enter.

The big day came, and as Val and I were getting ready to go, she was having problems getting her jeans on. It was to the point where we literally had her lie on her back across the bed while I pushed her tummy in and buttoned them. I figured we must both be putting on a couple of pounds as she was a very good cook. My brother came by with Denise and picked us up, and off we went. We ate at Spaghetti Factory, and on the way back, my brother and Denise sat in front while Val and I sat in the back. As soon as we sat down, Val whispered to me that she must have eaten too much, so she unbuttoned her jeans. My brother knew the route to drive so Val wouldn't see everyone's cars parked on the next street. As we approached the house, knowing what lie ahead, I tried to persuade Val to button up. She was uncomfortable and couldn't see it, particularly since, from her point of view, it was only going to be the four of us in the house. I was sweating bullets as she still had her pants unbuttoned as we pulled up to the house. We were literally on the house steps, and I was frantically trying to persuade her, when finally at the last second she got them fastened just as Denise swung the door open in front of her and everyone jumped out and yelled, "Surprise!" Little did they know the real surprise they all came so very close to getting! Of course, Val would have killed me!

The night before our wedding, the fellows took me out to my favorite Mexican restaurant. Yep! The very one in which I could not get a table on our first date. Meanwhile, Val was having a good ol' time with her girlfriends doing heaven only knows what. I was not aware at the time about the apparent tradition that the groom could not see the bride on the actual wedding day until she pranced down the aisle. Obviously, Val knew about it because I was banned from the apartment that night. Although I drink some alcoholic drinks from time to time, I have never really gone out to purposely get drunk in my life. However, I have been drunk on a few occasions. Usually, it is when the drinks and food slides down smooth and I don't pay close enough attention to myself. Thus, it was the night prior to our wedding. Admittedly, I've always had a weakness for tacos and margaritas. That particular night, I was having such a great time with the guys and the drinks tasted so good that the next thing I knew I had inadvertently dropped off the cliff and was pretty much plastered. And of course, they kept the drinks coming. Thankfully, I'm the basic happy drunk. Every single thing seems just hilarious to me. Afterward, the guys took me to Kevin's house—the best man—and poured me into bed for the night. Our wedding was at eleven o'clock the next morning, and it sure came quick! Poor Vicki, Kevin's wife! She had to scurry off to the store at the last minute to get me some white socks because I had forgotten to bring them with my tuxedo! Bless her sweet heart!

It is important to note that Val and I both took our marriage vows before God and those in attendance very, very, very seriously. This was it: for better or worse, sickness or health, no matter what, we were an inseparable team; nothing short of death itself would split us up. No matter what life threw at us, we absolutely *had* to address it and work it out between us; there simply was no looking back. Furthermore, Val and I were both committed from the very bottom depths of our hearts and souls to place our spouse's best interest first above our own.

The day after our wedding, Val and I took off for our honeymoon near Branson, Missouri, on Table Rock Lake in the Ozarks. Those were the days Branson was a small rural town. I had rented a cabin by the lake for the week and had planned on having a fabulous time on our honeymoon. Sentimental, romantic Dave couldn't wait!

However, the first morning of our honeymoon, Val was sick, so we really didn't do much of anything. The next morning, she was sick again, but we did manage to go to Silver Dollar City for part of the day. It is set up like an old-time town where you get to see them make candles, etc. and purchase the usual tourist items. Val bought some knickknacks, and back to our cabin we went. On the third morning, Val was still sick, and I was not only concerned about her health but also bummed out about our honeymoon. We decided to go back home without staying the last two days. Little did we know!

It wasn't long before Val came to me and said that she thought she knew why she was sick. Yep! She was pregnant! We were ecstatic! We had long ago decided between us that we had hoped to have two children. Since we both came from families of all boys, we really had hopes that we might have a girl, but of course as long as the child was healthy, we would be happy with either.

Now I'm Logical Dave to the nth degree. It only makes sense to me to thoroughly analyze things, get a good game plan together, and know the potential obstacles and possible solutions well in advance of taking any action. Yet it perplexed me to no end at what had just transpired of monumental significance in my life. And so I did a quick review of the time line: in January, I met a total stranger, Val; in February, we had our first date; in May, we lived together; in October, we had our marriage; and in April, we would welcome the birth of our first son. Wow! What was I thinking? Yet I was so very, very happy!

Furthermore, we had just begun a truly fabulous long-term marriage that *never* should have happened! Just think about it: I had totally had it with dating and repeatedly having women stomp on my heart and crush me. Yet I had always wanted to be married and had even been praying to a God that I wasn't even sure existed for a wife. It should have been absolutely impossible that Val's dad would be diving his truck on the same street where I worked and told his daughter to go and apply for a job there, particularly in light of the fact that they lived a good half hour away and she would have to make the commute twice a day. It was amazing that she actually did come and apply as she wasn't always prone to doing something like this just because he told her. In addition, as she would later reveal to me, she had just broken off a prior engagement solely because she felt that God wanted her to do so. And since that company had a no-dating policy, I could not even ask her to go on a date until she quit. But quit she did and remarkably accepted my request to go out on a date. Last but not least, I had totally kicked her to the curb following our first date. Yet undaunted, she would not take no and called me at work but then chickened out, only to have her mom hold the line and ask me to come to dinner. All combined cumulatively, it would seem to be far beyond the scope of mere coincidence and most likely impossible! Ah…but God had other ideas!

In the meantime, Val's dad had cut a deal to expand his trucking business. He needed drivers, and I was more than willing. It would mean virtually doubling my salary. However, it would also mean moving about sixty miles east to a much smaller town. At the beginning of the next year, Val and I made the move, and I went to work as a driver for her dad. I drove a tractor trailer on a peddle run with a load of department store goods to small town stores. Most of the stores were in small strip plazas of a grocery store, a dime store, and the department stores we served.

Just before we moved, we celebrated our first Christmas together in our little apartment. My brother at the flower shop got us a great deal on an artificial tree and some starter ornaments. If you recall, as a child, Val's family was involved in a church that did not celebrate any holidays. December 25 was no different than January 19 or any other day. Consequently, as a newlywed couple in our midtwenties, this was literally her first real Christmas. That first Christmas, I bought her a color TV set to replace her old black-and-white set. I was so excited! I wrapped it up at work with a red ribbon, bow, and the works and put it in the bed of a pickup truck that I was driving and headed back to the apartment. I could hardly contain myself!

Unfortunately, just prior to exiting the highway, one of the city's finest took exception to the joy expressed in my driving! He pulled me over on the off ramp and asked for my license, registration, etc. He came and gave them back to me and asked why I was going so fast. I explained the situation to him, and he could see the wrapped package in the back. He said that he noticed that the tires on the pickup were pretty new and that possibly the mechanics put the wrong size of tire on the truck which would throw the speedometer off. Following his lead, I said that was certainly possible and that I would check into it. He smiled at me, wrote me a warning, told me to slow down, and said, "You and your new wife have a merry Christmas on me!" God bless that man! It's funny about the differences in small town life compared to large city life. As the time approached for us to move so I could drive a truck for Val's dad, we took a weekend jaunt to the little town we would be living in to search for a place to rent. It was a little more than an hour's drive, and we arrived only to find out that nobody in the town played real estate on the weekends. It simply did not happen! Not only was that frustrating but I was a bit concerned about how we would ever find a place to live. Nevertheless, we picked up some newspapers and other information to help us call the following week to see what we could find from afar. While we were there, I went into the local grocery store to see if I could cash a personal check from out of state. I figured it would be a futile attempt, but I needed to know if I needed to set up a local bank account as soon as we moved anyway. Keep in mind that this was the first time I had ever set foot on this town's soil, and it was well before the days of everything being able to be verified online. The clerk looked at me, at my out-of-state driver's license, and at my check and inquired if I was going to be going to work for my father-in-law's trucking firm. I no sooner said yes than I had the cash in my hand. It was amazing how much they already knew about me! It was also fortunate that I had gotten the extra few dollars of cash!

As we drove home that evening discouraged, Val was sitting right next to me as she always did, and I had the headlights on, although it was just dusk and the dome light was on as she had the newspaper spread out to see what she could find for us. I was paying more attention to talking to her and not nearly enough attention to my driving. As a result, I was invited to meet another member of law enforcement. He gave me quite an education while we sat in his car and he ran my out-of-state license. He inquired about why I was going over the speed limit and what we were doing. Actually, I was not going that much over the speed limit, although I was over it, but the dome light caught his attention. I explained the situation to him, and he chided me for reading the newspaper while I was driving and wrote me a speeding ticket. Then came the education as he presented me with the citation, held his hand out palm up, looked at me, and politely but firmly stated, "That'll be eighty-seven dollars and twenty-five cents." I looked at him in utter disbelief and inquired, "Here and now? What ever happened to taking my license until I send my payment in?" He smiled with his hand still extended toward me and shook his head and said, "We don't do that here." Bottom line: if I didn't come up with the cash right there on the shoulder of the highway, he was more than willing to take me to jail! Val and I emptied not only my wallet, pockets, and her purse but the ashtray of the change I kept in it to scrape up the payment and went home with zero! But at least we were allowed to go home! After I paid him, the trooper sincerely looked at me and stated, "I live in this nice little town here; you might want to consider moving here." I thanked him for his suggestion, and back home we scurried, but well under the speed limit!

One of the overlooked areas about life that Val and I never compared notes about during our dating days was that of where each of us preferred to reside. I guess we both pretty much assumed that we would continue to live in the same Midwest city where we both grew up. Yet as life would have it, we were moving just a scant few months after our marriage. But we were both young and still wildly in lust with each other, so off we went. Now as it turned out, the move was more to my liking than hers. My idea of a perfect place to live is with my house on the center acre of a one-hundred-acre plot of ground. It turns out that I think Val always desired downtown New York City, although I doubt that she would have liked it had she moved there. So off we moved about sixty miles east to a small town of about 5,400 people, with Val five months pregnant to boot! We ended up leasing a small house from the local TV repair guy, and we were responsible for the rent and utilities.

As it turned out, that particular year, it was very hot in the early spring. And when Val, who was now *very* pregnant, went to turn on the air conditioner, it didn't work. When we informed our landlord, his response was that it wasn't summer yet, so we didn't need it. Neither Val nor I were happy campers—or renters—at that point. Val then discovered, as did our landlord, one of my little husbandly secrets that I had not yet shared with her. Years before, I had invested some money with a customer I had met at a bank where I was a teller. The investment did quite well. Despite his objections, we decided to withdraw it and purchase our first house at the other end of the same street. It turned out that we should have listened to my older friend, but it seemed like the thing to do at the time. He truly was looking out for our best interest when he advised against it!

While I worked for Val's dad, I drove a peddle run. I pulled a load out of the local warehouse in the wee hours of the morning and drove to the next state and delivered along a circuitous route to sixteen stores on an 865-mile route. Typically, I was gone for one and a half days, home a half day, and did it again. I did two runs one week and three the next, etc. Val used to pack a cooler for me from which I dined throughout the day, and I ate at a restaurant at night after the stores all closed and I could go no farther.

One day on the truck run, I was at the third store from the last one, and I was called to the phone. It was my brother-in-law advising me that they had just taken Val to the hospital as her water had broken. I kept the last two stops on the trailer and scurried home, per my instructions. My brother-in-law met me at the warehouse, and instead of taking me to see my wife as I wanted, he insisted, "She's not doing anything anyway. Let's get you cleaned up, have dinner, etc." I couldn't believe it! I was held hostage by my own brother-in-law!

When we finally got to the hospital, sure enough, he was right! Bless her heart, Val was having a very hard time and was in labor for many, many hours trying to give birth. Being the well-known chicken that I am, I sat behind her head, holding her hands, and giving her encouragement, "Push, push, you can do it!" etc. Finally, the doctor proclaimed, "We're going to have to get the baby out with a C-section." Then he looked at me and said, "I guess you'll be leaving." Recognizing my exit cue, I wished Val well, told her I loved her, kissed her, and went to the waiting room. Not long after that, I was the daddy of our first baby boy!

Sometime after our son was born, Val couldn't wait to go with me on a truck run. So off we went together, with her parents taking care of our young son for the next two days. By now I was accustomed to the run, but she was not. We left the warehouse around two o'clock in the morning as normal, and she immediately climbed into the bunk to snooze while I drove. Now the first ninety miles or so were on a major east-west interstate but across rural country. We had only gone about forty minutes or so when she piped up that she had to go to the bathroom. So I pulled the truck over on the shoulder, put the emergency flashers on, and parked. She looked at me in total disbelief. I explained that unless she could hold it for about another hour, there were simply no other options and that was where I went when I had to go. After pondering the situation a bit, reluctantly she agreed as long as I got out of the truck with her. So I stood guard in the middle of the morning with hardly a car in sight.

She took care of her business, and then it happened! As I stood on the shoulder, still on guard, I watched as my still fairly "new" wife, clad in only the bare underwear essentials, climbed up the steps of the truck tractor in front of me. Not being able to hold it any longer, I smiled behind her and reached up and goosed her, which led to her bursting out laughing hysterically, losing her grip and falling into my arms, and scraping her entire front on the serrated steps of the truck. I was frantic as I held my bloody but laughing—thank goodness—wife in my hands, scrambling for paper towels to clean her up in the early black morning on the shoulder of the highway, envisioning that a police officer was bound to pull up and cart me off to jail!

One of the areas that Val and I disagreed about all through our marriage was health care. Given my fear of white coats, I was not inclined to go to the doctor or dentist unless I figured that there was no way they could hurt me any more than I hurt already. Now that I'm older and have studied people considerably over the years, I think this may even be one of the many male-female differences. It seems to me that guys, as a general rule, are maybe more afraid of going to the doctor than the gals. Val used to tell me that she would probably end up with a dead husband only because I didn't go to the doctor in time. She, on the other hand, was inclined to take two aspirin today if she even thought that she would have a headache three days later. Val thought nothing of going to a doctor and pretty much didn't seem to have much fear about it at all. On the other hand, she was not at all interested in going to a dentist, and she seemed to be petrified of going in an ambulance. Many times when we were out and about together, if we crossed paths with an ambulance, she would say to me, "Oh my gosh, Dave, please don't ever let me have to ride in an ambulance." She never could articulate to me why she had such a strong disdain for them. While we agreed to disagree on the medical subject, there were times that I was concerned about her and, no doubt, vice versa. Despite that, she was great about literally holding my hand to comfort me whenever I really did have to go seek medical care. She was also great about explaining to our children that they had to get a shot, etc. to get better or ward off a potential illness. Even though I would go with them, I would sit in the waiting room while she took them in. I had to, as my inclination would be to take them and make a run for it! As a result, our children grew up without the self-imposed fears of white coats that their daddy had. I was so thankful for that!

I think one of the reasons for Val's mindset on health care was her background. When I married her, she came complete with her own set of medical anomalies which initially concerned me, but later I simply learned to live with them as she had. Among them, she would suffer from severe migraine headaches from time to time to the point where I would sometimes have to take her to the hospital to get a shot for some relief. In addition, every now and then, she would have heart palpitations in which her heart would race and she would have to sit down and wait them out. In the beginning, those made me a nervous wreck as I actually could hear her heart racing in her chest. Since the doctors could neither find a problem nor help with it, I learned, as she did long ago, to just be patient and wait them out with her.

One day, after our first son was beginning to investigate walking, I had just gotten off a truck run. At that time, our living room was arranged with the couch and love seat in an L shape and the coffee table in between them. I was sitting on the couch, and our son brought his favorite toy over to me, so we started playing together, with the toy on the coffee table. I noticed that if I moved it from the coffee table to the love seat, he would turn and take about a half step to get it. So I decided to move the coffee table slightly farther away and place the toy back on it. Sure enough, he turned and took a full step. So I did it again, and he took two steps. So I did it again, and he took two steps, slipped, and fell splitting his lip open on the table as he went down. I can't even describe how horrible and low that I felt. It was devastating. And off to the hospital we went to get him sewed back together. With this being our first child and without any instruction book, we did not realize just how resilient youngsters can be. Still, as a responsible young parent, it's still good advice to try your best not to break them yourself!

About a year and a half after our first son was born, Val was pregnant again. This time, we knew in advance that when the time approached, he would be birthed through a preplanned C-section. In addition, since we both agreed that we really only wanted to have two children in our marriage, we asked the doctor to tie Val's tubes after he had performed the C-section. This time, Val gained a considerable amount of weight and had a very difficult time with the pregnancy. I questioned her several times about the amount and types of prescriptions that she was taking while pregnant. Though I certainly don't have a medical degree, it just didn't seem right. She consoled me by telling me that the baby doctor prescribed them, so they must be okay. Still, I had haunting fears about it, and perhaps I should have acted on them, but still, he *was* the doctor.

Sure enough, about nine months later, the date, time, and place was set for the planned C-section and the birth of our second son. I took off work, took Val to the hospital, got her checked in, told her once again how much I loved her, kissed her, and went off to the waiting room. And I waited...and waited...and waited...and waited. A couple of hours later, I worried...and worried...and worried. All by myself, alone in the waiting room, I waited and worried.

Then the baby doctor came out in his surgical outfit and motioned for me to sit down and talk to him. He explained that he was having trouble with both Val and the baby not wanting to breathe for him in the operating room. He looked up at the outside window motioning to a helicopter flying away and told me that our second son was aboard being airlifted to a bigger, better-equipped hospital about one hundred miles away, in the hopes that they could sustain him and get him to breathe for them. Meanwhile, the doctor had essentially come out to ask me if I still wanted him to tie Val's tubes given the current situation. *Kablam!* Talk about totally destroying a semibrash, know-it-all young man's world! I cannot even describe the feeling of utter helplessness! I would not wish it on anyone under any circumstances. My feeble, little, totally fried brain was reeling! I was stunned beyond comprehension. Somehow I managed to mutter, "Yes, go ahead and tie her tubes. That was the plan." At that, the doctor scurried off back to the operating room, leaving me once again all alone in the room with my universe shattered in a zillion tiny pieces, tears cascading down my face, dripping on the floor.

And that was the time...a time of absolute utter terror and despair, with absolutely no hope, not a single thing on earth that I could do, not a single plan of action, not even knowing where I could start, even if I had a plan. Amid a steadily flowing stream of tears, finally, after twenty-nine years of living, I finally, totally, and completely humbled myself. And looking up to the ceiling, I cried in utter despair, "God, I obviously cannot do anything about this mess. But...if you do exist, please, please, please help my wife and my newborn son and let them live. Please show me that you are real and I will read the Bible or do whatever I need to do. I place all of us totally in your hands." Honestly, I didn't know if my simple little prayer was heard or if anything would come of it. The only thing I was really sure about was that I was a mere one breath away from totally losing the wife it took me so long to find and the second son that the two of us wanted so very much. That much was absolutely certain. And that, dear reader, is precisely the time that the God of the universe had me exactly where he wanted me—totally and utterly reliant upon him alone.

I determined at that time to read at least a chapter of the Bible each night, no matter what, and I did. Not long after that, out of the blue, a small inspirational magazine named *Guideposts* started coming to our house, even though we never ordered it. I tried my best to determine which kind soul sent it to us, but to this day, I still don't know. Not only that, they apparently paid for each subscription renewal for many, many years thereafter. My wife and son were in intensive care for a month each after the birth. We were on an 80 percent–20 percent insurance plan, so we incurred medical bills as a result that reached to the moon and beyond.

My wife got better first in the local hospital but was still not good enough to be discharged as they wanted to keep an eye on her. In an effort to get us all back together again, I succeeded in getting her to be allowed to transfer to the remote hospital where they had taken our second son at his birth. The problem was Val's fear of ambulances. There was no way she would go in one, and I felt confident that she would be fine in the car with me on the two-hour drive. Despite the local hospital pitching a fit and me having to sign what seemed like a zillion releases of liability, off the two of us went to check her into the other hospital. But sure enough, both my wife and our son not only survived the ordeal but were unaffected by it as well.

I thanked God and continued to read his Bible. Although I'm a good reader, I am a rather-slow reader. But I retain the information very well. I remembered that all the thee's and thou's and other words of a bygone age in my childhood Bible had both bogged me down and frustrated me to the point where I would simply give up. This time, I was determined not to let that happen. So I went to a Christian bookstore and asked them about the Bible. Upon hearing my concerns, they suggested that I select the New International Version of the Life Application Bible. I looked through it and purchased one. It was fabulous and just what I needed, complete with cross-references and notes about how it was applicable to real life today. I read, and I read, and the more I read, the more fascinated I became. Granted, I did not have a full understanding of everything that I read in it, but I prayed about it and continued on. It was amazing to me. The same Bible that I could not begin to grasp as a child was now extremely interesting to me. Slowly but surely, many of the questions about this life became very clear to me. The more I read it, the more I understood about *real* life and the more I wanted to read more and understand more. How very exciting it was! I remember at one point it dawned on me, "Wow! This is it! The very Word of God, the Almighty Creator of all of us and our entire universe. His instruction manual for all of life!" How very gracious and loving of him to provide it for us! And at this point of my life, having studied it and seen it actually at work in my life after so many, many decades, I am absolutely certain of it! And so, dearest reader, I don't know where you are in your life at this time, but I want to take just a brief moment to plead with you: please, please, please don't wait for such a drastic event such as this to occur in your life for God to use to get your attention. Please at least consider and research the God of the Bible and come now. He waits for you with arms wide open. You need only to humble yourself as I did and reach out to him in simple faith. Ask him to forgive you of your sins, for he is faithful to forgive *all* sins and take you in! After all, it cost him his dear Son's very life! Please accept Jesus as your Savior today, for you do not know whether you will see tomorrow's dawn or not! This is fabulous news! Because God is so very merciful and forgiving. No matter where you are currently in your life, you can be free to come to him, seek his divine forgiveness, and begin life anew with him. The moment you accept his Son Jesus as your Savior and start fresh doing life his way, you will be blessed from that very moment forward through all of eternity with the grandest eternal adventure you could ever have! Now that doesn't mean that from time to time, you won't have struggles and difficulties because you surely will, but those are designed to help you grow, painful that they may be at the time. However, now God will be right there to help you through them and to teach you the important life lessons that will help you with the future. And from time to time, you will sin and fall short of God's design and desires, but he will be ready and willing to forgive you and help you with them if only you ask.

Given these newfound revelations, I wanted to find a nice church to go to with Val and the kids. Oops! I had miscalculated. Given Val's childhood background with the only organized religion that she knew, she was not in the least interested in that action! Several times, I attempted to get her to go during our marriage, and each time, she would rebut with "No, thank you! And I don't want you to get any ideas about becoming a preacher." The couple times I actually succeeded in getting her to go, I messed up and got a bit too enthusiastic, only to have her back off and rebuff me again. So as the kids grew up, I became somewhat of a lone-ranger Christian, studying the Bible on my own, listening to good Christian talk radio, and finally heeding my daddy-in-law's warning about watching very carefully who I listen to and verifying them against the biblical text. His advice was invaluable through the years as I began to find out that not everyone who fancies themselves to be a "man of God" can be trusted to correctly reveal God's truths as stated in the biblical text.

Interestingly, one of the things that I found as this new adventure began was that I still sinned and messed up. Yet so did the great men in the Bible! With all my newfound excitement about getting to know God better and better, I now had my little growing family all at home, and I continued to drive the truck. A month or so later, in the fall of that year, my last grandparent, my dad's mom, passed away. A couple of months after that in the dead of winter, the holding company of the company we were contracted to service with our trucks informed us that they had sold that company since it was not earning them enough profit, so after we cleaned out the warehouse, we would no longer be needed as the new company had their own fleet of trucks. Uh-oh! Oh my! The warehouse would shut down, and it was the third largest employer in this tiny town. My job was about to evaporate, and I still had a house with a thirty-year mortgage and medical bills beyond description. Yikes!

And so we worked that last month to clean out the warehouse. We put our house up for sale, but the stark reality of it was that with the third largest employer shut down, nobody wanted to buy our house. Remember my investment friend who had warned us about withdrawing our money to purchase a house a couple of years prior? Now it appeared that we were about to lose it all! While Val watched the house and the two young kids, I went back to the large city to live with my parents while I looked for a job. Oddly, this time, even though to some extent I was at my wit's end over it all, it was quite different. I was strangely calm inside. I couldn't quite put my finger on it. It felt so strange and so peaceful, and yet we were in quite a pickle! I remember sitting in my parents' house, pondering the entire situation. I remember saying to God, "Lord, this is some great plan you have!" Then the thought occurred to me: Do I *really* believe *everything* I had been reading in the Bible? What about all the wonderful promises I had read? About how God loves and cares for those who love him! About how he works everything for the good of those who love him! About how he will never leave or forsake those who love him! *Really?* Deep down, did I *really* believe it? Well, *did* I? If so, should it matter whether the current circumstances are bad or good? And if he really *is* the all-powerful God who created the entire universe out of absolutely nothing, is *any* problem on earth an obstacle to him? The questions of true faith swirled in my head. Well, was I in or out? It was decision time! I took a very, very, long, deep breath and pushed *all* my chips into the center of the debate. I was *all in*!

And what was God's response? In very short order, we lost our house, our savings, everything! Thankfully, Val's oldest brother took over the payments of the house, so we didn't end up in default. But we did lose the down payment, etc. Even though my father-in-law did offer me continued work as a truck driver, I declined as it would mean spending a week or two on the road away from my family. I simply did not think it would be good for any of us. And so I was praying and applying for work all over the place. Every weekday, all day, I prayed, searched, and applied for work while staying with my parents. And every weekend, I made the two-hour commute to spend time with Val and the kids. Several weeks into it, I applied to an ad for a position as a dispatcher at a local trucking company. Although at that time I did think that I was qualified for the job, later I realized that I was not. Nevertheless, I think the owner saw an opportunity in taking a chance on this young ambitious lad at a very discounted rate of pay and hired me as well to perform odds and ends work for the company, and later they did make not only a dispatcher out of me but also enabled me to begin my ultimate career as a transportation safety professional.

And so we moved back to the large city into a two-bedroom apartment on a hope and a prayer! At one point, we were literally counting pennies out of the boys' piggy banks to buy them the next gallon of milk. In addition, since I was not being paid very much, I ended up having to tell my medical bill creditors that they would have to accept anywhere from a whopping one-dollar-to-five-dollars-per-month payment until I could earn more money or I would declare bankruptcy and they would get nothing. Amazingly, they all accepted, and it ultimately took me about ten years to pay it all off. Still, I held my ground and continued to faithfully believe and read the Bible. Again, the more I read, the clearer and clearer life became. In short, everything that I saw and had experienced in my own life was addressed in the Bible. And still, I had a very odd calmness about me through it all.

My many years of adventures in the trucking industry as a safety director for coast-to-coast trucking firms is an entire story all its own, and perhaps someday I will do a book about it as well. I used to tell family and coworkers that had I taken good notes from the beginning, I could probably produce a long-running prime-time TV sitcom about it all. There were so many interesting characters and situations that occurred on almost a daily basis.

While I would never wish such a traumatic medical situation as the difficult birth of our second son on anyone for any reason nor would I take any sum of money, no matter how large, for the experience, through it, I really did come to know the very real, very much alive Jesus of true Christianity. Slowly but surely as I read the Bible and continued diligently in my research, he revealed himself to me. As I would ask the questions that troubled me, slowly the answers would come to me.

I was led to such wonderful fellows as Hank Hanegraaff, who through his radio show, *The Bible Answer Man*, taught me that the more familiar you become with the Bible and real, true Christianity, the easier it becomes to find the all-too-numerous fakes. And he was right! After a while, it only took a few moments of listening to any preacher and I could easily discern whether or not he was teaching the *real* gospel of Jesus. Sadly, some of them are simply repeating misinformation that they themselves also bought into, but even worse, a vast herd of them twist and turn the real gospel message to garner fame and fortune for themselves, but ever so sadly, it taints the reputation of *true* Christianity, defames the name of Jesus, and reeks untold devastation on the people who believe their teaching. The Bible even addresses them and tells of their final fate. Many of the other true preachers of the Word of God, such as Chuck Swindol, Charles Stanley, Bob Russell, James Dobson, and others far too numerous to mention helped me along the way. They introduced me to guys like Lee Strobel and Guillermo Gonzalez, whose fine research paved the way for me to solidify in my own mind that it could actually be proven beyond any shadow of a doubt that the entirety of the biblical account of true Christianity was accurate. And furthermore, it was backed up by countless volumes of evidence in eyewitness accounts, history, archaeology, and precision prophecies predicted hundreds of years in advance.

Furthermore, I discovered that *true* Christians were *very* loving people. The more I read and studied, the more questions of mine were answered, and the more I began to realize the Bible really was very much God's instruction book for living *real* life today in any century! It was a book that was strangely and miraculously alive and active in everyday life! This, of course, meant that it was not simply an intellectual exercise of understanding the book but a very real lifetime of applying that knowledge to my life and allowing Jesus to live through me as I engaged other people and circumstances in my own life! It was so very refreshing and exciting, and still is!

I recall discovering within the pages of the Holy Scriptures that not only did they address the usual objections that people use against Christianity but the answers also aligned perfectly to what I observed to be true about the life that I was living and saw all around me. For instance, the Bible proclaims that no person—no, not even one—is good by the standard of a holy and perfect God! Not even a newborn infant! Now this certainly flies in the face of what the majority of the world believes, as we all constantly hear how innocent babies and little children are. But the reality of life is that most parents, and certainly not mine, don't teach their young children to sin, but they sure do it at a very young age. I did! And my two sons did as well!

One point of objection that many bring up about Christianity is true. Christianity is very, very exclusive! *But* it is also all-inclusive and for a very good reason! God is God, and we are not! It is his plan, *not* ours! The choice, however, *is* ours! God's desire from the very beginning of creation was and still is that everyone should come to know, love, and accept him and live with him for all of eternity. He desires it so much that centuries ago, he sent his only Son Jesus to earth to save us, and we brutally killed him! Given that, how could he *not* require us to humbly submit to Jesus as a prerequisite to gaining an entrance to heaven for an eternity of pure bliss? *But* just think about it: in God's eyes, all sins—every category of every sin—is an identical abomination to him. Every single sin is blatant disobedience to him and his holy plan. Whether it is one of our so-called "white lies" or adultery, which we downplay as an affair, or horrendous murder, *all* are equal in God's eyes. Granted, some are certainly more heinous than others, at least from our perspective, yet every one of them is disobeying a pure and holy God. *And* wonder of wonders, this is precisely what totally levels the playing field for all human beings of all time, positions of power, wealth, health, and any other circumstances. It simply does not matter if you live for twenty years or ninety, whether you are wealthy or destitute, an athlete or bound to a wheelchair. The bottom line is that every single human being who ever lived or ever will live is completely, totally, and absolutely equal at the foot of Jesus's cross. And oddly enough, that is the only place where everyone is absolutely equal. Every one of us is deserving of eternal punishment for disobeying our Creator, unless we humbly ask Jesus for his eternal forgiveness. Interestingly, the Bible also records that he is faithful to forgive us and give us his eternal life as a free gift, unearned and unmerited, and the Bible goes on to say that it is God's desire that *all* people turn from their sins and come to him!

There is literally *nothing* that we can do to earn his favor or merit. Think very carefully about it: he created us, this entire universe, and everything that is in it out of absolutely nothing. What on earth could we possibly give him that would merit his favor? Everything is his anyway. Sadly, many people delude themselves into thinking that they own all their little trinkets. The reality of it is they do not, and all that can be taken from them in an instant. That concept alone was so very refreshing and freeing to me when I discovered it. I own nothing. I am only a manager of the wonderful gifts, including every breath I take, that God has provided for me.

One by one, slowly but surely, the questions that had haunted me were being put to rest as I continued to read and reread and study and restudy the Bible. How can a loving God send anyone to hell if it is such a horrible place? The odd thing is that he doesn't! Rather, he invites all to come to him. But we are given a free will so we can pick and choose. It is important to note though that the moment we are born, we are in the automatic default position of having rejected him. Thus, each of us has to repent of our sins and humbly accept Jesus's sacrifice on the cross on our behalf to be accepted by him to spend the rest of eternity with him. Consequently, anyone who lands in hell for eternity chose to reject God and go there instead. I'm confident that it breaks God's heart every time it happens. However, for him to be a holy and just God, he simply cannot accept those who reject him. Not only that, think very carefully about it. How kind and gracious would it be of God to force people to spend eternity with him if they do not want to do so?

The knight in shining armor

We lived in the apartment for less than a year when my parents came to me and asked if we would be interested in moving into my grandparents' old house on the main floor while Dad's older brother lived in the basement as he was having trouble paying the utility bills, etc. Val and I discussed it as we did every major decision, and we moved in with my uncle. The two boys grew and entered grade school, and the years rolled on. I'll never forget the very first time Val called me her knight in shining armor.

We were still living in St. Louis, and our sons were in elementary school. I had covertly found out that she was planning on taking them for lunch on a particular day to a fabulous buffet-style restaurant named Trotters that was both fantastic and quite cost-effective. Those were days in which we did not have a lot of money, but we did treat ourselves every now and then. As is my nature, I didn't say a word about it, but I did arrange my schedule so I could be standing there at the front door awaiting their arrival. Unaware that I knew anything about her little adventure, she was totally amazed when she pulled into their driveway and there I stood at the front door. Talk about scoring points with the wife! And, wow, did she ever score quite a load of points from me by calling me her knight in shining armor! Not only that, much to my delight, she referred to me with that title many times as the years rolled on. Frankly, I can't think of any fellow who doesn't yearn to hear such loving words of affirmation from the lady he loves.

Over the years as I reflected upon it, I began to realize that, unbeknownst to me, my knighthood training actually began while I was a wee little boy child under my parents' care. That training was slow but steady and continuous. While most of it came from my mom, other family members had an influence on me as well. I was taught good behavior, values, morals, and etiquette. The lessons included such things as good sportsmanship: being both a gracious winner as well as a loser. I knew that I was always to try my best and capture the victory and not be haughty if I won but also to be a gracious loser and congratulate the better player(s). Though they all tried to make these lessons easy and fun for me, I still knew that they meant business.

Ever faithful Mom continued to slowly ramp up the training as I got older. As she prepared me to enter school, realizing that I would be away from her and Dad for extended periods of time, the training gravitated toward the areas that I might need on my own. Keep in mind that those were times when literally no one ran around with a cell phone in their pocket. Parents did not even have the option of calling their children at any time they chose. And so I was taught to memorize my address and phone number and Mom's and Dad's actual names. I had actually thought that those *were* their names! She showed me how to ride the public transit bus and read their schedules. Since we only had one car and my elementary school had no buses and was located about five miles from our house, I had to ride the public bus to and from school. I got to know "Big Red" the bus driver who watched out for me and several of the other daily passengers going to work.

Mom made sure that I knew the location of my secret emergency dime to use in the pay phone to call the police if I needed help. I knew that police officers, firemen, and public businesses were safe places where I could seek refuge and help in times of trouble. I was to ride my bicycle on the street going with traffic as far to the right as I could and to use the less-busy side streets and obey all the traffic laws. When walking, I was to use the city sidewalks when possible and to always walk facing the oncoming traffic so I could see them coming. Strangers were to be avoided at all costs, even to the point of crossing the street and walking on the other side, if necessary, and never ever get in or near their car. This training was so ingrained within me that I refused to get in the pickup truck of my friend's dad one day when he offered to give me a ride. In public, my brothers and I knew without even being told—and Mom was always available to remind us—that we were to immediately stand up and offer our seat to any adult who might come in later, especially the elderly and ladies. We were also to hold doors open for others. Mom would tell us, "That is what gentlemen do." And the years rolled on.

As we approached the high school dating years, the real knighthood training came, again primarily from Mom as she was with us more. Mom instructed us that when we took a young lady on a date, we were to always treat her as a young gentleman should treat a princess. She was to be treated with the utmost kindness and respect and valued as a treasure. We were to always remember that the young lady's dad was trusting us to bring her home on time and safe. We were to always hold her car door open when getting in and out as well as any other doors and pull out her chair when dining. In the event that we took a walk, we were to always walk facing the traffic with her being the farthest away from traffic so that we would be hit first. The bottom line was that we were to ensure that she would arrive home safe and on time, even if we did not. Thus, when Val referred to me as her knight in shining armor, it was a title that I held in high esteem!

Both of us had taken our marriage vows very seriously and honored them, our marriage, and each other. We went out of our way to place hedges of protection to prevent encroachment against our marriage or erosion from within.

I had worked at the previously mentioned company for about five years when it became evident that they were having financial problems. By now I had been reading the Bible for many, many years. So I began to pray in earnest that God would intervene and find a job for me. I began to answer "Help Wanted" ads and mail out résumés. This went on for quite a few months, and though I had a few interviews, still they did not yield a job. Meanwhile, the company's financial problems were looming larger! Still, I held my course and continued to pray and search. Out of the blue, one night as we were watching TV, the phone rang, and it was a voice of a fellow I recognized. He had hired me years ago along with the owner but had moved on to a different company about a year or two prior, and now he wanted to know if I wanted to go to work there as their safety director. The only problem was the company was located 250 miles away. It would mean uprooting our family once again and moving away from our extended family and friends, not to mention leaving my uncle alone again and our children having to change schools.

Val and I discussed it at length for some time. The salary increase the new company offered was going to be substantial and would position us to once again own a home of our own for the kids to grow up in. Still, it would mean moving so far away, and yet we could return anytime we wanted following a five-hour drive. She and I finally got down to the point of literally drawing a line down the center of a legal pad and listing the pros and the cons.

Now despite Val's disdain for organized religion, it turns out that she was a true believer in the God of the universe. Many times in our marriage, she would come to me and ask about a particular situation and ask me what I thought God would think about it. I would look it up in the Bible and read it to her and explain it further if she wanted me to do so. One of the vexing texts in the Bible occurs when the Bible addresses married couples and directs wives to "submit to their husbands." Sadly, so many couples read that, stop there, and get all up in arms about it. But it does *not* end there. The very next verse states that husbands are to lay down their lives for their wives! You cannot have one without the other as well as the entirety of the rest of the Bible! It is not a "buffet" in which you get to pick and choose what you want and reject the rest. It is all or nothing. While certainly not perfect, Val and I both understood those principles and modeled both very well in our marriage. I solicited and encouraged her input in every major decision, and she gave it liberally. I often felt that God spoke to me through her, so I listened intently to her thoughts on these decisions. Then she would give me the courtesy of making the final decision, both of us recognizing that the ultimate result would rest on my shoulders. More often than not, I decided to go with her suggestions, and almost without fail, they worked out wonderfully for both of us. The few times I chose to go my own way on a matter, she supported me graciously.

In the meantime, given the circumstances, I thought it best to consult my dad to get his thoughts about it. Deep down, I was seeking either his endorsement or his disapproval. What I got both shocked and dismayed me. He looked at me and asked for my analysis of it. I told him our list of pros and cons, and he continued to look at me and said, "Well, my son, it looks like you did your homework. I sure hope you pick right. Let me know what you decide. Don't worry about your uncle. We'll take care of him once we know how you decide." What? Who was this guy? What happened to the sage advice of the dad who loved me? Years later when we discussed it, he explained to me that he was being the very best dad he could ever have been to me at that time, by forcing me to choose for myself. And he was right! Choose we did! We decided that it was in the best long-term interest of our little family to move to Southern Indiana. In retrospect, I now know that it was the best thing that we could have done for both Val and me, but I will forever wonder if it was the wisest decision for our two sons. It turned out that moving was a lot easier said than done!

Susan

Meanwhile, my adventure continued.

After teaching in the Virginia Beach area, I was restless, and my adventurous spirit led me to a place much closer to home. I accepted a job in Williamstown, New Jersey. I was hired to teach second grade but was asked just before school started to fill a position in the K5 classroom—all the children in this class were five-year-olds—and I accepted.

Dad and Mom moved me again, but this time since it was so close to school starting, I had not found a place to live, so all my furniture and belongings were stored in a room at the church basement. One of the church families had an extra bedroom available because their daughter had just left for college, so I stayed with them until I was able to find an apartment. I found a very nice one-bedroom apartment about five minutes from the church and school.

Men from the school and church were able to move my belongings to the apartment, and I took the next day off to unpack and get things set up. I was totally exhausted and slept soundly until about seven o'clock the next morning when I was awakened by loud banging on my apartment door. Being alone in the apartment, I did not have my landline phone connected yet, so I was a bit perplexed on what I was to do. This again was before cell phones. I put on a robe and peeked out through the peephole. I couldn't believe it—it was the principal of the school! He had come to ask me if I could possibly come in and teach that day because he could not find a sub to take the class. I laughed and said, "Are you kidding me?" He replied, "Well, at least you see the humor in this situation." I told him to give me an hour, and I would be there. At least I would have the weekend to finish unpacking and find where everything had been put.

Teaching twenty-five kindergartens was quite the experience. I was so thankful that the school hired a full-time aide for me. She was a tremendous help, and we ended up being great friends. At the end of the year, the principal asked me if I would want to move up to third grade, as that position was going to be available. I didn't even have to think twice about it. I said yes! Little did I know at this time that I was to stay at this school for sixteen years. It was during those years I began to write journals of my everyday life as a teacher and as a single person. In fact, a few humorous stories ended up in my journals as a result of my many years as a teacher.

And…time rolled on.

CHAPTER 5

Go East, Young Man, Go East

The move

After I worked my two-week notice of resignation, the company I was going to work for flew me and put me up in a motel while I looked for a place to rent, and Val stayed with the kids at our home in St. Louis. It seemed like a fairly simple chore for me, but what a nightmare! The economy was booming following President Reagan's term, and by the time I got a newspaper on Sunday, the rental houses had already been rented. In those days, medium and large trucking companies often provided the use of a company car as part of the salary package offered to their safety director, and thus, it was for me. So I was driving back home each weekend to help pack, etc. As the weeks dragged on with no success in finding a place for our family to stay, I felt like I was meeting myself coming and going just as I had in our dating days.

I finally found a little house for rent, but when I called the owner, she already had five other applicants and really could care less about me or my family. I did get her to agree to allow me to come and see the house. My friend who hired me took me to see it. It was pretty small with no basement, but at least I would finally have my entire family back with me. I inquired what might make my application stand out and make it first in line among the other five, and as I had hoped, the bottom line was money. Sadly, neither my friend nor I had much at the moment as we had both left our checkbooks back at work. I asked if a twenty-dollar bill would put my application first if I brought her the security deposit and first month's rent the next morning. She agreed, and we packed up the family and moved. Of course, the actual move was just the beginning. After that, there seemed to be an endless number of other chores that accompanied it: getting the kids enrolled in school, finding the location of places such as grocery stores, and locating a decent doctor, dentist, etc. The house we rented was on the Southern Indiana side across the Ohio River from greater Louisville, Kentucky.

Some of our early exploits as "foreigners" in this new land were quite hilarious, such as watching the expressions on the locals' faces as we tried to explain a product that we just assumed was available everywhere, when they had never heard of it. I vividly recall Val approaching a grocery store cashier to inquire the location of C&H Sugar within the store. We assumed it was everywhere given the commercials on TV in St. Louis. As the conversation went back and forth, a bit-frustrated Val even performed her version of a Hawaiian hula dance for the clerk just like the commercials we had watched. As I witnessed all this, I found it quite amusing as obviously the cashier did not have a clue what on earth we were talking about and wasn't overly impressed with the dance. So I turned to Val and said, "C'mon, honey, looks like it's dominos in aisle 7 or nothing!" It was also evident that some of them apparently never crossed the state line their entire lives. Again, the facial expressions were priceless as I asked directions to a restaurant located in Louisville, Kentucky. The local Southern Indiana people would look at us in total disbelief, as if we had just arrived from Mars, and say, "You know, *that's* across the bridge!" By "across the bridge," they meant the bridge across the Ohio River, a whopping five miles from our house. I mean we just moved a family of four 250 miles across two state lines in addition to all our belongings. I was pretty confident that I could make the five-mile voyage across the Ohio River and back safely to enjoy a family dinner out!

America's best dentist

After we moved, much to my amazement, I succeeded in finding a wonderful dentist whom I dubbed "America's best dentist." He was great! He would stop working immediately with the least little movement from me. Of course, he knew by my long yellow feathers that I was "America's biggest chicken" when it came to the white coats! It was a bit of a drive to go see him, but he was well worth it. In addition, he and his staff introduced me to an interesting little tool that they used for chickens like me. It is called nitrous oxide. It is simply fabulous!

I'll never forget the very first time his assistant gave it to me prior to having a cavity filled. I suppose they determine the amount to be administered based on the size of the patient. Little did she know! Perhaps because I very rarely take even an aspirin, I've always been very sensitive to many drugs. Even a half tablet of Tylenol 3, with codeine, is enough for me to orbit Saturn many times! In fact, I used to tell Val to check for Tylenol 3 if I ever became a drug addict because that's where I would head! As it turns out, the nitrous oxide is a much better product! I think doctors are missing the boat by not using it on creatures such as me.

At any rate, the assistant put a nose cone over my nose and told me to breathe deep. The next thing I remember she was frantically telling me to talk to her. I vividly recall that my arms and legs all felt like they weighed ten thousand pounds and that I simply could not move them even if I wanted. While I was a bit concerned about it, I simply did not care! I also remember thinking that the polite thing would be to answer her, but frankly, I saw no point to it. I knew one thing, I was oh so happy! While she kept trying to get me to talk and adjusting her dials and gauges on the nitrous oxide, my knee started to itch, and on the one hand, I really wanted to scratch it. But I could neither get my arms to move, nor did I really care, so I gave up on it. As the assistant was becoming more and more distraught that I wouldn't talk to her, I decided to mumble something to her both to prevent her from having heart failure or something but also to humor me. Once she got me to carry on a conversation with her, the dentist came in and performed the procedure going slowly and explaining every step, as if I could have cared at that point what he did to me! Cut my head off? Great! Have at it!

To my dismay, the procedure ended, and they cut off my supply. But amazingly, I was immediately able to hop right up, walk to my car, and drive off. At that time, my white-coat phobia was still in full bloom. But I had not yet realized the full extent of Val's embarrassment about her crooked bottom front teeth. Since she had no problems going to the doctor, it perplexed me that I could not get her to go with me and the boys to the dentist no matter how hard I tried.

It turned out that the local elementary school was the next block over from where we lived, which was wonderful. And as an added bonus, the local public swimming pool was next door to the school, where our sons spent many a summer day. In short order, not only were our kids going to school there but Val was a volunteer helper for a fifth grade teacher, and later, they hired her to be a cafeteria monitor. The experience really helped bring her out of her shell.

Even though the owner of the little house had warned me that she would probably end up selling the house, it still came as a bit of a shock to me when she announced the impending sale only about eight months after we had moved in. And so began yet another search for a place to live. What an adventure that was!

The owner graciously allowed us the first option to buy her house. We declined as it was obvious that it was way too small, particularly in light of the fact that the kids would grow. By this time, we had succeeded in paying off our portion of the enormous medical bills from our second son's birth. We owned everything that we had free and clear, which wasn't much, but it was ours. We had no outstanding bills, other than rent and utilities. In a sense, it was utopia. However, neither did we have any credit cards or credit of any type. Try getting a house loan under those circumstances! And so the search began with time running very short as the owner had found a buyer, and the closing date was, well, closing in on us rather quickly. With every waking moment, we packed up the boys and searched and searched not only for a house but for financing as well. Everyone was trying to help us. One of the mechanics at work told me of a little town about twenty miles from the city with good affordable housing, pretty much just what I was hoping for. However, on the trip out, the four of us had just climbed the first steep hill heading away from the city in the direction of the little town when Val turned and looked at me and said lovingly yet firmly, "I'll tell you right now, buddy boy, you had better turn this buggy around because we have gone far enough!" That scuttled that trip.

Meanwhile, we went to see a mortgage lender, and as we waited, I spied an ol' familiar "friend" in his office—a copy of *Guideposts* magazine! "This could be great!" I thought. When we finally got to meet with the fellow, I explained our plight and asked if he could help us. He specifically told me that he could not make any promises, but if I wanted to write it all down and submit it to him, he would at least make an effort on our behalf. A couple of days later, I showed back up at his office and handed him a nineteen-page handwritten document that detailed our situation, all we had been through paying off the sky-high medical bills, etc. I thought he was going to faint right there in front of me. But many days later, he did give us a loan! It is truly sad the way our financial markets work today. Here we were—the stable young couple with an income and absolutely no debt after paying off a horrendous amount of medical bills, and lender after lender had told us that we were essentially stupid to have paid it all off, stating that we should have declared bankruptcy as then they would have given us a loan. Huh?

While all that was going on, we had finally settled on two houses. One was not far from our rental house, perhaps a couple of miles, and the other was on the same street at the other end, just like the first house we purchased years ago. I wanted the first and Val the second. As was the case in all our major decisions, we thoroughly discussed the pros and cons of each and prayed about the decision. I listened intently to Val, and she graciously allowed me to have the final decision. I knew she would support me no matter what I decided.

Afterward, I felt strongly drawn to her house, so we met with the realtor to make an offer. The owner was an elderly man who was heading to a nursing home where his wife had been for a while. His son who resided in New York had power of attorney for the mom. In the tit for tat between the two realtors with our contract, our eviction date loomed nearer and nearer. We eventually had to agree to pay full price, but we were hung up over the FHA inspection. They wanted us to pay for any repairs, and we wanted them to pay. I finally suggested to my realtor that I was going to walk down the street to work out an agreement with the elderly owner. I thought she was going to have a hemorrhage! "That's just never done without the realtors present!" she stated. I informed her that since this was a free country, it would be pretty difficult to stop me. I later agreed to wait a couple of hours while she scurried to get the other real estate agent to meet us there. We came to a very reasonable agreement, and the contract was set. Thankfully, we were allowed to move some of our things to the basement of the house prior to the actual possession date. Once again, this was a huge obstacle for the real estate agents, but it is amazing what suddenly becomes acceptable in the light of possibly having the sale collapse out from under them!

And so eventually came the day of the actual move, and once again, poor Val! Bless her ever loving heart! We had several people come to help us, and we had a truck to move our larger items down the street. We literally moved the same day that everyone else had to move as well. So the elderly man was moving to the nursing home while we moved into his house while a younger childless couple moved into our rental house. It had the makings of quite a circus. As if that was not bad enough, long before we got the notice that our rental house was being sold, I had paid for a weeklong seminar in Chicago that began the very next day! When we all arrived at our "new" house at the other end of the street, we were pleasantly surprised to see that the elderly man was already gone. But there was one teeny, little problem: all his furniture was still in the house! I frantically called my real estate agent for help, only to find out that it was all ours! "Didn't you read the contract?" she questioned. "That was why they wouldn't budge off the asking price. The agreement was that all the appliances, etc. came with the house!" Yikes! Neither Val nor I had any idea! So we worked to cram everything into the house full of his appliances, furniture, etc. And literally as I threw the last box in to the house, I kissed Val goodbye and told her how very sorry

I was to leave her once again, with a mess as well as the kids, etc. And off I went to Chicago. Despite all that, buying that house was one of the best decisions that she ever led me to make!

Upon my return, I was quite concerned to learn that our next-door neighbors were an elderly couple with a small dog named Spike. We briefly met them, and as we did, I noticed that their house was immaculate. I thought, "Oh, boy! I wonder how this is going to work out with us having such small kids, grade-school age." It turned out to be wonderful! Not only were they fabulous neighbors but they loved us and our boys and turned out to be more or less surrogate parents for Val and me as well as grandparents for our boys.

I have found it to be very odd but quite comforting the way God paves the way for those who truly love him. Sadly, we still sin, still fall far short, still have many trials and tribulations, yet he is always there to comfort us and hold us. Around this time, I became acquainted with two fine works authored by Dr. James Dobson of Focus on the Family. The first was *When God Doesn't Make Sense*, which deals with one of the most vexing questions about Christianity posed by believers and nonbelievers alike: "How can a loving God allow bad things to happen to the very people who love him?" As I read and absorbed it, little did I realize how much I would be needing the information Dr. Dobson presented in a relatively short time later in my own life. The second book was titled *Life on the Edge*, written for youngsters between the ages of sixteen and twenty-six. So I was a bit old for his targeted audience, but I was so glad that I read it. I only wish someone had given it to me when I was about fourteen or fifteen. It would have made that tumultuous time of my life a whole lot easier on me. Yet even though those years were long since passed, it was still a comfort for me to better understand what I went through and why as well as how it all lined up with the Bible. I would highly recommend both works to everyone along with all the reference materials presented at the end of this book (appendix C).

Terry Tumor

During our second winter here, I developed an excruciating toothache. As usual, I put off actually going to the dentist until it was quite severe. I finally went to the dentist and told him that I had a bad toothache in one of my back teeth on the top right side. He examined me and informed me that nothing was wrong. I told him that something had to be wrong as I couldn't chew on it and it was keeping me awake at night. He suggested that I go to the doctor as perhaps something medically was wrong, but my teeth were fine. As usual, I had calculated that the doctor could not possibly put me through more pain than I was already experiencing, so I made an appointment to see her. Yep! I even try to find women doctors in the high hopes that they will be gentler than the guys! Unfortunately, following my exam, she proclaimed, "You are fine! Nothing is wrong." Again, I begged to differ, stating my case. And so a few weeks went by as I continued to be shuffled back and forth between the two of them. Meanwhile, my misery continued as I was operating on minimal sleep and not much chewable food. Finally, the doctor sent me to have a whole-head X-ray at the hospital.

While all this was going on, the night following the X-ray, I had yet another moment of brilliance and figured that despite my lack of an actual medical degree, apparently I was at least as qualified as both of them. After I got off work, I came home and announced to Val that I was going to get to the bottom of this that night. To say that upon hearing that she was probably petrified is an understatement. So I took a typical plastic-barreled BIC pen, went into the bathroom, and looked in the mirror as I positioned the pen between my right side two back teeth. *Chomp!* I bit down on the pen as hard as I possibly could. Nothing! So I moved it up to the second two teeth from the back. *Chomp!* I about went through our ceiling! But much to my astonishment, it was the lower tooth, not the upper as I had thought and had told the dentist. It just so happened that he had extended hours that evening, so I called his office and proclaimed that I had found the problem and that I wanted him to pull it the following day. Of course, dentists don't like to pull teeth except as a last resort, so he tried to talk me out of it. I then informed him that he could take his pick: pull it or I would have a mechanic at work pull it because I was finished being in misery over it. Reluctantly, he agreed.

The next morning, I arrived at work, once again with minimal sleep, in anticipation of finally having some relief later that morning. I had not been there that long before the morning got very interesting! The phone rang and it was my doctor instructing me to go at once to the hospital to get an MRI of my head. She had already paved the way for me. I thanked her but told her that would not be necessary as I had found the problem and the dentist was going to extract it in a couple of hours. She then told me that I didn't understand. They found something on the X-ray and I needed to cancel the dentist appointment and report at once to get the MRI. Now a proclamation such as that will get even a chicken's attention!

After hanging up with her, I weighed the possibilities out and decided that maybe I needed to heed her advice. Heaven only knows how many answering machine messages I left for Val, trying to find her. One thing I knew for sure, I had no idea what an MRI was, and I wasn't about to waltz in there unarmed! The minutes dragged on and on as I frantically left more messages, but still no return call. As if more messages would magically get her to call! Now I know intellectually as I type this, it makes no sense, and you, dear reader, probably believe me to be a lunatic. Correct! When my white-coat phobia goes into full bloom, my little brain suddenly just flips into escape mode. I agree it makes no sense, but it is what it is. Where on earth *was* Val? And then another moment of sheer brilliance! I called the MRI place, explained my problem(s), and then inquired, "So are you going to dope me up, or should I stop by my house and dope myself up?" Not exactly words that the white coats accept very well!

One of the problems that I have always had with many white coats is their apparent arrogance and lack of understanding about how the world actually works. For some very odd reason, they seem to believe that in the world's hierarchy, they are on the very top with God being some place far beneath and the rest of us stupid, stupid people way, way down on the bottom among the earthworms. In my world, however, as their employer since either my insurance policy or my personal money actually pays for their service, God is at the top of the chart, with nonwhite coats under him and the white coats under the rest of society. Doctor's *orders*? I'm sorry, what exactly is *that*? As their employer, I'm paying for information. I need the medical background of the situation, the array of potential possibilities, treatments, and outcomes, and I will make my selection(s). That whole line of thinking doesn't set very well with them either. But like it or not, it's the truth! This, of course, creates an inevitable huge collision between our two worlds. In all fairness though, it has been my experience that the younger white coats do seem to me to be considerably more congenial and compassionate. So the MRI folks did a fine job of chemically putting me at ease, and the MRI was done. The tooth was still in place aggravating me, and the next morning, the doctor called and told Val and me to meet her at her office after work that evening. That certainly did not sound like very good news! As it turned out, the MRI found a golf-ball-sized something, wrapped around my pituitary gland directly under where my optic nerves cross. And once again, poor Val! She was such a great wife to have put up with me! It became apparent to me that this was a situation that obviously the doctors and dentist were clueless about, and since neither Val nor I nor apparently any of them could cure it, I did what was becoming more and more natural to me—I placed it firmly in God's hands. I prayed to him often about it and asked others to pray as well. It seemed to me that either he was going to allow me to live or I asked him to watch over Val and the boys. And once again, throughout the whole ordeal, I was eerily calm about it all. As I went through it all, I learned a very important lesson about praying that *his* will be done. Sadly, for far too long and far too many times, I had been guilty of treating God as I sadly see other Christians do as well, as some sort of genie that you petition to obtain this or that. So instead of a "gimme, gimme, gimme" prayer list, I began to pray that God's sovereign will be accomplished no matter what the circumstances. Granted, it is a wee bit scary at first, but it is a much better way to pray when you really analyze it.

Given all that, in an effort to lighten the situation a bit, I developed a sort of cartoon character that I named Terry Tumor. Terry was a little boy with a red baseball cap and dark sunglasses who was a bit of a prankster who lived in my head and continually switched the wires in my brain to create mass confusion and mayhem in my brain. He was much along the lines of the old-time telephone operators with a switchboard gone berserk. Well, lo and behold, Val took a wee bit of exception to my new cartoon creation. But eventually though reluctantly, she relinquished, no doubt solely out of love for me, as she saw that it comforted me to think of it that way, but there were a few times when her frustration showed through about it all.

One time, my ever-faithful wife accompanied me to a three-hour nonstop eye exam that the neurosurgeon put me through in an effort to decide what I had. As the eye doctor looked in my eye through the scope, wonderful Val sat faithfully in a corner of the room solely to comfort me. At that moment, I piped up with "Well, is he waving to you?" Obviously perplexed, the eye doctor said, "Who?" And without missing a beat, I responded with "Terry Tumor!" Poor Val said, "Stop that!" I behaved the rest of the exam!

Many, many weeks later, the neurosurgeon decided that I had one of four possibilities—ranging from a tumor, an aneurysm, a clotted aneurysm, or a partially clotted aneurysm, encased in a thick wall of calcium that I probably had since conception. He went on to advise that he could do nothing with it as a surgery would most probably kill or blind me. So he wished me well, and thus, it remains to this day. Needless to say, Val and I thanked God and heaved a sigh of relief!

During my third year working at the company that had moved us, they were experiencing an upheaval of sorts, and the friend who had wooed us to move to Southern Indiana moved on to start his own trucking concern. I was a bit afraid that I might end up being a casualty by guilt through association with him, but they kept me on with them anyway. Not long after that, I was offered a job at a company with a strong growth record, and I gave notice and switched companies. I worked as their safety director as well, but I felt that the new company was in a much stronger position to grow and advance.

All through our marriage, I always was very careful about making sure that I had a strong fortress in place to protect it at all costs.

Given the lack of females in my background, I was fortunate to find very nice and helpful ladies at the companies where I worked to help me better understand the woman's point of view on any number of situations that I found myself in with Val. I always made it very clear to anyone that I was more than happily married but that I would certainly be very thankful for some tips and pointers.

It really helped our marriage in the long run, as I was often clueless that I had inadvertently wounded Val by something that I said or did at home, until a compassionate lady at work would enlighten me. Armed with the newfound knowledge, I would scurry home at night, stopping off for an appropriate flower or gift, to apologize.

I firmly believe that one of the things that made our marriage very strong was our ability to truly forgive and forget following a disagreement, even if we agreed to disagree. At times, it was even funny. I would get up early to go to work and give Val a kiss, and she would say, "Aren't I supposed to be mad at you?" following a disagreement the night before. I would usually respond with "Probably." And she would come back with "What about?" And I would remark, "I don't know." That would end it, never to be brought up again. I think during those times, both of us would hearken back to her dad's earlier admonitions that the two of us had to make up things to disagree about and that a day or two later they wouldn't matter anyway. Thank goodness, he cared enough for us to give us that advice. It was invaluable throughout our marriage. At any rate, in late 1993 when I switched to the new company, I met several new ladies who were gracious enough to continue to give me their feminine insight as the years rolled along. It was at that time that I was able to form friendships with several of them that would last for many, many years. One of those was a very dear friend to Val and me named Kelly.

The workplace

Mom and Dad did the very best they knew how to prepare us for the workplace, and they really did do a pretty good job of it. I remember to this day Mom telling me as a young man, "Honey, your daddy and me aren't rich, so you're going to have to work for a living. So make sure you pick something you like to do because you're going to have to do it for a long time." And both of them touted the importance of taking advantage of every little thing that an employer is willing to teach you as that may well be a springboard of opportunity either into a better position within that company or into a better job at another company in the future.

As a factory worker all his life, Dad was a staunch "union man," but ironically, each of his four boys ended up in a management career of some sort or the other. This, of course, evoked relentless teasing among us as Mom usually sided with Dad. One day after I had a difficult day at the ol' bus garage, I came home and related the frustrations to Mom, who looked at me lovingly and said, "Honey, don't you realize that as garage manager, you have the 'kindergarten run'!" She meant that my "bus" was the bus garage we all worked out of and my kindergarten students were all the bus drivers. While she meant this somewhat in jest, there was a lot of truth to it as well! Another piece of time-tested sage advice that she imparted to me was "Son, as you go through your life at work, just watch and see how many employers stupidly run championship thoroughbred employees into the ground to the point where they end up quitting or getting fired and go to be a shining star for the competition. Meanwhile, once they're gone, the employer suddenly comes to their senses and notices, 'Did (s)he do all *that*? Oh my, *now* who's going to do it?'" Yep! Mom was exactly right! I've seen it for myself over and over and over again! It is amazing the extremely helpful insight that trusted solid older people can impart to you if you simply take the time to listen to them carefully and ask them the right questions. It is quite sad to me that unfortunately not many of our younger guys' and gals' value that advice very much in this day and age. I have been very blessed to have the career that I have had. I really believe that the good Lord put me in that career as I was perfectly suited for it, and I literally fell into it with no foresight whatever. However, since I recognized it as a potential, great, long-term career path, I decided early on to work really hard at studying it very carefully and thoroughly to be the very best at it that I could be. And heeding Mom and Dad's advice, I gave all my employers much, much more than they either deserved or compensated me. Although being safety director for coast-to-coast trucking concerns is very intense at times, it was also very satisfying work. I was on call at every hour of the day or night to cover fleet driver accidents and injuries as well as hazardous material incidents. Consequently, even though I was at home most nights, at any time, I could be called to work an accident either by phone or at the site. Thankfully, Val was accustomed to the trucking lifestyle through her dad. The trucking industry as a whole is demanding on families to make adjustments. Many family events had to be adjusted or postponed because of the lifestyle.

It is very sad to me that the people of this great nation have allowed industry leaders and politicians to all but destroy our economy. We need only look in a mirror to see the problem. We the people elect every person sitting in office making our rules. Not many citizens fully understand what a privilege this is, and they neglect to use it. What a shame! How on earth do we expect to get any different results when we continue to reelect the exact same people to office who created this mess? In the same fashion, we work so hard to earn the very dollars that have the purchasing power to change history itself, yet we continue to support the very people and products that we complain about! Stockholders cheer and allow executives of large corporations to live a lavish lifestyle with huge bonuses, etc. while they ship the jobs of our very existence overseas and give the stockholders an extra penny dividend. Stop and *think*! Without jobs, who will continue to have the means to purchase the pricey little trinkets being made overseas and shipped back to us? How exactly do you think that one is going to work out for you in the long-run stockholders?

Our young college-educated executives or high-priced consultants, in an attempt to make a name for themselves, will change things simply for change's sake alone without listening to the people actually doing the work, with the down-in-the-trench knowledge of what actually makes the company function. While at the same time all workers and managers resist real, well-thought-out, constructive change under the guise of "but we've *never* done it that way." And yet we wonder why we have so many problems! It is all so very sad!

Yet what a comfort it was for me as I cringed at observing these things to learn that as a disciple of Jesus, I actually worked for him, even though my paycheck was signed by someone else. He alone was faithful to me. He alone saw the quality and quantity of my work. Even as others climbed the corporate ladder over me, under me, and around me, Jesus and my ever faithful wife Val both knew the *real* truth! And really, that was all that mattered!

I know you have heard it said before, but it bears repeating, "Life goes by so very fast!" It seemed like only yesterday that I had met Val for the first time. The next thing I knew, we had growing boys, we had moved many times, and life was passing us like a bullet. In keeping with the sentimental romantic that I am, I went way out of my way to create memories for her to cherish as the years rolled by. Only very rarely did she ever get just a simple present from me for special occasions. The majority of the time, there was usually just a tiny, little hitch to it. She might have to open up multiple wrapped boxes, one inside the other to get her present. She might have to go on a scavenger hunt to find it. It didn't take her long to solicit the help of our sons for those. She might open an empty box full of confetti, only to discover that it has a false bottom. One thing both of us knew, she never knew which direction I might come from. It was such a joy for me to have the ability to make her so very happy!

Although she enjoyed all holidays with our little family, the top honor was given to Christmas and our anniversary. I learned from our very first anniversary that we would probably never have the typical romantic ones that I really desired. Firmly etched in my mind was our first anniversary dinner, when I went to great lengths to get a babysitter, dinner reservation, etc. Val loved our children so much that all I heard was "I wonder what he's doing." Consequently, it was nothing for us to bring a whole herd of kids to our anniversary dinners, our own two plus whatever friends happened to be "camping" at our house that evening.

Later on though, we tried to make at least our every fifth-year anniversaries very special. For instance, on our twentieth, Val was working at a local pharmacy as a pharmacy technician. It took me a lot of planning and legwork that morning, but it was wonderful and well worth the effort to see her enjoyment. As usual, I kissed her in the morning, wished her a happy anniversary, and handed her a card, which essentially told her to be all gussied up and ready to roll by a certain time. Little did she know! While she was at work, I had three red roses delivered to her. After she got off work, she had several red roses greet her in the car. When she opened up the door at our house, she smelled red roses as there was a dozen sitting on the TV. I arrived home just prior to the appointed time to find her ready to go. I kissed her, placed a blindfold on her, and escorted her to our car. I took the blindfold off at a very nice restaurant—silverware and cloth napkins! The place was packed, so I excused us and escorted her to the front of line to the fellow taking reservations. To Val's utter astonishment, without me saying a word and without missing a beat, he looked at us and said, "Ah, Dave and Val, please step this way!" He led us to a table with a red rose on it and a wrapped gift at her seat! That one got me quite a truckload of points with her! Oh…the gift was a pair of diamond earrings that I knew she had wanted! What a wonderful, wonderful wife God had given me!

One of the wonderful fellows that I heard on the radio was a man named Gary Chapman who authored *The Five Love Languages* and has a website by the same name—https://www.5lovelanguages.com. I would highly encourage all couples to explore his material and research it in depth. I found it fascinating as I looked at our own fabulous marriage with that as a backdrop. I'm sure many people looking at our marriage over the years must have thought us to be quite an oddity on many fronts. One of those would no doubt be our celebration of anniversaries, birthdays, and the like. Val's primary love language was to receive a gift from me. It could be as simple as a single rose for absolutely no reason or as expensive as a pair of diamond earrings. My love language, on the other hand, was her gift of touch. Not even necessarily of a sexual nature, although that was certainly welcome! Just simply touching my arm, holding my hand, or any skin-to-skin touch would set my little heart racing!

Consequently, it no doubt seemed odd to outsiders when I would tell them that I got Val a nice piece of jewelry and she gave me a pair of socks! But the reality was that she could have given me a diamond ring, sports car, or pair of socks. None of those even mattered to me. All I really wanted was a simple touch, a hold of my hand, a thank-you kiss, etc. Any one of those were worth more than all the gold on earth to me!

Much to my astonishment, immediately after New Year's Day in 1999, the company in which I worked so very hard to help grow in size and maintain a great safety record announced that the owner had sold out to a huge conglomerate. I couldn't believe that the owner would find satisfaction in his life doing anything else, but sell it he did. Sure enough, as was their protocol, in no time, they laid off most of the management, including yours truly!

The one thing about it that stuck out to me was how absolutely calm I was through the whole event. In the bygone years, I would have been a nervous wreck. But now that I had slowly but surely turned over many of the parts of my life to Jesus, events like this just did not bother me anymore. After all, I no longer worked for the owner. I had worked directly for Jesus the whole time. There were even times at work when people would watch me respond to events that happened and come back to me later, scratching their heads, saying, "So you must be one of those Christian guys, huh?"

On one such incident, a longtime driver had lost a safety bonus of roughly a couple of hundred dollars because he had a preventable collision. Since I was the manager of those bonuses, he came into my office in front of our staff and a couple of other drivers to yell at me. In a fit of anger, he threw a wad of money he had in his hand, which turned out to be about one thousand dollars and told me to keep that as well and went storming out. Without saying a word, I calmly picked it up and went and turned it into the owner and told him the story. The audience was stunned, perplexed, and fascinated.

In the meantime, in a land several hundred miles to the east, unknown to us, the eternal grand adventure was playing out for another lady named Susan.

CHAPTER 6

The Susan Chronicles: Adventures in the Waiting Room and with Jersey Guy

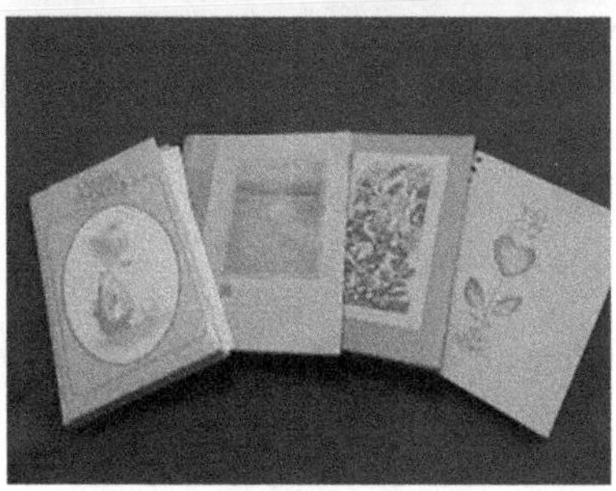

Journal Preface

I was born in 1954 in Pennsylvania. In 1977, I graduated with a degree in education from Liberty University. Throughout my journals, I often recorded thoughts and prayers for

> various typical day-to-day events, family members, friends, and students from time to time. Due to the very personal nature for some of them as well as the fact that they do not play an integral part of this book, they are not recorded here. However, for your sake, dear reader, I am allowing you to see the intimate details of my life as I lived it out before God and man. To that end, nicknames have been used in lieu of real names of the various people that came into my life.
>
> March 17, 1992: Teaching three years in New Jersey—twelve years total—now third grade. Student complained about someone praying for him. I remarked, "Wish someone would pray for me." Students then prayed daily for me.

I'll never know, but perhaps this might have been what led to my very first marital proposal. While cleaning up my desk after a day of teaching, I moved one of my books to discover a note scrawled on a piece of paper underneath that read:

> Dear Ms. Kobus,
>
> We been seeing each other ever school day. Will you marry me?
>
> Love, Yours Truly,
> Love Mike R.

And for your reading enjoyment, here are just a few more from my memories:

Following another student answering a question: "You just bought a ticket to youblewitsville." One kindergarten student to another while playing a classroom game: "Woman, stop your crying and just play the game." On another occasion, when one of the legs of a student's desk collapsed, the little girl sitting there attempted to fix it but failed. Immediately, a boy in the class came to her rescue, exclaiming, "Never let a girl do a man's work!" And just when you're up to "here" with some students, others will make you laugh. I was dealing with a problem, and when I returned to class, some of the students said, "Where were you, dear? We missed you! Yes, dear, we couldn't wait till you came back. Honey, we missed you so much!" We all then had a good laugh!

And now back to the actual journal entries.

> March 1992: Four students gave me love notes today. Dad and Mom are moving soon from childhood home. Please lead them to the right house, Lord.
>
> April 1992: Last Wednesday night, I blew front tire on curb. My friend and I sang a duet for our Wednesday night service. I lost my voice but did not have the resources to go to the doctor.
>
> I wanted to go visit my sister, Carol, in Minnesota. But I did not have money for the plane ticket.
>
> May 1992: Lord, please bless me with a husband who would have Christ first in our lives, a committed Christian, not to be swayed by material things. If God chooses to bless us with material things, we need to keep them in perspective.
>
> June 2, 1992: Three more days for the end of school, then I can go visit Carol. Thank you, Lord, for providing a way for me.
>
> March 1993: While cleaning out drawers, I came across some letters from a college friend. He had written letters of encouragement to me.

As I reread them, they brought me to tears with tender memories from the past with him as I pondered why God had not allowed our friendship to blossom into love. I could not understand why he had married another lady. I also wondered what it was about her and her qualities that she had and I did not possess. But that chapter of my life is now over.

March 13, 1993: The great blizzard of 1993. I stayed at home. Eight inches of snow in Williamstown, New Jersey had not been seen since 1983, but I arrived in 1988. I wish I could have gone home for the weekend as it is so lonely sitting at home as a single lady, but I did manage to burn up the phone lines.

March 21, 1993: A couple I know had adopted a baby boy, and he was in church. I was able to hold him. What a precious gift he is. It got me to thinking about how those who are married who want children but who cannot conceive can at least adopt them, although it is a long process, but those of us who are not married cannot do anything to change it. Even though some told me that I could adopt, I just couldn't bear the thought of bringing a child into my life who might not ever be brought up with a dad in the house.

January 21, 1994: A new year! The older I get, the years fly by faster. Just before going home for Christmas—a week—I had a difficult time about my life as a single person. It started when the church secretary who was making my skirt for the choir—she is also making her daughter's

> wedding gown—said, "What happened, Susan, that you never got married?" Of course, I said a few things, but I had such a despondent spirit after that. Then a few days later, we were talking again about kids, and she said, "Mothers will do anything for their kids, but you will never experience that." These remarks went to the bottom of my soul. I cried for about an hour or so that night—heartbroken that, yes, I will never experience little feet making pattering sounds coming to my bed, calling me Mommy or the words "I love you, Mama" or holding my own baby in my arms and knowing part of me is that little child. Seeing him or her grow up to be a child of God and serving him. Not only that but I may never experience the love of a man to love me for me, to walk hand in hand on a beach, to cuddle by a fireplace, to share our thoughts and dreams together, and to share the love of God and to serve him together. All these thoughts are on a back burner right now. My third graders do need me, but I still have these desires and dreams. We have been off school from January 18 to 21 because of ice and snow and record-breaking cold with temperatures zero degrees to negative eighteen degrees. It was a nice break, but I soon got cabin fever. It was nice of family and friends to call and check up on me. Thanks, Lord.

Often, in addition to the above, people would say things that hurt me just as much, such as "I can't understand why some young fellow hasn't snatched you up already" or "Just get busy, and before you know it, some guy will come along for you" or even "God himself will be your husband, just be content with him..." I know these people meant well with those comments, but I can honestly say that I would have to advise people not to make comments like those to single people. I found them to hurt me deeply by making me think that somehow I was not good enough for someone to marry. After all, being content is not the same as having a deep desire. It would have been far better for me had these folks simply asked how my current life was going, shown interest in things I was planning or doing, or if they could pray about something for me. Throughout my single life, I had to endure several conversations, similar to those previously mentioned, yet I felt the presence of God and just knew that he had a plan for my life. I eventually learned and treasured in my heart the teaching of the Bible that God's plan for every woman, whether or not she marries, is unique and designed especially for her.

> June 1994: School is over for the year. June 14 was the last day. I am looking forward to spending some time with family and friends.

> June 28, 1994: Mom and Dad are home from Poland.

My paternal grandparents were Polish immigrants to the United States.

> It would be nice to get my air conditioner in my car working, but it is going to take quite a bit of money. Lord, please provide.

> September to October 1994: School has started, and I have a great class of twenty students. Much different from last year. I am actually having fun teaching them, and I am trying new games and ideas. It has been a busy time with homecoming weekend, pictures, fire and bus safety programs walkathon, the missionary conference, and teachers' convention.
>
> The week of the missionary conference, I was having a hard time spiritually with my life

as a single servant of God. My eyes were on the missionary families with children. The couples were around my age and were serving together. This has always been a great desire of mine that I would serve the Lord together with a mate, not necessarily on a foreign mission field but someplace. I was feeling hopeless, crying, coming home in the car asking God why he has not fulfilled that desire. Then we went to the teachers' convention, and the first main speaker spoke on discouragement being sin and disappointment being the result of unfulfilled expectations. We are to focus on God who is the "I am." Put our faith in God and go forward for God (Numbers 13:5 and 1 Samuel 30). I had to put my eyes on Jesus and not others. Help me to remember that.

All of us teachers had a lot of fun and fellowship on that trip. It also helped me with the teasing I received about "Double A." Thinking about it, I get a warm, fuzzy, cozy feeling. I know Double A is younger than I am. Ten years? But it was fun. Twice, he chose to sit by me when we were eating. I had nothing to do with that because I was already seated. He does intrigue me. Sometimes he is real friendly and talkative, and other times, he is in his own world. I do hope we can become friends. Because of the age difference, I don't think anything else would happen, but who knows? Anyway, I can dream, can't I?

November 15, 1994: It has been a great year so far. I have had a lot of trouble with my car and getting it fixed. But praise the Lord for the extra money in the mail. It has helped so much.

Report cards this week, parent conferences, then Thanksgiving vacation. I have great room mothers this year. They have helped so much already.

January 22, 1995: A new year. What exciting things will happen this year? School is in full swing. Again, nothing is happening in my social life. Every year, I have a tiny hope that maybe this will be the year, but then nothing. When will it happen? I get so disappointed sometimes. An unfulfilled expectation.

February 11, 1995: Last Saturday, February 4, was our first snow of this year. The spelling bee held in February every year is always interesting. For my two top spellers, it seemed to go on and on. One of the girls in my class came in fifth in the state spelling bee.

April 1995: So much has happened. I had a touch of the flu in March. The teachers have been taking a computer class with Double A. It has been good to know the information, but it is so much to know. Sometimes he goes so fast with a lot of technical things. I don't understand it all. Of course, I have gotten ribbed in the class by other teachers which has just been good clean fun.

June 1995: School is over. What a wonderful year! I am tutoring this summer for six weeks. Thank you, Lord, for the extra money. Thanks for showing your provision for my dental work.

September 1995: A new school year. My eighth at this school. You have been so good. I have twenty-nine new third graders, and some of them are a handful. Lord, I need an extra dose of help this year. I am looking forward to great things happening this year. I hope I'll be able to write them down.

October 1995: October has been a busy month so far. The teachers' conference was good, but not a lot of good workshops, but I really enjoyed the main speakers.

Thursday night after we got to our hotel and changed, about eight of the ladies went for a walk, talked, played Skip-Bo, and talked some more until about twelve fifteen in the morning. We had a lot of fun. Of course, one of the topics was planning my wedding with "Jersey Guy," the new guy at church. He is divorced with kids—four—and sooo good-looking. I wish it wasn't so hard, but at my age—forty-one, they (are too young (Double A), or divorced (Jersey Guy) or happily married. What's up, Lord? Isn't there one for me?

We are back in the main grind of things. I have so many students who need extra help.

November 1995: Regarding Double A, what a nut! Ah, what a nightmare, after knowing him for two years.

November 7, 1995: Last Sunday in church, the pastor preached on the trials that Christians go through and that maybe the difficulty that you are going through may not be for you but for others. Jersey Guy was touched by the message as I saw him wipe a few tears. He did go up during the altar call. My heart went out to him. I wish I could be there for him, but I am in my prayers.

Jersey Guy has stirred a lot of feelings up for me. First, he is more my age, which makes a difference. I see that he is a good and kind father to his children and seems to make rightful decisions about spiritual matters. Then physically, I am attracted to him. His looks and body. Seeing him at church Sunday evening, I imagined myself sitting beside him with his arm around me. It just seemed to fit. I know I have these feelings. If he is not for me, Lord, bring someone into my life that will fill this void.

November 8, 1995: Wednesday evening, I sang the solo "There Is a Savior." When I had finished and was walking back to my pew, Jersey Guy looked at me and smiled a big smile at me. I felt like a teenager. It's been a long time since I felt that way.

November 19, 1995: Parent-teacher conferences. I was teaching this afternoon when a fourth grade teacher interrupted with a note from the school secretary, which contained Jersey Guy's name and phone number. I was immediately flustered. When I called upon a student to continue reading, I was informed that he had just read and that the story was finished. I tried to compose myself as I finished up with questions about the story. The students then began working on independent work as I left to go to the restroom and go speak with the secretary. As I walked into the office to ask about the call, she could not keep a straight face. It turns out that Jersey Guy actually *did* call and leave his phone number, *but* he wanted to speak to a church pastor. This was all a big prank on yours truly!

December 6, 1995: I noticed that Jersey Guy was talking to another lady at church. My mind immediately started analyzing: they are both divorced, so they will be able to relate to each other. She is quite pretty, etc. But wait! What about me? Does he even know that I exist and am available? Does he have no interest in me?

December 19, 1995: We had a church Christmas musical today. Jersey Guy was out sick with a strep throat. Rats! He would have been, should have been standing directly behind me in the choir! Something that I had hoped for! That being said, I decided to ramp things up a tad on my own. So since we were about to embark on our yearly two-week Christmas break and I would be spending it at my parents' house in Pennsylvania, I decided to put a little get-well card—unsigned—in Jersey Guy's choir folder for him to see upon his return. I later came to realize that in the long run, God designed us for the man to pursue the woman, and rarely, if ever, does it work out well when the woman pursues the man.

January 6, 1996: The Blizzard of 1996! Twenty-four inches of snow with more on the way! It had been snowing at a rate of two inches per hour! Needless to say, school was cancelled for a while.

January 9, 1996: Still snowbound! My neighbor and I did finish shoveling out my car.

March 3, 1996: Wow! So much snow since January! We have had five snow days off school so far. I had to come home early today for the apartment handyman to do a repair for me. But that didn't stop my little teacher comrades from teasing me about having a date with Jersey Guy!

April 14, 1996: Can you believe it snowed the first weekend in April about three inches? And I'm out of a car with a one-hundred-eighty-dollar repair on the distributor coil being replaced as well as car insurance coming due. Ouch!

Well, I did it again! I put a small encouragement card—also unsigned—in Jersey Guy's choir folder. And now I began doing some Jersey Guy observations as well. By observing him in choir and in church, he seems to be a sincere Christian fellow, and I simply love the way he laughs and gets others to laugh. This is crazy! But I'm in love! Will it ever come true? Or will this just be yet another one of my sad love stories? It has been seven whole months of a silent love.

June 6, 1996: On Wednesday night, a group of ladies had a prayer group. Afterward, as we all sat and talked together, somehow the conversation turned to me. As they continued to badger me, I asked if they wanted me to be open and honest with them. Of course, they all encouraged me to do so. I ended up telling them about putting the cards in Jersey Guy's choir folder. They simply loved it, and it took off from there. They all took a pinky swear—to not tell anyone else—and it became known as the Pinky Swear Club.

June 9, 1996: When we had choir practice today, I saw Jersey Guy quickly take a note—unsigned—out of his folder that I had previously put in it, and he read it. Of course, it would be great if I would ever be able to find a note in my folder from Jersey Guy, but I suppose that would only be possible if I would actually sign one of mine to him!

June 20, 1996: In the morning, I tutored two boys, and in the afternoon, I went over to a friend's house for a craft day. At least I was with other people there. Often, at events such as this, even though I am surrounded by other members of the group, still I feel so very lonely. They always talk about family, children, and husband things, and I just feel as if I have nothing to contribute.

Tonight I attended a ladies' singing group practice.

June 30, 1996: I was asked to sing to replace a scheduled singer who could not make it. After the service, as I was walking to the back of the auditorium, a lady stopped me and was talking to me about the song I sang. Jersey Guy happened to be in front of us and overheard us. He told me that I did a good job and that I did not look nervous. As I went outside, I saw Jersey Guy standing there, talking to his oldest daughter, so I walked over and joined in the conversation, and we talked together for about five to ten minutes. As I left, I saw another lady from the Pinky Swear Club who told me, "I'm keeping my eye on you!" Later, I wrote in my journal, "Yes! I'm finding more ways to naturally be able to talk to Jersey Guy!"

August 9, 1996: Last Wednesday at church, my friends told me that they saw Jersey Guy getting "Jersey Gal's" address. So of course, I felt crushed as I thought, "Well, here we go again! My heart is going to be broken!" I should have never been open and honest with my friends, as then I alone would know about the hurt. But they encouraged me not to give up! I hung around after church. Jersey Guy and I exchanged our courtesy hi's, and I met his younger daughter.

I went outside and saw Jersey Guy's mother, so I thought I'd go over and introduce myself to her. But Jersey Guy's older daughter came over and intercepted me, and we talked together about going shopping together. She thought that would be cool as she said that her dad would not let her go to the mall alone.

August 14, 1996: I baked chocolate chip cookies and put some in a tin with a note for Jersey Guy, which I took to the church. I figured if his truck was locked, it wasn't to be. However, I found that not only was his truck unlocked but the windows were down as well. Now this was pretty bold of me. I don't know what he thought when he got in his truck, but I hope he was pleased. But then I began lamenting again. He must not be attracted to my looks. He is distracted by my bad eyesight. My body type is too big for him. I may be too old for him. I might have some quirks that he does not like, etc. But I wish he would notice some good things about me. I have weak faith. Please help my unbelief. Hope then in God and lean not unto my own understanding.

April 25, 1996: Mom and Dad brought back photos and a video from their trip to Poland. I saw Jersey Guy in Sunday school class, and although

I didn't get to talk to him, he did wave to me on the way out. After the church Sunday evening, Jersey Guy motioned for me to come over to his truck where he was sitting. He thanked me for the chocolate chip cookies, and his daughter said that she liked them too. He went onto say that he had no idea who "SK" was that had left him the cards of encouragement. So he went to one of the pastors and asked him if he knew who it might be, and the pastor told him that one of the teachers who sang in the choir had those initials. I told him that I was in a baking mood and made some for my tutoring students and thought he might enjoy some too. Then he went to look for his son, and I went home.

December 14, 1996: While Jersey Guy and I had continued to see each other and exchange well wishes, etc., we still had never gone out on an actual date. However, I was getting to know him and his children better. Today I took his daughter shopping with me. I gave him my phone number and directions to my apartment so he could drop her off to go with me. Not only did he bring her over to me but he came in and spent a few minutes, and they met my cat Smokie.

Shopping with a teenager is *some experience*! When I took her back home, Jersey Guy and his other three children were not there yet. So I stayed for about fifteen minutes until they returned.

December 30, 1996: One Friday in December, I invited Jersey Guy's daughters to come over to bake some cookies with me. Unfortunately, I had to stay later than expected on that half day of school, so I called Jersey Guy to let him know. Later that day, Jersey Guy's two daughters and I had fun baking together, and my apartment and life felt so full of life and fun! I was thrilled to be able to minister to the two girls. After baking, we ordered pizza and played Uno together. Jersey Guy came to pick them up but did not stay. The girls gave me a hug and left behind two sugar cookies along with a note. That was so sweet of them!

January 1997: It's a new year, and I have been missing Jersey Guy, so I decided to call him. Just before I called, my stomach was in knots as I paced back and forth considering it. Once I actually called and began talking with him, I was fine. He answered and sounded terrible. I had planned on asking him and his kids over for a game night, but upon hearing him, I knew that he would not be able to make it. After we finished, I thought that I ought to do something like make soup and take it to them. Hindrance number 1: I don't have a large pot. Hindrance number 2: I have never actually made homemade soup before. Later, when I mentioned this to two of my friends, they said, "Chicken soup and we've got the pot!" So I made it along with some banana bread and took it over to them. When I arrived, he asked me to come in and have a seat. We all ate the soup, which was a big hit, and later watched some TV together. It was a great time! A couple of hours later, I thought I had better go back home. Jersey Guy walked me to the door and said, "Thank you. I really appreciate what you have done." On the way home, I seemed to glide along on a cloud all the way back home!

March 11, 1997: The past two Sunday mornings, I couldn't help but notice a lady coming to church with Jersey Guy. However, I found out that she was a friend of his family, but I don't know her relationship to him. I was feeling pretty bummed about this new event. During choir practice, the lady who normally sat next to me was absent, and Jersey Guy sat next to me. Since he did not have his music folder, he and I shared mine. He has a great voice, and I certainly enjoyed sitting beside him. After our practice session, I was speaking to his older daughter, and we talked about shopping, but she couldn't go with me this Saturday. But her younger sister piped up and said that she would like to go with me, so we made plans to do so.

After church Sunday night, there was a dinner, and I sat at the same table as Jersey Guy and his children along with another couple. When the couple left, I was able to talk at length to Jersey Guy, and he even opened up to me about his prior divorce. Unfortunately, he did not get to finish as another fellow came and asked him to help put away the tables and chairs, so I went ahead and headed for home.

April 28, 1997: Well, Lord, I guess I am now realizing that your answer is no. Jersey Guy's family friend, "Joy Bell," has been coming to church off and on with him the past several Sundays. She's thirty-two, single, living on her own, blonde hair, nice figure, and has taken to his kids very well. I suppose things will work out well for her. If you had wanted Jersey Guy and I to be together, you would have had it happen by now, right? My heart is crushed and broken, even being transparent to my family and friends. Hurt. When I wrote about a year ago, I wondered if this was going to be one of my sad love stories. Yep! I guess it's going to join the list. I felt that I have been stripped of myself at my own expense. I wait, have waited, and am still waiting. Why doesn't something click? Everyone else sees answers to this particular area in their lives. My heart is sickened because there is no hope. I feel unloved, unwanted, and uncared for. What kind of a pearl is that? No one wants that kind. It's not that I want to get married just to say that I am married, but I need to feel wanted and loved and know that I am a helpmate to someone, not out of obligation but out of love and care for someone. I've lost hope. Then I read the Scripture about hope, and then I am strong again. Inasmuch as I continue to struggle with my feelings of being a lonely single for so long, I have even petitioned God to remove my desire to be married, if it is not to be. Yet these feelings continue to come and go as time marches on.

May 1997: As school comes to a close, I'm going to miss my class this summer as they were a good class. I haven't seen Jersey Guy much, but just knowing that Joy Bell is around, I tend to hold back. I'm very hesitant about talking to him, even though I feel that he is still a friend.

June to July 1997: Tutoring has been going very well. In fact, it has paid for me to get an eye exam and new glasses, which I so desperately needed.

August 31, 1997: I saw Jersey Guy Sunday evening with—who else? Yep, Joy Bell. I guess they are an item now.

February 1998: Well, Jersey Guy and Joy Bell got married on Valentine's Day. I was invited to both the shower and the wedding but didn't go.

Fall of 1998: My class is going to be good this year. It should be a great year.

January 1999: I love my class this year. They enjoy learning so much! I'm getting to know two new single lady teachers better. One is in her midforties, around my age, and the other is in her midtwenties.

CHAPTER 7

The Dawn of a New Century

Dave

As the twentieth century was fading into history, our two sons were now becoming young men, though still living at home. And once again, I found myself jobless. I began to pray for God to send me another job, sent out résumés, and contacted friends, business associates, and the usual. A couple of months later, a good friend of mine who had been my prior loss control engineer for one of the trucking insurance companies from the bygone days called me and told me to call a certain insurance company, ask for a particular underwriter, and ask about a loss prevention position that he thought they had available. Not long after that, I was hired, and I traveled in a five Midwest state area assessing ensured companies' safety programs.

Although I was assigned to their Cincinnati, Ohio, office, I very rarely went there. Most of my work was performed at the ensured location, a hotel room, the company car they provided, or at my home computer. I was responsible for making my own appointments, schedules, etc. As long as my assignments were turned in on time, nobody cared what I did or when I did it. Most of the time, I would spend about a week on the road and a week or two at home. And then...*trauma*!

Because it crept up on us so slowly, going into it, we were pretty much blindsided. But to be perfectly blunt, for no apparent reason, Val had become quite the crab! She would go to the doctor, get a pill or vitamin or hormone or whatever, and be somewhat sociable for a couple of days but then revert back to being pretty hateful. Yep! She had a full-blown case of menopause! Now it wasn't as if I did not have some knowledge about it, but I had no idea! After a couple of weeks, I even went to her doctor with her. Admittedly, I was not at all a fan of this fellow. He looked at her chart and listened to us about what we were experiencing, and then he proclaimed, "Yep! It looks like she has menopause." At which time, I inquired, "So just out of curiosity, how long do you think it lasts?" My feeble little brain had reasoned that it probably lasts a couple of months or so. So you can imagine that I about passed out when the doctor piped up with "Oh, I guess she must have started about twelve to eighteen months ago and probably has another year and a half or two years more to go."

Again, not being overly enamored with this fellow, I went home to research it on the Internet. It was shocking! Everything that I was living was right there, in front of me on one website after another. Embattled folks like me writing in to the self-proclaimed medical experts detailing everything I was actually living. The expert answer? "Yep! It sounds like she has menopause. Good luck!"

Now I realize, of course, that I will never really know the true answer, but I would love to know—and I'm not kidding here—just how many arguments, fights, injuries, and, yes, actual murders occur as a result of this bizarre life event. What on earth happened to the love of my life? Who exactly *was* this beast of a woman living in my house inside the body and face of my wife? Val, where *are* you? Worse than that, I could only imagine what she must have felt like going through it all. Losing control over her thought process, body functions, etc.

On a typical frigid winter day at home, as I was inputting my reports on the computer, my wife would "barnstorm" in the front door, yelling, "Why is it so *hot* in here?" I quickly learned not to answer that one, but the reality of it was that I had not touched the thermostat since she left—that was her territory. She would race through the house stripping off all her clothes, dropping the thermostat setting like a rock, and flipping on all the ceiling fans. I would, quietly as I could, go get more clothes! It might not be fifteen minutes later that she would race through the house again, yelling,

"Who turned on all these fans? It's freezing in here!" You *know* I didn't touch that one! I can recall many times in those days of sitting at my computer with my "helmet and flak jacket" on, thinking to myself, "If this chick says one more word, I'm going to get up and choke her eyes right out of their sockets!" Of course, both of us knew that I could never lay a malicious finger on her, but it just felt so good to think it! Still, despite it all, deep down, I loved her so very much and felt so very sorry that she had to go through it. And a small handful of times during the next couple of years, in those very few brief moments of sanity, she would actually come to her senses, come over to me, hold me, and look at me with the same love that I saw so many, many times before and simply say, "Dave, I just want you to know that I still love you, but I just don't know why I do these things to you now." I felt so very sorry for her, and I did love her so very much! Even our two sons would come to me when she was gone in those days and sheepishly ask, "So, Dad, what's up with Mom?" I would explain it to them and then counsel them to "leave the house every chance you get, and please take me with you!" Sadly, I found myself literally living for my next weeklong business trip! But time waits for no man nor woman, and that too passed and was put behind us. Thank goodness! Once again, my loving wife was back, better than ever.

I had heard that the previous owner of the last trucking concern that I had worked for prior to its sale had opened up another firm sometime around the beginning of 2003. Around the Thanksgiving of 2004, he called me at my home and asked if I would be interested in coming back to work for him, as his safety department was in shambles, and he knew that I could correct it. At that time, I was still working for the insurance company, and although it was a good job and I did enjoy it, I did have to travel away from home quite a bit. And although I did realize that there was some risk in going to work for any newly formed company, I also knew that my wife and sons would probably like me to go back to a more routine job. Once again, I petitioned God in prayer, asking if this was what he wanted me to do, and Val and I discussed it at length. Finally, she looked at me with love in her eyes and said, "But really, Dave, you miss having your own fleet and your own drivers, etc., don't you?" Over the course of decades of being together, she had studied me so well that I often thought she knew me better than I knew myself. So I turned in my notice and made the switch. Little did I know what lay just a scant few years ahead for us!

As safety director for trucking concerns, I took the job very seriously, particularly since I firmly believed that I always worked for the good Lord himself. Consequently, I diligently studied my profession and made every effort to be the very best driver I could be as well as impart it to the fleet drivers. The last thing I wanted was for one of my drivers to see their own safety director get a ticket or do something foolish. How would I ever be able to effectively instruct them if I didn't lead by example? This was yet another lesson that I took to heart from my parents. Sadly, our country's leaders and industry leaders apparently never had the benefit of such parenting as best as I can tell by our society.

At any rate, during the winter of 2004, we had hoped to go to St. Louis for our yearly Christmas adventure to visit family and friends only to have it snow very heavily to the point where the highway was closed about halfway in between. One of the things that Val and I always had fun with was my driving ability and my occupation. Often, I would half teasingly but half seriously say to her, "Not to worry, your chauffeur is safety director. I drive for them all. You're in good hands with me. Let's go!" Thus, it was that winter. I told her that the highway was closed, but I saw no problem. I would simply reroute us south of the normal route and drive around the blocked highway, and I assured her that we would be fine. Neither of our grown boys opted to go with us that year, so we were on our own. The rerouting added only 70 miles on the otherwise 280-mile trip, but the snowbound highways turned the normal four-and-a-half-hour trip into a ten-hour extravaganza. We took our time and had the time of our lives! What an adventure! Neither of us would have traded our time together for anything in the world.

Ever since we bought our house, I often walked around the neighborhood to get some exercise. Many was the time that I would walk past a very nice-looking church about a mile from our house, and often, there would be people out on the back lawn playing ball, laughing, and having a great time. Several times, I considered going over to talk to them but never followed through on it. Anyway, I reasoned that even if I liked them, Val would never go for it.

As it turned out, not long after I began working back at the trucking company, I went to the grocery store on a blazing hot July day. The store was about three miles from our house. Within a block or two of leaving the store to head back home with a carload of groceries, there was an oil change business. The car needed the oil changed, but it was hot, and I had the groceries. Still, I reasoned, if I was first in line, I would stop and see if they would hurry it up for me. Lo and behold, I was first in line! When I went to pay, I noticed a paper sign sitting next to the cash register for a "free car wash" on that exact day and time at that same little church I usually walked past near our house. Well, the car did need a wash, but now the groceries had been in the car for a bit longer. Still, I thought, if I was first in line, I could ask them to hurry up. Well, lo and behold, I turned the corner by the church, and I was first in line, again! And that was where I met wonderful Dave and Mary, the young couple who were watching over a handful of teenagers who were washing the cars. I got out of the car and explained the situation to Dave, and he assured me that they would hurry. They all had such a good time washing it! After they had finished drying it, he turned to me and said, "Well, how'd we do?" I said it looked great, which it did, and asked how much I owed them. He responded with "Didn't you see our sign? This is a *free* car wash that we do every month to show the love of Christ to our community." I explained that I still wanted to donate to their church and that I needed to get going because of the groceries. For several minutes, we went back and forth. Finally, out of frustration, I stated, "If you won't even take a donation from me, then you must be nuts!" To which he responded, "Well, you could say that, but if you really want to donate, then I guess you'll have to do it on Sunday because today we won't take any money from anyone." He then wished me a nice day, and I scurried home.

When I got home, I relayed the car wash incident to Val and told her that either these people really understood the *real* Christianity of the Bible or they were nuttier than a fruitcake! She was quick to remind me once again that she did not want to hear about any church or organized religion, so I dropped it. Still, it ate on me and ate on me. After a couple of weeks, I could stand it no longer. I had to find out! I told Val that I understood her position but that I had to go to their church the following Sunday and find out. She wished me well but again cautioned me to leave her out of it.

The next Sunday, off I went on my little adventure. It was amazing! I could not have hand selected a more diverse, loving, compassionate group of people if I tried! Not only that, irony of irony, the pastor was a fellow who was also a St. Louis native, just like us! I went back and reported my finding to Val, who again abruptly dismissed me. I was so fascinated that I started attending each Sunday morning. I warned all of them not to bother Val. I was bound and determined to go very, very slowly with her this time, if I could get her to go at all.

I began going to a small group Bible study before the church service began, and that was where I met Kevin and Tammie, a married couple who had been going to that church for a couple of years. Each Sunday, Tammie would ask me how Val was doing and would say, "Well, tell her Tammie said hi!" So each Sunday, I would come home and tell Val, "Tammie said hi!" Of course, I had to explain to her who Tammie was. Several months later, I told Val that the church was going to hold a Thanksgiving pitch-in dinner for the congregation and that we had been invited, but since I knew she might not be interested, I would let her decide, and I would stay with her no matter what she decided. She looked straight at me at said, "We're going! I'm going to find out who this Tammie chick is!" Wonder of wonders, we went. She met Tammie and fell in love with her, Kevin, and the rest of the congregation. After that, I couldn't drag her away! It was fabulous! We went to everything together: church services, Bible studies, car washes, everything! Val even began studying the Bible on her own at home. She had finally found *real* Christianity, and she totally fell in love with it! I was so very happy for her!

And the years rolled on. Our two boys had graduated from high school, and though they were still living with us, they were both now strapping, muscular young men. In December 2008, we went to St. Louis to visit family and friends for our annual Christmas tour. As usual, we had a great time and returned in time to greet a brand-new 2009. Although Val had some previous trouble with her right arm, it became progressively worse, and she was diagnosed to have carpal tunnel syndrome and had an operation to relieve it in the spring of 2009. In the meantime, I began to notice more frequent fresh bruises on her hands, arms, and legs. She dismissed them, telling me that she had fallen that day or the day prior and that it was no big deal. While the carpal tunnel operation seemed to have not helped her right arm problem, her falling episodes were increasing in frequency, and now she was slurring some words. To say that I was highly concerned was an understatement.

From the time I first met her, Val loved children. Ours especially, but really all children. One of the things that she loved to do when she started regularly attending church with me was to serve in the nursery during the children's church or simply stop by and see the kids, hold a baby, etc. She was in heaven! One of the early things that was so very sad about her continuing digressing condition was when the church came to us and said that they could not allow her to do that as a preventative measure just in case she would drop a baby or fall on a child. Of course, they were correct in taking this precaution, and Val and I both understood, but it still broke her heart and, of course, mine as well, knowing how much she loved it.

Again, since I did not care for her doctor, I begged and pleaded with her to seek competent medical help. She tried her best to quiet my fears, reminding me that we had always come through these medical events together with God. I was praying like never before.

As summer and fall of 2009 came around, Val now had to use a walker to get around. Thankfully, our youngest son was home in the daytime to lift her back up when she fell as she no longer had the strength to do it herself. At that point, I challenged her with statements like "Val, if this keeps progressing, I'm apt to end up with a dead wife and the kids with no mom. Please get some decent medical help!" Again, she lovingly assured me that everything would be okay and that she was on a waiting list to see a doctor at the University of

Louisville. That was quite comforting to me as I knew they had some quality medical programs and staff.

On our trip to St. Louis for Thanksgiving that year, we had recently purchased a different car that was about two years old, so we took it on the trip. Heading back, we were in no particular hurry, but admittedly, I was probably about five miles per hour over the speed limit, and it was pouring down rain. I certainly felt that it was safe. As usual, Val was holding my hand and reading a magazine as we drove. From time to time, we would talk about whatever subject came up. We were about midway across Illinois when, out of the blue, a strong crosswind hit us and put the car at a forty-five-degree angle down the center of the highway for about a quarter mile. My little heart was pounding out of my chest! I got it straightened out, trimmed our speed back, and apologized profusely to Val for the whole ordeal, only to find her still nonchalantly reading her magazine. She looked over at me and said, "Huh?" Again, I apologized for sliding the car sideways down the highway, figuring my poor wife must have been scared to death. She started reading again and said, "Oh, that. I figured you and God could handle it." What faith! What a wife!

Not long after our Thanksgiving trip, Val and I were sitting in our living room one evening watching TV together, and she was having a bit of a Val pity party about her continually deteriorating health condition. I think the trip to St. Louis must have dredged up memories of better days and better trips. I lovingly looked at her and said, "Val, what if I were capable of knowing that you would have to be at your current level of distress with whatever you have, with trouble walking, slurring your speech, etc. for the next twenty years, but as a result of it all, one other person on earth, only one, would come to a loving, knowing, believing knowledge of Jesus. Would you be willing to do it?" Without a second's hesitation, Val replied, "Yes, of course." What faith! What a precious wife! At long last, in January 2010, we were invited to see a neurologist at the University of Louisville so he could examine, assess, and hopefully diagnose Val. Prior to going, we had to complete a sizable booklet of questions about the time line of her symptoms. The exam was quite lengthy, but at least I felt that she was seeing some championship medical people. The doctor asked for our permission to videotape the exam so he could review it later with the other doctors from his neurology group. We, of course, agreed. The exam was quite lengthy, and he went over the time line in exacting detail while examining her. By this time, her speech was slurred so bad that I had to be an interpreter for her.

Not long after that exam, we were instructed to see a different neurologist from the same group. Our youngest son took Val to the appointment, and the doctor called me at work to advise that it would be a lot quicker to render a diagnosis if we admitted her to the hospital that day rather than make multiple appointments and trips across the Ohio River to do the necessary tests over the course of many days. I had him put Val on the phone, and she agreed that would be better.

That Tuesday evening, I went up to the hospital to visit Val, and I was able to meet the neurologist as well. He was a fine fellow, even for a white coat! He took as much time as it took to explain to us in simple terms anything that we wanted to know. After he spoke to the two of us, I followed him out of her room to talk to him privately. We ended up in a tiny room together. I looked at him and asked him to promise to tell me, regardless of how painful it might be for me, the absolute unsugar-coated truth all the way. He assured me that he would. He went on to tell me that he wanted to take the time to do the necessary tests to make sure that he was giving the correct diagnosis. He took the time to explain to me the grave details and said that he would know for sure by the end of the week. Then he looked straight at me and said, "Dave, you asked for the truth, and sadly, the truth is that right now this minute I am about 85 percent sure. But for your sake, I want to run the remaining tests."

Usually, I shared everything with my loving wife, but I decided to wait in the high hopes that this too would work out okay. Val spent the next several days in the hospital while the tests were run. I spent the next several days praying that God would intervene. We were then advised that, on Saturday, the doctor wanted to speak to the two of us in her room.

CHAPTER 8

The Susan Chronicles: Adventures with Car Guy

June 9, 1999: Car oil pump has broken, and I leaked oil all over. I'm afraid to drive it now. The engine may go at any time. I've been getting rides to go every place.

Praise the Lord, I have gotten more tutor students than I had asked for! God knew that I would need the money. I also have the opportunity to work two weekends selling fireworks in Pennsylvania. What an experience! I worked six days for eighty-five dollars per day.

July 23, 1999: At this time, I am still carless. However, Dad had purchased a 1993 Spirit from a ministry that helps pastors. I asked Dad if we could check this out for me. A few weeks later, a friend of mine told me that she knew of a place in Pennsylvania that works with ministries to help them, so she gave them my phone number. Two weeks passed and I received a call from "Car Guy" who was connected with this ministry. It turns out that it was the same place where my dad had gotten his car.

July 25, 1999: Car Guy came to visit me to look at my car. When he knocked at my door, I certainly did not expect to be looking at a blond-haired, blue-eyed, good-looking fellow in his midforties. He talked to me about putting an engine in my old car to allow me to get around while we waited to see if his ministry could get a better one for me. By the way, he talked. It did not seem that he was married, but I did not want to pry since this was our first meeting.

July 30, 1999: Car Guy called. He found two cars that he wanted me to look at as well as another engine for my old car. I was able to hitch a ride back to my parents' home in Pennsylvania with one of my friends that weekend. Step by step, little by little, I see God working to get me a reliable car. While I don't have any expectations about what either of these cars might look like, God, you know what I need. With school starting in a few weeks, and having been without a car for the past three months, it is becoming more and more obvious that I need to find a solution to allow me to be able to do all the errands that will be needed while I teach at the school.

August 11, 1999: My friend and her daughters dropped me off at my parents' house, and Dad drove me to a small town about an hour away. The day was gorgeous, and we had a nice drive. Upon arrival, we asked where Car Guy was, and we found him out in the garage. My, oh my, he even looked handsome even in work clothes! He showed us a 1991 Dodge Spirit. Dad felt inclined to share with us some spiritual insights, and Car Guy seemed to enjoy this and joined right in! Listening, I could tell that Car Guy had a heart for spiritual things. Dad and Car Guy had to go back to the office to handle some paperwork. When Car Guy came back, he handed me the keys to go for a test drive. Lo and behold, he came along with me. Now that was quite a pleasant surprise! As I drove, I began to learn some things about Car Guy. He liked to fish. He loved the ocean, and he even owned his own boat. When I told him that I also loved the ocean and that we went to Cape May, New Jersey, every year for vacation, he seemed to be pleasantly surprised. He also worked on boats, and he made good money, but the more he made, the more he wanted, and he didn't have peace. So after learning about this ministry in Pennsylvania, he sold his boat and went to work for them. When we got back, Dad and I departed to go back home, and Car Guy said that he would check the car over next week and get all the little kinks out of it before I purchased it using the money I had saved up. Lord, my heart is overwhelmed and overjoyed in how you have worked in my life. Not only finding a car at a very reasonable price but also with the potential of a very nice and quite handsome single fellow around my age! This meeting was different because, Lord, you planned it. Little by little, step by step… Oh, Lord, I certainly wouldn't mind if you were to arrange a friendship between Car Guy and me and possibly transitioning it into a relationship.

August 15, 1999: Yesterday I got up enough nerve to call Car Guy about the car. I got his answering machine and asked about the car. Since his mom lived in New Jersey and he went back and forth a lot, he had offered to come and get me, if I ever needed a ride back home. Because he had previously offered, I did not hesitate to inquire if he could come if he would be in town the following weekend. He called me back and told me that he would be in town both days that weekend and that he could give me a ride back to Pennsylvania on Sunday afternoon. After he hung up, I was so excited yet nervous at the same time. I had one of my joyful fits. Lord, I want to believe that you are working something out, but I have fear and apprehension since there were so many other failed relationships—or the lack of—in the past. One thing that I have noticed about Car Guy is that he is asking me questions about my life, parents, and so forth, without me even having to initiate them. Usually, it is the other way around. I'm not sure if this is him just being nice to me or if he is really interested in me. One thing I know for sure, he had met Dad, and he really likes him!

August 22, 1999, Sunday: Sunday after church, I got home to find a message from Car Guy on my answering machine. He was going to stop by my apartment around six o'clock in the evening, but he needed directions. I was quite nervous, so I didn't even eat anything for dinner. Upon arrival, Car Guy remarked about how good it smelled in my apartment. The nice smell came from a lamp ring that I had. He asked to use the restroom before we left. Boy was I ever glad that I cleaned it! As we departed from my apartment, Car Guy offered to carry all my things, including my cat Smokie, which he didn't seem to mind that I brought along.

> While driving back to Pennsylvania, we talked to each other nonstop, and it was wonderful. When we stopped for gas, he remarked that it was a shame that we did not have more time or he would take me to see his mom. I remarked that I was not in any particular hurry to go back. But by the time we got to his mom's house, she had already departed to go to church. He seemed to be disappointed. I know that I was! As we continued on our journey back, we once again struck up a good conversation. I learned that we had so much in common. As we got closer to my parents' home, we saw a gorgeous sunset. As we drove through Valley Forge National Park.

Yep, the same place that Dave had previously stopped at to purchase a souvenir for his wife!

> I told him about all the deer and they were out and about at that time. He was so impressed that he stopped his van, and we sat there together and watched them. When we arrived at the house, he stepped in and met everyone and stayed with us for about twenty minutes before going on. Two days later, Mom and I had a good talk. She doesn't want me to get hurt again, but she did say that she wouldn't mind if something did work out between us. That really warmed my heart, and I am drifting off to sleep, so I will write more later.
>
> August 28, 1999: Dad got back from being in Poland, and on a Friday evening, he took me to pick up my car. When we arrived, we went to do the paperwork, and I didn't think I would get to see Car Guy. However, the car was in their

garage, and Car Guy was there! He greeted Dad with a hello and greeted me separately with a "Hello, Susan." My heart simply melted! Not only did I get a special hello but he used my full name rather than shortening it to a mere Sue. I have always liked the full Susan better! After we were finished, I spoke to Car Guy about making plans for him to come and pick up my old car in New Jersey.

September 7, 1999: The first day of school. I couldn't sleep last night just thinking about everything. I seem to have a nice class this year of nine boys and eleven girls. Of course, this is the only day that they all sit there bright-eyed and bushy-tailed! This whole week has been an emotional roller coaster. I left the lights on in my car, and it wouldn't start. I had to call the local pastor and have him jump-start it. I still haven't heard from Car Guy, and my mind starts reeling with all the negative thoughts about where he could be. Off on a mission trip? Too busy? What? I don't want these thoughts to come, and I try to push them away. I want to call Car Guy about coming to pick up the car. I don't need to know all the details, but not knowing anything is driving me batty! A general idea would certainly be nice. Okay, Lord, you brought him into my path. Did you do that just to tease me to let me know that this is what I could have but then you take him back again? I don't believe that is how you work! But I certainly wasn't looking. In fact, I didn't care if I ever met another man the rest of my life. I was fed up with guys and didn't need them, and then Car Guy walked into my life.

September 21, 1999: A lot has happened this past week. On September 14 around eleven twenty in the morning, the fire alarm went off at school. I knew we were not having a fire drill, but I reasoned that someone must have pulled the alarm by mistake. Nope, no mistake! This was a real emergency! One of the workers had hit a gas line, so gas was leaking in our building. We had to take our students across the parking lot to line up, and the fire chief said that it was not safe to go back in, so the buses were called to take the students back home. They could not even go back to get their book bags and other belongings. But praise be to God, at least everyone was safe! This could have been a real tragedy. By two o'clock in the afternoon, it was safe, and we could go back in.

Then on September 16, Hurricane Floyd hit, and for safety, all schools were closed. I'm still waiting to hear from Car Guy. I tried several times to call, but no answer, so I left a message on his answering machine. Last night, I finally heard back from Car Guy. He had been to a men's retreat and had gotten back home late. Since this retreat was in New Jersey, he did mention that he had thought of me as he drove past my exit on the freeway. Of course, this warmed my heart! Little by little, step by step! We talked for a while on the phone, not just about the car but other things as well. This was quite a comfort to me that we could discuss those things and not just the business at hand. I pray that our friendship will not end after the car details are wrapped up. Hope, yes! Trust, yes! But then there is always some lingering doubt. Please help me to trust you completely!

September 30, 1999: Friday night, I called Car Guy and got his machine. Monday afternoon, he called back and left a message on my machine. His message informed me that he would be around on Tuesday afternoon or evening. When I heard that, I thought, "Oh no! My home interior party is that evening!" On Tuesday, right after school, I rushed home to get ready for the party. One of my friends called to see if she could come early, and I said yes! At six forty in the evening, Car Guy pulled up in a flatbed truck. When he came in, I introduced him to my friend, and he informed me that his mom was in the truck as she had decided to come along with him for the ride. I asked her to stay for the party, but she declined. Car Guy and I talked car business. While he put the car on the truck, he asked me about school. During this time, the party demonstrator showed up, and my friend helped her carry her things into my apartment. Since previously Car Guy had told me that he had not been feeling well, I asked him how he was feeling now. He said the he has been feeling very tired lately and that he knows he doesn't really eat right without a wife to cook for him. I told him that I knew how he felt, as I don't always cook a lot since I am all by myself, but I usually do much better when I am cooking for someone else. Then Car Guy said, "Well, maybe sometime you could cook for me!" Wow! I wasn't sure I heard right! I started to ramble. After that, I really don't remember what was said! I sure had a hard time getting to sleep that night thinking about all that had happened!

October 26, 1999: To complete the registration for the car, I had to take it to get a state inspection. Sadly, it did not pass due to the left rear brake. So I contacted Car Guy as he had told me that he wanted to know how the car did. He was surprised that it had failed. Since I was coming home for Mom's birthday that weekend, I made arrangements to get the car to Car Guy as well. So in the afternoon, Dad and I took it up to Car Guy about an hour's drive. While were there, Car Guy told us that their mission had planned to revive my old car and ship it to Haiti for a missionary there. I can't believe it! My old car, on the mission field! Later that night, just as we were getting ready to take Mom out to dinner for her birthday, Car Guy called and said that he had found out that a cylinder was going out on the car as well. Since he would have to order the part, I would not be able to use the car, but he did have a minivan that I could use as a loaner.

He mentioned that he could deliver the van to me as he would be driving by our house in a few hours. When he got to our house and showed me the van, I got in the driver's seat. After he went over the location of some items, I asked if there was anything else that I would need to know. So he stood and leaned over me to show me the air-conditioning blower switch. Well, steady, my little heart! This was the closest we had ever been to each other, only a mere inch or two from each other's face! Just as he was about ready to leave, he mentioned that we would have to arrange a time for dinner. Wow! I said, "Absolutely!" Now I just have to wait for his call when he has my car finished. Previously, Car Guy had mentioned to me about his group going to Mexico on a mission's trip, and he had suggested that I consider coming with them. And so I began praying about that as well since I had never gone on one before. Not only that, this would help me to get to know Car Guy much better!

October 30, 1999: I spoke to the school principal about getting some extra days off around our Thanksgiving Day holiday to go on the Mexico trip. He said that he would have to think about it and get back to me on it. He finally said yes, and only then did I feel secure in sharing it with my fellow teachers and friends. All doors seemed to be starting to open, especially since Car Guy's ministry had given me a two-hundred-dollar scholarship to help with my expenses. Still, I was another two hundred dollars short of what I would need to be able to go. Lo and behold, Friday, as I was vacuuming my room, the school secretary walked in and handed me an envelope. When I opened it, there was only two one-hundred-dollar bills inside. No note, no indication of whom it was from. I had tears in my eyes! Praise be to my Lord who provides for my every need!

The following day, Car Guy called at my apartment while I was out doing errands, and he left a message on my answering machine that asked me to call his mom and let her know when I would be at home. Before I could call her, here he was knocking at my front door. He had brought my car and told me that it should pass the inspection now. After he left, I went to get my mail at the apartment complex office, and I noticed something black in my back seat. It was Car Guy's coat. When I finally got ahold of him, he couldn't believe that he had left it behind. He told me to hang onto it until we met up again. I hung it up in my closet and put a little thank-you note in the pocket.

November 14, 1999: A lot has been going on. Earlier this month, we had our teachers' convention, which had several workshops. I was asked to be a presenter with another teacher, and it was a hit!

I got my car inspected, and it passed, so I called Car Guy to let him know, and of course, he was glad. We talked roughly an hour about the upcoming Mexico trip and other things. Wow! The start of the trip on the 19 is fast approaching! This is going to be some experience! Lord, please help me handle the different culture and help me to be a blessing to all whom I meet. Also, please help me get through this week with report cards, conferences, etc. I guess this will be the last time that I write until my return after the trip.

November 19 to 29, 1999: The Mexico mission trip. Following parent-teacher conferences, I left to meet the others for the trip to Mexico. I was told that I would be riding in a van with others and that, much to my delight, none other than Car Guy was in charge of that van. We had a caravan of two vans, a school bus, and a motor coach. In addition to our team, the vehicles were filled with clothing and supplies. As we were preparing for departure, Car Guy asked me if I would mind riding shotgun—front passenger seat—to keep him awake. Now that was nice! As we got underway, our van engaged in a robust discussion while getting to know one another. As the others drifted off to sleep, Car

> Guy and I continued on in our discussion. About five hours into our journey, our van developed several minor mechanical issues. Thankfully, I was with a seasoned mission team that had made this trip several times in the past, and they were just about prepared for almost anything from having mechanics and meals on board and at the ready. Sleep was minimal, and bathroom breaks were sometimes few and far apart. Following several more breakdowns, we finally arrived at a Texas church that graciously fed us pizza. While at the church, we had a worship service at a little wooden chapel. Car Guy and I led the group in song. When we finally arrived at the Mexico border, one of our vans was not allowed to go through. So our van stayed with that van for about seven-and-a-half hours at the border, waiting for it to receive authorization to proceed across. Meanwhile, the others proceeded on without us. When we finally arrived at our destination on Monday, November 22, 1999, in the very poor village of Agua Fria, we stayed with some of the local families. They had no running water and no electricity, so I had to write my journal entries at night by candlelight.

Unfortunately, my journals did not reflect the exact date that we departed to return home, and due to the passage of time, I cannot recall exactly how many days we spent at our mission location. As best I can remember, it was somewhere in the vicinity of roughly ten to twelve days. While not every day was identical, much of the same type of work needed to be performed on a daily basis.

> During our stay, our men spent the majority of their time erecting a new church for the community. During that time, we ladies spent

our time cooking and doing missionary work with the children and ladies of the village, such as conducting Bible studies. In the evenings, we all came together to eat and worship together. Personal hygiene and bathing were rather interesting since there was no running water in the village. You simply went outside and stood in a bucket of water near a huge barrel of water. Bathing was accomplished by bending over and scooping out water with a washcloth. Not only was the water rather brisk but privacy was nonexistent.

During the day, Car Guy and I had very little time together, but sometimes at night, we would see each other and worship together or talk. It was great! One service, I wanted Car Guy to sit by me, but other people filled in the seats by me. So the next time, I made sure that I saved a seat for him!

One day during my time with the other women missionaries, I confided in another lady on our team that I had developed feelings for Car Guy. It was exciting to see the ever-increasing number of local residents attending our vacation Bible school for the children! We started out with only about twenty-five attending, but by the time we had to depart, it had grown to over one hundred! It was ever so sad when our departure date came. Though those people had so very, very little, they were so very loving and kind! But sooner or later, everything does come to an end. This time, I was assigned to go back on the bus, and praise be to God, Car Guy was on the bus as well! The return trip was relatively uneventful, other than the few minor mechanical problems.

When we finally arrived back at our Pennsylvania mission starting point, we unloaded and spent the night there. Ah, a hot shower! Car Guy was quite sick and retired early, but not before making sure that my luggage was all right. When morning came, he had a temperature of 102 degrees and had called to get an appointment with the local doctor. His lack of sleep and exertion had finally taken a toll on him. I went up to his apartment to bid him goodbye and return to my parents' house, but in retrospect, I wish I had stayed with him a little longer.

Tuesday, November 30, 1999: Well, it was back to school to find that my students had brought me some presents. I feel kind of surreal at this point. It is almost as if I'm still not really back yet. And I miss Car Guy, but I do want to give him some time to recuperate.

December 1999: It has been a busy month with all the church and school holiday activities. On December 20, I called Car Guy and left a message on his answering machine. Since I did not hear back from him, I called again on December 23 and left a merry Christmas message for him. Sometimes, it seems that I get mixed reactions from my family about my friendship or relationship with Car Guy. On the one hand, it seems as if they do not believe that this will blossom into anything for me. But on the other hand, it seems like they do want it to. At any rate, Car Guy seems like he wants to maintain our friendship. Now he is ramping up for a several monthlong mission trip to Haiti. But he still has not given me his mailing address so I can send him letters there. Should I bug him for it?

January 2000: As I sit here and ponder things, Car Guy did say that he wanted me to cook him a dinner prior to our Mexico trip, yet he has not returned my calls. Life has been happening so fast with the holiday activities following the Mexico trip, and now Car Guy is getting ready to go to Haiti for three months, and I will miss him. I was simply not able to write down during our trip all the many things that I have kept treasured in my heart during our trip to Mexico, such as how I felt when I woke up in the van to find that Car Guy had been looking at me while I slept, how I felt when he and I shared a blanket on the bus to keep warm, how I felt when his warm body left my side when he had to go work on the bus, or how I felt during our four thirty in the morning departure from Agua Fria with Car Guy in another van as he smiled at me when our eyes met. To me, each of these was such a special time that I have tucked away deep inside my heart. Perhaps they shouldn't have meant anything, but for a girl who has not had a special relationship, each of them meant a lot!

January 6, 2000: Car Guy returned my call about ten minutes after I had hopped into bed. Even so, I was overjoyed to hear from him. And I was even happier to hear him say that he could make it to dinner with me on Saturday evening at six o'clock. Afterward, I thanked the Lord for his answered prayer as it gives me hope!

January 10, 2000: When I got home from school, I found a message from Car Guy saying that he could not make it to dinner as their Haiti departure date had been moved to that very day. I was so sad I wanted to cry but forced myself not to do it, for I realize that although I don't understand it and certainly cannot explain it, I do know that it is God's plan for my life.

January 14, 2000: I received a message from Car Guy to thank me for the cake and calendar that I had sent him, and he gave me a Florida address as he said that he will be getting his mail from that location forwarded to him while in Haiti. He also said that upon his return in three months, he would have a lot to share with me.

February 8, 2000: The letter that I had mailed to Car Guy at the Florida address came back to me unopened. Apparently, that address had changed, so I contacted the mission board to get the new correct address, and I re-sent my letter. In addition, I sent him a care package of homemade chocolate chip cookies, some letters from my students, etc.

February 21, 2000: Well, my forty-sixth birthday has come and gone. Wow! Time jets by so fast!

February 27, 2000: The pastor and his wife have been taking groups of the school staff to dinner, and I just went with a group to a nice restaurant that he selected. He informed us that our school principal of many years and his wife will not be returning to the school. In addition, he told us that he and the new principal had hoped to bring our school up to a higher standing with more changes in the offing. I now know that at least I was secure for the upcoming school year, but what then? Will the new principal be satisfied with my work? Will we continue to need as many teachers in the future? Questions swirled around in my head. Up until the past couple of years, I had thought that I would be settled into this school for life. Perhaps I will, but this past year has begun to open up my vision to many other fields. It seems that when you are in one place for a long time, you get tunnel vision and tend to stagnate. It tends to not allow you to see a wider variety of other potential opportunities that might be available to you to pursue. My vision has now been opened up with the trip to Mexico and meeting other people. I now see other ministries to further God's kingdom in which I might be able to participate. I am beginning to feel a new burden and restlessness. Meeting Car Guy and seeing his vision has put a new perspective on things. I have begun praying that God lead me in my life and open up things as he sees fit. Of course, I certainly hope that Car Guy would be a part of it. And speaking of Car Guy, I sure do miss talking with him while he is gone. I hope he has enjoyed my letter, but he has not written back to me. It seems that he might not be much of a writer. Or could it be that he is afraid of developing a relationship with me? I'm not sure, but I need to know as I don't want to have my heart broken again.

March 3, 2000: I had a lot of errands to run today, so I didn't get home until later, around seven o'clock in the evening. When I went to pick up my mail, I found a letter from Car Guy! I was so excited that I even let out a little yell! Thank you, Lord! He even used the stationery and stamps that I had sent to him. In his letter, he expressed his joy in receiving that care package that I had sent to him. Now I wish that I had enclosed some more stamps in the letter that I had mailed to him this morning. Well, maybe I can write a short note to him at the end of this week and enclose some. Thank you, Lord, for answered prayer! It has been so hard to wait. Now he will be home in a month. Well, actually in under four weeks. Lord, I am now asking that he will make it a point to call and arrange a time to come and see me when he gets back home and gets rested. Please do it again, Lord. I am trusting one day and one step at a time!

March 12, 2000: I read part of Car Guy's letter to my class where he thanked them for all their letters and asked for their continued prayers for the people of Haiti. A few of the students asked if they could send him another letter and asked him to come to the class upon his return and talk to them. So I mailed their letters along with a tape and a letter of my own of a little more personal nature. I pray that he takes it well. He should be back home in three weeks. Lord, after a few days of resting, please help him remember to contact me. Trust. Hope. Belief. Faith.

March 21, 2000: Well, two weeks and Car Guy should be home, unless there is a change. I left a message on the answering machine at the mission headquarters to ask about the projected date of return, but I have not heard back from them yet. Lord, please prepare Car Guy's heart to contact me when he gets back. Please let me have assurance by what he says and does. Please prompt his heart to pray for me and our relationship. Hope! Trust!

April 8, 2000: Car Guy is back from Haiti, and I was finally able to talk with him. He mentioned that he would be moving to Florida, but he is not sure when and if it will be a long time. He said that he would come and talk with my class, but we haven't scheduled a time yet.

May 2000: Coming off a four-day Bible conference, it suddenly occurred to me that we only had five more weeks of school left. Since Car Guy had still not come to speak to my class, I decided to try to call him.

It should be noted here that these were the days of landlines only. Cell phones were relatively new and very pricey for both the phone and each minute of usage, so virtually nobody had one.

I did not get in touch with Car Guy, nor did I even get his answering machine this time, but I did get a message. It was from the phone company that told me the service had been disconnected. What? I couldn't believe it! Without a second's thought, I called his mom. She told me that he had rather abruptly moved to Florida and that even his sisters were upset with him for not telling anyone in advance. After I hung up, I was really depressed. I just couldn't believe that he had moved all the way to Florida without even telling me. I couldn't believe that our friendship could well be over. Was this another side of him that I did not know existed? Doubts, fears, and unbelief came flooding in. Didn't God know that I was falling for this guy and now my heart was breaking in two? I could not do a thing. I had to completely put my trust in God and wait until Car Guy contacted me. Two and a half weeks passed and still nothing. I thought if I don't hear from him in a few days after Mother's Day, I would call his mom back, as hopefully he would surely contact her for her special day.

Thursday, May 11, 2000: After school today, I had a lot of things that I had to get done. Upon arrival at home and checking the mail, I found a small package that I quickly opened up as I saw Car Guy's return address on it. Inside was a cassette tape only, no note, no letter, and nothing written on the case. So I drove to my apartment and put it into my player. I was so excited to hear Car Guy's voice! He had taped a letter to me and also to my class. In the letter, he mentioned that he still wanted to keep in touch. Thank you, Lord, for answered prayer! He also mentioned about me coming down and helping with the mission. Wow! I have been floating on cloud nine ever since! My students want to send a tape back to him, so I will include a personal letter of my own, but I think I will write mine.

Lord, your timing is not mine, but when I completely surrender, you always are there for me and have an answer. Step by step, little by little. Thank you, Lord, for the assurance that you are still working in my life!

May 30, 2000: On May 19, the class made a tape for Car Guy. I started it with a quick introduction, and they sang some songs and recorded their Bible memory verse, and about half of the class spoke on the tape. Upon returning home, I put a closing on the tape and wrote him a letter of my own. I enclosed three photos of my class and one of me during our trip to Mexico. And in my letter, I asked him about the Florida trip that he had previously mentioned on his last tape. I mailed it off the following day, so he should have received it by now. Lord, I pray that he receives everything that I said positively and that he responds back quickly. Wait. Hope. Trust. Faith. It would be so exciting and different to go to Florida this summer! What a great adventure and new experience it would be! At least one week, maybe two weeks. Not only would I be able to see what Car Guy is involved in, to be able to help in some small way, but hopefully we would be able to spend time together strengthening our relationship and have fun along the way! Asking in faith, hope!

June 3, 2000: High school graduation took place, and I was required to attend as usual. I always cry at these as they are such a happy and yet sad occasion for me. I sit and watch as some of my former little third graders graduate and head off to forge their own path in life. But it also seems to dredge up my own personal maternal time clock into full view. Will I ever be allowed to have my own husband and children? It is so very hard on me.

This evening, I ate dinner with the family of one of my students. She had asked me several months ago, and this evening was the date we had selected. After dinner, she took me outside, and she drove a motorbike with me perched on the back and took me through their family's peach orchards.

Decades later, through our Facebook connection, she told me that she was so excited to have been able to chauffeur me around that she had bragged about it the following day at school.

Lord, I am thinking about Car Guy again. I pray that he will write or send a tape back soon. He is in your hands, Lord. Please keep him for me. Help him think of me often and bring our relationship closer to serve you together.

June 10, 2000: This past week has been all half days, which has been great as it allows us to get our paperwork and cleaning completed. Thursday, the parents gave us a teachers' appreciation lunch at a restaurant.

Yesterday was the last day of school. We held a surprise luncheon for the departing principal and his wife. We had a time of reflecting back on our many past memories together, so tears flowed freely.

I hope to hear back from Car Guy about visiting him in Florida. If he really wants me to come, I need to know so I can start planning. When is the best time to fly? July or the first two weeks of August? What money will I need to fund it? This would be a fun working vacation for me. I really want to do this. So, Lord, please help Car Guy contact me soon. I would have liked to have heard from him by now, but it looks like I am going to have to wait again. Ways to go: (1) fly, (2) train, (3) car with Car Guy's mom, (3A) with Car Guy picking me up, and (3B) with my friend. I am looking forward with anticipation for this to come to pass!

June 20, 2000: I still have not heard back from Car Guy. I sent him a prepaid phone card in the hope that he would call me. Along with it, I enclosed a list of the days that I would be in New Jersey and Pennsylvania up to July 4.

Lord, please help him remember to talk to me about Florida. I would really love to go. I think it would be a wonderful experience. Lord, I need something to look forward to. Waiting again, Lord. Hope. Trust. I look forward to see how you are going to work this out.

July 5, 2000: I still have not heard back from Car Guy, and I don't know what to think. Lord, I really need to hear from him to know if this Florida trip is possible. As I said before, it would be a great summer trip—something to look forward to. Lord, I hope and pray that he took my letters okay. When I don't hear from him for a long time, doubts and fears come in. I need the assurance that he still wants me to come to Florida by giving me more details and encouragement. It is so hard to sit back and wait. Lord, remind Car Guy to *call* or write me this week. "Call upon me…and I will answer."

July 16, 2000: Lord, where is your answer? "Wait I say upon the Lord." When there is no news, does that mean no or wait? When I do end up talking with Car Guy, everything is all right. He is usually so busy he doesn't take the time to call or write—even his family. When I don't hear from him, a part of me gets upset and says, "Forget it," "Not worth it," "It is too hard," "He is not going to contact me," "Then I'm not going to contact him." But my heart says, "Keep working on it," "Don't stop," "It will be worth it all in the end. This is it this time." Negative thoughts flow so easily. I have looked for the positive—hope, trust, and belief—and I believe you, Lord, that you have given them to me from time to time. Where are you now, Lord? It is so quiet. I am forty-six now and have desired a good Christian husband and a family of my own for quite some time now, but it has gotten me nowhere. So when I finally give up and say, "I don't need a man," "I'm not going to look for one," "I'm fed up with them," "I can live without them," God drops one by my door, and thus begins a friendship. It is now a long-distance friendship which is so hard for me. I desire a deeper companionship, but I don't know what he feels because of the lack of contact. In a month, I will become very busy, but I still want to stay in touch. This is my free time, and I am willing to help him out. I know my other unmarried sister understands how I feel. Mom does in a way, but not as much. She is afraid I'm going to get hurt, and I am if it doesn't work out. I am also at a time in my life where a change in life would be good. I love teaching, but my heart is open for a change. Working in missions would be wonderful. I'm sure my teaching skills and experience would be able to be used in some way or another. I would miss the classroom, but not the daily stress and pressure.

Please, Lord, I need to hear from you and Car Guy. What attracted me to Car Guy: (1) his friendliness, (2) his desire to help others, (3) his desire for the Lord, (4) his desire to share Christ with others, (5) his love for the Lord even after a difficult time in his life, (6) when he asked questions about me and showed interest in what or how I was doing, (7) his beautiful blue eyes: I could swim in them, (8) his smile, (9) he calls me Susan, not Sue, (10) challenging me about missions, (11) his voice: music to my ears, (12) his care and concern on the trip to Mexico, (13) being able to be myself around him, (14) being able to talk with him freely about anything, (15) our backgrounds have so much in common: both of us are pastor's kids, (16) his love for music, (17) a hard worker, (18) his love and care for his mom, (19) his good looks: a handsome man, (20) his determination, and (21) his devotion to the Lord.

July 17, 2000: I had my first meeting today with our new principal. I was nervous but appeared poised and confident. We shared our background information with each other, and I answered his questions. After it was over, I felt that it was a good meeting. It will be different working for him. I hope everything goes well this year.

July 24, 2000: I still have not heard from Car Guy. I called his mom, and she gave me his e-mail address and told me that he was going to go to Haiti to work on generators, but she did not know when. I went over to a friend's house to use her computer to send him an e-mail. I was new to doing this and was amazed at how quickly it was sent. If he is still at home, I pray he will respond either by e-mail or by phone this week. I need an answer, Lord, a verbal one. Lord, I am hoping, waiting, trusting, and asking. It is so hard. I need assurance.

July 25, 2000: Well, I got my answer—no. Thank you, Lord. It was not one I expected. Car Guy quickly e-mailed back. He said he has been very busy and had found a new church and was making many new friends. Here is the part that broke my heart: he said one of his new friends have been helping with new ideas on his mission outreach, and he has enjoyed her company and was getting close. He also told his mom about her.

Since I was using my friend's computer once again, she asked how the e-mail was, and I broke down. She put her arm around me and told me she was sorry. She lives by a lake, and she has a beautiful deck by the lake. She told me to go out there and let myself cry until I was ready to talk to her about it. I can't believe it. It seems like a bad dream. Everything that I had hoped for, trusted in, had faith, waiting little by little, step by step fell away. Even though I was cautious, waiting for Car Guy to open up, waiting for him to say things before I rushed in. Like he said, I want to keep in touch. Why don't you come down to Florida. I believed him. I believed he really wanted me to come, but again I was waiting to find out details. Now I know why he took so long returning my letters. He was having a good time with her and didn't want to press the issue until he had to. I am so hurt!

Lord, my heart is breaking in two! I don't understand why you brought him into my life.

Now he is gone. Of course, I don't know that for sure, but it is pretty obvious. I pray that if she is not the best for Car Guy, that you will remove her. Lord, I'm having trouble sleeping, eating. I cry. I have a headache. Your child is hurting. I don't have the desire to do anything.

For two days, I must have stayed in my PJs almost all day. I couldn't go to church Wednesday night. I was to sing, but I had to get a friend of mine to do it. I don't want to be like this, but I'm human, Lord. You made me. You put these emotions in me. Please give me comfort. I don't know what you are up to, Lord, but this one really hurts.

August 3, 2000: Well, it's been a week since I heard from Car Guy. I had a nice long talk with Dad and Mom. They were sorry to hear about the news, and from meeting him a few times, they didn't have any reservations but one, and that was his divorce. Of course, they didn't have anything to go on, but there are always two sides. Dad said that he seemed to say things and then always had a hard time fulfilling them. Mom was really sympathetic, which really helped me out because sometimes she can get hard. Dad mentioned that we really don't know if it is a closed deal because two months is a short time to get to know someone. I did write Car Guy a letter and actually mailed it after four or five letters that I didn't mail. He should receive it today or Friday. Lord, open his eyes—convict him that he really didn't do this right. If I hadn't pressured him, he may have never answered. Lord, may he see that he does have a true and faithful friend. A friend that won't leave him, a friend that earnestly prays for him. Lord, if he is out of your will, if those are issues that he needs to deal with, please begin working in his heart. He is your child. If he is running from something, prick his heart to do what is right. Lord, he is in your hands. Help him to read my letter with an open mind. When he is ready, Lord, help him to come to grips with what he needs to do. Thank you for my family and friends. I need them more than ever. Lord, this has shaken me. There is nothing I can do but go on. I have many questions. I want to ask Car Guy many things. I may never know. That's the hard part. In my letter, I left it open for communication and friendship.

August 20, 2000: I am really starting to wonder about Dad's driving. It is so scary at times. I really think Mom should offer to drive more, but she doesn't seem to want to. I'm concerned about their safety. School will be starting again in two weeks. Lord, help me keep my eyes on you and seek your will. What do you have for my life? My dream is still there, but it is broken and bruised. Help me trust you. Show me the open doors. Again, help me be a faithful friend—praying, showing kindness and concern from time to time, expecting nothing in return. This is starting the third week since he has received my letter. Lord, help him reread it, pray over it, and seek your face over our friendship. Show me your power and your love for me. If somehow there is someone else for me, reveal him because I can't imagine how I would meet my soulmate. I really believed Car Guy was the one, and I was willing to wait for you to put it together.

September 10, 2000: School has started. I'm starting off this year with sixteen total third graders, seven girls and nine boys. I would love to go back to Mexico this year with the mission group, if it would be the Lord's will for me. Hindrances: cost (five hundred dollars), time, and getting the principal's okay. I sent Car Guy an e-mail a couple of weeks ago, but he has not responded. I would have thought that we could have at least stayed in contact with each other from time to time just to see what the Lord is doing in each other's lives. He has not replied. So either he is in Haiti, or he just doesn't want to talk with me.

November 10, 2000: Last Saturday, I had a little bit of a tough time as I remembered about getting ready for the Mexico trip last year and remembering Car Guy. Thoughts were running through my mind, and I began to cry. The next couple of weeks will be hard because of the memories. I do remember to pray for him and pray that he would at least e-mail or contact me just to let me know what is going on in his life. I had so much hope and trust in that relationship. It is hard to open up again to something new if it comes down my path. Right now I don't want to go down that road if it is going to lead again to hurt, to be broken, to lose hope—disbelief. Also, again, I have that same feeling: forget it, it's not worth having your heart torn apart. All I can say is that you did bring Car Guy out of nowhere for me, and it was working until...

July 19, 2001: Wow, it has sure been awhile. In January, I received a large brown envelope from Florida. In it was a general letter to family and friends from Car Guy and his girlfriend. Also a Christmas card addressed to me but no notice of their marriage. I had cried all the tears I could before, so I didn't cry when I read it since it was a general letter. If it had been a personal letter from Car Guy, I'm sure I would have cried buckets. On a personal calendar, they had their pictures. He had shaved off his moustache, and he looked older.

July 22, 2001: So far, it has been a great summer. The church that Dad was attending when he felt that God was calling him to become a pastor held their fiftieth anniversary celebration. Our whole family went to it. While I was there, I had a chance to reconnect with an old friend from my college days. He had been married but was now single. We talked at length, and it was fabulous. It brought back the fond feeling of being about to just be myself and enjoy a good conversation with someone who was really interested in what I had to say. But if this was to continue on, it will take God first and him second to make it happen. Sometimes thoughts of Car Guy continue to come up from time to time. I now realize that marriage to Car Guy may have not been good after about five years or so. I believe that God saved me from a potential bad marriage.

CHAPTER 9

The Susan Chronicles: Adventures with Dating Websites and California Ranger

September 2001: Another school year. I start with seventeen students this year.

September 11, 2001: Worse day in history in my lifetime. The school day had started as usual. About midmorning, a colleague of mine advised me that two planes had hit the World Trade Center and another had hit the Pentagon. I collected my students and got them back in their seats. We prayed for our president and our nation. The parents were notified to come and get their students if they wanted to do so. As the day progressed, we continued to receive updated reports from the news. By the end of the day, I think I only had three students left in the class with me. Upon returning home that evening and reflecting on this horrible event, it occurred to me that our nation had been free for so long, and we had become too complacent that something like this could happen to us. Tragically, many souls died prematurely today that did not have to. I wonder how many were now in heaven with our dear Savior and how many sadly did not make it. Such a shame. I did get a bit of good news though—my best friend from first grade is getting married!

December 2001: I attended my friend's wedding, and it was great!

For Christmas 2001, my parents bought me my first computer. As I learned to set up my own e-mail account and used Microsoft to type parent information letters, homework, and test schedules for my students, I began to explore Christian single websites. At the time, I joined two of these sites. As I explored the many profiles that were offered, I began to see a pattern of the guys that were on there. Some of the guys were on for just friendship. Others were looking for a godly marriage. Still, others were on for fun or to scam a gal. I learned quickly to ask questions that were not your typical questions. It seemed the longer that I was on these sites, that I was able to pick out the scammers that wrote to me. I learned to be wise in not writing back to them. Most scammers always had a previous marriage, whose wife died of a terrible disease or died in a car accident. They always had one or two children. Their grammar and sentence structure were atrocious. They always said they were on the site for a short time and wanted my contact information to keep in touch. They also used lines such as, "I knew you are the one for me because I can't take my eyes off your profile picture."

One of my friends gave me a website called Scam Watch, where you could type the name and see if they were on this site. I actually found two guys who had tried to contact me on this site. I reported them to the website I was on. On one of these Christian single websites, I became a chat monitor. For my volunteer time, my fee to be on the site was paid. I enjoyed my time in the chat room and actually met face-to-face quite a few male and female friends. A few of these friends later met and married. They are still married today.

But along with the success stories are the horror stories. It is those horror stories that I would warn people (especially females) to proceed with caution when on dating sites. First, be strong in your faith and your moral convictions. Don't fall for smooth talkers that make you feel good. Realize you are not a rescuer. Realize that just because you have waited so long for a mate that your defenses may be more vulnerable, and you could end up in real trouble.

Chat room antics—should I elaborate? When you meet for the first time face-to-face, meet in a public place. Make sure you tell your friends and family who you are meeting and where. Provide your own transportation. If it is long distance, make sure the guy visits you first and introduce him to all your friends and family. Determine beforehand what fences you will put into place. Here are a few horror stories I heard:

A gal from England met online a young man from the United States. They corresponded for several months, and he asked her to marry him. She said yes but wanted to meet him face-to-face before their marriage and her move to the US. After buying a plane ticket and arriving at his home, she knocked on his door. A woman answered and informed her that she was the Mrs.

What a shock this poor gal had, as well as a total waste of her time and resources.

Another gal met her husband online and, after several months, found out he was molesting her children. She took him to court.

Another gal married a guy she had met online, and right on the honeymoon, he said to her, "I don't want to be married to you and left her."

Being very cautious, I continued to search profiles and would write to several guys. Each of these would last a few weeks and then disappear. I was corresponding with a guy from Ohio, and we seemed to click. He finally told me after three weeks of writing that not only was he divorced once but three times. I told him I did not want to be his fourth wife. That ended our correspondence.

January 2002: I found out our principal may be leaving our school.

May 2002: I found out for sure our principal will be leaving, and another one has already been found.

May 22 to June 22, 2002: At this point, I had some experience on the dating websites, and I was highly tuned in to potential scammer profiles. However, as I scanned through the various profiles, I did come across a certain one that was of interest to me. That was the one posted by "California Ranger." After we had been chatting on the website for about a month, I had really enjoyed our conversations together. Of all the guys that I have been e-mailing, he stands far above the rest. My heart is drawn toward him, and I want to know him more. One of the things we have been talking about is how a person approaches marriage by getting to know the other person slowly and not rushing into things. This has been an interesting topic.

July 1, 2002: Well, I took a chance and asked him some questions, and he responded favorably. My family now knows about this new adventure of mine. And I got some sisterly advice, such as not writing too often at this stage. Of course, my heart wants to write to him every day.

August 7, 2002: It is just about three months now since I have been sending e-mails to California Ranger. He has been on vacation this week, and I really miss his letters. We moved on to Quick Messaging, which is great, and he even brought up the phone again. My heart did a leap! We need to decide on a day and time. Since he is in California, there is a three-hour difference in our time zones. We also decided to memorize Scripture verses together on the Internet.

August 10, 2002: Mom fell on Friday and hit her head. She was rushed to the emergency room but did not even get any stitches.

Now California Ranger and I are off to memorize another Bible verse together. I asked him to pick one this time. It is so cool memorizing Bible verses over the Internet with California Ranger together. Of course, it has to be on the "honor system."

June 10, 2003: Well, a lot has happened. Uncle Bill died. Dad was diagnosed with congestive heart failure. The war with Iraq. It was a good school year, praise the Lord! A wonderful blessing: California Ranger and I are still communicating after a whole year! California Ranger calls me more often now, and I enjoy hearing his voice. He is planning a trip to come and see me in the next month! It was to be this week, but it had to be pushed back. I am so excited yet nervous about meeting him. I know that I am "fearfully and wonderfully made." But to be honest, guys seem to want the slim Barbie look, and I am not that type. I have come to care about California Ranger in a special way, but I would love for this friendship to go to the next step. I have prayed for this my whole life since I had been a teenager. I am trying to guard my heart, but it is hard to do. I hope you will bless our meeting, and I pray that it will flow smoothly. May there be times of fun, laughter, and good discussions.

July 16, 2003: Well, California Ranger came to visit me! I was a bit nervous since I had never done this before. California Ranger flew into Philly on July 5. He was with me a total of five wonderful jam-packed days. We crammed so much into it, and it was all such fun: church in the morning and Atlantic City later to walk on the boardwalk, New York City: ground zero and Central Park, and Dad and Mom's house. Dad and California Ranger seemed to hit it off together. He wanted to see their basement as they have none in California. We also went to Lancaster, Pennsylvania: Amish farmhouse tour and dinner with Mom and Dad. At Washington DC, we went on Metro Service into the city, Washington Monument, on a bus tour, Arlington Cemetery, and the White House. We also went to Cape May, New Jersey, and toured the city, the lighthouse, and Washington Street Mall. Thursday was California Ranger's last day. I cooked dinner for him at my apartment. He had an early departure the next morning. Afterthought: "This is the Lord's doing. It is marvelous in our sight." Well, I would have never thought that this would have happened. Only the Lord would have made this possible. I have grown to care and love California Ranger through this year of e-mail. Meeting him helped make it so real.

Things that I admire and like about California Ranger: (1) his love for the Lord, (2) his willingness to memorize Scripture and to pray with me, (3) his care for me as a person, (4) a perfect gentleman, (5) his smile, (6) his blue eyes, (7) his warm hugs, (8) his skills to navigate and get around in new places, (9) he calls me Susan, not Sue, (10) his love for music, (11) I am able to talk freely with him and be myself, (12) I am able to have fun with him, (13) his voice is music to my ears, (14) a hard worker, (15) his love and devotion to his daughter, (16) sharing Christ with others when he can, (17) very good-looking, (18) being laid-back, (19) doesn't have a critical spirit, (20) a willing listener, and (21) management skills.

I would really like to know how California Ranger feels about me. Like me, he is close to being fifty now. I don't want to pressure him, but I need to talk it out more to get to know his true feelings about me. I know he is my friend. I know he cares for me. But how far, how deep, and to what extent does it go? I would love to be his helpmate, his soulmate, his wife, his lover. And

Mom is right, I would do anything for him. But isn't that the way it is supposed to be, a helpmate for your husband? I know I have a lot to learn in this area, and it might take me a year or so to get prepared for a good marriage. I loved the feeling of being fulfilled as I cooked dinner for him in my apartment and as we prayed together and talked together. I miss him so much. I know my limitations: I have arthritis, my eyes aren't good, and I need to lose some weight. These are my imperfections, and California Ranger knows them now. But what does he think of them? He is still my friend in spite of them, and I am still his friend in spite of his imperfections. Can I keep up with him? Will I slow him down if I am not as active as he is? We are totally opposite, but is that is what is attracting us to each other? Yet we have a common ground, and that is the Lord. As long as we keep you in our relationship, Lord, I know we can make it!

July 21, 2003: Lord, please keep California Ranger in the palm of your hand and bless our relationship together. Please let it grow sweeter and stronger. Ugh! It has been two days now, and California Ranger and I have not messaged each other. I miss him!

January 2004: Well, Lord, here it is, the new year! You have blessed me in so many ways! I have a fantastic class this year. They are a joy to teach and make me laugh. What a great bunch of kids. So far, I have been healthy. Just my knees giving me trouble. Should I get a cortisone shot? You have given my great friends here, also my great friends on the web.

California Ranger is still my best friend. He sent me a Christmas gift this year and a sweet card. In it, he said my friendship has been a light in his life, and he prays that it will continue. Wow! Our phone talks with prayer are getting sweeter every time. Lord, you have blessed me with a wonderful man, and only you could have done that through the modern technology. I am so thankful! Lord, keep California Ranger close to you. Don't let him go. Bring us both closer to you and to each other. In our own visions and purposes, may we love and serve you as a team to further your kingdom. May we be able to be together so we can serve you more efficiently than we can separately. Lord, bring us together again. Our love for you is strong. Bless our lives, Lord, for your glory. Lord, this has been better than anything I could have imagined, better than my choosing—the wonder of it all. Wow!

June 6, 2005: Wow! So much happened in the past year. School ended with me looking for a new job. After many résumés and applications, I was led to Valley Forge Baptist Academy to teach second grade. It was not my choice, but God sure led me through a tough transitional year.

I visited California Ranger in July 2004. Wow! California is so beautiful! What an experience. I felt California Ranger and I drew closer. I then moved from New Jersey to Pennsylvania and moved in with Dad and Mom. It was a hard thing to do after living on my own for twenty-five years. There have been some pluses: I have been able to save money. But I do really miss having a place of my own.

In September, Dad was diagnosed with lung cancer caused by asbestos (mesothelioma). It has been so hard to see him go down from being a very active man to just needing help get out of a chair or walking. We all as a family have had a tough time dealing with this. It is the hardest on Mom as she is his main caregiver. He has passed the seven months (they had only given him a six-month life span at diagnosis), and we are planning a family vacation to Cape May, New Jersey, in August.

During the month of November to December, California Ranger and I had a tough time. But we came through, and I went to visit him in March. I felt he really opened up more to me about his childhood and family. It was very special to me when we prayed that he would reach out and hold my hand.

Another special memory to me was, on my last night there at dinner, we talked about our dream house and what it would have in it. That was a lot of fun! Then in the motel room, California Ranger came in and sat and looked at the scrapbook I had made of our travels together.

Another memory was going to Yosemite. Then as we were leaving, it started to snow. It was so quiet and peaceful. Traveling back, we had a lot of fun playing a word game in the truck.

California Ranger is planning a visit here in August and hopefully spending a couple of days with us in Cape May. It is hard for me to relax and completely trust in you, Lord, as I know he still talks with D (another girl he had met) and plans a visit with her.

July 30 to August 6, 2005: Well, California Ranger could not come out and visit. I was totally disappointed. He had to get the transmission in his truck fixed, and it cost over three thousand dollars, so that ate up his savings. I had a hard time dealing with this as I know he *had* to get his truck fixed. But I also think, well, he just didn't want to come out, so he got his truck fixed instead. My feelings were so mixed. I totally want to believe him, but there is this small doubt, but I must believe the best of him.

Cape May, New Jersey, Friday night was spent packing the cars for the next morning. It was exhausting! Saturday morning, we finished the last-minute packing, and our small caravan departed around nine thirty in the morning for the New Jersey beach house. Although the week was a whirlwind, it so much fun having a family vacation with all of us together again! We had such fun together with games, such as Uno, *Balderdash* with words such as "squama" and "clinchpoop" that made us all laughed so hard, poker—my nieces and nephews taught me how to play, and I'm not sure I understand it, but I did actually win once—and puzzle, two thousand pieces. We had fine dining of home-cooked meals, Wendy's, and Lobster House. We had activities, such as family photos at the beach, sing-alongs, prayer and worship times, fishing—Dad simply loved it and wanted to stay all day—crabbing, shopping at Washington Street Mall, swimming in the ocean—we rented a beach wheelchair with really big wheels so Dad could go and put his feet in the water and feel the wet sand on his feet as Dad always loved the ocean—surfboarding, "walking the boards" at the Wildwood Boardwalk, miniature golf, watching the sunset at Sunset Beach along with their flag lowering ceremony. All in all, it was fabulous and went by way too fast!

Note: It should be noted that there is a large four-year gap in the journals here. I was preoccupied with many things during this time and did not do any writing as a result. Most prominent among them was the continuing deteriorating health and ultimate devastating death of my dad on February 13, 2006. It is also worthy of note that California Ranger and I went with a group from his church on a ten-day-or-so mission's trip to the Happiness Foundation Orphanage in Quito, Ecuador, in the summer of 2008. And sadly, he lost his job at some time near the end of 2008 and had embarked upon a job search. At the beginning of 2009, he had moved to the East Coast, in a coastal town, pursuing some job leads.

CHAPTER 10

The Susan Chronicles: Adventures with California Ranger on the East Coast

June 9, 2009: Lord, I am starting a new journal which will contain my prayers, talks with you, and my thoughts. Be with California Ranger tonight. Give him rest. Continue to lead him in the right direction for a job. I pray that he will get some inquiries from his résumé going out. May he really seek your face on the California job. Lord, if at all possible, keep him here on the East Coast. Keep the gals from Christian Café away from him. Our friendship is too sweet for anyone to come between us.

June 10, 2009: Thank you for this day—a day to be out and enjoy your creation! I had a wonderful time at Lake Tobias Wildlife Park. Lord, be with California Ranger tonight. I know he would have enjoyed where we went today. I pray that the jobs will start coming his way. May there be at least two potential job offers so California Ranger can process the pros and cons and not just take the job in California because it is "at least a job." By what California Ranger tells me, it is not his pick, but maybe you know better. Lord, for my personal reasons, I want him here on the East Coast, but I know how things go. Also, please continue to make our relationship strong and may California Ranger see that he has already "a lady in waiting," and he will lose so much if someone else comes into the picture. Lord, please help me with my weight. I am doing the walking, weights, swimming; and no change seems to happen. I need a miracle in many things.

June 11, 2009: Lord be with California Ranger tonight. Help him as he continues to look for a job. Again, may there be something from his résumé that goes through. I pray something promising will come up so he will be able to compare it with the job possibility in California. Lord, he just moved here. He spent all that money to drive across the country, rent a small U-Haul, and change his truck and bike licenses for two years. Lord, I know his desire is to settle down, not move month to month over some risky job. Also, keep him away from gals on Christian Café. Lord, you gave him to me, and I know that you can take him away, but my heart's desire you know.

June 12, 2009: Thank you for this day, Lord—stress free! Be with California Ranger as he flies to California and back. Be with him as he meets with this guy tomorrow at four o'clock in the afternoon. Help him remember to ask all the questions that he has. Lord, I can't pray that he does not take the job if it is offered to him. That would be selfish. I want him on the East Coast, but it seems you have other plans. I can't stop that. All I pray is that he will not make a hasty decision. My gut tells me the job is his, and he will go for it unless there is something when he gets back that is worth him staying. May he be able to come with us to New Jersey at least three to four days. I am going to miss him so much. He is so close, yet again it is not going to happen. Lord, I just don't understand. My heart's desire on this matter is never being answered. My hope, trust, again is weak. I need to see a miracle in my life. Lord provider, like Hannah in the Bible, I cry out to you night after night for my desire.

June 13, 2009: Lord, thank you that California Ranger arrived safe in California. I pray that all his questions were answered at this meeting. I don't know his feelings, but if it is a go, I know he will take the job. It just seems pointless that he wasted time and money to come here and changed everything legally just to move back less than a month doing all the changes over. I know I don't understand everything. All I can do is pray for wisdom on his part. Also, that there would be something in the next two weeks to make him look at all angles. Also, continue to bless our relationship. I need reassurance, and if possible, in your still-small voice, speak to him about commitment and marriage. May he see more and more that he can't lose me and he can't live without me. I know I love him very much, and I want to spend the rest of my life with him.

June 14, 2009: Thank you, Lord, for this day. The little ones in junior church were actually good today! Thank you for California Ranger calling me. I feel good that he calls me to share and to talk things over. I know he needs someone to just talk and vent things. I am glad that he feels comfortable in doing that. Lord, unless you intervene in some way or speak to California Ranger in such a way that his heart wants to stay in the East, then I know that he will take this job. It just tears at my heart because I feel that I am losing him again. Our times together will not happen. Cape May, New Jersey, is a no for him. Lord, all I wanted and desired was to spend quality time with him, relaxing and enjoying God's creation—the ocean and sunsets, walking along the beach—but you are closing the door again on my desires, making the heart sick. I know I am not perfect. I disappointed you many times, but it seems you take away the things I desire the most. I have lived fifty-five years. I could care less about movies, TV, games, sports. What I care about is relationships. Family is here now. I am with them all the time. I desire my own now. It doesn't matter about money or material things. I care deeply about California Ranger and would be more than happy to share a life with him. But more and more, we always seem to be pushed farther away. I accept whatever you have.

June 15, 2009: Lord, be with California Ranger during his return travels to the East Coast. He will be in very late. Give him rest and peace. Lord, this is a hard decision for him, and I know he wants to make the right one. My feeling is that he will take the job because (1) it is a job, (2) he is bored, (3) this gives him a new adventure again, (4) he is guaranteed the job for six months, and (5) it is a job he will like. My heart says stay, and that is because (1) he just has been here a month, (2) I want to see him more, (3) my heart is involved, and (4) I want him to come to Cape May. But I know that he will choose a job. If he does, Lord, I am willing for the adventure of traveling back with him and then flying back, but all this is done quickly, too quickly. I say, Lord, give him wisdom and peace.

June 16, 2009: Thank you. California Ranger arrived safe and sound through the thunderstorms. Thank you for his call today. I know he is bouncing off his thoughts and ideas with me, and I like that, Lord. He needs a good friend to do that with, and I am so glad that he has chosen me. I know he will ultimately make the decision. Thank you about these other two calls about job offers on the East Coast. It will give him something to compare and go by. I pray for his interview at eleven o'clock in the morning. I pray that it will go well and that they will not leave him hanging for a week but get back with him as soon as possible. I pray for the other interviews he has to set up, and we know nothing right now about this job. Guide and direct, give small signs to California Ranger so he can say, "Ah, okay, I know what to do." Be with him tonight, give him peaceful sleep, and may the angels watch over him. Help him to know and realize I care and love him dearly.

June 17, 2009 (Wednesday): Thank you, Lord, for this day. I woke up with a bad headache, I think from all the stress and tension. I know you are in control, but I know you also let us make our own decisions. Please let that company let California Ranger know as soon as possible by Friday. Also, be with him on this other interview. May you give him peace about his decision. Lord, I need reassurance from you also that our relationship would move quicker if California Ranger was here on the East Coast. It may make him realize how worthy I would be to him as a wife. I know it wouldn't happen right away, but by seeing each other more, we would grow closer, keeping you first in our lives as Hannah prayed, so I do pray for California Ranger as my husband.

June 18, 2009: Thank you, Lord, that California Ranger and I have been texting. It is fun to keep in contact that way but better on the phone and in person. Lord, he said he talked to his brother, and it helped him see things a bit differently, but he has not made a decision yet. I am not sure what his brother told him. I could guess but am not sure. I pray for wisdom on his part. Yes, I want him to stay, and I know I will be sad and disappointed if he goes back, but there is nothing that I can do. I know he would like to be settled somewhere, and at his age of fifty-four, I just don't think it is wise for him to be moving all around, no benefits to start off with and no guarantees this job will take off after six months. I am baffled, so I leave it in your hands to guide him.

June 19, 2009: Thank you, Lord, for this day. Help us as we get ready for our vacation in Cape May. Lord, I pray for California Ranger tonight. Give him a good sleep. As the time gets closer, make it clear to him what he should do. I pray it will be the right decision. I have to rely on you, Lord. You know my thoughts, my heart. If he takes the job in California for six months and it does well, then it will be just our yearly visits again. He is moving all around, nothing settled. If he takes a job here, he can get more settled, and we could see each other more. And hopefully, it would be a positive thing with a future involved. So not sure what his brother had to say to him but may he rely more on you than on him.

June 20, 2009: Thank you, Lord, for the call from California Ranger. Yeah! Now he is staying and has interviews! You know the job I think is right for him, and I pray that interview goes well. Thank you for the advice that his brother gave him. May you bring him to believe in you. Thank you that California Ranger will be in Cape May. Help him to pick the right dates. I know for us it would be better after the fourth, so if you could please place that in his heart, that would be awesome. Thank you so much for answering prayer. Now he needs the job.

June 21, 2009: Thank you for this day. Keep us safe in Cape May. Thank you for the decision that California Ranger made. May you continue to give him signs that he did the right thing. I pray for his interview on Friday. I think that job has potential, and it is in Pennsylvania! One of my desires was for him to move to Pennsylvania, so this could be a good thing! My desire also is that we see more of each other and he will miss me and want to be near me. I desire him to then realize that even though I am not perfect, I am a great catch with a lot to offer him, and my greatest thing I offer him right now is my loyalty.

Thank you so much for answered prayer that he is still here on the East Coast.

June 22, 2009: Thank you, Lord, for this day—a good day. Help me with my knees. I want to be able to walk on the beach without much pain. Continue to help me with my weight. I pray for California Ranger. I pray that he doesn't get discouraged but will continue plugging away and sending out résumés. I pray for the interview on Friday. Lord, may this not be a hiring from within but may the person actually be looking for someone outside of their company to hire. May California Ranger be the right candidate this time. May he get called back to interview the second and third time. I am excited that he might get this job, and dare I ask that he might even be transferred closer to me. May he continue to pursue our relationship to a deeper level even though he had said that he doesn't want to remarry. May you change his heart as you have changed the king's heart. My desires, like Hannah, I cry out to you.

June 23, 2009: Thank you, Lord, for this day. It was fun to e-mail back and forth with California Ranger today. I'm not sure if he applied for the New Jersey job. The only concern that I have is the high cost of living and taxes there. But it is in your hands, Lord. I pray as he prepares for the interview this Friday that the person will be impressed and want to interview him again. I pray that you would give him confidence and peace. Lord, bless our time in Cape May. I am not too happy with him spending July 4 with other friends because I never know if they set him up with someone or if this "Sunrise" person will be there. Lord, you will have to take care of that for me. I am extremely happy that he will spend a few days with me in Cape May. Best after the fourth, hopefully at least three to four days. Lord, continue to bless our friendship, and may it grow stronger and take the next step. You have to prepare him for that.

June 24, 2009: Thank you, Lord, for this day. It was different but good. Be with California Ranger tonight. Give him rest for his body. May his cold heal quickly. Continue to help him as he job searches. May you open those doors to the right job. Be with him on Friday as he travels to his interview. May it go well. I pray that he will be able to stop here on his way back for an hour or two. May he come just at the right time for Cape May, and may he enjoy his time with us more that with his other friends. Guide and direct in all job searches and interviews, and may he have a job by mid-July. Continue to guide and build our relationship toward "one." Continue to speak to his heart about marriage and dispel his fears and insecurities about it.

June 25, 2009: Thank you, Lord, for this day. Help us remember everything that we will need for our vacation. Help us to arrive safely. May it be an enjoyable and relaxing time. Keep us safe from any injuries and disasters. I pray that California Ranger will spend at least three days with us. May it be the best time ever for him. I pray that you will keep him safe as he drives tomorrow for his interview. Prepare the hearts of those he will be talking with. I am trusting to hear good news.

June 26, 2009: Thank you, Lord, for this day. I am excited about going to Cape May. We all need a break, and it will be fun. Keep us all safe. Thank you that California Ranger is coming. I am soooo excited about that. I know he will enjoy himself with me and the family. Help us also get some one-on-one time at the beach or the boardwalk or when you see fit. I know I'm not that great in a bathing suit, but help him to look past that and see the person I am and that he will want to be around me more. Thank you, Lord, for his interview. I pray that they will keep him as one of the three managers they need to hire. It would be awesome that he would be here in Pennsylvania. Hoping that this would be where he would stay as our relationship gets closer to a possible marriage.

June 27, 2009: Thank you, Lord, for this day. A lot was done today to get ready for our vacation. I pray that you will get us all there safely. I pray I will remember everything. Give Mom sleep tonight. Be with California Ranger. I pray he will be able to join us for several days which he says he will. Keep him safe in all his driving. I pray that the company will offer him one of the manager positions for the end of July. Give us all rest tonight. Amen.

June 28, 2009: Thank you, Lord, for this day and for the safety you provided for each of us to get to Cape May. Be with California Ranger tonight. I am not sure why I could not get ahold of him, but he is out doing things. May he hear soon, and may he get a job by the end of July.

June 29, 2009: Thank you, Lord, for this beautiful day. We had a great day at the beach. Thank you for California Ranger calling me today. Continue to be with him, and may he hear good news.

July 1, 2009: Thank you, Lord, for this day. Be with California Ranger and keep him safe and continue to be with his job search. May he hear back from that one company. I pray he will not move back to California. Be with him as he travels here next week. May we have a great safe time.

July 2, 2009: Thank you, Lord, for this day and for keeping us safe so far. Continue to put a hedge of protection around us. Be with California Ranger and continue to help him on his job search. May he get the right job before August. Be with him as he travels here for a few days.

July 3, 2009: Thank you, Lord, for this day. Be with California Ranger tonight. Let him hear back from the company that interviewed him. Bring him here in Cape May, New Jersey, safely and let us have a relaxing fun time.

July 4, 2009: Thank you, Lord, for this day. Thank you for the freedom we have here in America. Help us to never to take it for granted. I am so thankful to be an American. Be with California Ranger tonight. I hope he had a nice time at the church barbeque, but it would not be too nice if there were single ladies there or if he had time with this Sunrise. I pray that she just keeps away from him and help her friends not to hook him up with her. Anyway, Lord, keep him safe and continue to be with him on his job search, and may he hear from that one company for another interview or a phone interview. I pray that he will at least be able to spend three to four days with us. Help him to really enjoy himself here with me and the family.

July 5, 2009 (Sunday): Thank you, Lord, for this day. I am a bit disappointed that California Ranger isn't coming until Tuesday, but I am happy that he is coming. I get this awful pit in my stomach that he will head back to California. Lord, he has been working so hard at finding a job. Please let there be a breakthrough, but not at job W. Ugh! Even though he says he is not crazy about the guy at job A, it would be a great job for him. I don't want him to go back to California. Lord, I also have my heart involved here, and I need you to show me signs of his loyalty and commitment and care and love for me. Give us a fabulous time, something for him to say, "Wow, I miss Susan and her family."

July 6, 2009: Thank you, Lord, for this day. I am so excited that California Ranger is coming today. I am so excited. I pray that he will have a safe trip. Help us to enjoy each other's company and have a fun time. May all the food prep go fine, and may he enjoy the food. May he relax and enjoy our family. I pray that this will mean something to him, and may he miss me when he goes back.

July 7, 2009: Thank you, Lord, for this day. Thank you so much for California Ranger coming. It brings so much joy to my heart. Help us to have an awesome time tomorrow—breakfast, the beach. I know I don't look the greatest in a bathing suit, but help me or others think negatively on how I look. Help us to have a great time. Help California Ranger not to be ashamed or not happy in how I look. Give me the strength in my knees tomorrow. Help California Ranger to have a great time and want to stay another day. Help this to help our relationship grow. Help me have a restful sleep.

July 9, 2009: Thank you, Lord, for these past three days with California Ranger. It was awesome! I know he had a great relaxing time. I had a great time at the beach with him—just in the water a bit but loved the lying on the towel in the sand, just talking. I loved just sitting and watching the sunsets with him. I took him to Wildwood, and we walked the boardwalk together and played a game of Skee-Ball. We also played *Putt-Putt* and had ice cream with my two nephews. The Marsh Safari Tour was great. We learned so much. I asked him if there was any change in me since we had met. He told me, "No, you are a very loyal friend. Steadfast, like a rock." He said that he has needed that in his life and that I am the only one that he could count on. That meant a lot to me. God, what an awesome guy you have provided for me. He admitted that he knows he has let me down on occasions, but I have always stood by him. Lord, I just pray, hope he would change his line of thinking of friendship to an actual relationship. He has said that he doesn't want a relationship to spoil a good friendship. I don't believe that it will. I think that it would strengthen it. Anyway, I pray for a job for him in the next month or two. Help him continue to trust in you.

July 10, 2009: Thank you, Lord, for this beautiful day. I went to the beach with my sister for three hours, and we saw dolphins playing. I sent California Ranger a text message, shopped, and watched a movie. All in all, a great day. Be with California Ranger during his interview tomorrow. I know it is not the job that he wants, but he will take it if that is what you want and it is offered to him. Help us to see each other again in a few weeks. May our friendship grow deeper, and may he see I would make a great wife. I know I'm not perfect. Again, thank you for the compliment he gave me.

July 16, 2009: Thank you, Lord, for this day. Reflecting back on the last day, Sunday, at the beach was great. We all wish we were still there—so relaxing. Thank you, thank you, thank you for the job offer that California Ranger accepted with job W. Not his ideal job but, praise the Lord, he has a job that in time could move up to manager, even transfer closer, but he is here now for a longer time—two hours away. I am so happy. Plus, he is coming here again within two weeks to help me move my classroom. I pray that he will at least stay three days or two and a half days. Lord, continue to bless our relationship. May he see that, although I am not perfect, I do have a sincere heart and I love and care deeply for him and want to spend time with him. May there be time we can see each other even though he is working now.

July 21, 2009: Thank you, Lord, for this day. Help me prepare for school with a theme and also develop a presentation. Lord, be with California Ranger. I don't know what he is doing or why he won't text me or call back, but I need to know when he is coming so I can plan when I can do things. I pray that he is safe and not holding things from me, as in seeing another gal. I pray that he will be truthful and open with me. I care so much for him and want to spend time with him. You are in control of our lives. The thing is, does California Ranger understand that with the choices he makes? Help him not take me for granted but love, cherish, and respect me as your precious daughter. May he see the gem that I am with some cracks in it.

Note: After teaching second grade on my first year in 2005 at Valley Forge Baptist Academy, the following year, the third grade teaching position became available, and they asked me if I would like it. I took it as I had previously taught third grade for many previous years in New Jersey, and I simply loved the interaction with students in that age group.

July 25, 2009: Thank you, Lord, for this day. Be with California Ranger and help him see you are at work in his life. May he make the right choices with his friends. Keep other gals away from him. May he miss our talks, prayers, and Bible study. Lord, you brought him this far to the East Coast. Now you need to work in his heart for a wife. Help me not say anything that would cause him to run the other way.

July 26, 2009: Thank you for this day. Be with California Ranger. I pray that he made it back home safe. I know he will call when he is ready to talk.

July 30, 2009 (Friday): Thank you, Lord, for these past two days California Ranger was here. Thank you so much for all the help he provided—moving my classroom, helping with the desk, which is a huge job which I really appreciate so much. We also had fun swimming and playing games and watching two movies. Lord, thank you so much for his friendship. I am so relaxed around him. Yet I am still nervous about telling him my real feelings. I love and care for him so much it hurts. I miss him already, and I want him to come back as soon as possible. Lord, what can I do about my feelings of love for him? The more we are together, the more I want to be around him. To let him know how I really feel about him is so scary, and I don't want to lose him by him running away from me. I want to snuggle up to him, but I am scared he will reject me or move away. It is so hard. I love him teasing me, and he sure did a lot of teasing this time. Lord, be with me and my emotions. Be with California Ranger and help him relive our time together and help him say, "Wow! I miss her too. I can't wait to be with her again." Help him on Monday with his new job as it will be different at first. May this be a step closer to him moving to Pennsylvania.

July 31, 2009: Lord, thank you for this day. Be with California Ranger tonight. Help him sleep well with his shoulder issue, which I did not know about before. Help his mind relax and not worry about his new job. Lord, I tried my best to talk to another lady who is near and dear to me about my feelings for California Ranger, and all she would say was that I would have to keep my feelings in check. And she brought up the weight thing, and it is not like she is thin, but it bugs me that she thinks that is what is holding him back from a relationship or marriage. So she gave me no encouragement but to say, "I give you credit for accepting how God made you." Well, there is nothing to accept. This is how my body is made. I don't care for it, but there is nothing I can do to change it, except what I have been doing—trying to eat right and exercise. So it is hard for me, even though I don't show it or complain 'cause I know it will get me nowhere. I can come to you, Father, and ask that you see my heart and my desire and that as you are working in the life of California Ranger and my life, that you will continue to bring us together and open up his heart to accept me not only as a friend but as a partner for life in marriage. May his views change even though I can never change him. You can by tugging on his heartstrings about me. I know this move was a big step and a step needed to bring us closer to each other—not only in distance but in our relationship. I am not sure when I will see him now, but I pray it will be within this next month even before school starts. Help him realize that I am a precious gem waiting for her prince to pick the gem. Again, I refer to Hannah and her consistency in her prayer for a son. Mine is for a mate for the rest of my living days here on earth. What exciting things will you have in store for us?

August 1, 2009: Lord, thank you for this day. Thank you for junior church. The little ones are precious. I pray for my dental appointment, and I pray that the dentist doesn't find anything. I am a bit nervous that he will. I pray for California Ranger. Tomorrow is the *big* day. He is starting a new job in something he is not comfortable. I pray you will give him confidence and peace. Give him a good night's rest so he can wake up refreshed. Lord, again I pray for California Ranger and the relationship I have with him. I thank you so much for bringing him into my life. I am so blessed. It is just so hard as a single woman not to have feelings for this wonderful guy. Yet it seems I am just to put all on a shelf, so to speak. It seems he doesn't ever want to get married, yet he wants me in his life. He enjoys my friendship and wants to spend time, but not as a married couple. Only you can work on his heart. May he see I am someone he can't live without. I know it would be work—gosh, it is just work trying to date him, yet I love his company. He is helpful and caring, yet in day-to-day living, I don't know. But neither does anyone else before they marry. Again, I pray like Hannah in the Bible.

August 2, 2009: Thank you, Lord, for this day. Yes, I knew that I would probably have a cavity, and it looks like maybe a root canal. Ugh! If it is, help me go through it without too much pain or discomfort. I try to take care of my teeth properly, but somehow the bacteria seem to get in there. Thank you that the first day went well for California Ranger. I can tell that by the reply that he sent. I pray that he will call tomorrow as it is his day off. Lord, help me tomorrow get some things done: walking, school project, tutoring in the afternoon, and maybe a swim. Hmmm...

Lord, I pray that you will help me with this new school year—fifteen new third grade students to train. Help me find new things and challenges for them. Help me the first week, for teachers such as me don't care for it, as it is so very hard setting up the classroom, getting the students adjusted to the rules, etc. Be with Mom and give her things to do and help her get some rest. Continue to be with California Ranger and help him realize that he has a wonderful friend who wants to spend the rest of her life with him. Again, I pray as Hannah—believing in you, trusting—hoping that my prayer will be answered.

August 5, 2009: Thank you, Lord, for this day. I knew I would have to do something to the upper left tooth. Lord, I pray that the filling does the job for a few good years. I don't want the root canal. I pray that the medicines work, and I won't be in pain. Lord, right now I feel blah, and I don't know why. Could be the ending of summer, missing California Ranger, getting ready for a full-packed year of parts that I am not looking forward to: sitting in meetings, conventions, etc. I do thank you for this relaxing, laid-back summer. There are still things I would like to do. I pray you will help me with my class this year. I pray for those who may have academic problems that I will be able to help them. I pray for attitudes and Christian growth in the class. Be with California Ranger this week—his first full week of on-the-job training. Give him rest. Help keep him strong in the faith and his walk with you. Keep the evil ones away from him and his mind. May he think of me often and miss me.

August 6, 2009: Thank you, Lord, for this day. It was a good day, and I got a few things done: school and school preparations, Bible study, walking and weights at the Y. Help me wake up in time for walking. Lord, continue to heal my tooth. I don't want to go in again so soon for a root canal. Take any pain away. Keep it from getting infected. Help the medicines to work. Thank you that I have been able to take care of my teeth. Help me, Lord, as I go back to school. Be with California Ranger. Continue to help him get adjusted to his new job. I pray that you will give him peace. Keep his mind on you. Help him stay strong.

August 7, 2009: Thank you, Lord, for this day—haircut. Thank you for the find of the black skirt. Lord, help my tooth heal and for me not to have a root canal, and if I do that, it can wait till next cleaning. Be with California Ranger. Give him rest tonight. I am not sure of his hours. Keep him spiritually strong. Help him flee temptations. May you protect him mentally, socially, and spiritually. Not sure of this Sunrise person, but keep her busy and away from contacting California Ranger. May you, as you have done before, keep California Ranger in the palm of your hand. I am so blessed to have him in my life. Lord, show him that I would be good for him and he would miss the gem set before him. Again, Lord, you know my thoughts and heart. My hope, like Hannah, is in you.

August 8, 2009: Thank you, Lord, for this day. It was a good day. Thank you that California Ranger called. I know it is tough for him this week and next week. I pray a hedge of protection around him for his spiritual warfare against Satan at the workplace. The people who are there—they are not Christians—even the lady who he works for seems to have a bad attitude and didn't even check on him for break or lunch. I pray you will give him a good eight-hour sleep. I pray for his shoulder and tooth that there won't be any pain again. I pray that he will miss me and our talks and he can't wait to talk with me again. I pray that even the story he heard about the missionaries' marriage will spark a light under him. My prayer would be that, as the year progresses, he will see how much he cares for me and he will have that desire to be married and he will propose to me. Hannah's prayer.

August 9, 2009: Thank you for this day. It is your day. Let us rejoice and be glad in it. Please forgive me of my sins. I pray that you will help me stay strong in you. Thank you for helping me get a little of the schoolwork done. I pray for this year and my fifteen students. I pray that I will be able to help them grow. Be with my tooth. I pray that it will heal and not be sensitive to the cold. I pray the gums will heal and the medicines will work! Be with California Ranger. Give him a good eight hours' rest tonight. Help him readjust his body schedule for working. Keep him strong in the faith at work. Help him not fall into temptations. Keep him pure in mind and body and soul and spirit. May you continually be working in our lives to bring us together. Hannah's prayer.

August 10, 2009: Thank you, Lord, for this day. It was a full long day. Be with California

Ranger tomorrow as he works and trains. I pray that the general manager will check on him to see that he gets his breaks and lunch. I know this is not the ideal job for him. Help him get through the tough part. Help him remain strong in you and that he will be a light there in that store. If another job opens up that would be better suited for him, then have that available. If he gets transferred, help it be a store closer to Pennsylvania and even close to me. Hannah's prayer.

August 11, 2009: Thank you, Lord, for this day. Thank you for the rest. Thank you for the time spent at the pool. Thank you for giving me motivation to start the Cape May scrapbook. Help me tomorrow to get things done. Keep me safe. Lord, help my mind and keep it pure. Be with California Ranger as he works. He is learning so much, and I know at times it must be overwhelming. Help him as he travels for training. Lord, if you want him to pursue another job, then make one available to him. If not, I pray he would get transferred to this area. Lord, keep his mind pure. Help him stay strong in you. May he miss me again and want to see me again as soon as possible. May our friendship continue to grow into a romantic one. Hannah's prayer.

August 12, 2009: Thank you, Lord, for this day. It was a good day. Thank you for the rain this afternoon. Lord, help me get up and walk and do the weights tomorrow. I also need to do blood work this week, schoolwork, and scrapbook. Some cleaning also. I pray for my class that we will have a good year. Help me have exciting things for them. I pray for California Ranger.

Give him peaceful rest. Help his tooth not to pain him too much and also his shoulder. Help him as he takes in all the new things for the job. I pray that you will keep him in the palm of your hand. Help him to be strong spiritually, and may his light shine for you. Lord, help him to know I really care for him and I keep him in my prayers. Lord, if possible—and this is a *big if*—I would like to see him. Not sure how it would work but it is a small request that does take some planning. Ask and it shall be given to you, and, Lord, I am asking this request and the request that I keep asking daily: may like Hannah, I see my prayer answered.

August 16, 2009: Thank you for this day. Lord, my tooth is cold sensitive, and I need to call the dentist. It looks like a root canal. Ugh! But I can't have this pain. I pray that he will be able to fit me in, not Wednesday, and that this will be what it needs and nothing more. I pray I will be able to pay for it. Lord, help me get some more school things done and the closet done. Help me start preparing for the flooring. Be with California Ranger tonight. Help him get the proper rest. Keep him safe as he travels for training. May you continue to be with him on his job search. Lord, continue to be with our friendship, and may it grow. I know California Ranger is stubborn on doing things his way in a sense, but help him realize I could be such a great help to him. I am hoping to do my walks in the morning before school and swim in the afternoon after school. Hopefully, this will help and make a difference when he sees me next. I have hope, and yet sometimes that hope is so dim. Lord, I am asking in faith. I sure don't understand your timetable.

August 17, 2009: Thank you for this day. I did get a lot done. Lord, I pray for my tooth. Please heal it. If not, the root canal will be next Tuesday. Help me as I prepare to start school next week. This will be my thirty-first year as a teacher. Wow! Be with California Ranger tonight. Help him get a good night's rest. Keep him close to you. Help him avoid temptation in his mind as a man. Keep him socially, mentally, and spiritually pure. Keep us close, Lord. I pray he will think of me often and want to be near me.

August 18, 2009: Thank you, Lord, for this day. Good news on my blood work. Now, Lord, just waiting for my tooth to heal. I pray I don't need the root canal just yet and that it will be what the dentist said—it just takes time to heal since the cavity was so deep. I pray I will get a lot of school things done tomorrow. Be with California Ranger and give him a good night's rest. Give him two good days off. I pray that this lawn work with this guy doesn't work out. It doesn't seem promising going into partnership with him with not a lot of work promised. I pray you will open up a job where he can have his weekends off—preferably closer to eastern Pennsylvania. Help me not bug him, but I do miss him and want to spend time with him. 1 Samuel 10–11, Hannah's prayer. Lord, remember your daughter and grant her request.

August 19, 2009: Lord, thank you for this day. Lord, I am trying not to take any pain medication tonight. Help me relax and sleep and my tooth not to be in pain. Help it heal completely in these next four days. Be with California Ranger. Help him with his tooth and shoulder not to pain him. Help him answer his e-mails. I miss him so much and need him in my life.

August 20, 2009: Thank you for this day. It went better. Thank you. Be with California Ranger. Lord, I haven't heard anything from him for the past six days, and that bothers me. He hasn't e-mailed or returned my texts. I am worried something has happened. Help me rest in you. Continue to bless our relationship. Faith. Hope. Trust. Continue to heal my tooth so I don't have to have a root canal.

August 24, 2009: Thank you for this day, Lord—a long, hard, tough one—but I got through it. Be with California Ranger. Give him peace and rest. I pray he did the right thing. Please send a good job his way, preferably in Pennsylvania. Lord, be with him as he helps "Lumberjack" out with the tree-cutting business. I pray that we would be able to see each other over the Labor Day weekend. I pray that California Ranger would be open to that.

August 26, 2009: Thank you, Lord, for this day—another tough one—but I got through it. Sometimes I feel like my head is going to explode with all the information being thrown at us. Be with California Ranger and help him find a job that is more suited to him—not retail. Bring the right job to him. Lord, help him be open to spending some time together over the Labor Day weekend. It would be nice if he came to me for a day and a half, and then I could go with him back to his coastal area for a day and a half. Help us work something out. I would love to be able to go to his church.

September 2, 2009 (Wednesday): Thank you, Lord, for the beginning of school—a rough start—but we made it. Lord, thank you that California Ranger was okay. Help him realize that I am a part of his life, and when I don't hear from him in days by e-mail, texting, or phone call, I get very worried, and it is just because I care so much for him, and I love sharing my week with him. When I can't, I feel that some part of me is missing. Lord, help him be able to be with me this weekend. Help us figure out a plan. Again, I would like to visit where he is, and I expressed that to him once already. It could work this time because of the time I have. Anyway, any time I can spend with him would be awesome. Help me with this rest of the week. Be with the family and keep them safe. Amen.

September 3, 2009: Thank you, Lord, for this day. It was a pretty good day. The students love history, and I am glad. Help them tomorrow on their history quiz. Help us have a good day. I pray that California Ranger will check his e-mails and get back with me as soon as possible and that he will spend some time with me and not tell me he has this or that on the weekend. I pray again for our relationship and that he will see that we both need each other in our lives and that we could be a great team for serving you. He is the only one for me, and I can't even imagine someone else in my life. Life is too short to start all over again with someone new. May you grant the desire of my heart like Hannah in the Bible. May we all have a good night's rest.

September 6, 2009 (Sunday): Thank you for this day of rest. Thank you for your love and care. Lord, help me this week at school to be the teacher with a caring heart yet strong and firm. Help me guide these little ones spiritually and academically. Thank you, Lord, for California Ranger getting the new job. It is more in his line of work, plus he has the weekends off. I also pray for the tree job, and although he is not getting paid, he is learning a lot. Lord, help him be true to his word about coming. I don't want to pressure him, but at the same time, he should want to spend time with me. If not, then it tells me that there must be someone else, or he just doesn't care. I just don't know. I get confused. Lord, I love him and want to spend time with him, but I can't make him love me. Help me trust and believe you.

September 7, 2009 (Monday [Labor Day]): Lord, thank you for this day. I got a lot done today cleaning up: closet, floors, and clothes. Help me with the class as I try to bring them up to speed. Be with California Ranger as he works for Lumberjack. Keep him safe as he starts his new job next Monday. Keep him strong in you as he will face temptations of sculpted, athletic-looking, young ladies who will charm their way into his life. Keep him strong from Satan's tactics. Help him see that I am for him and I do love and care for him. Hannah's prayer. Keep me in the faith—trusting, not doubting.

September 9, 2009: Thank you for this day and all that was done. I do pray for my class. Right now I see them in need of some guidance in several areas. Specific students need extra help in certain subjects. A few seem to be daydreamers. Lord, please help me give them the guidance that they need to mature and academically as well. I pray that I will reach their hearts and that they will want to try harder.

Be with California Ranger tonight. Give him rest. Help him as he works for Lumberjack this week. Lord, I earnestly ask you to speak to the heart of California Ranger about our relationship. I really believe that if I knew that we were dating with regard to a deeper commitment in the next year or two, I would feel so much better. But being in limbo is so hard. Lord, I desire a closer intimate relationship. May you grant me the desires of my heart.

September 10, 2009: Thank you, Lord, for this day even though I wasn't feeling my best. I pray that you will help me with my class tomorrow and their special needs. I pray for this weekend with all I have to do. Help me get it done yet have free time. Be with California Ranger tonight. Give him rest for the weekend before he starts his new job. Thank you that he is making the effort to stay in contact by e-mail. I will know more if he calls Saturday. I pray that he will come soon to visit. I need to see him. Help him realize that through our communication and seeing each other, that we do get closer. Help him to enjoy our times and desire to see me more. I continue to pray Hannah's prayer—believing and trusting.

September 11, 2009 (Friday): A pretty good day, Lord, thank you. Two students were absent; one was tardy, and two left early today. Two of the boys will need extra help this year. Lord, give me wisdom on ideas to help these little ones. Lord, I have a lot to do around here: apple picking and making, weeding, cleaning, going through my things, and doing some schoolwork. Help me not get overwhelmed. Lord, be with California Ranger. Give him the desire and initiative to come here. I don't want to pester him and make him come, but I want him to be willing to come on his own. Put a desire in his heart, Lord, to want to see me and spend time with me. I earnestly pray.

September 14, 2009: Thank you, Lord, for this day. Thank you for helping with devotions for school. Now I just need a quick one for Thursday. With prayer, Lord, as my car is inspected, I pray that it will pass without spending too much money. Lord, I pray for my students. Thank you that the one little boy came in today. Help him get used to the class procedures quickly. Thank you that California Ranger has a decent job now. I pray his first day went well and that he will excel in the job. I pray that he might even consider a transfer to Pennsylvania. Lord, help me know what to say to him concerning our relationship and the right timing. I pray his heart will be opened to the possibility of regularly seeing each other with a goal to see where it will end up. May you grant my desire.

September 17, 2009: Lord, thanks for this day. I have quite a challenge with my class and their academics. I pray for each student that not only will they grasp the concepts but they will mature. Lord, I pray the cost of my car inspection will not be a lot, less than three hundred dollars because I will need new tires in a few months. Lord, when our friends come to visit in October, I would love to have California Ranger over as well. Please have things worked out for him. Also, please help him invite me to come and see him on the East Coast. I feel that he is so close, yet we are really not seeing each other enough. Put a desire in his heart to visit more. Lord, my hope is in you. Let it not be deferred as my heart is so sick. Is there stubbornness in California Ranger that he does not care? I care deeply for him.

September 18, 2009: Thank you for this day, Lord. Thank you for being able to chat with California Ranger on Facebook. Lord, I pray when he calls tomorrow that we will have a nice—great—talk. Lord, I need to see him again soon. I pray that you will open up doors to let that happen soon. Lord, you brought him to the East Coast. Now I need another miracle. Lord, I really don't think it is too much to ask. Lord, give me rest. Help me to get done what I need to get done. I pray my hair will turn out okay tomorrow.

September 20, 2009: Thank you for the call from California Ranger yesterday. It was early, but it was great. We got to talk for an hour. Lord, be with him this week as he works for Lumberjack. I pray you will send him a great job with benefits. Lord, again I pray for our relationship. May it continue to grow, and may he desire to be with me. My heart has waited so long. May California Ranger see my heart.

September 21, 2009: Thank you, Lord, for this day—a bit crazy—but things were accomplished. Be with California Ranger and give him rest. Keep him healthy as he has no benefits. Lord, he needs a good-paying job. Send him one here in the tristate area. He can't go back to California. You brought him here this far and our relationship this far. Bring us closer. Lord, continue to give me direction. I need California Ranger in my life and would be honored to have him for my husband.

September 23, 2009: Thank you for this day and everything that was done. Thank you for helping me with the students. I pray that you will give me insight on how to help each student progress through the year.

Be with California Ranger. Continue to put your hand on him as he searches for a job with benefits. I pray you will keep him safe and keep him from temptations. Lord, touch his heart and make him see me as a mate for him in his later years. I love and care for him.

September 29, 2009: Lord, October is just around the bend. I love fall—the crisp mornings, the leaves changing, fog in the mornings. Thank you for this day. Thank you for the past couple of days of getting things done. I am starting to catch up, but there is still so much to get done. I pray for the right weekend for our friends and for California Ranger to all meet up here together. May our friends observe the tenderness California Ranger would show to me during our time together, and may the husband of our friend say something to California Ranger. Be with California Ranger. Give him rest. Keep him from temptations. Help him stand strong in his faith and trust you as a man. Give him the desire to see me and be with me. May he soon invite me to visit him—just have to find the right weekend.

October 2, 2009: Thank you, Lord, for this week—a long week, so much to do each week. I have to remember to take one day at a time. Thank you, Lord, for helping me walk three days this week. I need to do four. Help me get all that I can get done with schoolwork. Be with California Ranger. Help him with his job search and the job he has now. I pray that you would put a hedge of protection around him. Guard his heart with others trying to match him up or other strange women. Keep him from temptation. Lord, help or prod him to surprise me in some way. I need for him to show me he cares a lot for me. Lord, I want it to go to the next level, but he has to want it also. I pray for my miracle. May hope still reign.

October 5, 2009: Thank you, Lord, for this day. I pray for the one little boy in my class who was out of hand and silly today. I also pray for the two boys who are sick that they might get better soon. Be with California Ranger and help him with his job search. May *you* bring him to the right job. Lord, help him not to overdo things with the tree business to make his shoulder worse. Lord, I need to get real serious with you and California Ranger. We need to see each other soon. Lord, you brought him to the East Coast, close to me—two hours. He could have gone to New Mexico or close to where the other lady was moving, but you took him away from that situation. Why? So he could move here. You brought us this close. Now we need to work more on the relationship. I have waited and waited and a thousand times waited, and I am sure I will wait some more. I have seen your hand in this, but now it seems it is at a standstill—nothing. I know my plan and your plan are not on the same time line, but I need to see you working in our lives again as a couple. I just have a hard time understanding him wanting to live the rest of his life alone. I know he likes his alone time—we all do, but we are also social people, who need to be with one another. I cherish and love the time I spend with him. I don't want to share it with anyone else. Lord, my desire is for Mom to be able to enjoy my wedding experience. I want her to be part of it. She is not getting any younger. My heart is not into meeting a new guy to start the dating experience all over again. California Ranger has always been the one to make my heart melt. It is not a phase, a crush, or puppy love. It is my choice that I chose him. We both are not perfect. Sometimes he has different views than I do, but he is an awesome Christian guy who I adore so much. I have so much love to give so much to enhance his life. I just don't know if he just doesn't see it or chooses to look at my flaws which are many and says, "Hmm… I can't live with that, so I will stay single." It is so hard to figure him out, yet that is what intrigues me—a mystery. I can see our life together: he a help to me and I to him, serving and worshiping together as a couple. Having a Bible study in our home—the possibilities are endless, yet time is wasting away.

October 6, 2009: Thank you, Lord, for this day. It was a different mixed-up day. Thank you for the improvement that the one little student is making in math. I also pray for the other student who has failed three math tests. I don't know what is going on. I pray for the other student with the spelling problems. Also, we need a leader to emerge from this class. I pray for California Ranger as he continues to search for a job. I pray that it would be one that would bring him even closer to me. Lord, I pray that you will prick his heart about me and our relationship—that we should grow closer as a couple and that he will want to pursue me as a mate. Lord, it is time after all these years for something to happen. I earnestly pray for a miracle. Hope and trust.

October 8, 2009: Thank you, Lord, for this day. A lot was done. Help the one student in my class catch up on the assigned work. I pray you will give me ideas on how to display the history items. I see their excitement in learning about American history. I pray that they will catch on in math. Be with California Ranger as he continues to job search. Bring one right job to his attention, and may he choose to accept it. Lord, help him choose me as a mate. I just don't understand—we get along great, enjoy each other's company, love to do things together. It just seems that he has a problem with it on a daily basis, which is key to marriage. I pray for him to make the right choice. May my desire be fulfilled and not the hope deferred.

October 14, 2009: Thank you, Lord, for this day. I was sad to hear that one of my students in my class will be leaving the school. Also, I pray for California Ranger. Give him rest. Also, as I hear of new jobs and I pass them along, I pray that California Ranger will prayerfully consider them.

October 22, 2009 (Thursday): Wow, Lord, what a whirlwind week. The field trip to the farm was fun but wiped me out. The lady there was so helpful and generous to the students. Then being in the library was stressful for students and teacher. I am just glad it is over for this week. Be with California Ranger. Thank you that he agreed to come and help Mom with yard work. May we be able to spend some time together just hanging out. I would love for him to come to church with me. Lord, help him stay until Sunday afternoon at least until after lunch. I pray he won't use the excuse "Oh, I just have to be back Sunday morning." May he also keep his word about Thanksgiving. I am thankful that he is going to this men's retreat. May there be something for him as a man that would help him spiritually and in his daily walk. Also, may there be something there also with relationships that would make him have his ah-ha moment—something that he would use to bring us closer together or something that would make him realize what a wonderful person I am and he needs me in his life more and more.

October 25, 2009 (Sunday): Lord, I am hurt—very. It seems all my praying and crying out to you is for nothing—no answers. In fact, California Ranger just told me over the phone that the answer is a big no. It really hurts—all these years. Everything I have done. I have put myself out there. I have invested many hours and much money. My love for him has been strong. Yet nothing. He says we are two different people, different lives. He is so active. He said that I would not like him gone all the time. I have shared so much with him. Now he is sharing with another woman. I just don't know how to pray about it. My heart aches. California Ranger says life is unfair. It doesn't go the way we want it to. Yes, true, but he is calling the shots. He wants to be friends but wants me to understand this is where his life is right now. He wants me to be happy for him. It is too hard because as I have prayed before I truly felt you put him in my life, and now it seems you are taking him away from me. I know I am not perfect. I don't have clear skin on my legs. My eyes are not good. I have arthritis. I can't keep up with him, but he can't seem to overlook that. I feel like a misfit to him. He can't seem to accept me for who I am although he says he respects me as a person, but that is it. He says he enjoys my company but then finds someone else who he would rather be with. He says distance has been an issue, but I don't believe that. He just doesn't want to date me. He is not attracted to me that way, and it hurts. The prayer is still unanswered—as I prayed like Hannah. It is silence from you. You, Lord, seem way too far away, not giving me the hope. Hope deferred makes the heart sick. My heart is sick. I think the reason it really hurts is because I know he is much closer now and someone else gets to enjoy what I have known all along. He wants to spend the time with her, not me now, and I know that sounds selfish, but it is how I feel. It is going to be so hard to tell people "No, we are not together anymore. He is dating someone else." He won't come and see me. I don't know what else to say.

October 27, 2009: Lord, today was a little better to go about my day. I am still hurt and wounded and not sure how to handle this. I need your wisdom on how to handle this. California Ranger has made his choice and, in doing so, has hurt me. As friends, even our communication will slow down some, and he won't come to see me. It almost feels like a death. It never seems to work with me, Lord. So many people say, "I want to marry my best friend," or they have said, "I did marry my best friend." Mine is always the other way around. My best friend married someone else. It hurts. It stinks, and it is unexplainable. I have to be strong for my own sanity. This lady must be beautiful for him to fall so much for her so quick, and he must feel like he is her knight in shining armor as he gives his guidance to her situation. I am sure that, in time, the pastor there will mention of them being together. Lord, give me the strength, courage, and wisdom to talk with California Ranger on Thursday and just tell him how I feel and what I need to do to heal. Then, Lord, if this is your will for California Ranger and he goes through asking her to marry him, I pray you are already preparing someone better for me who will love me for who I am, flaws and all, someone who will have that spark when they see me. Seven years wasted but also a learning experience. Maybe I am not seeing what you see, Lord, and California Ranger maybe would not treat me the way he should after a few years of marriage. Maybe he would stray away from his vows because I would not be physically what he wants. So many thoughts: I am baffled and confused. Give me rest.

October 28, 2009 (Wednesday): Lord, thank you for this day. I pray for my family members and thank you for them and for their love of me. They want me to be happy. Lord, give me the wisdom and the words to say to California Ranger tomorrow. Help me be wise yet letting him know how I feel about the situation. Give me the words, the understanding of this strange relationship we have. I pray that he will also see what I have been through. Help him see that I have no control over who he dates or goes out with, but it stinks when the heart has gotten involved with all the time we spent together. He has made his choice, and therefore, our relationship will suffer because of it. I know nothing of this lady, and I am sure she is a gem. Most are. I just don't want her controlling him. Give me grace to endure this trial, and may my heart heal to love again.

Note: The journals jump in time at this point, but I did have a "define the relationship" talk with California Ranger over the phone.

CHAPTER 11

Another Chapter Unfolds

Dave and Val

And so, dear reader, at long last, we arrive right back at the very beginning of this book.

It was winter, January 2010, and there we were…all alone… holding hands…just as we had for so many decades. I'll never forget the feel of her lovely, soft, warm little hand nestled securely in mine.

And then it came from out of nowhere—the bombshell. *Wham!* And our entire lives and world exploded.

The neurologist stood in front of us and slowly and compassionately explained that he had kept Val for those several days and ran every conceivable test possible in an effort to be able to tell us anything but what he had to now tell us. He told us how very, very sorry he was, but Val had ALS or amyotrophic lateral sclerosis (Lou Gehrig's disease). Short of a direct miracle from God, it is fatal in all cases. We were shell-shocked. To make matters worse, though Val wanted so very much to go home with me, it was impossible. She had digressed to the point where she would need around-the-clock care. I'm sure Val reflected on how we had all worked hard to make accommodations at home for her condition. She knew that she was only a call away from assistance by me or one of our sons. At that time, she had the capacity to get up from the couch, although sometimes she needed assistance, and take her walker down the hall to the bathroom. I would help her get into the tub to take a shower and come and get her out when she was finished. I'm sure she thought if she could only get back home, her life could resume as normal. But the sad reality to the rest of us though was that over the few weeks in the hospital, the disease had continued to take its toll on her body, and it was more than obvious that she no longer had even that capacity.

Just to be absolutely sure, I contacted a nurse that I had lost contact with for several years, but I had remembered that her husband also had ALS, so I asked her about it. She lovingly told me first how very sorry she was, but also that even though I wanted so much to take Val home, the logistics of the disease was such that neither me nor our boys would be able to handle it. Sadly, in retrospect, she was right. Once again, I placed our family in God's loving hands. I now knew that this came as no surprise to him. He knew from the beginning of time that we would be at exactly this point at precisely this time. He also knew the ultimate outcome. Still, we prayed and petitioned him that *his will* be done.

Although it was extremely painful to me, I felt compelled to take Val's beloved "trash can" wedding ring from her due to her inability to either call out for help or defend herself. I know it hurt her deeply, but I also knew that it would devastate her if it had been stolen. I assured her that I had it in a safe place and that nobody could get it. Still, in a sort of tit for tat, there was a short time that she wanted me to take mine off as well. I did take it off for a couple of days and kept it in my pocket, but eventually I was able to convince her that she might not want me to have it off as I "wandered the public streets alone." Thankfully, she allowed me to wear mine again as I had always worn it as a sort of badge of honor to have her as my wife. My ring was actually her dad's, but inside, she had it engraved with "I'll always love you—Val." It meant the world to me!

At any point previous to this in our marriage, if you had asked me to rate my love for my wife and our marriage, on a scale from 1 to 10, I easily would have assessed it at a 9 or 10, depending on the date and time of the survey. Even during the rough, tedious menopausal years, though stressful, still I loved her so very much! It absolutely astounded me to learn as we went through her battle with ALS hand in hand to discover that, as a result, our love had the capacity to soar to unimaginable heights well above the perfect-10 mark! I cannot even do it justice with mere words on this page, but I will endeavor to give you at least a partial taste of it as we proceed.

Our marriage was always a triune adventure: God, Val, and me, in that order. I know that both Val and I gave everything we had to our God, our marriage, and each other. And I would think that accounted for about 20 percent of the success of our marriage, combining each of our efforts, with God injecting the initial 80 percent. I knew full well that God had the ability to cure Val if that was his will for us at that time. But that was the question. There was *no doubt* in my mind that at any point in time, if it was his will, Val and I would walk out of there hand in hand—as we had done so many times in the past—to the utter astonishment of the medical community. Neither Val nor I would have been a bit surprised. But would *that* be his will? I also knew that Val was only "on loan" to me and that, at some point in time, I would be required to give her back. Still, I had no idea it would be so soon, and it broke my heart. It was ironic to me yet somehow comforting as I reflected on it all that God gave Val to her parents, who gave her to me, and now it appeared that I was going to be required to give her back to God. On the one hand, though it seemed impossible, I knew that God would love her much more than ever I did. I loved her so very much, so how on earth could I deprive her of that? Yet to get there, I also knew that it would mean suffering through this dreaded disease. It simply broke my heart. Once again, just like at the birth of our second son, I felt so very, very helpless, and the reality of it was that I *was* completely, utterly helpless. Though my heart was breaking all the way during our walk through that terrible dark pit together, it felt as if I was living in a sort of twilight zone episode. I was oddly calm about it, despite having some Dave pity parties and having my heart breaking into a million pieces with no way to avoid it, yet it seemed that God surrounded us with so many people and circumstances to help us through it. I have always felt to be so very fortunate that God gave me the ability to see the bright and even humorous side of life as well as the somber, painful parts. Our adventure together through this phase of our marriage certainly contained a considerable amount of more pain, but it was seasoned with some wonderful times as well.

I have often reflected upon which is better—to lose the spouse or other loved one suddenly such as in an unexpected fatal auto accident or to lose them ever so slowly, gradually watching them fade away before your very eyes. I have reached no conclusion as I see both benefits and problems with each. I think God is very gracious to all of us in veiling our time of death from us. One of my sadder reflections on this whole event was watching Val go through the realization that she would never be going home again, following what was supposed to have been simply a doctor's office exam. Sadly, that determination became apparent while she was in the hospital being diagnosed. They had a Port-A-Pot positioned alongside her bed. This enabled either a nurse or me to sit her up on the side of the bed, help her stand alongside the bed, and simply turn her a ninety-degree turn and sit her on the toilet. Sadly, two nights in a row, she slid through my arms onto the floor, and I had to get help to get her up. It is a lot like trying to hold up a huge mound of Jell-O that is the same weight as a human being. The final straw came when she slid through the arms of a trained, qualified nurse the following day. But of course, Val still desired to go home with me. It broke my heart every time I had to leave her there alone at night.

I should note at this point, for the readers who are not aware, that ALS, better known as Lou Gehrig's disease, is a relatively rare neurodegenerative disease for which there is no cure at this time, although research has been ongoing, and recently, they have made some pretty good strides at understanding it. It is not hereditary, except in very rare cases, estimated by some at less than 10 percent of the known cases. It attacks the nerves that control voluntary muscle movement, including muscles that control speech and swallowing, yet the patient's brain remains alert and active. The patients usually die from the many complications that occur as a result of the muscles shutting down, such as from pneumonia, suffocation, starvation, etc. On average, most patients die after about five years postdiagnosis.

It was amazing to me the number of decisions that needed to be made when this kind of predicament rears its ugly head. To further compound things, Val was becoming harder and harder to understand to the point where even I was having some trouble with it.

Despite that, I was bound and determined to do everything possible to love her and help her to the best of my abilities. In addition to contacting my friend, the nurse, and getting some good information from her, I contacted the ALS Association, and they sent me some good information as well. One of the things that I learned but has always been difficult for me was that, first and foremost, caretakers, such as me, had to take care of themselves in order to be able to assist their loved one. While I agree that is true, I had put God, Val, and our marriage first for all those years!

I spent every possible minute at her bedside trying to savor every single second I could with her. She spent about six weeks at the University of Louisville Hospital. The neurology staff kept her as long as possible to try to help her and study her as long as they could. But the time ultimately came when logistically she had to be moved to a nursing home. In the interim and all through the disease, her neurologist repeatedly went over and over her time line of symptoms with me. He often told us, "You two are beyond a doubt on the bullet train for this disease. I've never seen anything like it." To that end, I think God was very gracious to us as it is a very ugly disease. At the doctor's urging, as soon as I could, I went and signed Val up for Medicare, Medicaid, and any other program that I thought might help her. I'm so glad that I did and so thankful for their assistance. Very early into her continued stay at the hospital, her doctor advised us that we would have a couple of days to discuss and come to a decision about several issues: whether or not to insert a feeding tube at this time, whether or not the hospital should attempt to resuscitate her in the event that she could not breathe, etc.

Many times during our marriage, I attempted to discuss such issues with Val, but she never thought it to be important enough to talk through. Although the issue was now being forced, still she was somewhat reluctant. Ultimately, I saw the deadline looming directly in front of us, and just as I had done all through our marriage, it was my deepest desire to make all our decisions as the united team that we were. The day before the deadline, I was sweating bullets through the workday, knowing that I would have to nail these issues down that evening, come what may. I dreaded having to do it!

When work ended and I was on my way to the hospital—yep, across the Ohio River bridge—I felt like a zombie simply going through the motions to get to her room but definitely *not* wanting to go in and have *this* discussion! As I opened the door to her room, lo and behold, there sat Laura, our assistant pastor's wife who also was a registered nurse! She looked up at me and politely stated, "Well, I better be going." Poor Laura! I practically tackled her, saying, "Have a seat! You're just the person I've been looking for!" How amazing!

There is no doubt in my mind that God sent her on that specific day for that specific reason: to assist both of us, with her trusted medical knowledge, to make the decisions that we needed to make. I know, I know, Laura is one of those dreaded white coats! 'Tis true! But still…she is wonderful, loving, fabulous Laura! Bless her heart! She sat with us and explained what we needed to know, and what I had been terrorized about for days became a very easy event with her help. The following day, we reported our choices to her doctor: Val wanted the feeding tube inserted, did not want to be resuscitated, etc. There are multiple pros and cons to each of these decisions, each with various repercussions, so the choices are not all that easy.

One of the things that caretakers and others say in the information about ALS is that the disease affects each patient differently, which is one of the reasons that it is so difficult to diagnose. That is certainly correct. Every day that I went to visit Val, I never knew what I might be confronted with. My older son would later say to me, "Dad, spending just three or four hours with Mom is like working a ten-to-twelve-hour job; it's so exhausting." He was right. As a compassionate caregiver, you were constantly trying to guess what the next problem might be and how you could possibly short-circuit it before it happens. It was nonstop.

Although the feeding tube was inserted a few days later, Val had not deteriorated to the point where she actually had to use it yet. However, eating was one of the truly intriguing things to me throughout this event in our lives. As time went on, it became more and more difficult for Val to eat. As her loving husband, it broke my heart to see her in this plight. Strange as it might seem, I quickly became Val's sole "certified" feeder. It seemed that the rest of the medical staff was not all that willing since we had signed the "do not resuscitate" order. They were afraid of her choking and dying. As her loving husband, I would take as long as it took to chop up each item into teeny, tiny miniscule pieces and put them on the very tip of her fork and feed them to her. For her to be able to drink, I would have to give her a cup with just the very bottom barely covered to keep her from choking on it. Every few bites or so, I would have to check her mouth and tease her about hiding her food in her mouth from me. The sad truth of it was that she simply was not able to get it all down even though it was chopped up so fine. It got to the point on the weekend days that I would be with her all day, and about all we would do is go from meal to meal to meal. About the time she would finish with one meal, the next one would arrive not long afterward.

The hospital staff was always so gracious to me. Sometimes, due to her condition, they would send up a tray of pureed food which she hated, but they would also send up a regular tray in a few minutes when I would go ask for it. Not only that, more often than not, the tall food delivery guy would bring me a tray of food, just for me, as well. The hospital food was simply delicious, much to my amazement!

Early into the event, her right arm became the first victim. This was the arm she had previous trouble with and the one on which they performed the carpal tunnel surgery. In retrospect, I highly suspect that it was misdiagnosed. Everyone had to be careful when they moved her in bed as the arm remained quite tender and had to be babied, but it was also dysfunctional. She could not move it at all. Countless times when they came to move her, I would lovingly cradle her arm in mine and ever so gently move it out of the way.

One Sunday while I was in her room at the hospital, I heard the sound of singing outside the room, down the hallway. A nurse came in a while later, and I inquired about it. She asked if we would like to have them come in and sing to us, and we responded yes. A little bit later, in walked six or seven gentlemen impeccably dressed in their Sunday finest suits singing their hearts out with the ol' time gospel songs. One of them came over and held Val's hand, talked to us, prayed for us, and then sang some more, singing as they left her room. I cried then, and I'm crying as I type this. Sometime later, I asked another nurse about them, and she informed me that they had been doing it every Sunday for years. She said you could "set your watch by them." What a fabulous ministry those fellows have! Sure enough, the last few Sundays that Val was in that hospital, every Sunday morning, they would come to see us, and once again, Val would have her very own private serenade and church service right there in the room! I was able to talk to them later and found out that they were called the Walnut Street Zion Legion and had actually been doing this every Sunday since the midsixties!

One Sunday afternoon after the singing troupe had departed, Val was tired and went to sleep, so I decided to go out in the hall to a visitor waiting room that the hospital had down the hall. More often than not, there would be people camping there, awaiting word on their loved one's condition. This particular hospital is well-known as a premier trauma medical research facility. At any rate, I sat in there placing phone calls to family and friends to give the latest report on Val's condition. Every so often, I would wander back to Val's room only to find her sleeping, and I never had the heart to wake her up. As the afternoon wore on, I became hungry and pondered whether to wait to eat with her or go find something on my own. Since I usually ate last with her having to take so much time to feed her, I decided to go find something. This hospital was *huge*. Val was on the eighth floor, and the cafeteria was in the basement at the opposite end. In short, it is like the journey to the end of the earth, but off I went.

After my long hike, I found the cafeteria and went in and found a tray and some utensils, etc. I grabbed a granola bar or two, anything that I thought I could take back up and see if I could get Val to eat some. And then it hit me—quite the eerie feeling—there I was inside this *huge* cafeteria, all alone. The doors were wide open, and there I stood absolutely all by myself: no other paying customers, no workers, just me! Talk about a strange, bizarre feeling! I really didn't know quite what to do. I decided that since it was Sunday, perhaps the workers were off on break or cleaning something, so I would try to find something a bit more substantial than a granola bar. I found a short hot food bar with actual hot food in it, which comforted me since somebody would have to be there to watch over it. They had about four dishes on display, and as I viewed and pondered the selection, out of nowhere came a fellow about six feet four inches tall who walked right over to my left side and practically stood on top of me, literally arm to arm.

Once again, talk about a strange feeling! I mean, I'm a fairly sociable guy, but after all, this was a complete stranger not only in my comfort zone but practically invading my body! And once again, I really didn't know quite what to do. Where *were* those cafeteria workers anyway? I tried ignoring the fellow, figuring he would go away. Nope! No such luck. So very, very slowly, I looked up to see his smiling face beaming down at me. No words, just a big smile! I smiled back and managed to eke out a meager hi. Again, nothing. He just nodded and continued to smile at me. I pretended to look back at the selections and was relieved as another person walked behind the counter while the smiling telephone pole remained glued to my left side. I ordered the herb-roasted chicken, and while it was being prepared, I hazarded another glance up at "Mr. Smiley" and quietly inquired, "Can I help you?" Still smiling wide as ever, he continued to look down upon me, shook his head, and just as quietly responded, "No, no" and kept on smiling while glued to my left side. I thanked the counter person, snatched up my chicken on my tray, and scurried off to the cashier.

After paying a rather-exorbitant price, once again I found myself to be the sole living creature in the *huge* dining area with many wide-screen TVs all around. My herb-roasted chicken leg tasted terrible, but I choked it down anyway, not cherishing the thought of ever coming back to their little twilight zone area and then went back to the safety of Val's room to thankfully find her awake. I sat next to her and relayed my little saga, which she got a big kick out of, and we awaited the arrival of her dinner. As part of passing the time with her, I said, "Let's look and see what's on your supper menu!" Take a guess at what the main course for the night was. That's right! Herb-roasted chicken! I couldn't believe my eyes. I thought, "Oh no, poor Val!" Just as the thought entered my little head, who should waltz in her door but, yep, Mr. Smiley grinning ear to ear! *Then* the ol' brain kicked in! "Oh my gosh!" I exclaimed, "*You're* the food guy!" "Yep," he responded. "I tried to get your attention downstairs at the cafeteria, but I guess you didn't recognize me. I couldn't say anything to you down there by the other workers, but you don't have to pay their high prices. Don't I always bring you a tray and take care of you?" Needless to say, the three of us all had a good laugh at my expense. Not only that, as usual, Val's herb-roasted chickens were cut up, in a sauce, and wonderful! If only I had waited, I also could have dined on the great patient food!

When the time came that the hospital could not continue to keep Val there, they notified me that I would have to talk to the group health insurance that we had through the company where I worked and get authorization from them to move her to a nursing home. After several days, I was presented with a choice of two nursing homes, both in small towns about thirty miles from our home. I couldn't believe it. Try as I might, I was forced to select from the two. Once again, the ol' brain cells finally kicked in—my beloved friend, Kelly, from the earlier years! She worked at a hospital near one of the nursing homes. I called Kelly and explained my dilemma to her. She encouraged me to go visit both to see what I thought. She also told me that she thought the one by her hospital had done a fine job when they treated her grandmother, and in addition, if that was the one we chose, she would be just a short walk away during the weekdays. Knowing that Kelly is good as gold, I hung up with her, dialed the insurance company, hospital, etc., and told them all that we wanted Kelly's pick! Later, I thought good ol' Kelly was going to kill me for not having personally investigated the two. And so the stage was set. A couple of days later, on Friday, the move would be made. In the interim, on one of the last couple of days at the hospital, Val's old childhood chums made the long trek from St. Louis to visit her one afternoon. There they were: Denise, Debbe, and Sandy. Among many other things, they brought Val two dozen red roses! I took off work a couple of hours early to go be with them. About midafternoon, following the long drive, the three of them were hungry and began to inquire about the dining possibilities. I told them the tale of my adventure in the cafeteria, but they decided to embark upon the hike down there anyway. Amazingly, they returned in just a few minutes all excited. On the way down, they came across a fellow from Jimmy John's making a delivery to the hospital. I was astounded that they even knew about Jimmy John's. The only thing I knew about it was that it was a tiny, little store front sign that I passed on my way to the hospital each day. I had never investigated it, but it turns out that it is a delicatessen that also has locations in St. Louis as well as Louisville, and they all loved it. Hesitantly, I asked Val if she would want something, and she was all in.

It was great! Val had not been eating very much the previous few days, and I was a bit concerned about it, but when I cut up her sandwich into the normal teeny, tiny pieces, she ate a considerable amount, which, of course, took up a long time. But she had such a great time listening to her friends talk to her about the old days and their antics together. I was so very happy for her!

I had been dreading Friday, the big moving day for Val, and sure enough, it came right on schedule. Later that afternoon, the human resource director called me to her office where I worked. This was nothing new since we worked together on many different things. The bottom line was that despite no prior notices or indications after five years of work at that company and an additional six or so at that same owner's previous company, I was summarily fired. Once again, a shining example of why you should always work for Jesus rather than any person. Stunned, I departed and went to the hospital to prepare Val for the move. Any other time, I would have shared my misfortune with her, but under the circumstances, I could not bring myself to do it. It was a mistake though, and I should have done it.

I got to the hospital early as I had planned, went into Val's room, closed the door, and sat down by her bed as I had done many, many times before. I held her little hand in mine, probably more for my comfort than hers, looked lovingly into her eyes, and explained to her that I had come to prepare to move her to the nursing home. By this time, it was becoming more and more difficult to understand Val when she tried to talk. Bracing for the shock, I went on to advise her that the only way it could possibly be done was by ambulance. I assured her that I would be right behind the ambulance in my car, "glued to their bumper." I was amazed that it didn't seem to faze her, despite decades of her expressing her fear of riding in an ambulance. The medical staff helped me pack her things in my car, including the two dozen red roses that she had recently received. So the car was packed, and I sat in the parking lot awaiting the arrival of the ambulance while Val was still in her room. It got later and later, and I waited and waited. Finally, the ambulance showed up, and I waited outside for them to bring Val down so I could assure her one final time that I would be directly behind the ambulance all the way.

We arrived about forty minutes later at the nursing home around seven thirty on Friday night after the normal day staff had long since departed for the weekend. The night shift greeted us, and they were wonderful to us. The ambulance crew wheeled Val in, and we followed the night shift personnel to her room. It was sad to me that they put her in a room with two elderly ladies after having just come from weeks of having her in a room all to herself at the hospital. On the other hand, I knew that she had always enjoyed and gotten along well with older people. As they nestled her into her new bed, I began to unpack her things from my car. I gave the two dozen red roses to the night staff and asked them if they would mind putting them in water in the vases and make them look nice for her. Meanwhile, the two older ladies sat in their wheelchairs and watched the excitement of getting a new roommate. Several minutes later, the ladies came back and gave me the flowers, which looked beautiful. With three ladies now in the room, there really wasn't much space for any one of them. Each had a bed with a dresser, and they shared a restroom. I set the flowers on Val's dresser top and was shocked when she immediately threw a fit as best she could with her speech impediment. Still perplexed by her reaction, I suggested several other locations that I thought would meet with her approval, only to have her continue to be agitated. Quickly running out of places to put the flowers, I sat down beside her to study her responses to see if I could gain a hint of what she wanted so badly. The bottom line was simply that it was her deepest desire to give each of her two roommates a dozen roses apiece as a gift. Once I gave her flowers away to her two roommates, she was happy. The little old ladies didn't know what to think. They both looked at the two of us as though they had never received flowers as a gift in their lives. What a wife! I cry every time I think of how generous she always was to people less fortunate than her, even in her time of trauma at the end of her life. What an example she is to those of us still living on this earth today!

Although they had no idea that we were going to move Val that particular night, two of my brothers drove in from St. Louis that night and met us at the nursing home at midnight. My third brother went with me to "hold my hand" the following morning to sign Val in and make sure that I understood the mound of paperwork, etc. I made all the selections just as Val and I had previously discussed, and my brother sat there beside me and did his "duty" of explaining every little detail to me. Once we were finished, my brother wheeled around to face me and said, "Now listen to me close. I did my duty to watch over you this morning and help you, but if my day ever comes and I'm in even a remote situation like your wife, you had better sign me up for everything known to man to keep me alive as long as possible!" He simply couldn't understand why Val and I had opted out of some of the life-extending procedures.

Within a few days of Val moving to the nursing home, I met with my good friend Kelly at the hospital where she worked and walked across a parking lot to the nursing home. As is her nature, she immediately severely chastised me for selecting the home purely on her word without a visual inspection. I knew that one was coming, yet I would do it again and again and again if a similar situation ever arose! I introduced Kelly to the nursing home staff and let them all know that "Kelly is good as gold, so if she says anything to you, it's as good as if I said it myself." Bless her heart, Kelly supplied us with a little yellow book with blank pages, which I immediately dubbed "The Kelly Book." Her intent was that she and I could use it to leave notes to each other of our visits to see Val, jot down notes of how she was doing and so forth. I always left it out in the high hopes that our church congregation members and other visitors could log their visits in it as well. For better or worse, it quickly became more of a "Dave Diary," where I wrote my deepest thoughts and observations to God, myself, and anyone else who chose to read it as I went through the dreaded disease process with my beloved bride. Often, I would resort to reading and/or writing in that little book as I sat by Val while she slept. I simply could not bring myself to wake her up, but neither did I want to just leave, and that little book became such a comfort to me. All through our marriage, I spent countless hours just watching my wonderful wife sleep. I simply loved every single teeny, tiny atom of her, just the way God made her. And I might add, he made her an absolutely perfect fit just for me!

The nursing home staff was ever so gracious and loving toward both Val and me for the several months that she stayed with them. Since ALS is not that common of a disease, many of them were not accustomed to treating a patient with it and had to become educated about it as we went through it together. I told them that I had lost my job and that the health insurance benefits would probably run out soon and asked them not to tell Val since I wanted to let her know myself once she had a chance to get acclimated to her new surroundings.

Val had not been in the nursing home for very long before they moved her to a two-person room in one of the corners of the building. That room was closer to a nurses' station, and they felt that they could watch her more closely from there. Most of the time, she was in the room alone as only once for a short time did someone occupy the other half of the room. She had not been in that room very long when she suddenly became quite agitated with me during each of my visits and would often order me to leave, for no apparent reason. This sudden change in her perplexed me and concerned me along with disappointing me. How could my beloved wife be doing this to me? After analyzing it a couple of days, I came to the conclusion that she must be doing it out of her love for me, desiring that I get on with my life. So I devised a plan of action to hopefully thwart it. The next time she did it to me, I got up, picked up a chair, and carried it barely across the line into the other unoccupied side of the room and sat in it facing her bed. I pointed out to her that I was now out of her room, and there I sat the rest of the time. When it came time to go, I put the chair back, went to her bedside, lovingly held her hand in mine, and gently told her, "You can go ahead and be mean and ugly to me and order me out of your room if you want, but understand this: I signed up to love you for the rest of our lives, and that is *exactly* what I intend to do. So each and every day, I intend to show up here to visit you and love you as best that I can no matter what you may do to me." That ended it! I once again had my loving bride back!

Although the entirety of our circumstances was both so very sad and overwhelming to me, still I knew that God was in control of it all. And as I had come to expect over the years, I still had that strange calmness within through it all. Yet to further compound the issue for me, for the first few months, Val simply did not want to accept that she could not come home with me each night, despite her clearly progressing condition. Though I would try to comfort her as best I could, she would attempt to escape each night. I'm sure she thought that if she could just get home, everything would go back to normal. Since it was evident that she would fall helpless on the floor with every attempt, the nursing home would have to take the added precautions of both lowering her bed near to the floor and placing soft mats on the floor by the bed and eventually put her in a bed with side rails.

With the advent of modern technology, it is wonderfully amazing some of the things that nursing homes now have at their disposal to assist them with the myriad of patients' needs. Since Val was essentially defenseless and unable to call out for help or assistance if she needed it, as a precaution, they put two alarms in her room so that they would be alerted every time anyone entered her room. Her escaping from the room was not a worry as once she hit the floor, she was completely immobile. Even though I was thrilled that they treated her so well and took all these precautions for her, as her loving husband through all those years, it broke my heart every time I had to leave her there all alone at night.

I spent the next few days searching for another job and went to see her each evening as if coming after work. I had the high hopes that I could find work before having to tell her about being let go. With each passing day, communication was becoming more of a chore for my poor wife. I would have to really pay close attention to every detail of her, and even then, sometimes I could not understand her. To make matters worse, she is right-handed, and her right arm was the first to give way to the disease, so she could not even write a note to me. While she used to have beautiful handwriting, the last few documents that she signed looked like they were scrawled by a first grader. Her signature would literally take up the entire eight-and-a-half-inch width of a normal piece of paper. Sadly, the day came when she looked so very concerned when I walked into her room and persisted in asking me questions about work. Though I tried to dodge them as best I could, she persisted and finally point-blank asked, "You lost your job, didn't you?" I told her that I had and tried to reassure her that everything would work out okay and that God would provide for us as he always had in the past. She was calm about it after that, and I'm sure she probably spent many hours in prayer about it the next few weeks. It seemed that all my life as one job went away, God always opened another opportunity for me, with only one exception. This time was not that exception. Since the economy had pretty much tanked out and my typical job search efforts seemed to be falling flat on their face, although calm, I was beginning to wonder what I was supposed to do. Perhaps I should be staying every second with Val. Out of the blue, the thought occurred to me to simply send blind e-mails with résumés attached to all the local trucking concerns. I decided to start with A and go down the list alphabetically. I don't think my e-mail had left my computer even thirty minutes after one of the first B companies when the owner called me for an interview. I told him the entire story about Val, and within a couple of days, I was back at work again. Not only that, the job was a pretty good fit. I worked four days on and had four days off. Every day, I went and spent as much time as possible with Val in an effort to provide as much comfort as possible for her.

Every day and every night, I would pray that God's will be done for Val as well as our little family. I knew full well that he could cure her with but a tiny, little thought, but I wondered if that would be his will for her and our family. I also knew that I had seen many of his miracles in my life and that, as a general rule, his timing seemed to always be much later than the timing that I hoped for. To that end, the fact that the days were slipping by into weeks and months did not mean much to me other than watching the disease slowly but surely have its devastating effects on my wife's bedridden body. I know that thousands upon thousands of people were praying for her and our family, and even many people who we did not even know. It was such a comfort to us. In addition, Val received a constant barrage of support cards at our house. My goodness, did she ever love having me open them for her and read them to her, showing her the pictures and handwritten notes. She got them from far and wide: family members we had not heard from for years, friends, church members, and others. Our little church house congregation helped us so much in so many, many ways. I have no idea how many times they would make the thirty-mile journey just to spend some time with her and pray with her. Sometimes they would bring their children to see her. She loved all the children so very much her smile would light up the city! Many was the time that the men would shake my hand in the hallway to say goodbye while at the same time palming me money "to buy gas or whatever." What a blessing they all were to all of us! Since giving Val gifts was her primary love language, I would often give her jewelry for her special days of the year. In addition, she had quite a collection of costume jewelry that she purchased for herself, mostly to wear as a fun novelty for the children at the local elementary school where she worked. She had earrings for almost any occasion. Since she was also quite a crafty person, she made many things herself, and she often enjoyed giving them away to unsuspecting people. Many was the time in better days when we would be shopping and she would give the jewelry she was wearing to a total stranger if the person showed an unusual interest and admiration for something she had on.

And so it did not surprise me very much when the day came that she insisted that I bring her all her costume jewelry to the nursing home. Since her speech was so impaired, she also had me make a sign to put on the cases she kept them in. When a beloved staff member of the nursing home would care for her, she would show them the cases with the signs which told them to take a piece of jewelry for their own use. Not long into her new little program, I had stopped at the local Wal-Mart to pick up some items when a nursing home staff member stopped me in the parking lot. She inquired, "Do you know that your wife gave me a piece of jewelry the other day?" I told her that it did not surprise me, and I went on to inform her that it was hers to keep as a gift for taking such good care of Val. I could tell by her reaction that she was thoroughly perplexed.

And the weeks rolled on. Every day of my four days off, I would spend as much time with her as possible, and on the four days that I had to work, I tried to at least spend a little bit of time with her as well. Sometime in May 2010, I received word that the insurance company would authorize a transfer to a nursing home considerably closer to our home. Needless to say, this was fabulous news! And so, sometime in May 2010, off we went once again with Val riding in the ambulance for the second time towing me in our car, "pasted to their rear bumper."

This, of course, made life considerably easier on me with the nursing home now a scant few miles from our house. Ever so sadly, the beloved little yellow Kelly Book was somehow misplaced, lost, or something, vanishing forever more. So I went out and purchased a second little blank book to place by her bed, which I summarily dubbed "The Kelly Book: Second Edition," and it resumed the role of serving as a journal for me and a log of any other guest visitors who chose to write in it. That little book was such a comfort and joy to me as her disease continued to slowly consume my wife's body. As time slipped by, everything that I had read during my research of this horrible disease was coming true right in front of me. Every day, I went to visit Val in her room, and the only thing that I knew with absolute certainty was that the day before was marginally better for her. Slowly but surely, bit by bit, I watched as Val's body was being shut down. First, her right arm, then her right leg, then her left leg and left arm, and so forth. Each time as I approached her room, I braced myself for what might be lurking on the other side of the door.

Even though my faith in our Lord Jesus never wavered, the seemingly endless, ongoing, unrelenting grief that I endured during this time period was such that there were several nights that I did hold my own Dave pity parties. Oddly enough, most of the time, I would leave the nursing home and make a beeline straight past our church pastor's home and pull up to Aaron L's house, a fellow member of our congregation. Aaron and his wife, April, were ever so loving to me—opening up their home with two little boys and welcoming in a sobbing, distraught Dave. Aaron would sit with me on his couch for hours with me crying on his strong shoulder. I love their little family so very, very much! I'll never forget the first time we saw them. It was Sunday, and Val and I were in our usual pew when they came in and sat directly in front of us. As the service continued and I watched as they tended to their young sons, I couldn't help but reflect on Val and I as we raised our two boys. So as the service was nearing the end, I leaned over and whispered to Val to see if she would have any objections to us taking them out to lunch with us to get to know them better. It turned out that they had recently moved from the greater Pittsburgh, Pennsylvania, area due to Aaron's job and were looking for a good church to attend. I suggested to them several in our area, in addition to our own church for them to consider. Not only did they end up attending our church but later, Aaron became our assistant pastor. And they added to their little family with twin daughters.

The evening of Friday, September 16, 2010, I stopped by briefly at the nursing home to see Val as I was quite concerned about her. She appeared to be half asleep, dozing in and out. I once again held her sweet little hand in mine and whispered in her ear, more or less begging her to take Jesus's hand if she saw him and go with him, as I knew that he loved her infinitely more than I ever could. I kissed her, and I reported to work at six o'clock in the evening as usual. At two o'clock the following morning, Saturday, I received a phone call at work from the nursing home informing me that Val had died.

Since I was the only person on duty at that time, I called to get a replacement and departed for the nursing home, partly relieved that it was finally over, partly lamenting what might lie ahead, yet happy that my sweet Val was now in the loving arms of our dear Lord and Savior Jesus, never to suffer anymore while at the same time so very sad for my own loss. When I arrived at the nursing home, a member of the hospice team was already there. When I walked into her room, there she was in her little bed, just like so many, many times before. I got a chair and sat beside her bed, and there I sat…and sat…and sat, for what seemed like endless hours. In retrospect, I really don't know what exactly I expected. Her body was there, but dead as dead could be, as she was gone to be forevermore with Jesus. And so I sat there. It was as if the entire world had disintegrated and only Val's body and I were there all alone, although I'm sure others were in the room with us. At some point, someone ushered me out of the room, and I was turned over to the "custody" of some members of our congregation.

[Appendix A contains a copy of the second Kelly Book that I kept while Val was in the last nursing home. In it I have captured and preserved my observations and prayers while going through the disease with my loving wife.]

CHAPTER 12

The Susan Chronicles: Spending More Time in the Waiting Room

January 24, 2010: Lord, here it is, January 2010. I am writing down my thoughts and prayers again. It has been a hard four months trying to heal my heart. Thank you for helping me make the right choice in telling California Ranger not to call me but once a month or whenever. It was hard, but I had to do it. California Ranger will always be in my heart, but he has moved on, and it is time for me to move on. As I am on eharmony now and searching profiles on Christian Café, there are those that catch my interest, but, Lord, they also have to be interested. Thank you for sending to me "Connecticut Yankee," and although it is just the "get to know" stage, I pray that maybe something I say may spark his interest that I am different from the others he is writing. I would like to get to know him more to even get a phone call from him, but again, I don't want to push or rush things. I am waiting for his answer on the question I asked him. I know that he and his brother are very busy right now taking care of their ninety-year-old parents. Give them wisdom and strength. Then, Lord, if you have me meet someone else, that is fine. I just want to start to enjoy knowing that person to share with my life. Continue to heal my heart from California Ranger, and since he has chosen this way to go, then our contact should only be on birthdays, holidays, and emergencies. Lord, help my doctor visit to go well tomorrow. Help me with school. Bring hope back to my heart.

January 25, 2010 (Monday): Lord, thank you for the good day in school. Be with the three students who need help taking their math tests tomorrow. Lord, give me the motivation to go to the YMCA at least four times, if not more, in a week and to stay away from bread and sweets. I need to get back to where I was in the summer. Continue to help my heart to heal. Bring a new male friend into my life with the potential of it growing deeper. Be with Connecticut Yankee and his brother as they help their parents. Help California Ranger to get a job that will pay benefits even if it means moving again.

March 2, 2010 (Tuesday): It is me again, Lord. I need to express myself. It has been awhile. Thank you for always being there for me. I have failed you so much and need your forgiveness. May my heart continue to heal from California Ranger as I know you have been helping me. He has chosen to move on, not even calling me, and that is fine because I know that now his life is entwined with the lady that he chose, and I am just a distant friend who filled in the gap for him. Yes, I learned so much. I pray that this is just a stepping stone to the man you have for me. Thank you for bringing into my life Canadian

Mountie from Canada and Connecticut Yankee from Connecticut. I seem to have a great rapport with Canadian Mountie. I love his letters to me. They are fun and informative, and he writes as if he enjoys talking with me. Canada, wow! Who would have even thought? I know he has two young teenagers, but, Lord, I know anything is possible—if it is your man for me. Connecticut Yankee is an interesting guy, and I don't know how to read him. Right now he is so involved with helping care for his ninety-year-old parents, so I am sure in his mind to get involved in a relationship would be tough. Yet he does write. He is in the States, so he would be easier to see, but I get a feeling it won't go anywhere with him. Lord, help me tomorrow with the students and then with the sixth-grade play tomorrow night. Help me with devotions for Thursday and then something for my presentation next Tuesday. I continue to pray for my health. May you give me the motivation, strength, and willpower to lose some weight that I have gained.

March 4, 2010: Thank you, Lord, for helping me these past two days. You are my strength. I trust in you. Lord, I seem to have contracted a cold. Make my body fight it. I don't want to be sick. I have so much I need to do. Give me the wisdom in knowing what to present on Tuesday. I want to make it fun. Help the class to buckle down and work hard. It has been a tough year to motivate them. Lord, thank you for my friendship with Canadian Mountie. I am finding myself smiling when I see a letter from him. Guard my heart. It has been just about three months. He seems very sincere, honest, and knowledgeable and cares for the things of the Lord. I don't know how active he is with church. As I think of things, I would love to be able to talk on the phone, but I know if our correspondence continues, then it will be a reality in your time. Lord, my heart yearns for a man for companionship, friendship, to be a team to enjoy each other to follow you together. As Canadian Mountie is much taller than I am, there is this hesitancy of him being too tall, but in the scheme of things, that is low on the list. His heart and character are the most important. Lord, if you see fit, help our friendship grow in the next month. Be with Connecticut Yankee. I am not sure what is going on with him, but if it is timing, then it will be worth it.

March 17, 2010 (Wednesday): Thank you, Lord, for this day. Lord, help me with my exercise and weight. I do try, but I am weak and fall to eating junk. Help me with my class these next two days. Help the one little boy with his math and spelling. Lord, be with my new friendship with Canadian Mountie. Thank you for giving me his friendship as I needed someone who I can share with. Wow! He is from Canada. I would have never thought I would have a male friend from there. Lord, yes, I want the friendship to grow, and I feel we need to now talk on the phone. May you open the doors to such a conversation that would lead us to talking on the phone. May Canadian Mountie be open to it. We have been e-mailing now for three months, and it is time for the next step. I pray he would write to me tonight.

March 29, 2010 (Monday): Thank you, Lord, for the great spring break. There is still more to do this week. Help me with my students to get them motivated especially for the SATs. They need to do a good job. Continue to be with me and my health. Be with Canadian Mountie. Keep him safe, and may he sense I am different from the others which will hold his interest. If he is on tonight, may he write me a positive note and even mention the phone. May our friendship continue to grow in the coming months. May he feel free to open up more with me. Give me the wisdom in how to handle this new friendship. Be with the team in India as they continue to work this week. Heal those who are not feeling well and bring them back safe to their families. Be with California Ranger. Help him to be open to search for a good-paying job. All I can say is that you kept me safe from his stubbornness and, possibly in the years to come, a big breakup. You taught me many lessons which I hope will help with Canadian Mountie or the person I am to be with.

March 30, 2010 (Tuesday): Lord, be with Canadian Mountie this week. I feel a pulling away, but I don't know. Help him write me and connect back. I need to know more about him. Help him open up to me. I want to be his friend. Help him see and understand that.

April 28, 2010: Lord, it has been awhile. Thank you for this day. School is just about over. Praise the Lord! It has been a tough year with this class. I pray that I have done my best to bring them up to where they should be when they enter fourth grade. They are an immature, silly third grade class with some strong personalities. I pray that their achievements list shows much improvement. Well, Lord, I know where Canadian Mountie stands for now. He is seeing someone local, which is fine. I did really enjoy his e-mails and the bantering back and forth. He always made me laugh. A new friendship has now developed with "Firefighter." As I process all that he has shared, he has a lot on his plate—a lot of drama. I pray for his upcoming back surgeries, that they will be successful with a good recovery time. I pray for the situation with his retirement pension. I pray the paperwork will be completed and move quickly so that he can see your hand at work. As we plan to meet, may the details and the meeting go smoothly. May we both go into it with no expectations but gaining a new friend, but seeing if there could be more. I am waiting for his call. I know he has a lot on his plate, so let me not be anxious or worried. Thank you, Lord, for new friends.

May 10, 2010: Lord, thank you for all you have given to me. Thank you for Firefighter, a new friend. Thank you that he did ask me to dinner. We met halfway in Lancaster at the Olive Garden. I was impressed that he dressed nicely: a blue-and-white-checked dress shirt and nice casual white-tan dress slacks. He did look like his picture: baldhead. He buzzes it as he is mostly bald anyway. Again, a lot for me to digest: some of his Christian beliefs are a bit different from mine, and he has two grade school girls. I am not sure what he thinks about me, but he does know about my health issues as well. He seems to accept me as a friend—too early for anything else. So here is what I need to know and ask: Is it proper for him to ask for a second date, or do I take the initiative and ask him to dinner? Hopefully when we are talking on the phone, this will come up. Lord, he is close enough to see every few weeks. I need to know if this is something I should agree to—get to know him more. It seems when I think I would like to get to know someone better on the Christian Café, like "Georgia Peach," few e-mails back and forth, then all of a sudden, it stops, and I never hear from them again. Georgia Peach is from Georgia, so it would be farther, but if he is interested, he will make a way. Lord, my desire would be dating in the summer with the outcome of going into a committed relationship in the fall, but I know you are in control no matter what.

June 6, 2010: Wow, so much has happened since April. Lord, my time has been taken up with other activities, so I have not had time to pray to you about my relationships. First, Firefighter has not contacted me, so it is almost a write-off with him. For some reason, he seems like he is withdrawing from me. Lord, I pray for "The Virginian" from Virginia. It seems our letters are very in-depth, and I wonder if you are changing his heart. I don't want to have false hope, but it seems to me he wouldn't share things about his ex, if he didn't start to enjoy our letters. So I do want to pray about this. Lord, all I need is *one* for me to put my whole heart into the relationship. Would you please send me that one so I will know how to proceed? Lord, begin to make it crystal clear. I am tired of reading all those profiles, sending out countless letters that are read, but I never hear back from them. I want and desire that magic.

June 7, 2010: Thank you, Lord, for having Firefighter contact me on Facebook in chat. He is fun to chat with. Just as I begin to think I will never hear from him again, he pops up. He does want to get together again, and that does make my heart smile. I pray we will be able to connect and plan something. Be with our family as we go to Cape May, New Jersey, for our annual vacation and keep us safe from accidents. Help us have rest and relaxation.

June 10, 2010: Thank you for this day, Lord. Help me continue to improve by going to the YMCA—walking and swimming. I need to see some results. Lord, be with Firefighter tonight. Give him a peaceful rest. Help this procedure to be successful. Lord, help us be able to get together before our trip to Cape May. Be with all our family. Lord, I pray for my future husband. Guard his heart, his life, his physical, social, and spiritual health. Lord, I do pray for California Ranger. He was such a part of my life. Although this chapter is closed, help him be the man you want him to be. If he is happy, then that is the best for him because I didn't make him fulfilled.

June 21, 2010 (Tuesday): Thank you, Lord, for this day. I pray that you will be with all our family as we go to Cape May. And while we are down there, keep us safe. Keep your angels around the house here. Let no harm come to the house. Lord, be with Firefighter. Help him see you are real and will answer his prayers. Lord, be with the new guy who has started to write. I don't know if he is just being polite or is interested.

Lord, you know my heart's desire—I only want one, and my dream will be fulfilled.

June (Thursday): Thank you for the thunderstorm. Thank you for keeping us safe in it and not losing power. Lord, be with Firefighter. Help him in all that is going on in his life. I am not sure where I stand with him. Lord, then the new fellow in eharmony. I am not sure if he is a scammer. I just can't put my finger on it. I will see what he writes back. Lord, if he is a scammer, make it clear to me. I pray that you will send me the one and only one for me. My hope has been dashed so many times. Lord, all I need is one.

August 1, 2010: Lord, thank you for this day. It has been a crazy summer. I enjoyed my two-week vacation at Cape May. Lord, help me make wise decisions in my life. Right now there is Firefighter. I am not sure of our friendship. Help us at least connect again. I need more than one date to know more about him. Be with him and his two daughters. Help him with the retirement issue and his back injury.

Lord, be with DC tonight. Lord, help him go on the Christian Café soon and open up his mail. Lord, guide his heart to want to answer favorably back to me. Help our souls to knit—to feel something when he reads my letter. Thank you!

August 30, 2010: A new school year started today. I pray for each of my students. Tonight I pray for two of the girls who need extra help in cursive writing. Give me the direction in order to help these girls. I pray for their behavior. Help them want to do what is right.

Lord, I was shocked by the e-mail from California Ranger. I never thought he would marry that lady. Apparently, he fell for her, and she is the right fit for him. Although it hurts, I am trying to take the high road and be happy for him. Lord, that along with all the people I know at school—teachers—getting married and even the church that my heart cries out to you. It has all been so hard for me. When are you going to send the one to me? It is a constant battle that even my family doesn't understand. I miss sharing my daily day with someone. I miss the intimate prayer times and Bible studies. I miss someone caring for me, sharing their day with me. It is an ache in my heart. Lord, I have been proactive, and I have just done nothing, and it seems both of these don't work. I have poured out my heart to you, cried, and prayed like Hannah, but still nothing. I desire a deep friendship with a male leading to marriage—you know the desire.

Lord, I pray again for DC. I would love to begin a friendship with him. What he wrote in his profile is from a man who loves you and has a good head on his shoulders. Lord, give me restful sleep tonight.

September 1, 2010: Wow, Lord, what a way to start the day in school! We had our first spelling pretest. Please help me this year with helping this class see the seriousness of school and help prepare them for the future, both academically as well as in the other areas of life. Lord, help me in my personal life. I am trying to do better in my walk with you. I pray that DC will be online again and for him to read my mail.

I pray for T. He responded—a good sign.

September 2, 2010: Today was better, Lord. Thank you for helping me today. Lord, thank you so much for helping my knees not to ache and feel swollen this week. I praise you for that. As I start to exercise again, help me be consistent and help the knee joints not to ache. Lord, I pray for my needs as a woman who hopes and prays for a man after God's own heart to want to pursue me. I have almost given up on DC. He is never online. Plus the one time he was, he never read my letter to him. Maybe T will be a new friend. Lord, I pray for my class tonight.

September 6, 2010 (Monday): Thank you, Lord, for this day. Well, I guess T will not be a new friend. I don't get it. He seemed to respond—a few e-mails—then nothing. So I tried the next age group up. "Gulf Coast" is writing now, good conversations. I just don't know how it will work out. Spiritually, he seems to be on the right page with me. He has an awesome testimony.

DC still has not been online since August 15. Maybe he is not the kind of guy I think he is. Maybe he is into the looks, party-type girl. I would just like him to read my letter and respond favorably. Lord, I know you have told me to wait, but it is like you have withheld this part of my life from me. I have even prayed before—take the desire away from me, but the desire is still there. Lord, give me rest tonight—a peaceful sleep. May the day be bright and happy tomorrow. Help me with my students at school.

September 7, 2010: Today was a good day, Lord. I pray for individual students of mine and for each of their specific needs which you know.

Please help each of them and help me teach them what they need to learn in ways in which they will understand. Please be with my heart. Heal the hurt and rejection, not only of California Ranger but of so many other guys who seem to look only on the outside first, then the inside. Grant me the desires of my heart.

September 8, 2010: Thank you for this day. Thank you for the mom of one of my students coming in today and helping. What a blessing. Once again, I pray for the specific needs of each of my students and ask you to help each of them as well as me. Lord, I am trying to live a Spirit-filled life. I desire your best and always have wanted a godly man. I have failed you many times, but I want to delight in you. My desires, hopes, and dreams have not yet been fulfilled. As I strive to serve you in my teaching and my daily living, grant me the desires of my heart. Bring that godly man to surface.

Lord, on the Christian Café, there are a couple of men I would like to know—Gulf Coast from Georgia and the other guy from there and DC. DC, for sure, but he is never online. I pray that he will read my e-mail. The guy from Canada tonight read my e-mail but did not respond. It would be nice if he would write back to me.

September 9, 2010 (Thursday): Thank you, Lord. It was a good day. So far, I am enjoying this class. Lord, I pray again for each specific student and their individual needs of which you are aware. Help me teach them what they need to learn in unique ways that will help them understand. Lord, I am so blessed with all the parents' help this year. Thank you so much for this encouraging part of the school year. Lord, I pray for the desires of my own heart. May you grant them as you did for Hannah in the Bible. I do pray individually for the few I am corresponding with. I pray you will keep them godly men, fit for your service. I pray that DC will soon be online. I pray that my letter will jump out at him and that he will respond favorably. I pray for my doctor visit on Monday. May it be a good report.

September 10, 2010: Thank you, Lord, for this day. It was a good day. Thank you for giving me the wisdom I needed to handle a couple of students in class today. I know it will not be easy, but we did have a couple of good weeks without having to send anyone to visit with the principal. Lord, I pray for my desire, and may you grant it. Just because recently a couple of guys have been writing to me online and it has been nice and both seem sincere, at any time, they might stop. So I simply cannot let my heart go out to them at this time. Twelve to thirteen hours away is not a short trip, and I don't know if either of them would be willing to make that long of a trip. I again also pray for DC who has not been on since August 15.

September 14, 2010 (Tuesday): Thank you for this day. Thank you for helping me with the presentation. I felt at peace, not nervous at all, and felt that it was a good presentation. Lord, as usual, I pray in behalf of my students and their individual needs. May you watch over them all. I also pray for the guys that I am writing to. It is nice that they do keep writing, but I wonder: Do

I bug them too much? I pray for them each as a man that you would help them in their Christian walk—spiritually, emotionally, physically, and socially. I pray that DC will soon be online again and help him notice my letter and respond favorably to it. I have to leave all this in your hands because once I make the contact, it is out of my hands. Grant me the desires of my heart, oh Lord.

September 19, 2010 (Sunday): Lord, first, cleanse my heart. Make me a clean vessel for you these next three days. Be with me in school tomorrow. Once again, I come before you in behalf of each of my students and their specific needs to help them academically and socially. May I help give them the life lessons that they will need. Lord, I pray for my own heart. I pray that you will grant me the desires of my heart. Guide me in not making mistakes. I pray for the fellows that I am writing to online. Guide their hearts and help them be honest. Keep them pure and help them this week. Lord, I pray specifically for the three that I would like to hear from. Give me rest tonight. Clear my mind. Sweet peace.

September 22, 2010: Lord, I pray once again for my students and each of their individual specific needs as I see them displayed in my classroom. Help me in that regard to be able to give each of them what they will need later in their lives—academically, emotionally, spiritually, etc. Lord, be with my desires. Yes, you know me. Yes, I have sinned and repented. I am not perfect by any means. But my heart's desire is to marry a born-again Christian who desires to have you in the middle of our relationship—that when there is a problem, we can come together and share and pray about it together. My husband will not be perfect. He will have flaws that only you can work on, just like my flaws. Lord, I pray that the new guy on eharmony is not like all the others, and I will hear from him and continue our e-mailing.

September 25, 2010: Thank you, Lord, for the teachers' conference. I really enjoyed myself this year. Thank you for showing me new friends. Lord, I am not sure what went wrong with my car. It should have been done. A part must not have shown up. Lord, my patience is really being tried on this one. Lord, give me rest tonight. Lord, I pray for myself. Keep me strong. Help me have the hope you have for me for a relationship, my mate. Bring that person soon. He will not be perfect, but grant me the desires of my heart as it says in Job.

September 29, 2010: Lord, I had a good time tonight with my friend at the Ben Franklin Institute in Philadelphia teachers' night-out event. Thank you for her friendship. I can feel free to talk with her about anything. Lord, thank you for the improvement with the class as a whole. And once again, Lord, I come to you seeking your help with specific student needs that I see demonstrated in my classroom. Help me help each of them in the best way that I can. Be with me as I teach tomorrow. Help also my social life. Guide me to the man you have for me. Lord, you also know about each of the men that I have been corresponding with online and my assessment of them. I don't know much about the new guy on eharmony. Please help him pray and seek you. Also, the fellow from the Christian Café from NH who seems very nice. I would like to know him more. He seems to be more of a fit for me, so to speak. And the man from GA who seems to be a bit older and more mature, but I'm not sure about him. Also be with the pastor from GA. Can I see myself in the role as a pastor's wife? With any of them, I wouldn't mind getting to know more about them. A phone call would be welcomed. Two of them seem to write and then back off for a while, so I just don't know. Lord, guide me to make right decisions.

October 9, 2010 (Thursday): Wow, Lord, so much has happened since I last wrote to you. Lord, help me with my class tomorrow. Lord, watch over my students and help each of them with their specific needs and help me help them in ways in which they will understand. Lord, thank you for the phone call from the one GA guy. I learned a lot about him, and it was fun talking with him. I pray our next call will go as well. Help me remember to ask him the questions "What is his goal on eharmony—friends, dating, or marriage?" and "Where does he see himself in a year or two?" I would like to meet him in person. How is his schedule for visiting here? I need to tell him about my health issues but also find out about any that he might have.

November 3, 2010: Lord, thank you for this week. Thank you for helping me get through last week. I pray for my class as a whole. May I see unity and leadership. I pray for each of the individual students and each of their specific needs.

Lord, help me be the teacher I need to be for them. Lord, now for me. This GA fellow did not work out because he is into this other gal. So at least I didn't get emotionally involved with him and didn't spend a lot of time with him. I can't afford the time to be wasted with someone who is not the right match for me. Lord, right now the man from Kansas is writing. Hmmm…he seems nice, so we shall see. On eharmony, the man from Vermont viewed my profile, so I looked at his and sent him a question. Not sure if he will respond. He looks handsome. His profile seems interesting. Lord, I am tired of writing guys for a month, and then they fall away. I want to be able to say and tell people in a month or two that God has answered my prayer. My prayer partners are waiting for a good report from me. I also have been waiting a long time.

November 4, 2010: Lord, thank you so much for helping me this past week. It was such an improvement over last week. There are still issues, but each has to be dealt with on a daily basis. I pray for my class as a whole that they will mature in their walk in the next few weeks. Lord, be with my new fellow in Kansas tonight. I am not sure where this new twist of friendship is going, but I am willing to see what happens.

November 8, 2010: Thank you, Lord, for protecting me when I tripped in the garage after school today. Thank you that my glasses were not broken. Be with my class tomorrow and help them with each of their individual needs. Lord, thank you for the Kansas man I am writing to. I pray for your guidance in this new friendship.

Because my guys are always long distance, I never know if they are going to work out. I hope and pray they do, and I work toward that goal, but I know you are in charge, and it is the guy who continues if he wants to. Lord, there is also a new one on eharmony for me from Florida—no picture. I am scared. His profile is sincere, honest, and almost too good to be true. But there is no picture, nor can he see my picture, and that is scary. I am taking a risk in communicating with him. There needs to also be some attraction on both sides, so I pray for him and his needs. Lord, only you know the outcome.

November 9, 2010: Lord, I feel stronger than ever. Keep me from sin and help me resist the devil's tricks. Help me when I am tempted not to act on that temptation. Lord, I pray for the new fellow from Florida. I am nervous about this one because there is no photo of him. I know many guys can talk and walk their faith, but I am not attractive to them. Lord, this is scary. I need to trust you that you are guiding the communication. I pray that you will know what is best and that you will give to me someone who is so handsome that I will be blown away by your goodness to me. I would pray that he would feel the same about me. May your hand be on this new friendship. My newest Kansas guy made it clear a long-distance relationship is not for him. For whatever it is worth, thank you for his friendship.

November 10, 2010: Lord, it seems the ones who don't follow your guidelines prosper. Yes, I am scared about the Florida guy, and now I get that little hurt in the pit of my stomach.

Okay, he read my answers, and now nothing, no communication. What is happening?

November 11, 2010: Thank you, Lord, for your guidance today. It was a great chapel service. The third grade did an awesome job. Be with the class tomorrow and help each of them. Help them shine their light in the afternoon. Lord, even though I said that I am scared about not knowing what the Florida guy looks like, I am starting to doubt because I haven't heard from him in three days now. I put my heart and soul into answering those questions, and then it is silent. I wonder, is it silent because he doesn't want to communicate anymore? Does someone else have his interest, or is he a bit nervous of what I look like? Is he waiting to post a picture, or has he not had time to respond? I do want to see where this would go. It is a mystery, and I pray he would be more than my expectations or more than I would ever dream and hope for. Lord, hear my prayer. I want to be able to share the good news to those who are praying for me. I am asking, seeking, and I am knocking, believing you.

November 12, 2010: A good day today, Lord. Thank you! Lord, I pray for my recent Florida guy without a photo. I pray that my sense of intuition from his profile is right. That he is a genuine, sincere person who loves the Lord and is a handsome man who would adore me and fall madly in love with me. Lord, maybe his free time on the site ran out—who knows—or maybe he has made his choice already. I pray I will get an answer soon.

November 13, 2010 (Saturday): Thank you for Thursday—for getting my hair done, for the deals I got at the store, for seeing my niece, etc. Lord, I have lived many decades now with most of my life being devoted to living the life you proclaimed in your Bible for those who choose to believe in you. I have read and studied your Word for many, many years now, and I know what it says about selecting a lifetime mate: "be not unequally yoked" and "how can light have fellowship with darkness," etc. And, Lord, I have been single my entire life, but for many decades now, I have longed and yearned and prayed for a good solid Christian marriage with a man after your own heart to share it with. But still…nothing. And yet, Lord, I have witnessed through being a chat-room monitor, participating in online dating myself, in my own personal relationships, etc. seemingly descent Christian people totally disregarding your very clear directions and choosing to date and ultimately select someone else. Still, I am holding the line for a fellow that you select for me. But, Lord, I just don't understand. The others seem to be happy and prosper despite clearly disregarding your very clear directions. And I pray and pray and plead and knock and knock and yet…nothing. Oh yeah, I get to write to guys for a month or two, and then they drop away. And yet I *must not* and *cannot* ruin my testimony for you. I have to be strong, and, Lord, I need your help. I am writing this with tears streaming down my face. I deeply desire that godly man for me to love and to cherish me and to hold me when I am crying and to laugh with me when we have fun. Grant my request. Again, I pray for the fellow in Florida. This is very strange—no picture, and yet I feel a connection. I am nervous about no picture, but I want to know more. As I read his profile again, he says, "If you can wait a few weeks…" I am not sure when those "few weeks" are: end of November to December? If he is the one, the waiting will be worth it. I am praying that it is more than I have ever dreamed of, 100 percent more than the last relationship, and this one will be the pursuer, even with the distance. I can't wait to see him and hear his voice. I can't wait to meet him. Give me peace, comfort, joy, and happiness. Show me your love and care for me, Susan. I need you, Lord, to answer my prayer.

November 15, 2010: Lord, thank you for this day. Overall, the class was good. But I continue to pray for the specific students who need your help and mine. Please help me be the teacher that I need to be to give them what they need to succeed. Be with me and heal my heart. I know you are in charge of my life, but you are silent while all those around me go ahead and make their choices. Yet I can't let myself go where they have gone—to the unsaved world to find their loves. Lord, I need answers to my prayers. I need to see you working in *my* life, so you can get the glory. Be with the unknown fellow in Florida. I will continue to pray for him to get a job, to help him in his daily walk with you as a man. I have no idea who he is or what he looks like. So trust does come in, yet it is scary. Help him be able to reveal himself quickly. Help me *not* to pray foolishly or in vain.

November 16, 2010 (Tuesday): Thank you, Lord, for this day and for another day to serve you. Thank you for life and my health. Thank you for helping me get back into swimming. May I be more consistent and may it work. Lord, be with the unknown guy from Florida. Sight unseen, but if this would be a match, then it is worth the wait. Lord, grant my prayer that also others will know you are working in my life. Besides my family, I know at least my two prayer partners are praying for me. I need to give them a positive answer. Lord, this has been the toughest thing I have had to endure. Lord, you know my heart's desire to have a godly husband who will cherish me as a precious gem—someone fun and loving and sincere and honest. I want and desire to enjoy life with someone. I need to trust you in this situation.

November 17, 2010 (Wednesday): Thank you for this day. Busy, yes; issues, yes, but thank you for the strength to get through the day. I pray for each of the needs of each of my students, Lord. You know what each of them individually need to progress for this year. Show me what to give each of them to help their understanding.

Be with the unknown fellow in Florida. If this is to be someone for me, then continue to open the doors. Help him find a job. Be with him in his spiritual walk as a man. Help me be attractive to him and him to me as he has no picture, nor can he see any pictures.

November 20, 2010 (Saturday): Lord, thank you for the harvest party and all the parents that showed up. Lord, I continue to ask you to give each of my students what they need according to each of their individual needs as well as for me to have the ability to teach those things to each of them in a way that will make sense to them. Lord, grant my request please for a godly man to enter into my life. Lord, I know you are soon returning, but it sure would be nice to have that Christian husband to walk along beside me until you return. I pray for the unknown Florida man. This is a faith prayer because I don't know who he is, what he looks like, and he has been silent for seven days now. I know in his profile he asked for patience for a couple of weeks. I just don't know when that couple of weeks started. I pray you will give him a good job, good benefits with the possibility of moving to—okay, let's say it—Pennsylvania. Help him be beyond my dreams as a man should be and look like. May I be pleasantly surprised by you, Lord.

November 21, 2010 (Sunday): What a great Sunday! Thank you, Lord, for both services! Lord, give me a peaceful sleep. Lord, be with me tomorrow. I pray for a good day. Be with each of my students and help each of them. As Thanksgiving approaches, thank you for the many blessings you have given me. Be with the Florida man and help him get a job. Help him as a man to live the way you desire for him to live. Again, I have no idea what he looks like, but, Lord, I am sure you wouldn't have put him in my path if I would not be attracted to him and vice versa.

November 22, 2010 (Monday): Lord, it was a good day in school today. Thank you for that. I pray that you will grant us a good day tomorrow in the classroom. I pray for my students who were sick. Keep me from getting sick the next couple of weeks. Lord, help me stay strong in my walk with you as the devil wants me to fall. Lord, grant my desire and request for a godly born-again Christian. I pray for the Florida man. Guide and direct his life, and may you have our paths to cross again.

November 23, 2010 (Tuesday): Thank you again for a good day in school. It was a bit overwhelming for about an hour when it seemed that all my students needed me at once for many different things. Thank you for the small gift that I got today. What sweet people they are. Help me in my lack of relationships. Lord, you know my heart and what I desire. I don't think I am asking for too much. Lord, grant my desire so that others will see the goodness of you in my life. Many people are praying, and I need to see your answers.

November 24, 2010 (Wednesday): Lord, you have been so good to me. You gave me a good day with my students. It was an easy day. The DVD was awesome, and they loved it. Lord, thank you for giving me assurance and peace. May you grant my request for an awesome, godly, good-looking man to begin a wonderful relationship. Give us safety as we travel tomorrow.

November 26, 2010 (Friday): Thank you for yesterday. Things turned out okay. I had a nice, relaxing time. Lord, it is quiet for me with nothing on the horizon unless the fellow from Florida makes the next move. I am not sure what is going on with him, his job or financial situation, but I would like to be able to communicate with him again. Open the door for that to happen. Other than that, no one else seems even interested. Lord, I just need you to show me an answer, give me a hope, grant my desire, and show me a sign that you are working in my life. I need to see you and trust you. Hope deferred makes the heart sick, and I sure have had hope deferred so many times. Again, I want to be able to say of my relationship it was God that brought us together, orchestrating two people who desire a godly partner. Lord, I waited so long to have a godly man in my life. It is humanly not getting any easier. If you would grant me my desire, could you please bring that person into my life soon. It would take at least six months to a year before marriage. I just want to be able to enjoy life with my mate before I get too old to move around and go places.

November 28, 2010 (Sunday): Thank you, Lord, for all that has been done this long weekend. Thank you for the time off. It went way too fast. Lord, I am waiting to meet the one you have for me. Where is he, Lord? You seem so silent in my life: no hints, no hope, just silence. Lord, I desire a godly man. Grant my request so others will know you are a God of miracles and you can do this.

November 29, 2010 (Monday): Thank you for this day. It was hard getting back into the groove of things. Thank you for helping me with the class. Please continue to be with each of my students and their individual needs to help them spiritually, academically, and socially. Please watch over and heal those who are sick. Thank you for all the moms who come out to help me—what a blessing!

Lord, now for my situation. I pray for the man you are sending my way. I can't wait to meet him and learn all about him. May you prepare him as you are also preparing me. Lord, I know this is a bit selfish, but could I meet him sooner rather than later? Grant my desire, so people will know it is you who has done this thing.

December 1, 2010 (Wednesday): Lord, thank you for this day. Thank you for protecting me as I drove to school in the windy, pouring rain today. Basically, it was a good day with some issues, but we got through it. Praise the Lord! I pray again for my individual students and each of their needs. Lord, my life is full, but there is an emptiness of that longing for love, but I *can't* take the devil's way of finding it. You know my heart's desire. May you give me the hope I long for, yet it seems unreachable. May there be a sign that you have heard my prayer and the answer is on its way.

December 2, 2010 (Thursday): Thank you for this day. Thank you for giving me the wisdom to handle issues as they came up. Lord, thank you for the peace you gave me today. Thank you for the prayer I received of care and concern for the issues that you know have been weighing heavy on my heart. May your will be done. On another note, I pray that I will continue to stay strong in my faith, belief, and trust in you and that you will answer my prayers. May that godly man be ready for my friendship, and may it then grow. I need to see you at work, and I know that you are. I guess, like Gideon, I need to see a sign. My happiness and joy is in you and only you. It sure would be nice to have a human person to have a relationship with.

December 4, 2010 (Saturday): Thank you for the day off on Friday. It was good to go to New Jersey where they were holding their holiday house fund-raiser and to see old friends. Lord, the concert was great. It was nice to do something different. Lord, I continue to pray for a godly Christian man for myself. I continue to pray for the unknown Florida fellow. I am not sure if he has lost interest or if this is still the waiting part. Help him to find a job in these tough times. If not him, Lord, then please send someone new to me so we may at least start on the friendship. Have that person like and love me for who I am and encourage me and realize that I will never be a size 10. With an encourager, we could set a goal. You know who is right for me. Bring him my way.

Note: This marks the end of my journals. They are all handwritten in journal books and range from March 17, 1992, to December 4, 2010, with some gaps dispersed throughout. At this point in my life, I did not take the time to journal. But much of the missing journal years are written in the other part of the book. It should also be noted that my unknown Florida guy ended up being yet another flash in the pan, and he simply never did reenter my life.

CHAPTER 13

Hitting the Jackpot: The Second Collision of a Lifetime

Dave

Dearest reader, you may recall that my childhood and family background have already been established. My first and only marriage to Val was simply wonderful, and we were able to raise our two boys during that time. Sadly, our marriage ended abruptly a mere twenty-four days short of what would have been our thirtieth anniversary when she succumbed to ALS, better known as Lou Gehrig's disease.

To say that her premature death left me shattered is a vast understatement. But I had to march forward: God would want it that way, Val would want it that way, and our two sons and my three brothers certainly encouraged me that way. Oddly enough, Val's dad was probably my biggest cheerleader, telling me I took good care of his daughter and that I needed to find a second wife. At that point, my life truly was in shambles, yet amazingly I was totally at peace with it all. I had lost my wife and my job. And additionally, my dad had dementia, and my mom was now in a nursing home. At the urging of my three younger brothers, I packed my bags and went to St. Louis to live with Dad while my older son watched over my home.

I spent a total of about a year living with my dad at his St. Louis residence. It was quite the adventure, to say the least! Although I had just completed roughly a year of being the sole caregiver of my wife while she was in the nursing home, I was not totally prepared for what lay ahead. While Dad was somewhat able to perform the physical tasks of daily life and hobble around with the aid of his cane, due to his dementia, mentally it was a lot like caring for an adult-sized three-year-old. I had to constantly be on high alert to know what he might be doing at any given moment. Thankfully, well prior to my arrival, he had driven to the local grocery store, which was only about two miles from his home, to pick up just a couple of items, and it took him over two hours to return home because he got lost. That little escapade both scared him considerably and was the catalyst for my local brother to take his driver's license and keys away from him. Consequently, due to his continued fear of getting lost, at least I didn't have to worry too much about him attempting to escape and wander off on me.

I learned early on, through both research as well as practical application as my new adventure unfolded before me, that setting up a daily routine is very beneficial for dementia patients. I couldn't help but chuckle to myself that our lives had evolved into mimicking the infamous *Groundhog Day* movie. Every single day, with scant few exceptions, I got up early to beat Dad to get the daily newspaper from the driveway and prepare his breakfast at the kitchen table. The exact same meal, the exact same prescription pills, and, of course, the daily newspaper. He would eventually wander down the hall, sit down, and read the newspaper over and over while eating. It didn't matter how many times he read it. Each time, it was brand-new for dear ol' Dad! At the appointed time, he would get dressed, and off we would go on a thirty-minute drive to visit Mom at her nursing home and have lunch together at their little café in the basement. I would wheel Mom down in her wheelchair while Dad hobbled behind with his cane. We would eat, and they would talk—sometimes for only ten minutes or so and sometimes for hours. I would patiently sit and mostly listen, sometimes nodding off, in and out of sleep. Sooner or later, Mom would announce that she wanted to go back up to her room, and off we would go. At the same time every night, Dad would eat the exact same TV dinner, watch some television, and go back to bed. And so it was—every single day, the exact same routine, over and over and over.

The only exceptions were on Sunday morning, when I went to church or when my local brother would relieve me so I could keep my own sanity. An unknown St. Louis person I had come across during one of our excursions had led me to investigate a fabulous church which was quite instrumental in helping me pick up most of the shattered pieces of my life and put me back together again. May God bless them, one and all!

During this phase of my life, I once again found it amazing as I reflected back to my life about a decade earlier, when we lived next door to our elderly neighbors. I remembered back to the days that as a young man raising my own two sons, I used to try to help care for the older couple next door who we loved so dearly. Since he loved to mow grass, he would lovingly "pitch a fit" whenever he caught me cutting his grass. Sooo I would lie in wait until I saw them leave and run over and cut it! He would usually question me about who cut it in his absence, to which I would reply, "I'm not really sure, but I must say they did a fabulous job!" I would also shovel off their driveway and walks while doing my own, hoping he wouldn't come out. As I did these chores, I would often talk to God and tell him of my concern about my own parents as they aged several hundred miles away from me. Little did I know that the day would come when I would be the one doing it. Though it was quite a chore, it was comforting for me to be able to assist them. Oddly enough, it was also at this time of reflection that I pondered upon having become the fellow that I wished I had in my life during my tumultuous years as a much younger lad that this book was born. I suddenly realized that I then knew the answers to many of life's most perplexing questions, and I desired to share it with any who might listen and be helped by it in their own lives. Little did I know at that time the long tedious journey it is from that time to the time that you are reading this.

About a year into it, the day came when a director of operations, with whom I had worked several years previously, contacted me and asked if I would be interested in an opening that they had in their safety department. I applied and got the job. Once again, my older son and I switched houses, and he took over as his grandpa's primary caregiver. Though it might seem a bit premature to some, please keep in mind that I had a good year to grieve and ponder the impending demise of my wife as her ALS slowly yet progressively took its ugly toll on her. So I began not only a job search but, after her death, I also joined a couple of Christian dating websites in an effort to look for another wife. It was quite an uncomfortable experience, to say the least. After all, I had not had to date for three whole decades! And this sets the stage for the continuation of the eternal grand adventure!

The newfangled computer dating was quite intriguing and perplexing to me, although I did have high hopes for it as admittedly I was never that good decades ago at normal dating. I had presumed that both men and women on the dating websites who had proclaimed that they were in search for a long-term marriage relationship, just as I was, were in fact looking for just that. Yet I quickly found that not to be the case. Either that or they certainly had a much different idea of what constitutes a great marriage than I did. But after all, I had just completed thirty years of a wonderful marriage. I had heard both the successes as well as horror stories of dating online. As I pondered the profile forms, I wanted to be as truthful as possible yet not give out too much personal information to any potential scammers. Yes, ladies, we men have our fair share of women scammers too! Or perhaps men scammers only posing as women! I was vexed by attempting to give any prospective matches some idea of who I really was yet avoid having them think that I might be a scammer. I decided that my best bet would be to lay out my track record of thirty years as a loving husband and dad of two boys and present that on my profile page. So I answered the profile questions as best I could and posted about six photos or so of our marital life—one of me currently, one of our dating time, one of our wedding, one of our family of four, etc. Oh my! Little did I know! As it turns out, my actual life apparently parallels the profiles many men scammers use: widower of a long-term marriage with a couple of children whose wife succumbs to a dreadful disease, etc. Although I was not aware of that little problem, I had thought that by posting photos of our marriage, it would show the legitimacy of my background. Wrong again! Many a gal would let me know in the opening response, "I would *never* go out with someone who would post photos of their dead wife!" Really? I would have thought it was a compliment to her life and substantiated the fact that we did have a great long-term marriage! Apparently, shame on stupid ol' sentimental, romantic Dave!

Throughout the course of our marriage, Val and I both felt very blessed to have married each other. We were partners, lovers, and best friends. We would tell each other that our partner wouldn't have anything to worry about if something were to happen to one of us, as it was obvious to each of us that we both knew how to make a marriage great. Val would tell me that single women would line up to marry me since I was such a good husband to her, and I would tell her the same thing. Since I had such a tough time dating prior to marrying her, I found that hard to believe. Perhaps that became a self-fulfilling prophesy as the ladies were not exactly beating my door down to go out with me.

Nevertheless, somehow I did manage to get a few local ladies to go out on dates that I met while online. One was about my age and had a couple of grown children with grandchildren, and she had been divorced a few times. For the sake of this account, I'll just call her "Kentucky Woman." We hit it off pretty good on the Internet, and e-mails progressed to phone calls and finally to actual live dates. During those times, I made no bones about my intention to date as many women as possible and slowly narrow down the field in an attempt to find the best fit for me as well as for her. I anticipated, and it seemed only logical to me that others on the computer dating sites would be doing the same thing. After all, to exclude all others after responding to the first match leaves you with a choice of only one out of one while leaving potentially millions totally uninvestigated. You had better hope that you found the right one! Yet I was chided for that as well!

Kentucky Woman and I got to the point when we decided to meet at a local restaurant for our all-important first date. We had a great time dining and chatting together. We shared with each other our core beliefs as well as our Christian backgrounds. These were always of critical importance to me as I know their value in creating a fabulous long-term marriage. After eating, we held hands as we chatted while walking around and investigating the restaurant's riverfront property and then strolled back to our cars. It was at that point that she became aware of just how serious I took my faith walk when she walked over to hug me, and I backed away, explaining to her that I was not comfortable getting that physical part started that early into knowing her as I felt that it was much too dangerous at that point. She respected that, and we continued on dating and having further computer and phone conversations.

One of my computer matches was a lady several hundred miles from me in Iowa. We exchanged e-mails for quite some time and were really getting along great from my perspective. We had been corresponding on almost a daily basis when I sent a response to her. In it I stated as a side note that I was still corresponding to several other women as well, just as I had told her from the beginning, but I wanted to assure her that as of that time, I thought that she was far and away better than the rest. Well, she abruptly told me in her next e-mail that she did not like "being compared like a horse in a race" with other women, and that was the end of it. No more e-mails, not interested in any explanation, or discussion—just the end of the journey together! Amazing! I thought that was precisely what everyone on those websites was doing! Furthermore, I thought that was the whole point of it! Everyone was on the websites to find God's very best partner for one another.

Another time, I asked for a live date from another local lady after many e-mails back and forth. She agreed to meet me for lunch at a local establishment, and I agreed to buy her lunch. At this time, I had been on several live dates with Kentucky Woman as previously mentioned, and we had been getting along quite well. And so this other local lady and I met for the first time. Talk about awkward! We ordered, and the longer she talked, all I could think about was "I wonder what Kentucky Woman was doing and how I wish I was with her at that time!" It was all I could do to contain myself. When lunch ended, she looked across the table from me and simply said, "I don't think this is going to work out. So are you still going to pay for my lunch?" I told her, "Absolutely!" It was probably the best money

I ever spent! I felt that God had been very gracious to me by quickly and soundly closing this door tightly shut. I had always prayed to him to do so as I only wanted his selection of another wonderful lady to share the rest of my life with. Not only that, the quicker I was able to eliminate the wrong matches, the faster I would be able to find and spend time with the right one!

The next couple of months, Kentucky Woman and I spent more and more time together and had such a great time. Once again, she had checked off all my items of importance for a good marriage partner. I spent time praying about it and felt that she was the right partner for me. And again, I asked that God would open wide the door if we were to marry or to slam it tightly shut if he did not desire us to wed. We had each visited each other's church and met some of the people and pastors there.

I proposed to Kentucky Woman, and she accepted and agreed to premarital counseling given by my pastor and his wife at their home. We set the date and went for our first visit. It went fine, and we had some items to work on prior to our second session. When we arrived for the second visit, the pastor's children were in bed, and the four of us sat in their living room. Not too long into the session, the subject of Kentucky Woman's prior divorces came up. And then once again, my little world came crashing in.

My beloved pastor, who stood with us throughout the illness and the ultimate untimely death of my first wife, announced that he was willing to marry me because my wife had died, but he was not willing to marry Kentucky Woman and me as he felt that she should reconcile with her prior husband and live out their marital vows. Wow! Talk about being blindsided! To say that I was utterly stunned was a vast understatement, and Kentucky Woman left in tears with me. Now as it turns out, my pastor and his wife, and even Kentucky Woman, all knew that remarriage following divorce was a long-standing Christian debate of which I did not have even a remote clue. I informed all of them that quite frankly I didn't care what any of them thought about the subject matter nor even what I did, but rather, I only really cared what God thought about it, and I was determined to get to the bottom of it before doing anything.

The next several months were spent discussing this issue with the pastor and Kentucky Woman separately in an effort to search for evidence that would convince me of what God's position was on the subject in as much as I could not find it directly addressed in the Bible to my satisfaction. And so the debate went on…and on…and on. We would share a vast variety of literature written by well-known Christian authors on the subject, and I would sit for hours and hours reading with that material in one hand and cross-referencing it with the Bible in the other hand while praying for God's knowledge and wisdom and asking him for his position on the subject. And so it went as the days turned into weeks and then months while Kentucky Woman and I kept in contact with each other. My pastor felt horrible about having to put me through it after coming off the death of my first wife, but nor could he go against what he firmly felt was the will of God. Quite sometime later, he told me that it broke his heart to have to tell me that he could not marry us. He said that not only had he and his wife discussed it but he had prayed quite a bit about it for guidance as well as discussed and prayed with the church elders about it. Furthermore, he told me that he performs very few marriages due to the numerous divorces in the United States at this time.

Several months into it, Kentucky Woman came to me with a little book titled *Marriage, Divorce, and Remarriage* by well-known author John Piper and asked if I had read it. I said no and asked if she had and if she agreed with it. She stated that she had. And so I read it. I asked our pastor to read it. As usual, he read it and gave me his notes which we later discussed.

In the meantime, I saw a movie on TV of two very young Christian couples who were all friends and got married around the same time. During the movie, the man and woman from the opposite couple committed adultery, which led to the ultimate devastation and divorce of all of them. In addition, it showed the aftermath. It was some place at that point that it was almost as if God himself spoke directly to me and said, "See, Dave, this is exactly why I hate divorce so much and why Kentucky Woman should go back to her prior husband." Furthermore, it was very clear that the book that Kentucky Woman had given me drew the same conclusion with clear biblical references. I went back to Kentucky Woman to reaffirm that she had indeed read the book and agreed with it, and she affirmed that she had. Now I'm not so sure how well she read it, but she seemed a bit shocked when I showed her straight from the book a very similar situation as ours and the conclusion that the book came to about it.

While this might not be the correct conclusion for everyone, it was clearly the correct conclusion for us and the one that I am confident God led us to. That being said, it also substantially narrowed the field of potential marital partners for me down to only widows and women who had never been previously married, which was not many around my age. Nevertheless, I certainly desired a second fabulous marriage and did not want to invite a train wreck of one. Please keep in mind that I truly wanted only God's very best match for both Kentucky Woman and me, and this lengthy little exercise we had just been through clearly indicated to me that God had slammed this door tightly shut!

In retrospect, I must say that I feel quite blessed and humbled that God selected my little family, of all people, and me to actually live through one of the most vexing questions of the Christian faith and one that so thoroughly perplexes some people to the point that they feel as if they could never become a Christian because of it. And that question? How can a loving God allow bad things to happen to his people that love him? But let's look at my situation up to this point: my first wife had died, having come to know and love Jesus, her Savior. And now she is in heaven, living with God through the rest of eternity, just as his Bible promises! Kentucky Woman had several divorces and had asked God to show her if any decent godly men were still around, when he led her to me. What she later admitted to me that she had *not* asked of him was that he would allow her to actually *marry* one! Still, it appears that I have been crushed twice and am devastated at this point. And in some respects, I was, yet I never, ever, lost faith in the God of the Bible! So please read on!

For whatever reason, though I suspect that God led me both to it and through it, I heard a radio show named *New Life Live!* I had heard it many times in the past, but on this particular day, they were advertising a new Christian dating site that they had created called His Match for Me (www.hismatchforme.com). Although highly skeptical at this juncture, I decided to give it a shot. I at least realized at this point that my field of potential partners had been severely limited to only widows and ladies who had yet to marry for the first time. And so the search began yet again of the time-consuming and tedious task of wading through potential matches, reading profiles, and so forth. Although I was much quicker in reviewing them, it just seemed so endless at that time. And of course, I kept on praying that God would send me his very best wife for me.

At one point, I remember coming across a potential match from a single lady who had never been married and was about the same age as me. She was a third grade Christian schoolteacher, whose computer name was "Teachgems."

I thought she sounded like a nice lady after reading her profile and decided to send her a canned computer response, so I scanned through the multitude provided in an attempt to find just the right one. I decided on a generic "Okay…you've got my attention" and sent it off to her.

Any time I responded to a potential match, I never really expected to get a response back, so I was quite delighted when the next time I checked my inbox, I saw that Ms. Teachgems had responded with an inquisitive "How did I get your attention?"

"Interesting," I thought. I reread her profile several times and replied with "All the above…" Thus began a flurry of back-and-forth exchanges as we began to get to know each other. We quickly let the other know that we were both exchanging correspondence with others. Specifically, she let me know that she had been e-mailing to one "Montana Cowboy" for several weeks at that point, and she wanted to see if it would go anywhere. I encouraged her to continue to do so as I wanted God's very best match for her as well as me, for to do otherwise would be to be inviting a train wreck at some future point. I informed her that I intended to continue to write to her until she kicked me to the curb, in which case I would quietly fade off into the distance and go away. My theory has always been if you don't have a ring and a solid commitment from another suitor, you are fair game to pursue a dating relationship. May you select the very best match for you.

Each successive round of e-mails got longer and longer. We quickly found out that the website limit was one thousand characters per e-mail. Although I told her that I was content to go at her pace, I did encourage her to swap personal e-mail addresses with me so we could send longer responses, as by this time the website required multiple e-mails to send a response. Still, she held me off, stating that she was not comfortable at this point, but would let me know when that time came. And so it went…on…and on…and on. Eventually, we did swap personal e-mail accounts and shared photos and even longer correspondences. Since I had been married previously, admittedly it was probably easier for me than her. While we had our share of fun, I continued to strive to bring out the really "down in the dirt" topics of a great marriage and a fulfilled life. As we progressed, I was beginning to see glimpses of what I had witnessed while dating Val. Slowly but surely, my checkboxes of things I needed to have in a wife were being checked off. And the e-mails got longer and longer. Still, I was a bit perplexed as to how this could culminate in a marriage as we lived hundreds of miles apart. After all, I reasoned I need some shoulder-to-shoulder, eyeball-to-eyeball time! Nevertheless, my older son encouraged me, as he had recently met a fabulous lady from Indonesia online, and they had married. He kept assuring me that if it was meant to be, it would work out. I attempted to persuade her to swap phone numbers with me, but again I was pushing her a bit too far in advance of her comfort line. When I finally got phone privileges, in no time, we were talking to each other on the phone for several hours every night while our e-mail exchanges became shorter and fewer and farther in between. Before I knew what had hit, all my wife checkboxes had been checked, and I thought, "Oh my…this could really be the one!" [As it turns out, Ms. Teachgems had saved all our e-mail exchanges, and they can be found in appendix B at the end of this book.]

Our first encounter began in early March of 2013, and summer was quickly coming upon us. I thought it was about time to ask for a face-to-face meeting, so I figured the July 4 weekend would be the ideal time. But Ms. Teachgems, who I had found out was actually named Susan, put me off, stating that her family would be out of town on a vacation. We decided that I would fly out to meet her the following weekend for an extended weekend.

The thought did occur to me that although she really might have been going on vacation out of town, she might also have invited Montana Cowboy to attend, so I was able to garner enough information from her to research the exact location of the house that they were going to rent for the vacation. I figured it would be in my best interest to protect my interest from afar. Oh, and lest you think I might be a bit of a weirdo, my career job over the past several decades involved performing extensive research of many different people, things, etc.

The day they left to drive to the vacation house, a small package that I had sent arrived at her home containing a card and small gift for her and a gift card for her mom. It never hurts to woo the mom over as well! While they were on vacation, I had to rely on Susan to phone me each night to ensure that she could get a good cell phone signal and was able to talk. And so the nightly phone conversations continued. And…oh yes! Ol' Dave sent her a bouquet of flowers to the vacation house as well! It also never hurts to remind the girlfriend, family, and any others who might have been invited of your presence from afar!

That week seemed like an eternity, but the next thing you know, I was on a plane heading to the East Coast to see her for the very first time. And…bless her sweet heart, when I arrived late at the motel, she had a fruit basket delivered there, waiting for me! Nice touch!

The next morning as I drove to her house, I went through Valley Forge National Park. It was strange to me that it seemed oddly familiar. It turns out that I had driven through it and had stopped at their gift shop while on a business trip many years before. I arrived at her house and, much to my delight, found her to be every bit the sweet lady I had fallen in lust with from so far away. Yep! That's right, I did say "lust"! Although Americans in general are quick to say that they "fell in love," I really do not believe that to even be possible this early into a relationship, not even the best of the best. *Real* love is a firm commitment to live life to its fullest through thick and thin, no matter what comes your way with your partner and to always place your partner's best interest ahead of your own, no matter what the cost.

I had the opportunity to meet her sweet mom in whose house she lived and, later, many of her other friends and relatives, all of whom seemed to be very nice people. So off we went to explore her land together while at the same time getting to know each other on a more up-close-and-personal way. It was simply fabulous! We had such a great time. It seemed as if time just flew by, and sadly, it did. During my weekend stay, we went to several restaurants and one night went to see a spectacular play of *Noah* at Sight and Sound Theater. It was amazing!

My extended weekend stay was like a whirlwind. We had planned several things we wanted to do together well in advance but did others at the spur of the moment. In short, we had a fabulous time together, and before I knew it, it was time to go back home. I could scarcely believe it, and it was all I could do to contain myself. The following morning, I had to depart early to go back home. It nearly broke my heart to leave her. And the long nightly phone calls continued. By now there were virtually no bounds on any topic that we wanted to explore with each other over the phone. It was wonderful having such a fine lady with whom I could share my heart on anything and everything. At this point, I was steering our conversations into the very deep issues of life as I wanted to be absolutely certain that we both held the same worldview, for I knew that this is one of the key ingredients into having a truly great marriage. By now I was quite convinced that unless God himself firmly shut this door, this was the lady I would want to have as my second wife. And so I pushed her ever onward. I told her that I thought she should come visit me since I had been to see her land, and she agreed!

Although with the start of school coming up quickly, she agreed, but a bit reluctantly, to come over an extended Labor Day weekend. So we began to make plans, and she searched to find a substitute teacher to fill in for her at school. At some point around this time, a couple of things happened that seemed to solidify my belief that I had found my next wife. One night while Susan I were talking, she asked me if I was still on the website, and it turned out that we both were. She then inquired if I had been getting any other hits, to which I responded yes, and I told her that I had just recently gotten one and that I would even share it with her if she wanted. She said that would be fine, so I sent it to her. Much to her surprise, as it had been to me as well, the name on the match for me was none other than Teachgems! Yep! Their website had decided to match us up, not once but twice!

Not many weeks later, I had driven to St. Louis to be with my family and friends over a weekend. As I was returning, I still had several hours to drive, so I called Susan just to pass the time in conversation. While driving, I asked Susan how it was going with her fellow, Montana Cowboy. She responded with "Yes. We need to talk about that." I told her to go ahead as I had several more hours of driving. She told me that she had to kick him to the curb because he always found an excuse to not come out to visit with her. Well, my little heart about jumped out of my mouth with that one! At this point, I could not have been any more convinced that sweet Susan was truly God's best selection just for me!

And so we began to plan out her trip to be with me over the upcoming Labor Day weekend. Some events were planned in advance, and some were just created on the fly during her stay. Unknown to Ms. Teachgems, I immediately went to purchase an engagement ring for her. After all, I had virtually a thirty years prior great marriage under my belt. All my checkboxes for a good wife had been checked. We had spent hours exploring the important things in life over the phone with each other. I had been to see her and her land in person, etc. In short—and in my mind—if I searched the world over, I would never be able to find a wife equal to or better than Susan! Furthermore, it was once again incredible to me that, for the second time in my life, God had virtually delivered her to me straight to my computer monitor! Not once but twice! So I sat down in my living room with myself and had a little heart-to-heart conversation with both God and me. I asked God for his wisdom and asked if indeed Ms. Teachgems was, in fact, his best match for me. And I envisioned that every woman on earth arrived at my doorstep and offered to be my wife. And I asked myself, "Well...do you really think any of them could even compare to what you have in Ms. Teachgems?" And I had to admit, "Nope! I certainly couldn't!" I had seen this before, at the end of my courtship of Val, and I certainly didn't need to see any more! The next day or so, I went out and bought an engagement and wedding ring set and had it gift wrapped.

Well, before we knew it, Labor Day weekend was upon us. I had gotten everything set up as well as possible but knew that I would have to wing some things on the fly as events unfolded. Susan was scheduled to fly into nearby Standiford Field in Louisville, Kentucky. Granted, by some standards—Atlanta, Chicago, Los Angeles, etc.—it is not a huge airport, but it does handle flights from almost anywhere. Her arrival flight was around midnight, and I was amazed at how empty the airport was at that hour. I had presumed that it was a hub of activity twenty-four hours a day every day. Just outside of the security checkpoint was a group of about twenty-five people, just like me, waiting for passengers to arrive. Other than us, the security guards, and some airport maintenance personnel, the entire airport was pretty much empty, and frankly, it was a bit spooky.

And so I waited for her to come down the ramp. Dressed for the occasion in my shorts and T-shirt, as soon as I saw her coming down the ramp toward the security checkpoint, I held my laminated, computer-generated sign that said, "PA Smokin'-*Hot* Chick"! She laughed when she got close enough to see me holding it and asked,

"What would you have done if another gal came over to you and said that she was the 'PA Smokin'-*Hot* Chick'?" Now that was something I never thought about! As I said previously, some things might have to be handled on the fly!

I took her to the motel room that I had all ready, brought her luggage in for her, and gave her the key to the car my son and I had brought up for her to use in case of an emergency. As I had hoped, she loved the bouquet that I had in a vase, the separate single rose and rose petals I had spread on her bedspread, the Andes mints on the nightstand, and the fruit dish in the refrigerator for her. We said good night, and I returned home as we had an early start the following morning.

It is funny to observe the difference of perspective people have in the various stages of life. My two sons were in their early thirties at this time, and my firstborn had not long since met a fabulous lady from Indonesia on the computer and married her. Intriguingly enough, our government does not allow you to immediately bring your new bride back to our soil for a couple years, but that is an entirely other story. At any rate, as they would watch me depart to pick up Susan for our date, they would cringe in dismay at the way I was dressed or where I might be taking her or if I told them that I had no plans at all and would have to just wing it. I would get comments like "Dad! You can't be serious!" To which I would respond, "Fellas, she might as well know early on the kind of guy she is getting involved with. I want her to see the *real* me!" And off I'd go. Yet I'd chuckle to myself on the way out, remembering those days of thinking those same thoughts.

Bright and early the next morning, we started off from the motel and stopped by the company where I worked so Susan could see it and meet some of the people there. Then we drove a few hours up to the Creation Museum near Cincinnati, Ohio, and had a fun day of it.

Friday morning dawned, and again we got an early start to make the most of our short time together. This was baseball day! In addition, Susan got an opportunity to meet my two grown sons and some other local friends of mine. We went and toured Louisville Slugger where the majority of the big league bats are made, and that night, we went to watch a minor league game of the local Louisville Bats with a fireworks display after the game. It was great!

On Saturday, we toured the local area but really did not have any daytime plans. However, Saturday evening, we had previously planned a dinner cruise on the Ohio River on the *Spirit of Jefferson.* But…my plans were a weeeeee bit more extensive than Susan knew!

We arrived a bit early, as is my nature. As I escorted Susan out of the car, I slipped a small box from the glove box into my pocket. Yep! It had been riding along with us only inches from her all day long! We sat on a bench, waiting for the boat to board, talking with each other. I simply love talking with her! As we boarded, they took a photo of us for a souvenir, and we had the first table seating six just inside the door with window seats across from each other. And yes, I got her a rose in a vase as well! The middle seats next to us were empty, and the aisle seats were occupied by a couple from Indianapolis, Indiana, who we did not know. The lady sat on my side of the table, and her fellow sat on the side that Susan was on. Behind him and off his left shoulder was a disk jockey and a very small dance floor. The center aisle was the location of a buffet-style dinner. The boat undocked, and off we went up the Ohio River.

We had not gotten very far when it started to rain heavily. Dinner was served, and the disk jockey explained that he would play some tunes, and after dinner, we could dance and make requests or announcements—just let him know. Oh, boy! Did I ever have an announcement for him to make!

After dinner, Susan went to the other side of the boat to take a picture of something outside that she found to be intriguing—and at my encouragement. I took that golden opportunity to write an announcement for the disk jockey to read and asked the unknown Indianapolis lady if she would deliver it for me. She read it and agreed. She quickly became my accomplice and did a fine job! When Susan returned to her seat, my accomplice asked if Susan wanted her to use Susan's camera to take a picture of the two of us together. After the photo shoot, she quietly kept the camera near her and later admitted that the only reason she did the photo was to gain access and control over Susan's camera for later on. She was a great accomplice!

Ironically, as we talked, Susan and I discussed the fact that neither of us danced. Not long after that, the disk jockey piped up and specifically announced that he wanted to ask the two of us to come up and lead the next dance. Susan and I looked at each other, and I asked her to go up there with me to see what he wanted us to do. When we got up there, Susan told the fellow that neither of us danced, etc. To which he responded by reading from the card he had been given, "So, Smokin'-Hot Chick, Dave would like to know if you would marry him." And then time stood still…for what seemed to be an eternity. I was beginning to sweat bullets and wondered if she was ever going to answer!

I pulled the box out of my pocket, handed it to her, and asked, "Well, will you?" I went on to say, "After all, we've spent countless hours talking, I've seen your land, and you've seen mine. I have nothing else to show you. At this point, I think it simply comes down to your decision." Finally, she accepted my proposal, and the whole boat applauded.

The final two days were a whirlwind of visiting the church I attend, local sightseeing, and then ending with going on a brief tour of the Falls of the Ohio fossil beds and sitting on a park bench watching a gorgeous sunset. We were now engaged, and once again, it nearly broke my heart to have her leave me and go back to her homeland in Pennsylvania!

Susan was very surprised by my marriage proposal because, although we had discussed the possibility of marriage, she had in mind that we might eventually get married later that following spring as she still had to finish teaching her class that year. I, on the other hand—once I had decided that she was well suited to me—figured that yesterday was a bit too late! Thankfully, Susan was surrounded by a wonderful, loving group of women, who became known as "The PA Smokin'-Hot Chicks' Club"! At any rate, the beloved women's group intervened and convinced Susan that the school could probably survive without her, and so the date was set for a December wedding, just a few months later, much to my delight! And so preparations began and, for the most part, fell squarely and thankfully on Susan's plate. Boy, did she ever have to scurry!

Meanwhile, the wonderful state of Pennsylvania had some intriguing rules. Their law dictates that you have to purchase your marriage license so many days in advance, and that starts the clock for a fairly narrow time line in which you have to have the ceremony and send the signed license back to them, or the license becomes null and void. This necessitated that I fly back to Pennsylvania over the Thanksgiving holiday just to take Susan to the government center to get the license with our credentials. One might think that in this day of e-mails, faxes, and the like, the state might have come out of the Dark Ages!

CHAPTER 14

My Knight in Shining Armor

Susan

One of my friends told me, "On to better adventures!" So I began my search again. I searched and searched but had quite a lengthy dry spell of around three years. During this time, I beseeched God daily and continued to read the Bible, books, etc. and wrote in my journal. I was able to date several fellows at this time, but they were short-term relationships as perhaps some of their names might reveal: "The Fireman Date." He was actually a fireman. "The University Security Date." We met at my old alma mater where he worked as a security guard for their football game. After driving a considerable distance to meet him, he neither paid for my lunch nor offered to get me into the football game. Despite telling me that we would meet after church the next day, I never saw him again. "The Businessman Date." We met and dined at Barnes and Noble. He asked a few questions, then reached out and shook my hand, and told me, "It was nice to meet you." And he left, never to be seen again. And the "Octopus Date." He was quite intent on getting some hands-on action, if you catch my drift!

As I look back on those years of being on the Christian websites, I thought I would be a lifetime member. In fact, several of us long-term members used to discuss just that while online. Although I enjoyed my time as a chat monitor for one of those sites, that too began to get old after ten whole years of simply making long-distance friends online. I wanted the real deal, as I was getting too old for dates that did not work out.

Around February of 2013, I began to exchange e-mails with a fellow I named Montana Cowboy and began a friendship with him over the Internet and phone. We seemed to click, and we sent each other daily texts as well as spoke with each other on the phone each week. I had a desire to meet with him, but I had already made up my mind that the guy should come to see me in my town first. Whenever we discussed this, Montana Cowboy always seemed to have an excuse why he could not come to see me.

About a month later while still communicating with Montana Cowboy, I received a very short note from a guy in Southern Indiana that simply said, "You got my attention." As I had learned to do, I very carefully read his profile and was a bit concerned as his profile matched that of a typical scammer—being a widower of a long-term marriage with two children that ended with his wife having Lou Gehrig's disease. But this particular profile caught my attention because it had one significant difference. Unlike the many others that I saw, this one had good spelling, sentence structure, and grammar. And so since I am curious by nature, I wrote back and simply asked, "How?" Thus began a series of e-mail exchanges with my "Indiana Jones" as well. As the weeks passed, we began to not only exchange e-mails but spent about two hours on the phone with each other every evening. My heart was drawn by Indiana Jones pursuing me. Never before in my life had I ever been pursued by a suitor, and it was the best thing I had ever experienced. Even though I told him early on that I was communicating with Montana Cowboy and did not know where that relationship would go, Indiana Jones was relentless in his continued pursuit of me. (For more about this, see our e-mail exchanges in appendix B.)

I never quite knew what to expect from him, this Indiana Jones. It was different and wonderful! I never laughed so much in my life as with him. A couple of months later, around May, he had delivered to my house a nice bouquet of flowers for "Freedom Day"! Now what exactly is Freedom Day? you might ask, as I did. Indiana Jones told me it was for once again gaining my freedom from the school children for the summer! To be perfectly honest, I had neither celebrated it before nor had I thought about it quite in that fashion, and that was one of the things that I found to be intriguing about Mr. Jones. He had such a unique way of viewing the world in which we live.

He requested a face-to-face meeting over the July 4 weekend. I declined and explained that my family and I would be out of town on vacation, so we settled on the following week. During our times on the phone together, we began to explore not only superficial things but the more in-depth subjects relating to the really important things of life. Although I was still a bit skeptical of Mr. Jones, I still found that he continued to check off the important items of my husband list that I had made up years before:

Susan's husband list

a born-again Christian
my best friend
a leader
a servant's heart
a man of character
a good sense of humor (must be able to laugh at the little things as well as be able to make me laugh)
emotionally healthy
a communicator
a fun, down-to-earth type of guy
handsome to me
plus blue eyes
a guy who would love me just for being who I am
an encourager

Over the next few weeks leading up to my first face-to-face meeting with Indiana Jones, my Montana Cowboy just faded off into the distance. When the family vacation week rolled around, Mom and I stopped by our mailbox on our way out of town. I was delighted to find a little surprise for both Mom and me in a small box sent to us by none other than my Indiana Jones!

While on vacation in Cape May, New Jersey, Mr. Jones and I continued our lengthy evening calls. One day in the middle of the week, a flower truck arrived and delivered a beautiful bouquet addressed to me at the vacation house that we were renting! Since I was the only one in the house at that time, I greeted the delivery man. He said, "Are you Susan Kobus?" I said, "I am." He handed me the most beautiful flower bouquet arrangement I had ever seen. I took them inside and quickly read the note. It was from my knight! What a guy! By this time, several others of my family were arriving back at the house, and were they ever surprised to see this beautiful flower arrangement. I could hardly wait to talk to Dave and thank him. I floated on cloud nine the rest of the week.

As I continued on this journey, I was blown away with the timing of the events. I was also amazed by such a godly man who actually lived out his faith. There was no doubt in my mind by this time that he was in this for good, and boy, did I ever enjoy his constant pursuit. I was sure that we would have a blast together once we met face-to-face. We had decided to have our first meeting in person the week following my family's return from vacation.

Mr. Jones arrived on a Friday and stayed for three days at a nearby hotel. During our three days together, we had *so* much fun. He always had me laughing, and I never quite knew what he was up to. On one occasion, we visited Valley Forge National Park. While at the visitor's center, we each signed the visitor book. I had already signed and was looking at a display while Indiana Jones was completing his part of the page. Since I thought he was taking a bit too long, I went to see what was up, only to find him with a strange grin on his face. When I read his entry, I laughed when I saw what he had written for his answer to the question, "Why did you come here?" There it was: "To see the PA smokin'-*hot* chick"! And so I will be forever immortalized as part of our national park registry!

I introduced him to my family and many friends, who liked him immediately and told me that he was a keeper. Among many other things that we crammed into those quick three days, he got to visit the school and see my classroom as well as meet the pastor of my church and several others.

During another of our adventures together, I had him take us to Lancaster, Pennsylvania. While there, we ate at one of the famous area Amish restaurants. The food was excellent, of course! As we got up to leave, my Mr. Jones gently leaned over and wiped a piece of food off that I unknowingly had on my cheek. This was very endearing to me, and it was at that time that I thought, "Well now, I certainly can't allow this knight to get away from me!" Sadly, the three days just flew by, and suddenly, it was time for him to go back to his home in Southern Indiana. Somehow I managed to hold back my tears as I watched him depart.

As we continued our lengthy nightly phone calls, my heart was slowly being captured. Although I did not know where our relationship would lead, as it turned out, God and Dave—also known as Indiana Jones—sure did! Oh my! He had told his local church family all about me, and at this point, they could not wait to meet his smokin'-*hot* chick from Pennsylvania! I was continually amazed at the Lord's handiwork in our journey together. Never in my wildest dreams could I have picked out a man who would be just the right fit for me. His heart and character is what I was falling in love with. Not that many weeks after he had left my state, we started making plans for me to fly to see him in his state around Labor Day weekend. School had started that year the last week of August, and I had my teacher hat on. I just couldn't see taking off the first part of the week of the school year and leaving my new class to a sub. As I discussed this dilemma with a dear friend of mine, named Bonniemae—who was my prayer partner for many years—she helped me see clearly that:

> The students will always be there.
> I needed to do this—the trip—for myself.
> This could well determine my future.

What did seem quite clear to me was that all the events that had happened from our very first e-mail exchange up until this point were clearly God designed:

> The principal of the school joyfully encouraged my visit to Indiana.
>
> A substitute teacher was quickly located, and she was delighted to take my class.
>
> And to top it all off, amazingly, the pastor's wife was so excited for me and stated, without reservation, that I would be coming back home with an engagement ring!

An engagement ring? She must have lost her mind! We had only known each other for six months. School had just started. I needed to teach these children the rest of the year. This is insanity will never happen! With those thoughts occupying my brain, I conjured up a much better plan: I would go for a visit in his state, and he could come back for Thanksgiving and/or Christmas and propose to me. We could get married after school was over! Yep! *Much* better!

So the arrangements were made! I was going off for an Indiana adventure right after school started, leaving my new class of third graders in the hands of teachers I trusted.

Continuing in pursuit mode, Dave paid for my airfare and motel room. Upon my arrival around midnight, I found out just how serious he was. Much to my surprise when I opened up the motel room door, there was a bouquet of roses on the bed, a vase of roses on the entertainment center, Andes mints on the nightstand, and a container of fruit in the refrigerator. Oh, and how could I forget about the sign that he greeted me with at the airport? There he stood, among all the other people in the middle of the night at the airport, with a computer-generated sign that said: "PA Smokin'-*Hot* Chick"!

It was truly a five-day whirlwind, including the Labor Day weekend. We certainly had a full itinerary:

a trip to the Creation Museum in Kentucky, near Cincinnati

a visit to Dave's place of employment to meet some coworkers

the Louisville Slugger factory and museum

a Louisville Bats baseball game, complete with fireworks after the game

several meals at restaurants

opportunities to meet some of Dave's friends as well as his two grown sons

a trip on the *Spirit of Jefferson* down the Ohio River

a visit to Dave's church on Sunday

a walk near the Falls of the Ohio fossil beds

a tour around Dave's town and the nearby towns, etc.

I remember thinking at that time, "This is great! Now I know so much more about the guy that someday I might marry." Ah, but little did I know what Dave had planned before I departed to go back home to Pennsylvania!

On Saturday night, we had reservations to go on a dinner cruise on the Ohio River on the *Spirit of Jefferson*. We boarded the ship and found our window table with a beautiful rose on the table for me. As the events unfolded that evening, I never expected what was in store for me. We made friends with a couple who traveled about a hundred miles to go on the cruise and sat at the other end of our table set for six. The middle two seats were empty. Following our meal, it started to rain heavily, and I went to the other side of the boat to take some pictures of items of interest on the shore. Little did I know that Dave sprung his plan into motion the second I left. He quickly enlisted the lady sitting at our table as an accomplice and asked her to deliver a note to the onboard disc jockey, all the while praying that I would not return too quickly. It worked! When I did return, our new friend asked to use my camera to take a picture of the two of us. Of course, I let her as I wanted to have a photo to remember the event. Normally, I would have asked her, but the mood that night had taken my sanity away.

After our photo shoot, Dave and I began talking. I was distracted and hadn't noticed that the gal sitting next to Dave had purposely commandeered my camera, thinking ahead for future use that evening. The conversation turned to remarking about the people dancing on the small dance floor. Lo and behold, after one of the songs ended, the DJ announced that "Dave is here with his girlfriend. Let's have them lead us in the next dance." We both looked at each other, and I was stunned, as neither of us danced! Dave encouraged me to go up with him to see what the DJ wanted. I looked at him and mouthed to him, "We just talked about this." Dave shrugged his shoulders and led me to the dance floor. We just stood there, and the DJ saw our dilemma and asked others to come up and join us. I heard the DJ say something about "Dave wants to know if you will marry him." I then looked at Dave as he pulled out a small wrapped box from his pocket and handed it to me. I started crying and asked, "Are you serious?" After making him wait for my answer—because I was so overwhelmed—I definitively said, "Yes!" The people on the ship cheered and clapped, but to me, it seemed as if Dave and I were the only ones on the entire ship. By this time, it was pouring down rain, and we had docked. The captain of the ship said that we could all stay on board if we wanted to wait until the rain let up. Many of the people leaving congratulated us, and one of the stewards told us that we brought a tear to the captain's eyes.

My dream proposal was a night to remember. It seemed like a dream, but it was not a dream at all—it was real! I was now engaged! This trip truly changed my future. Of course, that night, I had to call all my family members just to let them know. I was up until two o'clock in the morning! The next morning, Dave picked me up to attend his church, and I was introduced to people as his fiancée.

On Monday, my last day in Indiana, we went to see the fossil beds on the Ohio River and sat on a park bench to cuddle and watch the sun go down. As we snuggled together on the bench, he ran his fingers through my hair, and we kissed. It was very romantic, and neither of us wanted the trip to end.

Time was fleeting, and I had to fly back home to Pennsylvania the next morning. Dave did not want to let me go back. As we sat at the airport, Dave kept squeezing my hand between his two hands. When I asked what he was doing, his response was that he did not want to forget what my hand felt like in his.

Once I got back to Pennsylvania, it was a whirlwind. I was back to teaching, but now I also had to plan a wedding that in my mind would take place sometime at the end of the school year, about nine months later. As it turned out though, we ended up deciding to get married in mid-December. Talk about a short time span! It is now a mere three months until our wedding, and I had so much to do! Oh, boy, did my calendar ever fill up fast with school events and now wedding plans just around the corner!

Right out of the box, I was perplexed how I was going to be able to go shopping for my dream wedding dress, which would take quite some time, in addition to teaching and other responsibilities and plans I had. As I searched my calendar to find some potential available time, I spied a two-day teachers' convention that normally I would be required to attend. "Ah, this could be just the ticket!" I thought. So I went to our school principal to plead my case and requested that she allow me to take both days off to attend to my wedding plans. Lo and behold, she told me to go ahead! Yes, indeed, the Lord had blessed us both in so many ways!

Another long-term dream of mine came to pass that year. I had always wanted to mentor a young teacher. As it turned out, my class was the biggest one in the school that year, so they placed a young lady, Michele, in to help me as a volunteer. She had taught a short time after college closer to New Jersey, but her parents lived in our area and attended our church. For no apparent reason as school ended the prior year, she felt as if God was leading her to return home to be with her parents. Thus, it was that I was able to mentor her, as I prepped her to take over my class just prior to my marriage.

From September to December that year, my entire life was completely filled with teaching, church, assisting my eighty-two-year-old mother, planning our wedding, and, of course, the lengthy nightly talks with my fiancé. It was a whirlwind! Yet God was so very good to me in putting just the right people in my life to help me put all the wedding pieces together. It seemed that I knew someone who had expertise in every aspect of a wedding: a cake decorator, a wedding planner, musicians, and so forth. And bless their hearts, they all were willing to chip in and help me.

As the time got closer, I was the recipient of three wedding showers! That's right, three! Count 'em: one, two, three! The first one was given by my students, little third graders, and their parents; the second by the teachers at my school; and finally my church family. While my students were happy for me, boy, did they have questions: "Where are you going to live?" "Are you going to have children?" "Why can't your new husband come to live here?" "Are you going to live in *India*?"

Meanwhile, just two weeks before our wedding, Dave called and said, "I have some sad news to tell you." As you might imagine, my poor heart dropped down into my stomach. Then he told me, "I was let go at my job. So if you want to call this off, I will understand." I responded with "No way! I am all in! Our God will provide!" As I began packing up for this adventure with the man that God had provided for me, I realized that God's timing is perfect. Had I insisted on being totally in control, I certainly would not have had to wait this long to be married. Was it hard to wait, to truly trust God, with the unknown for so many decades? Oh yes! But it was so worth the wait to finally have a loving husband specially designed by our Almighty God just for me! This reminds me of the song "Trust His Heart" by Babbie Mason:

God is too wise to be mistaken.
God is too good to be unkind.
So when you don't understand,
When you don't see His plan,
When you can't trace His hand,
Trust His Heart.
He sees the master plan.
And He holds our future in His hand.
So don't live as those who have no hope.
All our hope is found in Him.

To think that the Almighty God, Creator of the entire universe and everything in it, had looked down on me and, in his timing, provided my very own knight in shining armor!

Our wedding day in December 2013 was a beautiful, warm, sunny day. As the time for our wedding was drawing closer, it had snowed the three weekends before, and we were so happy that the temperature was heading up to the midfifties. I had an early morning hair and makeup appointment that day. As I drove to that appointment, God gave me a beautiful sunrise which reminded me of how great a God I have. From that point up to our wedding ceremony, which was at two o'clock in the afternoon, there was a scurry of activities. In the meantime, Dave and his son, David, were staying at one of the church member's house close to the church.

With my wedding gown in the back seat, along with my suitcase packed for the honeymoon, I drove to the church to get ready. I suddenly realized that I had forgotten my charger to my phone at the house. I quickly called my brother and described to him where I had left it, when he said, "Oh my, we have already left, but I will turn around and get it for you." What a brother! After carrying my wedding dress in and several other things, I panicked. My phone! Where is it? I searched the bench inside the church, and I searched the car. It was no place to be found. All of a sudden, I reached back to the pocket in my jeans, and there was my phone! Whew!

My dream wedding was now here! I was on cloud nine! Sometimes it seemed like a blur, and other times I remember every little detail. God had sent me my knight in shining armor who was perfect for me. He also did it in his timing, as I would have certainly preferred it to have been several decades earlier rather than spending so much time waiting in his waiting room. But… I had determined to wait on his timing as I really did want only his very best selection of a husband, and I could hardly wait to see just how wonderful our marriage would be.

Our wedding ceremony was perfect, except for one little, tiny detail. As I walked down the aisle with my brother escorting me—he was filling in for my dad who had previously gone onto heaven—unbeknown to either of us, a cell phone had decided to take a ride on the train of my wedding gown all the way to the front of the auditorium. It turns out that a friend of mine from New Jersey stood up as I walked down the aisle, and just as she did, she dropped her cell phone, and it bounced out into the aisle just as I was walking past the pew she was in, right onto the train of my dress. So down the aisle, the three of us went—her phone, my brother, and me! Upon delivering me to Dave at the front of the church, my sister-in-law noticed the hitchhiking cell phone and told my brother, her husband, as he went to sit with her. He then went back and retrieved the mystery cell phone and took it back to their pew with him. It wasn't until two weeks later that we were told about the hitchhiking phone.

Dave

I've seen my sign.

As a thirty-six-year retired Christian elementary—primarily third grade—schoolteacher, Susan was surrounded by quite an entourage of wonderful people who were ever so faithful, gracious, and instrumental in assisting us through all phases of our dating, courtship, and marriage. And as our good Lord would have it, several of them had both experience and expertise in planning and creating the many facets to orchestrate and produce for us a lovely wedding and reception at the church where Susan not only worshipped but also taught her third grade class when I met her.

A couple of days prior to our big day, my elder son David—my best man and only groomsman—and I flew into Philadelphia to tidy up the few required last-minute items that go with having a wedding. One of the families from the church graciously allowed us to stay with them at their home. We arrived as planned and spent the next day picking up our tuxes at a nearby small town, etc. Meanwhile, the pastor from my Southern Indiana church flew to New Jersey to spend some time with one of his relatives. Susan's pastor was to be the presiding church official, but mine played an integral part in the ceremony as well.

Time flew by, and soon, David and I were en route to the church for a two-o'clock-in-the-afternoon ceremony. Of course, we had to arrive extra early for all the final details, such as the many photo shoots, etc. But first things first! I was escorted down a hall to a classroom that I was to use as my dressing room. As I entered, my first impression was that it must be a first grade classroom as the desks were low to the ground and quite small, all arranged in straight little rows all facing the teacher's desk at the far side. All the way across the far wall, above the blackboard, near the ceiling was the entire alphabet in capital and lowercase letters showing the students the correct way in which to write them. My son was sitting there, and my tuxedo parts were laid out awaiting my arrival. We greeted each other as I took off my coat and began to unbutton my shirt. As I did, my attention was drawn to a tripod at the front of the classroom that held a black poster board-sized sign. It had several sentences composed of printed white letters which filled up the entire sign. Scattered throughout the wording and glued to the sign were about ten or so boxes of candy and candy bars. Curious, I walked over closer to it and began to read it: "All my life I dated [Goobers] and [Nerds]. I finally met a [Hot Tamales] guy. He gave me love that was [Good & Plenty]." "What?" I thought. "Oh my! What on earth are they teaching these little kids at such a young age?" I continued to ponder this in my head. "I thought this was supposed to be a rock-solid Christian school, where my sweet soon-to-be wife taught third grade for so many years!" Now both perplexed and highly concerned, I read on: "And I wouldn't trade it for a [PayDay] or [100 Grand]. I never thought I'd [Skor] a man who makes me [Snickers]. I'm so happy that I found a great guy in this enormous [Milky Way]. I love you! Hugs and [Three Hersey Kisses]. Susan." Well, needless to say, I about laughed my fool head off while also breathing a sigh of relief! And I tenderly reflected, "Ah yes! That's my gal! Right up my alley! Clearly, perfectly designed by our Almighty Creator, God, just for me!"

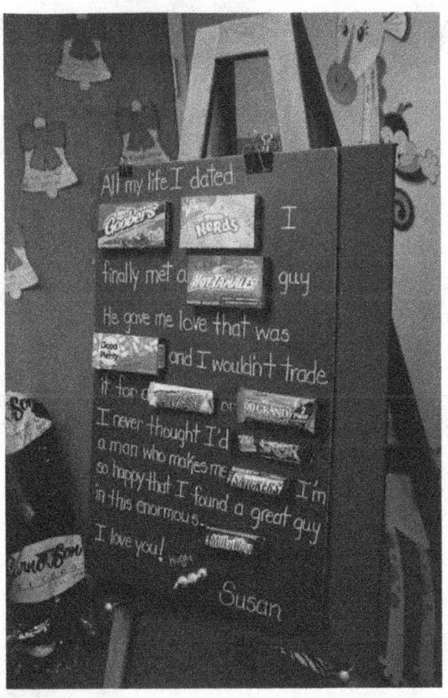

As the two pastors, my son, and I waited at the front of the church, I saw my wonderful God-selected bride glide down the aisle on her brother's arm just as beautiful as beautiful can be! The ceremony that my new wife and her entourage had orchestrated was lovely, and both pastors did a great job. Following the ceremony, we had a brief reception, the all-important photo shoot, followed by a meal at a restaurant with the family before heading off to a local motel near the Philly airport for an early flight out to our honeymoon on St. Thomas Island in the Caribbean.

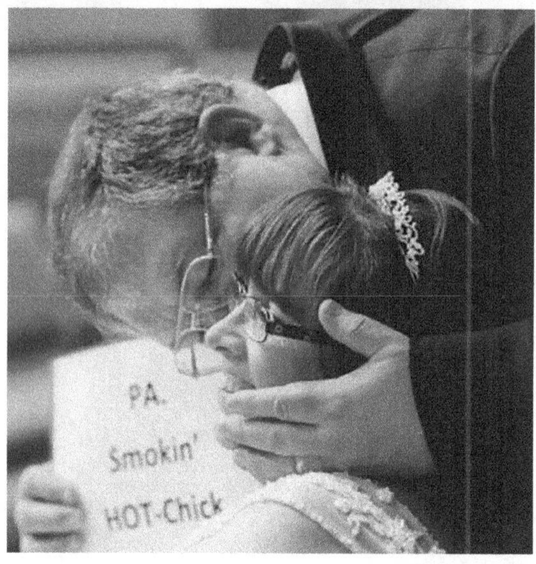

CHAPTER 15

Our Adventures as Husband and Wife

Dave and Susan

Ah…the married life! Oh, how sweet it is! Once again to have a sweet, loving wife to share my life with who God designed and provided for me. Now in partnership with that same eternal God who created all things, we could share our hopes, thoughts, love, and dreams. But dating and courting are one thing, and living side by side day to day is quite another! We still had so much to learn about each other. Our adventures started by jetting off for our honeymoon week on St. Thomas Island previously booked through a travel agent. Following our flight over, there was no need to rent a car as limo and taxi services are very competitive and quite inexpensive. But oh my! The rides zipping up and down the twisty, curvy little roads with vehicles using the left side of the road was quite exciting in and of itself!

We arrived at the check-in desk of the resort motel and were blessed to have donned our "Bride" and "Groom" baseball-styled caps that Susan had brought with us. Seeing them, the clerk excused herself, disappearing in the back, and came back to proclaim that since we were on our honeymoon, the motel had given us a free upgrade to an ocean-view room rather than our booked island-view one. It was great! With a view of the Caribbean and just below our balcony to the left, we could hear the little live ensemble playing their island music each night.

The first day, we came across a lady who helped us plan events for the entire trip capped off with a dinner cruise on a catamaran aptly named *The Cat* that was *wonderful.* Some of our other island excursions included an island tour that included a stop where a local celebrity lived, and we got to have our picture taken with her. She is none other than the sunglasses-bespectacled "Monica Lewinsky" the donkey!

During our adventure to Coral Cove, they had an underwater room where you could look out into the ocean. It was there that we crossed paths with a professor from Liberty University where Susan earned her teaching degree, although she never had him in any of her classes. In addition, the young diver of theirs was working his summer job while attending the same college. It is amazing how you can come across people you know or from familiar places hundreds of miles away.

On another outing, we had decided to eat lunch at an ocean-side café with outdoor seating. While we were eating and enjoying the saltwater breeze, we observed a storm brewing over the ocean and heading in our direction. As we scurried to get up and seek shelter, I saw an iguana nuzzled up alongside my foot, which was holding me hostage from being able to get up and leave. They pretty much roamed wild and free on the island, and you never knew where you might find one. As I was concerned about the possibility of being bitten, I attempted to slowly move my foot away, but every time I did, it would inch up next to it. Finally, just as raindrops were beginning to fall, I was able to safely extract myself from my captivity, and we made a run for cover.

Sadly, all good things eventually come to an end, and we departed back to our new reality as newlyweds. We rented a truck and a trailer, and Susan's two nephews loaded us up with Susan's car on the trailer and her beloved cat in her traveling cage, and off the three of us went on the slow two-day 650-mile journey across the Appalachian Mountains. Thankfully, when we stopped at a motel halfway across as well as throughout the whole trip, the little cat was a real trouper, and we all made it through the journey unscathed. Upon arrival back at our house in Indiana, some fellows from our local church assisted us with unloading, and I returned the rental truck and trailer. Susan has always had a spirit for adventure, and what an adventure it has been for us as we continue to grow together under our dear Lord's leadership!

Susan

As we sat exhausted after moving in, I was so overwhelmed as I looked around the man cave that Dave called home. This was going to be my home now. Oh my, how could I live like this? Yes, it was truly a man cave that desperately needed a woman's touch. Remember Dave and his two sons lived here before he married me. As all these thoughts danced in my head, I began to cry uncontrollably. I love this man so much, but so much need to be cleaned, organized, and discarded. Rooms needed to be painted, stained carpet pulled up. How would I ever manage? Dave cuddled me in his arms as I cried and told me that he would help in whatever I wanted to do. As stated before, just two weeks before we were married, Dave had lost his job. [Dave: It should be noted here that during our dating days, Susan had warned me that she was a crier, so it wasn't as if I hadn't been forewarned and had willingly signed up for these times. Thankfully, we had both been *totally honest* with each other about exactly who and how we are.]

So for two months, he searched for a job as we worked together to bring the house as a home. Slowly, it has been turning from a Dave's man cave into a Susan castle—his word for it. It is still in a work in progress, as any homeowner would know.

As I look back now, it was a good thing that Dave was out of a job for two months. Not only did we bond more as husband and wife but he was able to help go through things with me as we sorted out what needed to stay and what needed to go. We also painted one of our rooms together. Oh my, what I learned in that process of my new husband: my husband likes to ponder things through, and I am more of a person that dives right in to get the job done. So I learned a lot of patience. I only thought I had patience after teaching elementary students for thirty-six years. I also learned that we balance each other out. We learned from each other. I appreciate how he brings a different perspective to a certain situation. After painting the first room, we both realized we are not good painters and enlisted help in doing the other rooms.

In mid-February, God provided a new job for Dave. On one of my solo adventures during the day, I noticed that there didn't seem to be a lot of cars moving around, and even the stores I went into seemed deserted. I remarked to Dave later that night that I believe that I was living in Hicksville instead of Jeffersonville. Six years later, I believe that I now live in a thriving, growing city.

Dave

I had also known from the dating days that Susan was a south-paw (left-hander), *but* what I did not know was how it impacted daily living with her. It first became apparent to me when I went to turn on a lamp in our living room after work one day. Yep! The very same lamp that I had turned on for years with a family of four. But that night, for some odd reason, I could not find the switch up under the lampshade. What on earth was going on here! It turns out that my new lefty wife had turned the lamp around so it was now on the opposite side of the lamp! A while later, I also noticed that all of a sudden I began to have a difficult time untying packages secured with twist ties. This had never occurred before. Yep! It turns out that my new lefty wife turns them the opposite direction when tying

them shut and open again! We both got a good chuckle out of those and several others as time went by. And as her knight in shining armor—her title for me that I find ever so endearing—I just laugh about it and leave them be for her comfort, ease, and enjoyment.

It has also been amusing watching her get acclimated to her new homeland. As a native of the Greater Philadelphia, Pennsylvania, area, she is accustomed to colder temperatures with a lot more snow, whereas we panic with the first snowflake. She found it odd to be called "sugar" and "honey" by our store clerks and was concerned that our stores were in financial trouble due to the lack of herds of people in them all day.

It was both comforting and exciting to me as I saw this newly formed marriage slowly but surely take on the oh so familiar and wonderful tones that Val and I shared in ours. It certainly wasn't identical as it couldn't be, but it has the same essential elements and flavor. After all, we are older and have no children living under our roof. We study each other intently, and we each go out of our way to make life even a tiny bit better for each other. She continues to woo me toward her, and I continue in pursuit of her. We spend most of our time together and go most places together, usually hand in hand. After all, physical touch is my primary love language, and if we didn't want to share our life together, why get married? We try to surprise each other, and I go out of my way to keep her off balance and fill her up with special sweet memories when possible. However, sometimes I do ponder whether or not I might inadvertently be setting my sweet Susan up for some future pain of those same memories should I die first, having been previously vexed with some following Val's premature death myself.

The great kidnapping

A scant few months into our marriage, Susan was still trying to get accustomed to her new environment and surroundings, and the little church that we had been attending had encouraged its married members to sign up and attend a Friday evening and Saturday morning marriage seminar at a church in an adjacent small town. We signed up for it, and as the date approached, my devious little brain began to ponder just how I might be able to ramp it up a bit for my new wife and give her just a small taste of precisely who she had married in addition to give the seminar group a taste of what a truly wonderful marriage can look like.

I came up with the outline of a plan and realized that I might have to once again do some creative quick thinking as it played out. The Friday of the event, I elicited some help from one of the ladies at the new job that I had landed to be my accomplice. I scurried back to my office while she picked up her personal cell phone and dialed Susan who was at our house. My accomplice asked Susan if she had signed up for the seminar, and Susan told her that we had. The work lady then told Susan that she needed to pack an overnight bag to bring with her as she would be kidnapped and then abruptly hung up. While I was working, I thought the phone would surely ring with my frantic wife on the other end. But after about an hour went by and she did not call, I decided to call her, making up some excuse to call her. After we had discussed that, Susan told me that she was concerned about the seminar that night and told me about the phone call. I responded by telling her that I had also received a very similar call while at work, but I saw no reason to panic as we would be around many other people, but we would bring an overnight bag, just in case it was part of the program.

I spent my lunchtime and got off work a bit early to prepare for that evening. I typed a card for her and a card for me and placed them each in a separate envelope with our names on the front written by my accomplice. Just prior to going home to pick up Susan, I stopped off and got a single red rose in a small vase and took it to the church holding the event. The large room was all set up with the tables, etc., and I asked if there was assigned seating and was told we could sit anywhere. I selected a table and put the rose and her card at one seat, and in the seat next to it, I put my envelope. Then I went and got her.

While at home, she once again expressed her concerns. I comforted her as I packed and suggested that she do the same, which she begrudgingly did. I tossed the luggage in our car, and off we went. Upon our early arrival, we were given name badges on lanyards and other program materials, and we saw our pastor and a few others milling about near the entrance, and once again, I inquired about the seating. Upon being told to sit anywhere, we entered and scanned across the room for a table to Susan's liking. Seeing the lonely table with the rose on it, she asked why I thought just that one table had a rose on it, as I had suspicioned that she would. I suggested that we go over and investigate it. When we got to the table, we saw the two envelopes with our names on them. She read her card, which said something to the effect that the rose was a sign that she would be kidnapped that very night and that she could do nothing to prevent it, and it was signed "Zoro." My card similarly stated that my wife would be kidnapped and was also signed Zoro. By now the room was beginning to fill up, and several other couples from our own church had arrived, and of course, Susan was now very concerned and began to talk to several of them about it as well, including our pastor and his wife. Though none of them knew anything about my little plan, they also attempted to calm her down by telling her that our church had several jokesters, and some even stated that it was probably me. And so our little group was all abuzz about what this was all about throughout the event. At one point just before the start of the seminar, several even suggested talking to the husband of one of our members who was an officer in Louisville, Kentucky, about it. This is precisely one of the unplanned events where I had to do some quick thinking, and I interjected that it wasn't really necessary as I felt that we would be safe with all the people in attendance, and no doubt, this was a joke by someone in our church.

When that night's program was over and we were dismissed until the next morning and nothing out of the ordinary had occurred, several people offered to walk us to our car. Once again, I told them not to worry as the parking lot had plenty of people in it departing. We got in our car and departed. As we drove off with our bags still in the car, Susan was now relieved but did ask a couple of times about our route home sensing but not really knowing due to her unfamiliarity with her new residence that we were going back home in a slightly different direction. I sluffed it off, telling her that I had simply decided to go home a different way. But when I turned to go onto a highway, she called me on it and told me that this was definitely *not* the way back to our house. To which I responded in a gruff voice, "That's right, Missy, you should know better than to get in a car with a stranger! You *have* been kidnapped! I *am* Zoro!" And

I flipped over my name badge where I had written in large letters, "Zoro." I proceeded to whisk her off to the same motel where she had stayed when she first came to see me and we had gotten engaged. We spent the night there and finished the seminar the next morning.

Cape May, New Jersey, vacations

Each year, Susan's mom rents an oceanfront house for vacation in Cape May, New Jersey. It is a fabulous, fun-filled time as family members come and go over the course of her two-week stay. And though she is older now, she still thoroughly enjoys it. We laugh as every year we hear her tell us that this might be the last year since she is older, yet a few months later, she will tell us that she made the down payment for next year. Every year that we can, we pack our bags and jet off to Philadelphia where we rent a car and drive the remainder of the way to vacation there with whatever family members might be there.

Other adventures

Since Susan has an adventuresome spirit, often for our wedding anniversary, I will try to provide her with a memorable outing as part of my present to her. And since our anniversary precedes Christmas by only a few days, we often depart for St. Louis immediately after to spend the holiday with family and friends. During those times, she will do her best to try to pry the location out of me, but it is always to no avail as I tell her, "Sorry, it is in the vault!" And so it was on one of our first anniversaries. I had told her to be "all gussied up with bags packed and ready to depart" by a certain date and time. Off we went going north on Interstate 71 toward Cincinnati, Ohio, out of Louisville, Kentucky, with her trying her best to finagle the final destination from me. After a bit of "cat and mouse" dodging around the question, I finally told her, "Well, my dear, you like a good adventure, so now you're getting one! You choose! If you see something you like, just tell me and we will go there!" Admittedly, that was only a marginal fib, but I would have made good on it if she would have selected something. But since she didn't, we ended up going where I had really planned on taking her: to the Newport, Kentucky, aquarium, and we found a hotel to stay at and ate a nice dinner at a great Italian restaurant that the hotel suggested. She told me afterward just how much she enjoyed the aquarium even after yearly field trips to one on the East Coast with her students and helpful parents, etc. as on this trip she could actually enjoy and explore the exhibits without having to keep track of the entourage that she had taken with her for all those previous years.

The great shootout at "Ye Ol' Homestead"

One evening when I returned home from work, as usual I parked the car on our driveway. As I walked across the walkway up to the house, I noticed a plastic bag hanging from the doorknob. "That's odd," I thought. "Why hadn't Susan noticed it and brought it in the house?" As I got closer, I also noticed a note on the front door that read something similar to "Beware: I'm armed and somewhere inside on the main floor waiting for you! So arm yourself and prepare for battle if you dare! Loser pays for dinner. May the best shot win!" Well now…*this* is a gal after my own heart! I looked in the plastic bag and saw that it contained a brand-new Nerf pistol with three plastic bullets. Sadly though, with adrenaline pumping, I did not read the instructions and inspect my new firearm closely enough prior to entering the house. But in I went! Now I've never worked in law enforcement, but I have watched enough TV shows to know how they properly clear a house. So I crept through the house, sliding along the walls, opening up doors with my foot, pistol at the ready, going systematically room to room. I finally narrowed it down to inside either the back bedroom or in the hall closet. Pistol ready, I flung open the closet door, and due to my unfamiliarity with my new weapon, I was shot before I knew what hit me. Needless to say, it was a blast, and off we went to buy my wife a dinner of her choosing! It was fantastic!

An eerie night in a ditch

Susan

Every year in December, we travel to St. Louis, Missouri, to be with Dave's family for Christmas. As this time is so close to our wedding anniversary, I never know what Dave has planned for our adventure. As is our custom, after packing the car but prior to actually departing, Dave and I sat in the car and prayed that God would watch over us and bless us with a safe trip. And so it was just prior to embarking on this adventure as well. Christmas was spent that third year with Dave's family and with me meeting most of the family members for the first time in Val's family in Illinois. All of Val's family welcomed me with loving arms, and I felt strange but loved very much. That night, driving back to St. Louis to Dave's brother's house, it was rainy and very foggy. It was so foggy that it was hard to see even a few feet ahead of us. Dave did an excellent job of getting us there safe and sound. I was exhausted, so I headed up to bed, but Dave stayed up and talked to his brother and wife to almost two o'clock in the morning. The next day, after having lunch with the family, we headed to Indianapolis, Indiana, where Dave had planned our adventure for our third anniversary. As we drove, we talked and talked and joked with each other, and every once in a while, Dave's tire would hit the rumble strip along the side of the road. I hated to hear that sound and told him so. As the dark began to settle in, we had about an hour to continue to find a hotel in Indianapolis. I remember an eerie silence came over me as our conversation had stopped and my eyes were starting to close. All of a sudden, I jerked fully awake as I sensed and saw our car veering off the highway. As I glanced at my husband, he was totally asleep at the wheel. I yelled his name while hitting on his arm to wake him up. He jerked awake, and his adrenaline took over, but it was too late. We were headed for the ditch in the middle of a four-lane highway, going seventy miles per hour. We both had our seat belts on, and I remember us bouncing down into the ditch, turning left, then right, then up the hill toward the oncoming traffic. I know I was shaking and praying that somehow we would not end up there, when all of a sudden, the car turned to the left as Dave was turning the wheel. After several more turns, the car stopped in the middle of the ditch. I began to shake uncontrollably, and tears flowed from my eyes. I looked over to Dave. He was not hurt, but he kept saying, "I am so sorry. I am so sorry!" He asked if I was hurt, and I told him no. He immediately tried to move the car, but it was stuck in several layers of mud. He then called AAA, and as he was on the phone, a police car pulled up to the side of the road, and an officer came down to talk with us. The officer called for a tow truck to tow us out. As we were waiting for the tow truck, an ambulance came, and the EMTs asked us if we wanted to go to a hospital. We declined. I was amazed, as it seemed to me we had been cushioned in a bubble that protected us from harm. I knew it was God protecting us all the way. The officer stayed with us until we were pulled out of the ditch and safely down to another exit. He examined the car and said there was not a dent or scratch on the car, and the rumble we heard was mud caked up in the tires and frame of the car. We thanked him, and we were now continuing our way to Indianapolis for the night. I think I must have cried the rest of trip, but it was just tears squeezing out of my eyes realizing we could have died that night. I had never experienced a car accident before, just a few fender benders that amounted to nothing. So this was very dramatic to me. Before that night was over, we did find a car wash that was open to try to get some of the mud out from under the car. When we finally arrived at our hotel for the night, we were so happy to finally lay our head on our pillows. We talked, cried, prayed, and thanked God for sparing our lives. The next day, we explored Indianapolis and went to the Children's Museum which was the original destination, and it was wonderful.

As I relayed our ditch story to my family, my sister-in-law told me that I needed to find out if Dave needed to do a sleep study. I Googled "narcolepsy" and began to see that Dave had shown signs that were unfamiliar to me. When I showed Dave, he was amazed that he showed several of these symptoms. Now getting Dave to see a doctor is quite the challenge that I didn't realize that I would have to face. Even though he knew something had to change, he was very reluctant to make that appointment. After weeks of research and lively discussions and me sometimes in tears because I knew this would benefit his health and our safety, he had his first appointment. This now went into several home sleep tests and a sleep study performed overnight at the hospital. He was diagnosed as having sleep apnea and was given a BIPAP machine. Oh my, the first year was such a learning curve for him to use the machine successfully. I know many times he just wanted to quit and throw the machine away.

I told Dave that I now can see the benefits of him using the machine, and I am so happy he went through with his appointments. He is more alert during the days, and he is not consistently falling asleep in the middle of our conversations. It was tough going through this, but that is what makes marriages stronger—going through the tough times together.

Dave

Needless to say, that little adventure was nothing I would ever have wanted for anyone, much less my beloved wife, and I felt such shame and humiliation from putting her through it. Sadly, unknown to her, I knew full well from my job the symptoms of sleep apnea, but I was in a clear case of denial. In addition, though certainly not an excuse for my bad behavior and decisions that I made, I had several things working against me that helped me dismiss the obvious symptoms and do nothing about them, which could so easily lead to our potential premature deaths. One was my aforementioned enormous fear of the white coats and medical procedures. In addition, I knew full well the costs of the tests and the adverse impact that it had on drivers with a commercial driver's license in the trucking industry. And finally, I simply could not even begin to imagine having to try to sleep with that contraption strapped to my face all night long.

Nevertheless, this event certainly put this front and center in our marriage as it should have been. And so ever so reluctantly, off I went to get the studies performed, and it was not much of a surprise to me that sure enough I was diagnosed to have sleep apnea, and tethered to a machine all night long I would be. Grrrreat! Wow! The learning curve was *huge*! And I *hated* it! However, I had promised my sweet and ever-so-loving and patient wife that I would do it. I was determined to master it no matter what it took. I studied it and studied it and tried and tried. Lo and behold, ever so slowly, I made some progress. Thankfully, over time, I was in fact able to figure it out, and I can honestly say that it has made all the difference in my life and our marriage. As a result, I am finally able to stay wide awake and alert. Now I would highly encourage anyone who might struggle with this to get those studies performed and get the machine.

Another covert adventure

I learned early into my first marriage to Val to make plans and purchase gifts well in advance of special events. Though it takes a lot of thought and planning, it is certainly well worth the effort to surprise her. And so it was on yet another of our anniversaries. The prior Thanksgiving, I had privately informed my brother and his wife in whose house we stayed and who normally hosted the family get together that no matter what they did don't host it on the Saturday before Christmas, and no matter what I said or did between then and Christmas, we definitely would *not* be there on Saturday. Well, lo and behold, a few weeks later, my wife asked what I thought about them doing it on Saturday. And just as I had told them, lying through my teeth, I said, "Whatever, it doesn't matter to me."

On Friday morning, I gave Susan a card in which I had written "Be all gussied up and ready to roll by [a specific time]." She knew from prior events that this meant we would be departing at precisely that time in the early evening. From her perspective, we had our packed bags in the car and were heading off to St. Louis for the family Christmas. As we departed greater Louisville, Kentucky, on southbound Interstate 65, she questioned me about where we were going as she said we were going the wrong way. I attempted to get her to believe that I was simply taking a different route, but instinctively, she wasn't buying it. As the questioning continued with her trying to extract the destination from me, I told her that she had plenty of signs about whether or not we were heading toward St. Louis, referring to the setting sun—west, we were going south—as well as the highway signs, one of which had said "Bardstown, Kentucky."

Not long afterward, we were on the ramp and heading to Bardstown. As we entered the town, I pointed out the local train station to her. Shortly thereafter, to her amazement, I checked us into a hotel there and told her that we needed to find a nice place to have our celebration dinner. As we had about a half hour to kill, I told her to select a nice location where she would like to eat and even handed her a town map that I had gotten at the hotel. As I drove aimlessly about the little town, with one eye on the road and one on the clock,

I pointed out many things to her and several times asked if she would want to eat there. She was perplexed and told me that she knew nothing about any of this.

When the appropriate time arrived, I drove back to the train station that now had a line of people on the parking lot. I remarked that since she had not chosen a place, we could try the train station as it looked to be pretty popular with all the people. So in we went, and I parked the car. She was hesitant due to all the people, but undaunted, I got out and ushered her out of the car and into the back of the long line. As we slowly inched forward, she continued to express her concern about getting a table due to the large crowd. When we finally got inside and were standing at the podium inside the entrance, Susan cringed as we were asked if we had a reservation. I gave the hostess our names, and she promptly handed me our tickets to the event. Susan had quite the surprise as we rode the train on a "Murder Mystery" dinner train ride that night. It is so very important to fan the flames and keep the sparks flying to keep your marriage alive and vibrant as the years pass by!

Coaching married and dating couples

Dave

Since both Susan and I have only been exposed to fabulous marriages and have diligently studied the entire phenomenon for decades now from the single life through dating leading into a wonderful marriage, it has become our hearts' desire to help as many people as possible to achieve the joy we have in our lives going through the process. In addition, we also have known the pain of going through the breakup of bygone relationships, and it saddens us to see so many around us go through it as well. And so we now find ourselves attempting to coach as many as possible who might be inclined to listen to our wisdom in these critical areas of life.

One such event happened on March 17, 2018, when Susan and I were shopping at Fresh Thyme in Louisville, Kentucky, on a

Saturday afternoon. As usual, she went to the fruit and vegetable side while I went to the bulk aisles to search for nuts and stuff. As I pondered my selection, I noticed a young couple moving toward me from the opposite end also scoping out the bins. As they passed me, I heard the young lad say excitedly to his lady, "Oh, look! They have Albanese chocolates. They are so good!" To which the young lady gave a rather-nonchalant oh and attempted to walk on. The fellow then said to her, "Don't you want something?" And the response came back, "No, I'm fine," and off they went. I short time later, I happened to be behind them at the checkout counter, and I motioned to the young gal and said to her, "Please take a tip from a guy who's been married longer than you've been alive. When your fellow calls your attention to something and then inquires, 'Don't *you* want some?' that is his way of politely saying, 'I *need* some of *these*! What's *your* problem?'" She said oh, and while she was thanking me, the young gent standing behind her was giggling and beaming with delight. When she turned around and saw him, he motioned to me and told her, "He's right!"

CHAPTER 16

The End?

Not at all! While it certainly is true that we are now on the last earthly chapter of our eternal grand adventure, just like everyone else, the following chapters will occur just as soon as we depart from this earthly existence. For us, it will mean an eternity with our Lord and Creator, for the Bible declares in chapter 1 of the apostle Paul's letter to the Philippians 1:20–26: "I am torn between the two: I desire to depart and be with Christ, which is better by far; but it is more necessary for you that I remain in the body. Convinced of this, I know that I will remain, and I will continue with all of you for your progress and joy in the faith."

Dearest reader, it fills our hearts with joy that you have chosen to accompany us to the very end of this book, and we sincerely hope and pray that you will choose or have chosen already to be with us throughout the rest of eternity, for it will be fabulous beyond any earthly description! If so, please mark your calendars to celebrate the following:

January 1, 1,000,000,000
Dave and Susan and Val
One billionth New Year's celebration

We look forward to seeing you then! Until then, may Jesus bless each of you!

Sincerely,
Dave and Susan

APPENDIX A

The Kelly Book: Second Edition

Val

November 29, 1954–September 17, 2010
Battle with ALS (Lou Gehrig's disease)
July 25, 2010–September 17, 2010

Edited by Dave

[The original yellow "The Kelly Book" was given to us by Kelly as a means for me and her to communicate to each other about our visits to see Val when she stayed at Scott Villa Nursing Home from January 2010 to May 2010. Sadly, after they moved Val to Hillcrest Nursing Home in May 2010, the original book was lost, misplaced, thrown out, or something else and was later replaced with this second edition. The following is the typed version of the entries from that second book. Hopefully, this will help someone else. Editor's notes are in brackets throughout.]

Sunday, July 25, 2010

May our dear Lord Jesus Christ our Savior, the heavenly Father, and Holy Spirit—the triune God of the entire universe—be praised and honored throughout eternity! May his holy will be accomplished forever and ever! It is both an honor and a privilege for our family to serve him, even through this most difficult and challenging time. He has provided so very much for us—his gracious salvation through his sacrifice on the cross, he has blessed our marriage and family for almost thirty years, he has allowed us the privilege to serve him through this dreaded disease that has overtaken Val, my beloved wife, etc. Through our faith and hope in Jesus, we continually beseech him through prayer to heal Val completely of Lou Gehrig's disease (ALS) which has come upon her. However, may his most holy and perfect will be done always and forever! Should it be his divine and holy will to take her home to him, though it will break our hearts, we ask that he take her both swiftly and gently. In the interim, we sincerely hope that as many people as possible would come to know him as a result. May his praise and glory be proclaimed forever and ever and ever!

—Dave

Saturday, July 31, 2010
Hey, girlfriend Val pal:

Sitting here with you now and watching you peacefully sleep brings Denise, Sandy, and I, Debbe, a sense of peace also just being here at your side. Friends to the end always we'll be and beyond. We've gone over a lot of old memories and fun times we've had so many of and always brings laughter to all of us, and that's the good treasures in life—memories and one another. We each feel the pain and hurt for you and wish we could each take some to ease your discomfort. We love you and always smile when talking about all our times together. Boy, do we have history to tell. I could ramble on and on but pray every day you'll be okay soon and happy with no pain and worries! We'll all be together again at the end, and we can have a whole lot of fun again together starting stuff. You can drive! Love you, girlfriend. You've got a number 1 hubby and great sons watching over you. We all need to be thankful of the good times. I am. See you again for our second life together.

Love ya,
Debbe [St. Louis, Missouri]

Saturday, July 31, 2010

I came to honor my friend. I will always cherish the wonderful memories of all the fun we had growing up. My heartfelt prayers are with her now as well as her family. I'm thankful Val was given such loving family to care for her. God speed to Val.

—Sandy [St. Louis, Missouri]

Saturday, July 31, 2010

Funny thing about writing this note! I have no trouble verbalizing how I feel. Putting it down on paper seems to be impossible. I love you much, Val, and struggle when I don't know how to help you. *Use* any and all tools available to communicate. Our memories will continue in our mind even after the Alzheimer's takes my brain—ha! I know our times together are always going to bring a smile to our faces. I love your smile and how your eyes glisten. Be patient with your husband, sons, family, and friends because we love you.

Dave, David, and Gregory, I want you to know what a good friend your mother is. If you ever want to hear some stories, just call me!

—Denise [St. Louis, Missouri]

[Debbe lived in one of the two corner houses on Primm Street in St. Louis; Denise lived in the other corner house, and Val lived in a middle house—all on the same side of the street in the same block. They grew up, and all three went to the same grade school and high school and remained friends, along with Sandy Vavak. Denise was the maid of honor at Val and Dave's wedding, and Debbe was one of the bridesmaids.]

Sunday, August 8, 2010

[The Zion Legion of West Chestnut Street Baptist Church has a singing and praying ministry that dates back to around the sixties. They sang and prayed several Sundays in a row to Val while she stayed in the U of L Hospital while being diagnosed. Graciously, they came to her room at Hillcrest Nursing Home on this date and gave a private concert and prayer session for her with Dave and David J. present. May our dear Lord and Savior Jesus richly bless these gentlemen, their ministry, families, and church!]

They signed this book as follows: Kenneth Frye, Thomas Jackson, Dewan A. Heines—"God bless," James Shively, Larry Wales, and Darby

Powell, the Zion Legion of West Chestnut St. Baptist. May God bless!

Sunday, August 8, 2010, at 7:15 p.m.

How I love Jesus, my dear Savior, and Val, my wife! Going on three decades now, it has been the three of us! God has truly blessed us with so many loving, compassionate people! May he be glorified as a result of their ministering to us, and may he bless all of them! Although I would not wish our plight on anyone on earth, I do hope first and foremost that God receives glory and honor somehow as a result and that somebody somehow, someway, somewhere come to know him or know him better as a result to his honor and glory. And although it rips my heart out, I feel deeply honored that God chose my little family for this mission. May he comfort, sustain, and support us as we continue through it.

—Dave

Tuesday, August 10, 2010, at 1:05 p.m.

Here I sit again while Val tries to sleep. I hope she can, as it's been a rough couple of days and nights for her. The hospice [Amedysis] nurse and person who bathes her were here earlier, and wonderful Danielle, the Hillcrest nurse, is on duty today. All of them are wonderful and have helped us so much! May God bless all of them. Poor Val has been battling a sore spot between her legs and has been "gurgling" due to the phlegm, etc. in her throat. How I wish I could take some of this pain and agony for her! I love her so very much!

—Dave

Wednesday, August 11, 2010, at 1:30 p.m.

This morning when I got here, I was delighted that Val wanted to use the computer [lovingly donated to us for our use through this ordeal by the wonder ministry of Voice for Joanie] to "talk" to me. She, not being any kind of techno queen, is a reluctant user at best. I was a bit perplexed when the message was "gift." When I finally got down to the bottom line, she thought today was our thirtieth anniversary (October 11, 1980). Once I explained to her that it was only August, she was fine with it. How I love her so very much! Long ago, I've placed her in Jesus's loving and capable arms, yet still it hurts so much. I do have comfort in knowing with certainty that he loves her more than I ever could, though that seems impossible. So here I sit, waiting for his will to be done. I want so much for him to perform yet *another* miracle in my life and totally heal her. Of course, I realize it is a selfish request. Still, I ask it for his honor and glory. Nevertheless, if it is his will to take her to his eternal home for her, I obediently relinquish her to him, though it hurts so much. I've never been too good about beloved people going out of my life.

—Dave

Hi, Dave. We came by to see Val. I think she was in some pain, so we didn't stay long. We prayed with her and shared some scripture with her. We love you, guys, and are praying for you all.

In Christ,
Tyler and Beth [Rolling Fields Church]

Monday, August 16, 2010

My heart is breaking, cracking open, and letting my life juices run out. I find myself in a unique yet precarious position at this point. What could anyone do to me? Nothing! Rob me? Beat on me? Kill me? *Nothing!* If I die, I will be there to greet my beloved upon her arrival—not too bad! She can barely move her left (good) arm now. I'm so scared for her. Who will be there to scratch her itches while I'm at work, etc.? I know it's selfish, but I love her so very much, maybe too much. But Jesus loves her even more. Intellectually, I know she was only "on loan" to me, but still… I know if it's God's *will* to cure her, he will do it on *his timing* (which is usually at the last possible second or later). Still, it might be his will to take her back to her *real home*. I know he loves us. Still, I'm so *chicken, chicken, chicken*!

—Dave

Wednesday, August 18, 2010

God bless all the wonderful, wonderful people he has put in our lives to help us through this: the congregation of our little church house [Rolling Fields], the staff at Hillcrest and ScottVilla, friends like Kelly, our families, the hospice [Amedysis] staff, etc. David J., our son, is probably taking this better than Gregory [our second son] or me. I just hope he is okay inside.

The night of the 16, I held such a huge Dave pity party that half our church responded, or so it seemed. May God bless them all! I had no idea this would be so very hard. I love her so, so much and hate to see what this is doing to her. Though it is selfish and even if I'm the last soldier standing and even if the entire world population believes me to be foolish or stupid, *still* I *will* petition my God that it might be *his will* to perform yet another miracle and cure her. I simply *refuse* to give up that hope all the way until she draws her last breath. But if it is *not* his will and he decides to take her home to him, then so be it. May God's sovereign will be done! I love her so much!

—Dave

Wednesday, August 18, 2010, at 1:15 p.m.

Gary M. [Rolling Fields] stopped by on his way to work for a while. Bless his heart! He and Brenda [his wife] are worth their weight in gold! I *love* them so much. May God love and bless them!

—Dave

Val

Val, my dear, sweet wife,
Remember when you came into my life.

Three whole decades ago
Seems like yesterday…you know.

Together we married at God's altar,
Pledged our faithfulness would never falter.

United as one we went our way,
Did our work and had our play.

Together with Jesus, our love grew.
Along came David and Gregory too.

Raised God's children through the years,
Had our share of laughter and tears.

My sweet love, how the years have flown.
Thank you so much for the love you've shown.

But now we arrive at a sad, sad part.
Please, my dear, hold me tight in your heart.

Day upon day, I pray for you still
And place you in God's loving will.

Forever and ever you'll be my wife.
Thank you so much for sharing your life.

Love,
Dave

Thursday, August 19, 2010

Dear sovereign Lord, our God, here I sit again with the love of my life, truly a special, special gift to me straight from your loving hands. I do love her so very much, and it is so painful to watch her suffer so day after day after day. I try the best I know how to ease her pain and comfort her, but it is never good enough. Oh, loving, merciful God, though we're truly sinners and not at all worthy, still look with grace upon us—a faithful husband and wife joined as one at your altar so many decades ago. Please forgive us our many sins and grant us your faithful pardon and mercy as it is written in your sacred Word of long ago. You know both of us and our plight even before the dawn of time. You knit Val in her mother's womb. You know all the parts of her and how they work. You also know what has gone terribly wrong. You alone, dear God of creation, can go deep inside this gift of yours—the wife I love—and repair the damage. We have nobody else to whom we can turn or trust. Though we are not worthy, but only to your great glory, please consider healing her completely and give us more fruitful years ahead. Nevertheless, we acknowledge that you alone are the great "I AM," the alpha and omega. Therefore, we faithfully accept that your will be done.

Love,
Dave and Val

Thursday, August 19, 2010, at 5:00 p.m.

About Val—I mean Mom—she was found laid back in the recliner when I arrived today. I could tell that she was uncomfortable. She was breathing in and out loudly as if she had been under water for some time. I asked her several questions in an attempt to get to the bottom of her discomfort, with no clear response granted. So I decided to raise the back of her chair. She still gasped for air though. The nurse walked in the room and asked me if she needed to be put back in the bed due to the fact that dinner was approaching and the aids would be busy feeding these people for quite some time. So I asked her, with no response, and thought about it for a few minutes and said to put her back to bed. She proceeded to leave and went to the bathroom, and when I came back, she was unconscious. I guess that's why they say Moms know best.

—David [son]

Sunday, August 29, 2010, at 6:00 p.m.

This evening, the wonderful Rolling Fields church house came to worship with Val. Sadly, I had to work, but David (Hoo 1) graciously stood in on my behalf as well as his own. By all accounts, it was great! May our dear Lord and Savior be praised and glorified forever and ever!

—Dave

Wednesday, September 1, 2010

It's hard to believe this year is two-thirds gone, harder still to believe that the past three decades have flown by. Today when I got off work, David and I came to visit Val. I pretty much lost it. I had thought I was beyond being shocked by much else. But when I saw her lying there, unable to move, with oxygen (new addition) and a cool blow call pipe (although I didn't know what it was at the time), and her heels covered with caps to prevent bedsores (another recent event), I cried most of the day. It is like being sawed in two, ripping your heart out and stomping on it or being in a tunnel with a high-speed train coming at you with no way out.

In the evening after I took David home, I ended up at Dave and Mary's home, but they were out. Thankfully, Mary's Chinese mom, Chang, let me in. Mary came home, and shortly, Ray and Mike came to "babysit" me. We drove all around. Later that night, I had an audible conversation with the good Lord Almighty, creator of our universe. It was a lengthy session into the morning. At one point, I told him, "I'm walking in faith to you." In short order, he firmly but lovingly informed me that, in fact, I was not, or I wouldn't be holding such a pity party. I got a Bible, did some research on faith, repented, and slept the few hours left soundly.

May our dear Lord and Savior Jesus be praised, glorified, and honored forever and ever.

—Dave

Friday, September 3, 2010

Soon, it will be over. One way or the other, God will either heal Val completely, or he will allow this disease to take her home to him. May his will be done! In many respects, this mission has seemed surreal. To go so quickly from a complete, long-standing, loving marriage to the potential death of my loving wife within such a short two-year period of time seems impossible. Yet here we are. We anxiously await God's will. We stand by to serve him and accept his will, whatever it may be. Either way, may he be praised and glorified forever and ever!

—Dave

Saturday, September 4, 2010, at 11:00 a.m.

This morning, I came to see Val alone, as David decided to stay home this round. She had just gotten a new air-ride mattress late yesterday. When I got here, they were changing her as diarrhea was everywhere. Afterward, she was breathing very hard. Jasmine had the respiratory nurse evaluate her, and they decided on a game plan. All things I have read about this ugly disease are sure true. Each day, it is a new adventure as you never know which way it will twist and turn next. I sure wish I could take all the suffering for her as I hate seeing her go through it.

—Dave

Monday, September 6, 2010, at 11:30 a.m. (Labor Day)

Here I sit once again while my beloved snoozes. Although I wish she would awake so I could be actually involved with her, still I'm happy she has some relief. I wish I knew what she dreams about and thinks about during her many long lonely hours. I love her so very much! Today I brought in our marriage certificate and wedding album. I hope we can look at them together later. I was amazed when she said I could bring them yesterday as, up to this point, she refused me several times. I hope it will not be too painful for her. Over the years, what joy they brought us as we looked at them on many, many occasions!

—Dave

[It should be noted that due to the disease, Val had not been able to actually talk for many months at this point. Every question had to be presented to her in a yes-or-no format, and at best, on a good day, she could barely move her head to answer the question. David used to remark quite frequently and correctly that a mere four-hour visit to see Val was as physically, mentally, and emotionally exhausting as actually working an eight-to-twelve-hour work shift anywhere else. Note: Thankfully, Val did wake up that day and did look at the wedding album and other photos with me. It was great!]

Monday, September 6, 2010, at 4:00 p.m. (Labor Day)

Dear Lord Jesus our Savior, heavenly Father, and Holy Spirit, please hear our prayer. Though we are not worthy to say a word, yet we humbly beseech you to forgive our many sins by your holy divine sacrifice on our behalf that we humbly accept. Please look down with favor on your servant, Val, my precious wife who you gave me as an undeserved, treasured gift so long ago. Oh, Lord, our God…hasn't she suffered enough? This afternoon, they inserted another catheter to try to stop the leak. Please, dear Savior, who suffered so much on our behalf, ease her pain and discomfort. Hold her failing body in your loving arms and comfort her as only you can. Fill her mind with thoughts of the indescribable glory awaiting her in eternity with you. Please hold her and ease her into eternity with you, if that is your will. Still, my Lord and Savior, please consider healing her. You alone can cure her to the utter astonishment of everyone on earth, except those few of us who believe. May your holy will be done now and through eternity, for you alone are the mighty, wonderful alpha and omega, God of all creation. May you alone be praised and glorified forever and ever!

Love,
Dave and Val

Tuesday, September 7, 2010, at 7:00 a.m.

Here I sit once again while Val sleeps so peaceful and sound. I have to go back to the work house for the next three days. How I hate it! Still… I have faith that God will watch over her as he always has! Yet…how much more time will he allow me to have with her? I love him and her so very much!

Dear Lord, please bend your ear down toward us who want to be your servants—undeserving forgiven sinners by *your* holy sacrifice on the cross. Please continue to watch over Val and give her your peace and comfort. Please watch over our little family as well as all the wonderful family at this facility, our little church house, all our friends, relatives, etc. as well as the complete unknown strangers—believers who are praying for us. Please, dear Lord, bless them all to *your* glory and honor forever and ever.

—Dave and Val

Tuesday, September 7, 2010, at 7:15 a.m.

Please, dear Lord Almighty, creator of the entire universe, please hear the plea of this undeserved forgiven sinner, who loves both you and his ailing wife so very much. Please help me, lead me, strengthen me, and give me your wisdom to know what to do. What am I to learn from this? What do *you* want me to do? Please, dear Lord, help me! May *you* have *all* the glory and honor forever and ever.

—Dave

Thursday, September 9, 2010

Val, my mother and my best friend, I will miss your guidance and laughing with you. Making you laugh by saying something stupid or making you happy by saying that your shirt looks fine, finding something for you, or cleaning something for you. I'll miss you embarrassing me in public when you always strike up a conversation with a stranger out of the blue. Me helping ya find the matching earring when ya have hundreds of other pairs that you could wear just as well. Or a matching sock that has its own separate piggy compartment for each toe. Thinking your rules are stupid, for I now try to impose.

—David [son]

Friday, September 10, 2010

This day was pretty ugly all the way around. Six o'clock in the morning ended my last workday. I got to the nursing home around noon, and David went with me. He suctioned Val out again, as he had done countless times in the past. [For some time now, Val had to have her mouth or throat suctioned out due to mucus, etc. buildup in her nose, mouth, throat, lungs, etc., making breathing very hard on her. Being the chicken that I naturally am, I could not do it to her as it caused her to gag and was uncomfortable to her, yet it had to be done. Thankfully, our son David was able to perform the suction routine on her and did it frequently during each of our visits while I held her hand in an attempt to comfort her through the process.] Suddenly, she threw up a huge amount and had diarrhea, and her feeding tube site started leaking stomach fluid, etc. All this occurred more or less simultaneously.

At two o'clock in the afternoon, I met Shara from [Amedysis] hospice at Chapman's [Funeral] Home in Clarksville to make the arrangements, should our dear Lord decide to take Val home to him. The hospice crew sent Amber to wash Val up, and the various medical teams assessed her and decided to turn off the feeding machine and

> let her get emptied out. Sadly, one of the proposed theories is that her stomach muscles may no longer be capable to process her food. This presented a new twist that I hadn't counted on. I love her so very much!
>
> —Dave

[It should be noted that giving any ALS patient the correct nutrition is a very delicate balancing act for any medical team. Due to the various unexpected twists and turns that the disease takes on a daily basis, in addition to the degree of immobility of the patient and various other variables and factors, patients given too much may become too obese, which will adversely impact them. And if not given enough to sustain life, the body will resort to using up fat and more muscle mass to sustain itself, which is, of course, the very problem that the disease brings on.]

> Saturday, September 11, 2010 (one month to the day from our thirtieth anniversary)
>
> I've pondered what I could possibly get for her at this stage. The lady who cut my hair this morning suggested having a video made out of our wedding album. Today was significantly better for Val. When I got here around eleven fifteen in the morning, she was hungry but alert. They started the feeding tube up again at ten cubic centimeters per hour for four hours. (She had been at sixty-eight cubic centimeters per hour.) After four hours, she had no residual matter in her stomach, so they increased it to twenty cubic centimeters per hour for four hours. And again, no residual matter. It was at thirty cubic centime-

ters per hour when I left for the day. Praise and glory to our Lord and Savior forever!

—Dave

Sunday, September 12, 2010

When I arrived this morning, they had to turn the feeding tube off as they had sixty cubic centimeters of residual from her stomach. Thankfully, Danielle was her nurse. She said they had gotten her up to sixty cubic centimeters per hour last night. Meanwhile, bless her heart, Danielle *thoroughly* suctioned the phlegm out of Val and *thoroughly* brushed her teeth and cleaned her mouth and tongue. God bless wonderful Danielle! She loves Val so much! I wish she was Val's nurse all the time!

Three forty-five in the afternoon. Here we sit, waiting with the feeding tube off. At five o'clock in the afternoon, Danielle will see how much residual is left. I hope and pray it is none.

—Dave

Monday, September 13, 2010

This morning, Rob from hospice brought two lady volunteers to meet Val and me. Bless their hearts, they are willing to sit with her when I'm not able to be here. What a blessing! On a sadder note, I found out this morning that the residual in Val's stomach following her throwing up last Friday was eight hundred cubic centimeters, so she probably had about one thousand cubic centimeters in her stomach at that time, which is about twice what is normal. Consequently, David suctioning her out may have triggered it, but it did *not* cause it as it would have occurred sooner or later anyway. Sadly, this means her stomach is beginning to have trouble digesting food, and the problem will only progress with time. So they started up the feeding tube again today at forty cubic centimeters per hour to see if she can digest it and tolerate it. Sadder still, today the nursing home fired Danielle, who is certainly one of the finest nurses they had on their staff. *Unbelievable!*

Gary M. came by this afternoon for a few minutes. Bless his heart!

—Dave

Tuesday, September 14, 2010, at 10:20 a.m. [entry found on the very last page]

Hi, Dave. Just thought I'd come by for a little while to see Val. I guess you've already gone home to sleep. Val is sleeping very well right now. I probably won't disturb her when she's resting this well. I'll just sit and be with her. I think sometimes when we're so sick, we can feel another's presence even when we're sleeping. There's something comforting about that. I became involved with hospice because I wanted to volunteer to something worthwhile. I hope to be a helping hand and friend to you and Val. I love God with all my heart and being. I so earnestly pray that he will bless you and your family and certainly Val. Whatever use I can be to you both will be a pleasure to me. Anything I can do to ease your burden. Hope you don't mind my writing from the back. I left you your space. I want to be helpful and leave you your space. God bless you today as you can't be with Val.

—Sue R. (Amedisys [Hospice] volunteer)

Wednesday, September 15, 2010, at 11:50 a.m.

Dave, I'm here visiting Val. She was sleeping comfortably when I came in, so I took a few minutes to look at all the cards and letters she has around the room. She is so loved. I also noticed the picture of you two together. You make such a beautiful couple!

While the nurse was in giving Val her meds and changing her tube feedings, she seemed to be a little distressed, so I stroked her forehead and hair, and she calmed down and returned to sleep. I'm about to go now, and she is still resting comfortably. Rob is going to check in on her this afternoon. Please let me know if there is anything else we can be doing for Val, you, and the boys. We all keep you in our thoughts and prayers always.

—Shalia (Amedisys Hospice)

Thursday, September 16, 2010, at 7:20 a.m.

Shalia, thank you so much for the note. It really helps me in more ways than you could possibly know. I love her so very much! This morning, they had to turn off the feeding machine (currently at forty cubic centimeters per hour) as she is retaining both the food and stomach acids. The residual draw a few moments ago was less than fifty cubic centimeters. I'm *so scared* for her now. Thank you again.

—Dave

Thursday, September 16, 2010

Dave, I dropped by to say hi to Val for a few minutes around eight fifteen in the morning. I read a scripture and prayed with her and gave her an update on what's happening with us. Blessings.

—Beth McGowan [Rolling Fields Church]

Thursday, September 16, 2010, at 2:50 p.m.

Dave, I came by today to sit with Val. She was sleeping and very comfortable. I said prayers for her and read Psalm 23. What a beautiful lady! Dave, looking at your picture with Val on the wall blessed me. You both seemed so happy and in love. Dave, she is so blessed to have a husband so faithful and committed as you.

Peace,
Rob (Amedisys chaplain)

Friday, September 17, 2010, at 2:45 a.m.

My sweet Val died early this morning. I freely give her to our dear Savior, Jesus. May he love her more than I possibly could have throughout eternity.

—Dave

APPENDIX B

Dave and Susan's Dating E-mails

March 9, 2013, at 3:05 p.m.
From: Knight 777 [Dave on His Match for Me]

Okay…you've got my attention! [website canned icebreaker message]

March 9, 2013, at 7:47 p.m.
From: Teachgems [Susan on His Match for Me]

How did I get your attention?

March 10, 2013, at 6:44 p.m.
From: Knight 777

Teachgems—all the above! I'm not really sure how many characters this gives me to respond, but here goes. In general, I note that you and I have many mutual interests. In addition to that, I'm not sure how much you know about ALS (Lou Gehrig's disease) that took my wife, but it is a devastating disease. I slowly watched her waste away over the course of about two years, knowing the last year that—short of a miracle from God—she would surely die. So in many respects, my wife and I had that year of grieving together at the ultimate loss of each other. Still, I know for a fact that she is now pain and problem free in heaven awaiting my arrival some day in the future when God is finished with me down here. Yet I've asked God to send me a second wife for a second fabulous marriage. And...the answer is that I only get one thousand characters. So...wish you God's very best at this point and more later as long as you continue to respond. Take care for now!

—Knight 777

March 10, 2013, at 8:44 p.m.
From: Teachgems

Thank you for that brief yet, I am sure, still-painful reply. I am sorry for the loss of your wife and know it must have been very painful for you to see her go through so much. I do not know much about ALS. How long has she been in heaven?

Thank you so much for viewing my profile and for taking the risk in writing to me. I am rather new to this site, but I am also on Christian Mingle. As of this time, I have been corresponding and talking on the phone with a guy, Montana Cowboy, for the last three and a half weeks. I am not sure where this will be going, as his last question to me was "Would you be willing to pack up and move if things keep progressing?"

So for now, I need to see where the Lord is taking me and what he has in store for me. Since there has not been a committed relationship as of yet, I still have my profile on here. In fact, I think New Life gave me extra time—lol.

Anyway, may God continue to bless and heal your heart.

—Susan

March 11, 2013, at 9:04 p.m.
From: Knight 777

Susan, I truly do wish God's very, very best for you, me, and all the others out there looking! To that end, I would encourage and urge you to take your time and talk to as many as possible before narrowing the field. After all, a choice of one out of one really isn't much of a choice now, is it? And always keep in mind that on these Internet sites, you will meet some decent folks as well as some with not-as-decent motives. Please be very careful and investigate whatever reference you can. To that end, I will offer as many as you need or want, should you choose to proceed on.

But back to your question(s): My wife went to heaven well over two years ago. To some degree, I suppose I will always grieve her early departure to some extent. Yet I held her hand all the way through roughly two years of it prior to that, so I am through the really bad part of the grief process, and I know that our dear Lord, she, our sons, and others want me to carry on with my life.

—Knight 777

March 11, 2013, at 10:10 p.m.
From: Teachgems

Thank you so much for your kind words and words of wisdom. Yes, believe me, I have had some doozies, and yet I do know what I am looking for. I am not opposed to corresponding to several at one time to get to know someone. I just like to be open and honest as to where I am in my correspondence to others. I feel that it is only right so the other people don't start to feel that I am the only one for them at this time. Much time I believe must be spent in corresponding, especially at a distance.

One of my concerns with someone losing their spouse is that I would be compared to this wonderful wife that left earth early, especially if they had a loving and godly relationship.

May God bless you.

—Susan

March 11, 2013, at 10:27 p.m.
From: Knight 777

Susan, ah…well said! I well appreciate your thoughtful comments and have pondered them as well. Please rest assured that I did have a fabulous marriage, which I would hold out as my track record. However, understanding exactly your concerns, I have already predetermined in my own mind that I simply cannot and will not allow that to happen. A second quality marriage would necessitate: (1) Jesus centered—as was the first, (b) a completely different but wonderful second marriage with no "comparisons" allowed, (c) thus, a grand new adventure for both under the guidance of the Holy Spirit as it should be! My wife and I were both convinced that we had the marriage that never should have occurred, except for God's intervention, and I've learned that his holy selections are *always* better than mine! Thus, I always ask him to open and close his doors on any decisions that I have to make.

Take care for now. 'Tis getting late here (11:20 p.m.). Wish you well!

—Knight 777

March 12, 2013, at 7:39 p.m.
From: Teachgems

Thank you for your response and for sharing with me how you would go about your second marriage. I also believe that God is in control and knows much better than I who is for me.

As of now, I continue to correspond with the one I told you about, and I am praying that God will begin to show where it may be going. Being old-fashioned, I wait for the guy to begin the next step in a relationship. With long distance, it is a bit tough with work schedules and just life. So we shall see.

Thank you for your thoughts.

—Susan

March 12, 2013, at 8:47 p.m.
From: Knight 777

Susan, I know what you mean. I also am old-fashioned. I'm not quite sure how this

Internet dating process goes as I feel that, at the end of the line, I need some eye-to-eye, elbow-to-elbow time, and I'm not sure how you can ever get that with the distances in between. Now then, with that as a backdrop, my oldest son of thirty-one years just got back from his third trip to Indonesia in an attempt to bring back his Indonesian wife who he met online about a year ago and married over there last December on his second trip over. Believe it or not, he had to return to physically show their government his driver's license which he had left over here the previous trip just to get a certificate of marriage. Meanwhile, our government has not been very helpful either. My heart goes out to both of them!

Best wishes to you and take care for now!

—Knight 777

March 13, 2013, at 8:47 p.m.
From: Teachgems

Oh, wow, and we talk of distance. How did he ever do it? Most guys I write say they don't want to travel more than two hours, and they write a person off just because of that. As his father, were you skeptical of the whole thing? Do you believe it will work for him? I could not do international online dating.

So what is your real name? All I know you by is Knight.

It is late here, and I am tired. I have had a long day.

—Susan

March 14, 2013, at 8:40 p.m.
From: Knight 777

Susan, bless your heart! Hope you had a good night's sleep! It was wild! It has been interesting watching God work in the lives of my little family over time! My oldest son has longed for a good wife and been beseeching God for one, yet he had pretty much given up hope of finding one. Out of thin air, this lady, one month his junior, contacted him online. Due in part to my prior coaching and not knowing who she might be, my son's opening e-mail was something along the lines of "I'm looking for a good Christian wife, so know that I'm not going to send you money... Are you in or not?" Lo and behold, after a year of progressive e-mails, they did indeed tie the knot! I've both read several of their e-mails and did a couple of my own with her, and I think she's a keeper! I can't wait for her to come over here.

To the extent that you're comfortable, please share some about you. Take care!

—Dave

March 15, 2013, at 9:02 p.m.
From: Teachgems

Hi, Dave,

That is my brother's name. ☺

Oh, wow, that is amazing about your son. I would have been so skeptical of any international dating. I am glad God gave him a good wife then. I myself would not go that far to find a good Christian man. Just too scary.

Hmm, what would you like to know? My dad has been in heaven now for seven years. He passed away with lung cancer caused by asbestos. He was eighty years old. He was in World War II in the navy and worked in the engine room. He could have gotten it there. God gave him a great long life. He served as the founding pastor of a small Baptist church in Harrisburg, Pennsylvania. That is where I grew up. Had a great childhood. We were not rich, but Dad and Mom saw to it that we did enjoy the simple things in life, like camping, the beach, watching the airplanes take off, and feeding the ducks, as a few of the activities we did. I graduated from a public high school and went on to college at Liberty University. Oops, I see my allotted words are up.

—Susan

March 16, 2013, at 5:31 p.m.
From: Knight 777

Susan, thank you for being so open with me! I can't wait to hear more of the Susan story!

I was raised the oldest of four boys by a middle-class couple in a St. Louis, Missouri, suburb. Mom (Catholic) raised us in a Catholic grade school and public high school. Dad worked long and hard to support us. Sadly, he recently died about a month ago, just shy of turning eighty-four. Sadder, taking about God was never on the table with him. I once wrote him a lengthy letter detailing my own Christian adventure to knowing the real Jesus, and his only response was "Well, they live, they die, you bury them, and that's pretty much it." How very tragic. Dad was such a good guy! I hope sometime, at the end, he finally figured it out.

My brothers are spread out across the country in Colorado, Missouri, and Florida. Despite that, we all love one another very much, and all have long-term marriages, except for me, being the widower of a marriage which fell just twenty-four days shy of our thirtieth anniversary.

Hope to hear from you soon!

—Dave

March 16, 2013, at 9:12 p.m.
From: Teachgems

Hi, Dave,

Ah, four brothers. Glad you all get along, but sad that you are all spread out. I am the oldest of four. I have two sisters and one brother who is the baby of the family. All are married but me. My one sister just got married two years ago. My other sister married a guy from her college years. When we all get together, we have a blast. Sisters live in Pennsylvania. My brother lives in New Jersey. Right now, I live with Mom who is eighty-two years old. I had moved from New Jersey to help her when Dad got sick and just continued to stay with her after his passing. She is very independent and still drives. Mom has a dog, a cockapoo, and I have a cat that I adopted. Do you have any animals?

Well, I can never tell how much space I have on here for writing. Take care.

—Susan

March 17, 2013, at 1:48 p.m.
From: Knight 777

Susan, I was raised to love animals, and my wife used to say, "You think God created dogs just for you." (She was allergic to cats.) It is true! Dogs just seem to gravitate to me. We had several pets during childhood. My favorite was a border collie.

Have you had any long-term romances, marriage prospects, etc.?

Always know that I will only want God's very best for you, so if you should ever decide that we part ways, please just be up-front and say so, and I will vanish. And know that I am content to proceed at a pace in which you are comfortable. To that end, let me know if you ever want to swap offsite e-mail addresses where we won't have space limitations.

'Tis a blustery, cold, snowy day coming your way. Take care for now!

—Dave

March 17, 2013, at 4:11 p.m.
From: Teachgems

Thanks, Dave. I have always found that cats were easier, especially since I would be gone all day at school. Then I would travel during the summer. Can't always find someone to care for a dog, if you can't take the dog with you. I do love dogs and mostly all kinds of animals, except snakes and bugs. Lol!

I don't mind writing and appreciate you wanting to go at my pace. I am still writing to another guy, and again I don't know where that will end up at. So I don't think there is any harm in writing. You can't have too many Christian friends.

I did have one long-distance relationship, which I will gladly tell you about in a longer e-mail. So yes, here is my e-mail address: [e-mail address redacted].

Have a great evening.

—Susan

March 17, 2013, at 8:49 p.m.
From: Dave

Susan, thank you for sharing a better format with me! As I've said in prior e-mails, I truly do want only God's very best for you as well as me. I think our culture and specifically Hollywood and the media in general has been largely responsible for our unbelievable divorce rate in this country. In addition, I think the church universal has not done enough to educate people about the dire consequences, etc. I feel that God has blessed me beyond belief as my parents sustained a fifty-nine-plus-year marriage until Dad's death, and my three brothers and I had long-term marriages as well with only our youngest brother having the only divorce early into his first of two marriages.

It has always perplexed me why people of both sexes go on one date and then want to exclude everyone. It would seem much better to me for them to date as many as possible, then start paring down the herd to the fewer and fewer who are more in tune with them until the best of the best of the huge herd becomes apparent. I would think that would produce a much better selection process for all.

Now please understand that I firmly believe that if Jesus is the central part to a marriage of two firm Christians, he can produce an excellent marriage. I thoroughly believe that was what I had with my wife. People looking on at us didn't know quite what to make of us. Her dad would often remark, "I have never seen anything quite like you two. It's almost as if she breathes in and you breathe out." And that really was what we had for all those years. Yes, we did have our disagreements, but we also knew how to resolve them. I say all this to let you know that I would never want to stand in the way of you having the best that God would have for you, whether it is to remain single or marry me or any other God-selected fellow. And to marry someone outside of that is certainly inviting a potential train wreck. Why go there?

I'm so thankful that we can now exchange thoughts, ideas, etc. on a forum in which I don't have to wonder at what point I will be cut off.

And yep, cats are considerably lower maintenance. But…they are also much more aloof, and that is why I prefer dogs. But most critters are fine and, might I add, also God's creatures!

Just out of curiosity, do you play chess, and if so, do you like to play it? And yes, I would like to hear about your past to the extent that you have comfort disclosing it to me. Please know that it will go no further than these e-mails. I think that was one of the things that always kept my marriage alive and vibrant. My wife and I never quit exploring every teeny, tiny crevice of each other—our individual daily experiences, thoughts, hopes, dreams, etc.

Well, that's about enough for now. I still have some laundry to do, and my oldest son is here spending a few days with me from St. Louis. Yep! The same lad who went to marry the lady in Indonesia.

Hope to hear back from you soon. Take care for now!

—Dave

March 19, 2013, at 8:36 p.m.
From: Susan

Hi, Dave,

I did get this e-mail. Just has taken me a day to reply. Sorry about that. Yes, this is better, no limit on how much we type, and we can also share pictures.

I always want to be up-front and honest on who I am communicating with. Yes, I do see your point on selecting the best that God has for a person, and yet he does allow us to choose who we think is the best fit. He trusts that we choose *his* best for us.

I also firmly believe that if Christ is the center of a marriage, that marriage has a better chance of survival. I have seen good and bad marriages. The ones that seem to stick are those that show respect for each other, have Christ as a foundation, have fun together, and never stop learning about each other. It seems that when a marriage is in trouble, they have taken their eyes off the Lord and are in a very selfish mode.

Now I did promise to tell you about my one long-distance relationship. First, let me say that I never dated until I went to college. I think the boys at my dad's church were too afraid of him. Lol!

I have been on single Christian websites since my late forties. I have been on a site called Christian Café where I am a chat monitor, which means I am on there for free for my volunteer work. It was on there that I met California Ranger from near San Francisco, California. We seemed to hit it off and e-mailed about three months before talking on the phone. It was after seven months that he flew over to see me. This was my first online experience, and I was scared to death. But the Lord blessed our friendship, and we grew stronger and stronger in our bond of friendship. Many miles were flown back and forth over the course of the five years we were friends. When we talked, I would always ask him where he thought our friendship was headed. He would always say to me, "Susan, relationships are hard. Friendships are easier. Let's just continue and see what happens." I totally believed him and continued to be the best friend I could, even through the long distance. We would have so much fun together when we were together. He spent four days with my family and me on our family vacation, and I even went with his church to a short-term mission's trip. On the fifth year of our friendship, he lost his job in California and started to look here in the east. One day, he called me to tell me he was in Maryland and had found a job and would be moving there. I was so excited. Now I knew we would be seeing more of each other. That was true for about four months. He then began to make excuses to not see me, and I finally found out that he had started to date a lady in his new church. Then nine months later, he e-mailed me and said he had married her. I was so devastated. So many of my friends and family who had met him thought we would get married. Yes, I would have married him if he had asked. God must have better plans for me that I know not of. It has been five years since he got married. I don't regret my time spent with him as I learned so much, but it sure did hurt.

Since then I have had a few dates here and there through the Internet, mostly local and one from Virginia. All have been who their profiles said they were, but they just were not what I was looking for. The guy from Virginia I actually went down to see. Never again will I go and visit the guy first. He was a jerk. Never offered to pay for my meal (we went dutch). Never came to say goodbye to me after I went to his church (he sang in the choir). He could have slipped away for a few minutes and said, "Thank you for coming."

So my best online dating experience was with California Ranger, and he broke my heart.

Scammers come a dime a dozen. I can smell them coming even before I open up their e-mail. Lol!

So I am open to long-distance friendships or relationships. I proceed with caution.

How long have you been doing online dating? Have you dated anyone locally?

Please tell me a little bit about Jeffersonville. Is it a large city? If not, what large city is it near that I might know? I have been to Hammond, Indiana, to visit friends when they lived there. They are no longer there now.

On your profile, you say you are in transportation. What type of work do you do in transportation?

It snowed just a dusting here last night, then had a wintry mix most of the day today. Nothing stayed on the ground. This afternoon, the sun did come out for a while. Most of our winter has only been dustings of snow. We seem to have missed the big snowstorms. All I want is spring to come now!

Have a good night.

—Susan

March 19, 2013, at 11:14 p.m.
From: Dave
Subject: Have a happy Wednesday

Susan, I'm so very sorry that your relationship with California Ranger fell apart. I well know how painful that can be. I grew up the oldest of four boys to middle-class parents in suburban St. Louis. As a child, I was an introvert, and to make matters worse, I had to change from Catholic grade school to public middle school in eighth grade. Around family, I was, of course, too young to be with the adults, yet older than most of the family children. At school, all the cliques had already formed, so I was more or less odd man out on most fronts. When high school rolled around, all I really wanted was an opponent to play chess, and I really didn't care too much about the rest of society, although I was always polite, etc.

Beyond a doubt, I was not a very good dater, and I had a very difficult time with it and dated very little. My very first date was taking the scout master's daughter to the junior prom. I had zero girl experience and zero dating experience. Yet as a young man, I was in lust over her. We went out several more times, but for whatever reason, she moved on, and I had no idea. (There should be a law that you have to advise the other sex that you are moving on!) So devastated, I didn't date again for some time. In fact, you could probably count on one hand the number of ladies that I dated. I was always the one getting crushed!

My wife, on the other hand, dated prolifically and was actually engaged prior to me. We married in our midtwenties and, as I've told you previously, had a truly fabulous, God-orchestrated, and God-centered marriage of just shy of thirty years before she succumbed to ALS in September 2010.

Sadly, the last nine months of her life, she was confined to a nursing home. I would visit her every possible moment that I could every day. It broke my heart to see her waste away before me. Our local church, family, friends, and even strangers were amazing throughout, supporting us in unbelievable ways. I learned so much through the whole ordeal, yet I would never want to go through it again, nor would I wish it upon anyone else on earth.

Among other things, if you would have asked me to rank our marriage on a 1-to-10 scale with 10 being the highest, I would have placed it someplace around 9 overall, including the three years of menopausal hell! However, never in my wildest dreams did I ever imagine that it would soar to heights that I would place at about a 15 (yep, off the charts) going through what we had to go through together during her ordeal, but it did! She was amazing! Prior to diagnosis, I had asked her if she would be willing to go through what we then thought was something much less as bad or worse if it meant just one person more would come to know Jesus, and she told me that she would without hesitation. I revisited the question many months later when she couldn't talk and had been bedridden for months following the ALS diagnosis, and again, she indicated that she would go through it if it meant one more person would be saved!

At any rate, I had about two years to ponder the fact that I could well end up a widower quicker than I would ever have wanted. So I did some online dating on a couple of other websites just a few months following her death. Her dad was my biggest supporter. He had lost his wife on our fifth wedding anniversary many years ago. Having observed our marriage, he told me I needed to be married, unlike him who is very comfortable living by himself. He is right! I love the marriage life and hope and pray that God will allow me to have a second loving wife in the future. Yet his will, not mine, be done!

Just as you remarked, it was perplexing to me that so many women that I swapped e-mails with on those websites stated that they wanted a decent guy and a good marriage, but the bottom line was that they did not want to do what it takes to have one. However, there was one local lady with whom I did end up having a very good relationship with. We ended up having many great dates and decided to marry. We went to marriage counseling with my pastor (her choice) and his wife. We returned for session number 2, and in short order, he informed us that he was comfortable with me getting married again, but not to her as she had been divorced previously. Furthermore, he provided scriptural references to back him up, and he had solicited the church elders' opinions as well.

Both of us were brokenhearted. I had read the Bible many, many times and was not convinced that he was correct, so I embarked on a two-month mission to discern what I thought was God's intent on the subject. I read and read and read the Bible and other commentaries, etc. I cross-referenced them with one another, etc. It was amazing to me the number of different points of view on the subject matter. At long last, my fiancée herself brought to me a John Piper book entitled *Marriage, Divorce, and Remarriage*, which she claimed to have read and claimed it was her position on the subject. I read it, which included the scriptural cross-references within it, and I came to the conclusion after many readings, prayer, etc. that my pastor was correct! I firmly believe that Mr. Piper was correct. I need to restrict my prospects to unmarried or widowed ladies, and I firmly believe that is how God designed it, despite what our society might believe today. Having suffered that blow, it is only recently that I have embarked on the quest once again, but this time with a much-narrowed selection process. You are currently the only one that I am corresponding with at this time.

Now please understand that I do have both male and female adult friends, but they are that and only that. In fact, the lady I almost married and I remain friendly and only friends as well. To that end, they all know how I am about marriage (holding it in sacred high esteem), and thus, I have a multitude of references for a prospective second wife to research. Thankfully, earlier in our marriage, several female work friends, primarily "Wonderful Kelly," were quite helpful to me as sideline coaches from the female perspective in helping me over a few rough spots (where I messed up due to my lack of female knowledge). God bless them one and all!

Jeffersonville, Indiana, is just across the Ohio River from Louisville, Kentucky. In fact, if you were to drive north on Interstate 65 across the Ohio River into Southern Indiana, immediately across the bridge you would take Exit 0 to come to see me. Yep! There is literally an Exit 0!

You could almost say that Jeffersonville, Clarksville, and New Albany, Indiana, are almost like Louisville, Kentucky, suburbs. They are all pretty, quiet, small town yet with the larger city amenities, such as malls, etc. very nearby. Personally, I would have preferred a house in the middle of about one hundred acres, but my wife thought downtown New York City would have been a good place to live, although I doubt that she would have liked it had she gotten there. Thus, this turned out to be a great compromise for us, and after living here a short time, you could not have dragged her away. I offered several times to move back to St. Louis, but she wouldn't have it.

I began my transportation career as a part-time school bus driver in St. Louis while attending college. I ended up becoming the garage manager of a fleet of 65 buses out of a total fleet of 4,900 buses spread out across nine states as a contracting service for many school districts. My wife's dad was a truck driver turned truck owner, and I hired her as a stranger applying for a job.

When we married, I went to work for her dad as a tractor and trailer driver. Currently, I am the safety director for a fleet of roughly 230 tractor trailers operating across our country and a small part of Canada. Once again, God has truly blessed me and my family as I had no clue such a job even existed, yet I love every day at work. Yep! There are certainly days that I want to pull my hair out, but overall, I just love this line of work!

Yes! Gotta love the mild winters! Actually, around September and October every year, I start living for April!

Well...hopefully, I have addressed all your questions to your satisfaction. (Heaven only knows that I would have been cut off many paragraphs ago on the His Match for Me site.)

Anyway, my son went back to St. Louis earlier today, so I do miss him already, and it is quite late (about 11:15 p.m., EDST), so I need to head off to bed for work in the morning.

As always, I do enjoy hearing back from you and eagerly await your next e-mail. Take care for now!

—Dave

PS: Based solely on your e-mail address, I guessed that your last name is [redacted]. Is it?

Friday, March 22, 2013, at 9:22 p.m.
From: Susan

Hi, Dave,

Thanks. Yes, it was painful, after spending so much time with him and he kept giving me mixed signals. It is a part of my life, but I have moved on.

Anyway, I am officially on spring break this coming week. Whoo-hoo! Lol! Teachers sure love their spring break, even though it feels like winter. Brrr. How is the temperature there in Indiana? Thanks for explaining where Jeffersonville is.

Ahh, I was very shy in school, never dated. Of course, my dad was a pastor of a small Baptist church, and I know the boys were scared of him. Lol! I didn't date till college and had two serious relationships, but neither worked out. Then through the years because of teaching in a small Christian school, there was not the opportunity to date from the small churches I attended. In my forties, I got on the single Christian websites. Other than California Ranger, I had a few other dates, but they all seemed to have issues.

Yes, my last name is [redacted]. My heritage is one-fourth Polish, one-fourth German, one-fourth English, and one-fourth French. How's that for a mix? Lol! My dad and his youngest sister were the only two out of the ten siblings born here in the US. All his other brothers and sisters were born in Poland. Dad actually led his mom to the Lord using a Polish Bible. His dad died when he was just thirteen years old. I grew up not really knowing my aunts and uncles on my dad's side because of our different lifestyles of being a Christian. Later in their lives, some of my dad's brothers and sisters did accept Christ. What is your heritage?

Oh yes, I do believe everyone has male and female friends. I am going to lunch tomorrow with a male friend of mine who is dating someone he met online, but she lives in Ohio. We have been friends for about four years, and every so often, we go out to lunch with each other.

Thanks for telling me about the lady you almost married. She sounds like a lovely lady.

It has been a long week, so my letter tonight is short. Have a good weekend.

—Susan

PS: I am attaching a picture of my siblings and me from 2012 Christmas. I am the shortest and the oldest. My brother is the baby in the family. My two sisters are one year apart, and I am eight years older than the sister in the red. We all try to get together over Christmas.

Saturday, March 23, 2013, at 12:39 a.m.
From: Dave
Subject: Ah, another weekend!

Susan, just gotta *love* the weekends! That being said though, I am on call at all times. Thus is the lifestyle of a transportation safety director. As a normal rule, nothing happens, but on the other hand, anything is possible. Currently, I am our fleet's first line of defense. But about a month ago, I hired Christina, one of our fleet drivers, to train as my loss prevention specialist. She is well suited to the job and is both progressing well in her training, in addition to chomping at the bit for me to turn her loose (allow her to take the off-hours calls, etc.). However, as I've explained to her, I would not be doing either her or our company justice if I allowed that this early into the training process. She is quite a bit younger than me and full of youthful excitement, which

I can understand, but this job requires a considerable amount of knowledge and expertise, lest something go horribly wrong. Over the long haul, I have high hopes for her, and she will set the company quite well for my ultimate retirement or demise.

You have a lovely family. My mom was a pretty good amateur photographer but pretty much drove my brothers and me crazy, taking multitudes of pictures throughout our lives at family functions. In addition, she was very good using the thirty-five-millimeter cameras, etc. whereas I never understood them and, quite frankly, had zero interest in them. Just give me the new digital point and shoot and I'm fine. Consequently, I have very few recent digital photographs. My oldest son, on the other hand, was quite reluctant in coming to a working knowledge of using the computer but became very interested once he found and began wooing his Indonesian wife online while living with and taking care of my dad prior to Dad's recent death. Throughout that ordeal, he photographed prolifically and had some very humorous ones. I think he got my sense of humor and his mama's artistic bent. I've included a few photos for your viewing pleasure of my life. Hopefully, they will not exceed any capacity limits on your computer. One is of our marriage, the second of our twenty-fifth anniversary, and the last from this past summer of me and our two sons when they both came in to visit me.

My wife used to always tell me, "Dave, I got the pick of the litter and the runt of the litter." She was referencing the cold hard fact that she was five feet and four inches, I am five feet teen inches, and my three brothers are all over six feet tall. And as you can see, I'm *still* the runt of the litter as our two sons outgrew me as well! Oh, well! Throughout the course of our marriage, she would inevitably have to ask me to get things down off shelves and other higher places for her, and I would always tease her with a quick quip of "Well, if you would *ever* grow up, you could reach this or that!" We had a ball together as well as with the kids.

We were always the neighborhood "block house." With very, very few exceptions, I would arrive home from work to a yard- and/or houseful of kids: our two "domestic" and those I dubbed as our "foreign" kids. We had such fun with all of them!

My dad was the youngest of three brothers. Don, the middle brother at one point in his life, spent several years researching our family heritage and got it all the way back to Switzerland in the 1600s. Apparently, part of the family left there and arrived in French Canada, and part eventually migrated down to St. Louis, Missouri. We found and still communicate a bit with family members in Switzerland (my middle brother and cousin actually visited them there), some in Washington state, and others. They are all such a loving great group of folks, though sadly not all of them are Christians.

Well, my dear Susan, 'tis now Saturday at 12:30 a.m., EDST, and I'm flat bet, although I do love exchanging these e-mails with you! However, I am going to cut this one off and hit the hay. I wish you a wonderful weekend! Please write to me as you can! Take care for now!

—Dave

Sunday, March 24, 2013, at 11:07 p.m.
From: Susan

Hi, Dave,

Ah yes, weekends are great, but spring break is better. I am off this whole next week for spring break. It sure doesn't feel like it weather-wise. We are expecting snow around midnight into tomorrow, maybe two to three inches or maybe just rain. They haven't predicted a snowstorm right all winter season this year. So I am going to be able to sleep in a bit…yeah!

Wow, being on call is very hard. I remember one summer I worked up at a camp for rich kids. I was on call twenty-four seven, in case they needed to be taken to the doctor or pick up medications or for any other minor injuries, like bee stings, falling off a horse, and needing to rest. I was a caretaker for them. I had to take a CPR class and a first-aid class in order to be hired. I did not like the job because I was mostly alone, unless one of the teens needed me. But the money was sure worth it. It helped me pay for a secondhand car that I needed at the time. So ugh…sorry that you are on call all the time.

I hope the new girl works out for you and that, in her enthusiasm, she does her job well. So what are your plans for retirement?

Thanks so much for sending the three pictures. The wedding picture was very nice, very sweet. I can tell that you adored her. Now which one of your boys is the one that married the international lady? Both of them look very much like you. What is the other son doing in his life?

I just finished watching the new series on the History channel called *The Bible*. Have you seen any of the episodes? I think it is done very well, considering Hollywood. But at least the message is out, and hopefully, someone might become a believer because of it. Question for you: Do you think Marcum became a believer after Jesus put back on his ear? I had never thought of that before and thought it might be possible.

Thanks for your compliment on my family. I have attached a picture from school. We had a fun day celebrating Dr. Seuss Day, so I got my picture taken with one of my students. I love taking pictures, and one of my hobbies is doing scrap booking. I usually have more time in the summers to work on it because it does take a lot of time, but I love creating the pages to put the pictures on. I love creating memories.

What type of a church do you go to? Tell me a little about it.

Time for bed as my eyes are starting to droop. Have a good night.

—Susan

Monday, March 25, 2013, at 9:20 p.m.
From: Dave
Subject: Spring break in the wintertime

Dear Susan,

It seems like winter refuses to release its icy grip on us this year. I'm happy that you get spring break, summers off, etc. It must be wonderful!

I've only been with this company for a bit longer than a year now, but it is great! Our owners are two fine Christian fellows, as is our general manager (my boss) and many of the folks there. We start every weekday off with about four of us on the ground floor and about seven in the second floor conference room doing a fifteen-minute Christian devotional and prayer time. It's great! And a great way to start each workday! I get the typical two-week vacation, plus a personal day each quarter off, but we are allowed to save them year to year. And with a full line of benefits and a nice salary, I'm quite happy with it, not to mention I love the work! The downside is having to cross the Ohio River Bridge to and from each day as it is always congested.

Retirement: I don't know that I could ever really retire in the sense that most Americans view it. I would have to do something! I suppose my dream retirement would be to have a ministry of some kind with my wife, if God allows it. Sadly, the way the economy and country seem to be going, I might have to work just to survive, although I do have a meager 401(k), etc., which hopefully will be enough to suffice. Time will tell as it always does, *and* God has always taken good care of me throughout my life despite my silly, sinful self!

The first marriage and family: Someday, hopefully, I will be able to share some of the stories of our marriage. Yes, I did indeed adore my wife. We were truly the marriage that never should have happened, but for the grace and orchestration of God. Ironically, we both thought that we married up! Oddly enough, it just happened (or God ordained that as well) that I knew lots of folks in the wedding business at precisely that time. The photo that you viewed was taken by a professional photographer that I knew and worked with named Jack who gave them to us at cost as a wedding gift. My mom was a part-time professional cake decorator who provided the cake. My brother worked for a florist and gave us all the wedding flowers. The bottom line (literally) was that we bought her a one-hundred-dollar JCPenny dress from their catalogue and bought the invitations, and that was about it. Our reception was held in my parents' backyard. Our love was all that really mattered to either of us, but all through our marriage, I always wanted to give her memories, little realizing that she would depart this earth prior to me. As you get to know me, you will find that I am an over-the-edge, die-hard, sentimental romantic to the nth degree!

Our sons: As you view the photo that I sent, our youngest son is on the left and the older on the right, closest to the door in the background. He is going to be thirty-two soon and is the one with the Indonesian wife. The youngest is coming up on his thirtieth birthday this summer and is a bachelor truck mechanic.

I love the History channel but have never seen *The Bible* episodes on it. I'm very careful about what I watch on secular media relating to the Holy Scripture as I've found that they rarely do a good job with it. As to your question, I assume that you are referencing John 18:10 when the mob came to arrest Jesus, and Simon Peter whacked off the ear of Malchus, the servant of the High Priest. I honestly don't recall the Bible giving any further reference to Malchus nor giving us any other hints about whether or not he became a believer. However, if you know of any, please let me know as I would be interested.

Photos: Great photo of you and the school child as Thing 1 and Thing 2. Ironically, early in childhood, I dubbed our two sons as Who 1 and Who 2 of "All the Little Whos in Whoville" from the *How the Grinch Stole Christmas*! Many years later when they were in high school or so, I asked them if they preferred that I start calling them by their real names, but both told me, "No, Dad. Let's just keep it at Who 1 and Who 2. Actually, we changed the spelling to Hoo 1 and Hoo 2.

"Ye Ol' Church House": You know what they say, "A picture is worth a thousand words." Admittedly, our church does not have the best website, but you are more than welcome to visit there: www.rollingfields.org. What a wonderful, wonderful group of loving Christians! Their loving care for my wife and our family as we went through her battle with ALS was fabulous.

Hopefully, I have adequately answered all your questions. Though hundreds of miles apart, I do enjoy these times we have together typing to each other. (I never knew just how valuable high school typing class would be all these decades later!) Sadly, it's getting a bit late, and I need to get to bed for the work adventures tomorrow. So hope I hear from you again soon. And as always, I wish God's very, very best for you! Take care!

—Dave

Tuesday, March 26, 2013, at 9:25 p.m.
From: Susan

Hi, Dave,

Yes, it seems like I am on winter break, although the temperature today went to fifty degrees. Now that felt like springtime. I did get quite a bit accomplished these two days…taxes done, bills paid, science test graded and put in the grade book, made sure all grades were in the computer for third marking period because report cards go out next week, and went swimming at the YMCA for both days.

Tomorrow is going to be a fun day, shopping at the outlets in Lancaster, Pennsylvania, which is about an hour away from me. It is where the Amish live, so I will see lots of horses and buggies.

I try to go swimming (which I love to do) at least three or four times a week. It helps with my arthritis in my knees. Swimming is good for the joints, plus is good exercise. During the school year, it is sometimes hard to make it the four times because of meetings or just doing after school things. I do feel it is important to maintain some sort of exercise in a person's life. I sometimes walk, but I get bored with that. I am also on thyroid medication to maintain my thyroid. I get checked once a year through blood work on that. I am also doing some protein shakes to control my hunger. I have lost thirteen pounds doing the shakes and have not put that weight back on. It is a constant struggle.

Thanks for answering my questions. Retirement for me is out of the question right now. If and when I do retire, I would probably like to either work part-time or substitute in schools and even doing one-on-one tutoring in the home. Sometimes during the summer break, I tutor students that might need extra help in a subject. I usually stay with the elementary kids though. Lol!

Sounds like you have almost the perfect job with Christians as your boss and fellow workers. That is awesome that you can start off with prayer. It also sounds like you have a great salary and benefits.

Ahh, then I picked right when I picked which son was which.

I also did a bit of investigation. Lol! I went on Facebook to see if I could find you, but I found your son first. He has a picture of him and his wife on his page. She is beautiful! Hope you don't mind that I was snooping. Lol!

Thanks for your church's website. I did look at it. It is very nice. I had to download Spotify to be able to hear the songs, but for some reason, it is not allowing me to hear them. I might have done something wrong. Oh, well.

Here is my church's website: http://www.vfbt.org/main.html. You can go and browse around. It is very fundamental Baptist, and sometimes I wish we could sing more worship songs, but that is okay.

Have a good night.

—Susan

Wednesday, March 27, 2013 at 9:27 p.m.
From: Dave
Subject: Simply swimmingly

Dear Susan,

You have a lovely church house! It is certainly larger than my local church. We currently only have an active congregation of about seventy or so.

Our family's homeland is St. Louis, Missouri. And when I visit there, I attend a huge church house (approximately 3,500) that is also wonderful, that one of the locals pointed me toward a couple of years ago.

Following the untimely death of my wife in 2010 and the loss of my job at that time, my three brothers encouraged me to stay in St. Louis with my early eighties Dad with dementia and my mom who was in the hospital at that time.

So my oldest son held down the fort at my local residence in Southern Indiana while I stayed with Dad. When my current local Louisville, Kentucky, job was offered to me, my son and I swapped houses. Dad died a few weeks ago, and my son is still at his house while his grandma (my mom) landed in a nursing home. However, now that my dad died and we will probably be forced to sell his house to support Mom in the nursing home, my son is debating whether to get a job in St. Louis and stay there or come back to live in Southern Indiana. Nevertheless, God will assuredly work it all out for the ultimate good of his kingdom!

Snoopin' around: My wife and I have always been pretty much an open book to anyone who would want to look at us. I still maintain that stand in the ultimate hope that I can either help someone come to know Jesus, or it I could be of assistance to anyone who will listen to my adventure with the dear Lord. To that end, feel free to ask, snoop, whatever. While I do have a Facebook page, please know that I don't really use it or check it, and honestly, I would get rid of it if I could only figure out how to do it. In some sense, I do have some tech savvy, but in another sense, I don't. I can create a pretty sophisticated Excel workbook, but I'm not much of a fan of Facebook. And while I've used a cell phone dating back to the old eighties, "monster cell phone" (safety director of an over-the-road trucking concern), don't expect me to respond to a text message! Hey! It's a *phone*, so *give me a call*! Just kidding, but you get my drift! My son, on the other hand, has a great sense of humor and has taken some pretty funny photos that he posts on his Facebook, so you will probably get a laugh there.

Swimming: You're a lady of my own heart! I *love* to swim, or anything else in the water! Sadly, I haven't done it in a while. There used to be a public pool adjacent to our local elementary school (approximately a half mile from my house on the next block). When the kids were in grade school, we used to get them season passes, and they would walk to the pool in the summer. My wife was the cafeteria monitor there for about seventeen years and did volunteer work in the fifth grade class. That pool closed several years ago, but they did build a public pool and skateboarding park about a mile away. Now that things have finally simmered down in my little life somewhat, I'll probably end up getting a pass for that. I could certainly stand to drop some weight. To that end, I'm very happy for you in your weight loss as I know the struggle of which you speak!

Games: Do you enjoy playing games? Specifically chess or other family-oriented games, such as *Pictionary*, *Balderdash*, *Trivial Pursuit*, *Euchre*, or the like?

Favorite things: What are some of your favorite things? Colors, foods, etc.

Love languages: Are you familiar with Gary Chapman's *The Five Love Languages*? If so, what is yours? If not, you might want to Google it!

Sing a song: I assume from your e-mail that you can sing. Sadly, as I probably already divulged to you, I am artistically in the negative (arts, crafts, songs, etc.). That was always the realm of my wife and oldest son. They both amaze me. It was a thrill and a half when, during our dating days, I discovered with delight how fabulous it was that my wife and I both had similar life values and goals but were quite different in other ways and that we could play to each other's strengths to complement each other in our marriage. It was great!

Good night. Well, I suppose I could talk to you on and on and on and on…but it is getting to the time when I will need to scurry off to my bed for some rest for work tomorrow. Please know that I thoroughly enjoy your e-mails and getting to know you better with each one. So please write when you can. Good night, for now, sweet Susan! And may God gift you with only his very, very best!

—Dave

Thursday, March 28, 2013, at 9:06 p.m.
From: Susan

Hi, Dave,

Yes, the church runs around one thousand, and we have two services in the morning. It is the same place that I teach. Most of the churches that I had attended in my several moves for my teaching career have been churches of three hundred or less. The only other place I attended that had a large congregation was where I went to college in Lynchburg, Virginia. In my last church in New Jersey, I was involved with the choir, ladies' groups, duets, and even solos. I even made a nonprofessional CD of a few songs for family and friends. If I can find them on my computer, I will send you the attachment. In the church I am at now, I sing with another lady (duet) on Wednesday nights every three months. Because the church has so many talented people, we are put on a rotation schedule. I am not in the choir at the present time because it takes so much commitment to sing both morning services, night services, and all the special meeting services. My dad was my biggest cheerleader in my singing. Sometimes in the summers when I had off school and he still was filling in for other pastors, I would go with him to sing before he preached. I love music and have never had any professional training, but it is all for the glory of God, and as my dad used to say, "It is from the heart."

Oh, wow, your dad just passed away recently? My sympathy goes out to you and your family. Wow, that was nice of your son to stay with him while you went back to work. How old is your mom? My dad passed away seven years ago, at the age of eighty, and Mom is now eighty-two and very independent, although she is slowing down some. She still drives locally and, every once in a while, will drive the forty-five minutes to see my other sister. I am so thankful for her sound mind (she does forget things sometimes, but don't we all) and for the Lord giving her the ability to do most of her things herself. My family and I have talked about the future with her, and if I ever marry, then my other sister would build on to her house a parent apartment with a walkway into her house. My sister works from her house, so it would be a great arrangement, if it comes to that.

Oh, a question for you: I was reading about the ALS disease that your wife had. It says that most people don't last three years after being diagnosed, but there are some that last ten years, and there is one lady who has had it for seventeen years. I was wondering how long she had it before she passed away. From reading about it, it is not a pleasant thing to go through because it does say you still have your mind and feelings. Did she go through many years of having it, and was it painful in the end?

I hope you don't mind me asking about it. My other question for you is: How do your sons feel about you looking for another wife?

Ah, so you're not good at texting, huh? Lol! Oh my, I don't think we are a match then. Lol! With being a teacher, I have to be up on the most recent things as much as possible, and even then, I am not up on all the latest gadgets. I do have an iPhone and use it to text. Many of my school parents will text me to tell me things.

I use the cell for everything. I just cancelled my landline phone as all I was ever getting was political calls and unavailable calls. I have a desktop computer with scanner and printer that I use a lot for schoolwork and personal use. I also have the first generation iPad which I bought at a discount from a family at school. I am thinking of trading it in a stepping up to an iPad 2 because mine is so old now that it doesn't support many of the new apps.

I am glad you didn't mind that I snooped. Lol! My nieces and nephews got me onto Facebook. It is a great social media. Many of my former students have befriended me, and it is great to keep up with them and what is going on in their lives.

Ah, well, maybe you could get back into swimming or walking. Yep, a daily struggle.

Games. I love playing games when I can. Chess…umm, no way…don't understand it even after several people have tried to teach me. Lol! Checkers, *Rummikub*, *Balderdash* (haven't played that one since before Dad passed away), any type of card games (some I have to be taught all over again). Lol!

Uno, *Apples to Apples* is a fun game! I am not good at puzzles. I get bored with them trying to find all the right pieces. Lol!

Love Languages, yes. I did read that book about ten years ago. From what I can remember, my love language is quality time and touch. What are yours?

Wow, favorite things, huh? Okay…um, let me think… Colors, I don't have one favorite, but I like very bright, vibrant colors, and for house decor, I like warm colors. Hmm, foods…well, just about anything, except for very fishy-tasting fish, sushi… I don't like very hot spicy things. My favorite restaurants are Olive Garden, Applebee's, Panara Bread… Bahama Breeze. Any type of a good café with great sandwiches and soup. We have one here called Zoup. They let you sample the soup before you buy it. I know there are probably some more, but that is all I can think of right now.

I love the beach, having my chair at the water's edge where the waves wash up over you, walking the beach, sunsets…the warm sun, but no humidity—lol—the smell of a warm summer rain, the brisk fall weather, filled with pumpkins, colorful leaves, hot apple cider, waking up to a quiet snowstorm when I didn't have to go out and shovel. Lol! Well, that is all for now. What about you?

I think I wrote a book this time. Lol! Have a good night.

—Susan

Friday, March 29, 2013, at 11:07 p.m.
From: Dave
Subject: The Susan Saga book

Susan, *I love it*! Thank you ever so much for being so open in sharing with me! You are such a lovely, lovely, kindhearted lady! *Thank you* for simply being the very best Susan that God made you to be!

My goodness, you gave me some chores to share back with you. Let's see if I can get them all.

Sing a song: Although I'm admittedly artistically challenged, I would *love* to hear you sing, so please send me a copy if you can. If I were with you right now, what song would you sing to me?

Dad: Yes, he died about a month ago or so. Having gone through the death of my wife, it did not crush me as bad as it did when she died. However, it was so very sad to me that, to the best of my knowledge, he never did come to know our dear Lord. It was never allowed to be a topic of discussion with him. About two years ago, I wrote him a long, long letter (roughly fifteen typed pages) of my life and the Christian walk, and all he would say was "Well, they live, they die, you bury 'em, and that's pretty much it." How sad, sad, sad.

Mom: Eighty-three years old and confined to a wheelchair in a nursing home. Still hanging in there, and we all love her but does have her "senior moments."

ALS: *Brutal! Yet God is so very, very good* and has *blessed me so very, very much*! He was so very loving and gracious to my wife and my little family as we went through her battle with it. Her neuro (a brilliant, compassionate, Christian fellow) questioned me relentlessly about the time line leading up to her diagnosis. He would shake his head and remark, "Well, you two are on the bullet train for this disease… I've never seen anything like it…" The bottom line was that she started exhibiting symptoms roughly a year prior to diagnosis and died about nine and a half months later.

You are correct on your assessment of the disease. To this day, nobody knows what causes it or how it works, although recent research indicates that it might be that the body somehow quits processing certain proteins correctly. The disease itself is only about 10 percent hereditary, but not in her case, and not contagious, etc. It appears to be nondiscriminatory in who it selects. You either get it or you don't, but if you do, it is the death sentence. Furthermore, it is very erratic. I visited her every day, for as long as I could, and every day when I walked into her room, it was a new adventure. I never knew how I might find her or how it had affected her since the last time I was with her. Essentially, the patient's body just starts to disintegrate piece by piece. But yes, the brain remains unaffected throughout. In her case, she had right arm problems for quite a while, and in retrospect, I now suspicion it was an early sign, although it was not recognized at the time. That is another problem with this disease. It is very, very difficult to diagnose. Her doctor once told me that they usually back into the diagnosis. Once all other possibilities are eliminated, ALS is all that is left.

At any rate, she began to fall while walking for no apparent reason and slurring her words. Once diagnosed and confined to the hospital or nursing home, her right arm gave way first, then her right leg, then left leg, and finally left arm. Early into it, she got to where she could not talk. She opted in to having them put a feeding tube in, but I tried my best to feed her actual food as long as I could. There was about three to four months or so we would literally go from meal to meal to meal all day because it took so long to cut it all up into teeny, tiny pieces and feed them to her only a scant few at a time on the very tip of a fork to keep her from choking on them. Because she had also opted in on a "do not resuscitate" order, ironically I was literally her only source of feeding as the nursing staff was afraid of choking her, and of course, they had neither the time nor patience to devote all day to her.

As far as pain goes, I asked her repeatedly, and she always told me that she was not in any pain. Now please understand that it is a very delicate balancing act for the medical staff to keep those patients medicated, fed, etc. to keep the body free from pain, nourished, etc. and yet allow me to have a functioning wife rather than a zombie. About ninety days prior to death, hospice (who is *wonderful*) was called in, and around that time, she had her final doctor appointment. At that time, the doctor wrote a prescription for morphine, as much as she wanted and anytime she wanted it. When we returned to the nursing home, I thought they were going to have a coronary over it!

Sadly, she died around two o'clock in the morning while I was at work. To this day, I'm not really sure what ultimately took her. A couple of weeks prior to that, her digestive system stopped working, and she threw up a bunch of feeding tube food, so I was somewhat ready for what I already knew was the ultimate end short of a miracle from God.

All through it, I asked God to perform that miracle and allow us to walk out of there hand in hand as we had so many times before, but it simply was not his will this time. "Selfish Dave" wishes I had her, but "Loving, Faithful Dave" is so very happy that she is with Jesus and free for all eternity of pain, trial, tribulations, etc. If God allowed me to have her back this minute, I couldn't do it to her.

The second wife: I cannot adequately describe to you how much I long for another wonderful Christian wife, selected by God for me, just as she is. I just love having a wife to share life with, explore life together, love, cherish, play with, help, provide for, etc. and, yes, even share tears with and sometimes disagree with! It is simply fabulous! Oddly enough, my wife's dad (about eighty-three now) is my biggest fan about getting the second wife. "Davey Boy," he tells me, "you need to be married. It suits you well, and you are so good at it…" His wife died on our fifth anniversary, and he has remained single ever since. My two sons, family, and friends are also in agreement. They witnessed it. I hope this doesn't sound like I'm bragging too much. But to that end, as I've told you, I come complete with as many references as you choose to have. Just ask and I will provide you names, phone numbers, etc.—whatever you would like.

Wow! Talk about a long book. This would have taken a year and a half on the His Match for Me site!

Love languages: I wish I had known about these much earlier into our marriage. It was comical for my wife and me. Hers was gifts. It didn't matter what or the cost, just the mere fact that I gave it to her. Over time, I came to know that good jewelry was always a winner. Good Christmas ornaments for her birthday—again, a surefire winner! Various cute knickknacks along the way—major points for me! Heart-shaped anything—winner! His 'n Her cutesy things—winner! For me, touch—anywhere, any time!

So…a typical mutual event—such as Christmas, anniversary, Valentine's Day, etc.—

went something like a card for each. A few times, we even unknowingly selected the exact same card for each other. The first time it happened, I thought she had found my card and was tricking me! I would give her a gift-wrapped gift, usually with a string attached (i.e., sometimes she would have to go on a whole house hunt for it with the kids with clues previously scattered throughout the house, etc.) She would then gift me with my usual pack of underwear, work shirt, or nothing. She could have given me a speck of dust or a new car; it wouldn't have mattered to me as long as…she *touched* me! We held hands everywhere, sat side by side, often with her long hair (aptly dubbed "husband's delight") wrapped around my neck. And of course, we would talk and share about anything and everything!

Miscellaneous favorites: Dark green for me! However, my wife always wanted me dressed in blues. And since I'm artistically in the negatives and hate shopping for clothes (for me) and since she is no longer with me to coach me, I pretty much wear black pants with a variety of blue shirts to work, church, etc. and comfortable shorts and T-shirts as much as possible elsewhere.

Fishy fish: I agree. *No, thank you!*

Phone service: Both, residential landline [phone number redacted]. Feel free to call me if you desire! It is an even better venue than typing all this, but I will leave it totally up to your comfort level. Cell phone: [phone number redacted]. The caller ID will say, "[name redacted]," the brother of my wife, who gave me the phone so we could communicate through her ordeal and has graciously continued to allow me to use it. Now that is the primary on that I use for personal use, but my work has also provided a company one for works calls, *but*...it is one of the newfangled ones, and I have not had a chance to swap over all my contacts yet. So right now, I'm strapped with carting around both!

Well, my dear Susan, it has grown quite late once again. And so I must scurry off to my bed once again, although I just love talking to you, and I could go on and on and on... But, alas, 'tis bedtime! So again, I wish you only God's very best! Sleep well! Please write to me as you desire (or, better yet, call)! Take care!

—Dave

Saturday, March 30, 2013, at 9:43 p.m.
From: Susan

Wow, Dave, I think you outdid me by writing a saga. Lol! Aw, thank you so much for your kind words. Yes, I did find the songs on my computer. I have attached two of my favorites from the CD. When you click on them, there will be like swirls, etc. I don't know how to get them off and put something else on. I hope you enjoy the songs.

Hmmm, what would I sing to you? Wow, depends on the moment, I suppose...probably a kid song. Lol! I know a lot of them. Or a worship song or a silly song, like...if we were really getting serious, "You Are My Sunshine." Lol! A few years back, one of my students gave me the title of "Song Lady" because I was always singing a song in class. Sometimes I even sung their spelling words, if I can think of a song that would go with it.

Oh, wow, Dave, as I read your account of your wife's ALS and all that you and her had to go through, it reminded me of my dad and how painful at the end it was. He died at home…that is where he wanted to be. So we got a hospital bed and put it in the dining room, and that was his bedroom for the last month of his life. We also had hospice come in at the last week of his life. They are awesome! At night, my siblings and I would take four-hour shifts to be with Dad. On my shift, I would always sing to him—okay, tearing up a bit here… I don't know how I ever made it through with teaching that year. Only by God's grace. Another little tidbit about me—I do tear up over sometimes the silliest things…or even very sentimental things. Even watching a movie that is sad or even romantic I cry.

Anyway, when you mentioned morphine, I remember having to give that to my dad at different times. Wow…it was tough. Dad died of lung cancer caused by asbestos. The doctor had only given him three months to live…but he lived about thirteen months. He was a fighter. He probably got it during World War II on the ship, working in the engine room. The asbestos can live in your body for sixty years, and you don't even know it. It must have been tough for you not to be with your wife when she passed away, but as you said, you knew it would not be long.

That is great that your family and friends are supportive of you finding the second wife. Ah, no need for phone numbers of family members…yet. Lol! Thank you for your phone numbers. I will write them down, and yes, when I feel comfortable maybe in a week or two, I will call. When are the best times to call?

Aww, sweet on all the different things you and your wife did for each other. That is what marriage is all about—caring, respecting, helping, having fun together, praying together, etc. Of course, I have never been married, but I have watched good and bad marriages. I want a marriage that will stick to the end while doing all the above and even more than I can imagine. All I can go on is the long-distance relationship I had with California Ranger. He and I were so compatible, and I loved the quality time I would spend with him and always wanted more because he was so far away. We would always hug and kiss on the cheek, and I sure did love those hugs. I am a hugger. We would pray on the phone together, and when together, we would always hold hands when we prayed. There was no sex involved because both he and I believed that sex was for when a person is married. So yes, I am a virgin, even at my age. Usually when I tell a guy that, I always get great respect for my decision. Most can't believe it, but they do respect me for it. Okay then… I did need to tell you that.

Ahhh, dark green, huh? Do you have anything dark green, or is it just the color you like?

And I *love* shopping. Lol! Oh, I love flowers…all kinds. Tulips are one of my favorites. But I love carnations, roses, lilies, sunflowers, and just an assortment of them. I love to fill the house with either real or fake flowers.

Well, let me know what you think of the songs.

Have a wonderful, blessed Easter!

—Susan

Sunday, March 31, 2013, at 8:32 a.m.
From: Dave
Subject: Happy, happy, happy Easter!

He is indeed risen! *King of kings* and *Lord of lords*! May *he bless you* and *your* family!

Lovely singing voice! You can sing to me anytime! I liked both songs about equally well.

I'm thrilled every time I get an e-mail from you, so it was such a pleasure seeing this one on Easter morning. I felt like a kid finding an Easter egg!

At any rate, I'm getting ready to go to Ye Ol' Church House, and I just wanted to wish you a morning happy Easter before I left. I will send you a longer e-mail later this afternoon or evening in response to your latest one.

So for now, sweet Susan…have a lovely, wonderful, happy, happy, happy Easter! Take care!

—Dave

Sunday, March 31, 2013, at 3:22 p.m.
From: Dave
Subject: Hippety-hoppety happy Easter (continued)

Wonderful Susan,

Let me continue the saga…

Sing a song: As I've probably already told you, I'm in the negatives artistically. Rather, I pretty much operate on pure logic. That being said, although I went kicking and screaming, bless my mama's heart, she did see to it that I had a well-rounded education. To that end, though I can't sing, dance, or draw worth a hoot, I do admire the skills of those who can. I love, love, love the Carpenters from way back when, and so I now give to you one of my all-time favorites: "Touch Me When We're Dancing" at https://www.youtube.com/watch?v=K6HNp1pLDP0. Just copy and paste it in your browser, and it should start playing.

The ALS adventure: Despite that, *God really is good*! Through the course of my life, I have been through several traumatic events, but wonder of wonders and glory of glories, he has been faithful in holding my hand through them all. Sometime in the future, hopefully I have the opportunity to share them with you. While I would wish none of them on anyone, God has used them to mold me into the critter that he designed me to be.

I did type and save an almost-completed book of the ordeal (about 135 typewritten pages) at this point. I still need to add a few details, cross-reference it with scriptural references, etc. I have high hopes of having it published at some time. Perhaps someday you would be willing to help me finish it up! Meanwhile, life and times have gotten a bit in the way.

My Christian walk: That is also an interesting tale that I hope to share with you in detail someday. In retrospect, it has been interesting to see how God orchestrated it. Despite the fact that my dad-in-law had their family involved in a less-than-desirable church throughout most of my wife's childhood, he was very instrumental in me becoming a decent Christian believer. But thus is the irony of the God that we serve! How wonderful it is!

Phones: Please know that I am more than willing to go at a speed in which you are completely comfortable as I am well aware that I am new to you and that there are a vast multitude of strange folks on these websites. I thoroughly understand. Many say that they want a fabulous marriage such as the one I had, but not many are willing to invest the time and energy that it takes to get it and sustain it. That is precisely why I hold out to you my track record and references. That being said, my logical brain believes phone conversations to be a much better communication venue and the next logical step, not that I am in any way trying to rush you, but some things that I would want to tell you are simply too long to type, even in an e-mail, and admittedly, I do long to hear your voice!

Since I am on call at all times for work, I always have my cell phone nearby. I am on EDST time zone, the same as you. Any time during the weekend or on a holiday is good to call me as well as evenings from about five thirty in the afternoon to nine o'clock in the evening. Due to the way my job is structured, while you can call me during work hours, sometimes I will not be able to answer, but usually I will answer and only be able to talk a short time or tell you that I will call you back later.

Favorite things: I just like the dark green color more than any other. I don't necessarily have anything in particular but prefer it and dark blue over most others, although my car is what I would call dark red, but women (and the manufacturer) seem to think it should be called burgundy for some reason!

Sentimental romance: Yep! I'm also a sentimental romantic to the nth degree! And yep! I've been known to cry from time to time. I shed many, many, many tears over my wife.

Dating and marriage: First, let me say that California Ranger was a fool to let you escape! What do you think happened there?

Also, let me assure you once again, lest I scare you, at any point, all you have to do is tell me, "Dave, this isn't going to work" and I will vanish from your life. However, please know that is usually a one-way street with me as the parting is too painful to play the yo-yo back-and-forth games.

Please know that I am somewhat up-front and at times just outright blunt. To that end, I hope that I made it clear that I entered the His Match for Me website in search for a second God-provided decent Christian wife and that I really do want God's very best for those potential ladies as well as for me. I know from prior experience that in doing so, the resultant marriage is fabulous, and to not do so is courting a disastrous train wreck.

Because of that, the dating or courtship with me is probably a bit out of the ordinary for most ladies. By that, I mean that until the time comes when we would mutually decide to exclude all others, I will constantly encourage you or others to date other guys, seek the guidance of family and friends, etc., investigate all the fellows' track records and references, including mine, so that you get the very best for you! I have actually been at a restaurant on a date and told my date that if she saw another guy who she found attractive, to let me know and I would get his contact information for her. While that may sound a bit bizarre in today's culture, when the time comes to exclude everyone else, I want to make sure that my wife-to-be has had every opportunity to devote the rest of our lives to each other without any regrets or reservations. My wife and I had just that: we knew that we were "lifers" and we trusted each other explicitly with absolutely no hesitation or reservations. It was *great*!

And to that end again, I hope that you are slinging e-mails, etc. back and forth to other suitors in an effort to get God's very best for you so that he can lead your sweet, loving heart to his best fit for you! I have learned to ask him to open and close the doors on any big decision that I have to make. That is yet another reason that I miss my wife so very much. I found through our many years together that often our dear Lord spoke to me through her, and I miss that so very much.

Now despite seeing my oldest son culminate an e-dating experience literally across the globe into a marriage, I'm not so sure how that will play out for me. I will definitely need some elbow-to-elbow, eyeball-to-eyeball time prior to such a commitment. You pointed out that you are still a virgin, and I also applaud your decision and commitment!

Please know that I was not as stellar a Christian fellow when I met my wife and that we did have sex prior to marriage, which is a funny story in and of itself, which hopefully we can share at a later time. However, also know that in both of our minds, we were as good as married at that time, and rest assured that she was my one and only sexual partner—I was twenty-six then—and will continue to be until God provides me with a second wife or takes me home to be with him, whichever comes first.

It is also important to know that if we were on an actual face-to-face date while I would probably hold your hand, I can't say that I would be inclined to kiss or even hug at first. I need to be absolutely 100 percent certain that we can be good friends as well as romantic and marriage partners. Consequently, I tend to hold dates at arm's length at first as I recognize the slippery slope that can occur with more intimate moments.

Now…after marriage, that is a whole other story! Please keep in mind that "touch" *is* my love language!

Well, my sweet, sweet Susan, once again I have typed a virtual book! And I just realized that I forgot about the laundry I had going in the basement! *Yikes!*

I can't wait to receive your next installment back to me as I enjoy them so much. Please tell me more about you and sing me an e-song and flip it to me, if you are so inclined. And so I now leave you with an Easter bouquet, and may God bless you always!

—Dave

Sunday, March 31, 2013, at 9:38 p.m.
From: Susan

Awww, Dave, thank you so much for the virtual tulips. I smiled when I saw them. Yes, you did tell me that you are in the negatives artistically, but I am sure you have other great qualities that make up for it. For example, I can tell, all I did was mention that I like tulips, and you found a picture and sent me virtual tulips. Now that is sooo very thoughtful of you. I like that. I can't draw a straight line or even cut a straight line, but my students think I am the best drawer. Lol!

I trust you had a very happy Easter, celebrating the resurrection of our Lord. Wow, yes, you have written so much, not sure where I should start to respond.

I love the Carpenters. When I was a teen, I fell in love with their style of singing. So sad Karen had to end her life the way she did. Growing up as I told you before, I think I was brought up in a strict Baptist preacher's home. We were not allowed to listen to rock music or even go to movies. As Dad aged into his late sixties or seventies, he mellowed out. Of course, we were all adults then and could choose what we wanted to do. I remember listening to them on the radio when he wasn't around. Yeah… I was a bit rebellious, although not as bad as my siblings. Lol! Awww, that song is sooooo romantic… Love it.

Okay, I have attached another one of my songs from the CD for you to listen to. I am glad you have enjoyed the other two. This one I sang at my dad's funeral, which again I have no clue how I got through it but by the grace of God.

Yes, I do agree that the phone would help with the long letter writing. I have an idea: because of your crazy work schedule, why don't I give you my cell number and you can call me when you are able. I am mostly free during the weeknights after six thirty in the evening because if I go swim, I get home around five thirty-ish, then dinner, and clean up. Only night that wouldn't work right now is Wednesday night. Most weekends, I am free unless I go out to eat. Then I could say I would call you back. You must learn to text! Lol! My cell number is [phone number redacted], an easy one. Yes, it would be nice to hear your voice also.

Would love to hear more about your Christian walk. I know, even though growing up on a pastor's home, my walk with the Lord has had some doozies. One where I almost gave up on teaching. That in itself was a huge trial and testing in my life. Someday I may share that with you.

Wow, why did California Ranger and I never work out? I am not really sure. He was a wonderful spiritual man. My dad used to love talking with him. California Ranger would carry around a paper that my dad had given him about some spiritual insights he had thought California Ranger would enjoy. I think I was different than most girls California Ranger ever dated, and he didn't want to lose my friendship. Romantically, I just don't think he was into me. In a way, I think that was the only thing that was missing from our relationship. Also, my gut feeling is that although we were the best of friends and he didn't mind being with me, I think my body type was just not for him. I just didn't seem to wow him enough. I know I was more into him than he was into me romantically. You see, I wanted him to be the first to kiss me on the lips. I was not the kind of girl who would do it first. Even though we would have late-night talks on the phone and when we did see each other and spend hours and hours talking and having fun, he didn't pursue me in a romantic way. As I told you before, I had not dated much, so to even have this much from a guy long distance, I was so smitten that he would commit time to spend with me. One February, when he flew out to visit me while also looking for jobs, he gave me a very special cross necklace. Now to me, it means something when a guy would give you jewelry and especially for Valentine's Day. So I got mixed feelings from him. When we finally did get to talk about it, he said, "Susan, you are very special to me, and our friendship means a lot, but that is *all* it means—friendship." Of course, I was crushed and started to realize that this was never going to go any further. Well, it is in the past. I learned and have moved on.

Yes, I do agree at some time some room and face-to-face time would be the next thing after phoning for a while. I know I have more time available in the summers, but again I am old-fashioned and feel if the guy really wants to meet me, he needs to make the effort to visit me first. Lol! I laughed when you said, "I hope you are slinging e-mails back and forth to guys." It is a strange world—the Internet dating experience. Right now I am only talking to you and to a guy from Montana. You came on the scene about four weeks after talking to him. We have talked about meeting, but both our schedules are making it hard to meet. So I don't know what will happen there. He will either try his best or just let it go as pen pals—only the Lord knows. Other than that, my e-mails to other guys get ignored, or the polite ones will say, "You seem like a nice lady, but you are too far away." Or they will say, "Sorry, I am only looking for someone who is within one hundred miles from me." Some of them will read my e-mail and ignore it, and then they are off the site or on only for the free days. Some of them, to me, are only on there to see who the next best girl will be, not really being serious about finding a life mate. I am on three sites: Christian Mingle, His Match for Me (where you started writing to me). I had been on that site for four months and have only gotten three guys to look at my profile. I have been on Christian Mingle for about three years and have had a few dates. One I call my "Octopus Date" and will have to tell you about that later. I laugh about it now, but at the time, I didn't like it. I am also on Christian Cafe, which I am on for free because I am a chat room monitor. For my volunteer time, I am on there for free. (That is where I met California Ranger). Since then on there, I had only one other date, which didn't work because the guy had too many issues to deal with.

Well, yep, it is getting late, so I will end this for now. Have a great Monday.

—Susan

Monday, April 1, 2013, at 9:17 p.m.
From: Dave
Subject: Wow!

Susan, so *great* to hear your voice for the first time! *Thank you* so very much for having the courage to share your phone number with me. You have my absolute guarantee that I will never abuse that privilege nor the trust that you have placed in me. The time passed so fast. It seemed like only a second!

I hope you have success in writing your paper and a good first day back at "Ye Ol' Schoolhouse" tomorrow.

So sweet dreams for now, my sweet Susan!

—Dave

[Note: It is worthy to note that once we began phone communication, our e-mails began to dwindle off.]

Tuesday, April 2, 2013, at 8:53 p.m.
From: Susan

Awww, Dave, thanks again so much for the virtual tulips. Yes, it was nice to hear your voice. By the way, I did get your message on my phone. I hope you had a nice dinner at your pastor's house.

I did get my letter typed and printed out, and everything was ready for today. Tough getting back the first day after a long break. Even the students were tired. I am tired after the long day, and we also had an all-staff meeting. Those usually go long. We have them the first Tuesday of every month.

My e-mail will be short tonight as I am tired. Take care and have a great day tomorrow.

—Susan

Tuesday, April 2, 2013, at 9:20 p.m.
From: Dave
Subject: Bless your sweet heart!

Susan, thank you so very much for sending this e-mail! You made my night. I just got home too, so I'll respect your snoozing time and just flip you this quick thank-you!

Sweet dreams to you, sweet Susan! Take care!

—Dave

Wednesday, April 3, 2013, at 6:53 p.m.
From: Dave
Subject: Happy, happy, happy Wednesday evening!

Susan, just wanted to say hi! I reread your e-mail of phone instructions and saw that Wednesday nights were not on the phone list, so I assume that you have Wednesday night church or some other activities. Still, just want to touch base with you!

Hope you had a lovely day and a better evening and tomorrow!

The weather is starting to warm up here, so I hope I'm sending it your way!

I can't wait to chitchat with you over the phone again, so always feel free to call me.

Take care for now.

—Dave

Saturday, April 6, 2013, at 7:50 p.m.
From: Susan

Hi, Dave,

Just thought I'd shoot you off a quick e-mail. Sorry I had to go and get the other call coming in. If I didn't think it was important, I would have ignored it.

This morning, I had a lazy morning, then a haircut, then some errands. Now I am doing laundry.

I hope your day was good. Beautiful sunny day, a bit chilly, but no need for a coat when doing errands.

Anyway, I am attaching the pictures I had done at Life Touch for our church directory. The one they put in the directory is more serious but with a nice smile. They give you a large one free, so it was too big for me to scan and send that to you. So the other two fun pictures they took, I thought I would send them to you. Plus, it will remind you of my hair length. Lol! My hair looks very auburn. It all depends on the light. Let me know what you think of them.

Have a great Sunday.

—Susan

Saturday, April 6, 2013, at 10:19 p.m.
From: Dave
Subject: Bless your sweet heart!

Susan, thank you so much for both your note as well as the photos. You are such a lovely lady and have a great smile. So sorry that I did not call you earlier as I had wanted, but... I also ran some errands today and...ate a late lunch and...fell asleep! When I woke up, much to my amazement, it was ten o'clock in the evening!

I started off at Ye Ol' Church House where I am a mentor for a twenty-year-old boy in a jobs-for-life class that we have been holding for the community, ran a variety of other errands, and ended up eating later around two thirty in the afternoon at a Mexican restaurant I had never been to before. I was tired and planned on taking a quick siesta, and as I said, lo and behold, it was ten o'clock in the evening when I woke up! Hopefully, I can fall back to sleep in a couple of hours so I don't end up getting my sleep schedule out of whack.

Hope you sleep well and have a great day at church in the morning!

As always, I wish you only God's very best for you! Take care for now. Hopefully, we can have a phone chat tomorrow!

—Dave

Sunday, April 14, 2013, at 12:55 a.m.
From: Dave
Subject: Happy, happy Sunday to you!

Susan, just wanted to be the first to wish you a *happy Sunday* today! So sorry I didn't give you a phone call Saturday as I always enjoy our chats, but it's obviously a bit late or early for that at this time. At any rate, as always, I hope your weekend is going well and that today goes even better and that you enjoy today with our dear Lord! Take care for now, my wonderful Susan!

—Dave

Friday, April 19, 2013, at 9:34 p.m.
From: Dave
Subject: Happy weekend!

Susan, I know you are having a family weekend, but I just wanted to say, "Hi! Thinking about you!" I hope you have a fabulous weekend, and as always, I wish you God's very, very best! Take care!

—Dave

Sunday, April 21, 2013, at 9:23 p.m.
From: Susan

Hi!

Sunday, April 21, 2013, at 10:28 p.m.
From: Dave
Subject: Wonderful Susan…

Susan, *love* the rabbit! *Thank you* ever so much! Wish I could take her with me! *Not* as good as *you* and would *definitely* rather have *you* with me, but still…*very* nice touch!

If it were not so late, I would call you. To that end, I will probably try to call you while en route from work to the pastor's house tomorrow evening. We are scheduled to meet at his house around seven thirty in the evening, EDST. Following his sermon this morning, I asked for some quality "Andy time," and that is what he set up. On the table will be:

a) Pascal's wager [Pascal's Wager: In general, Blaise Pascal (1623 to 1662) postulated that it was more beneficial and logical for people to believe in God than to not believe. His argument was along the lines that if God existed and you believed, not only would you have a good life while on earth but you would have an eternal life in heaven as well. On the other hand, if you believed but God did not exist, then at least you would have had a good life while on earth. To the contrary, if you did not believe and God did exist, whether or not you had a good life on earth, you would not have an eternity in heaven with God, thus losing out on all of eternity for only a relatively short life span while on earth.]
b) very loose Dave translations: Book of James—we are cautioned not to be like corks tossed to and fro on the ocean with respect to our faith.
c) Jesus's instruction to his disciples to go out and proclaim the gospel hither and yon but to shake the dust off their sandals of the nonbelievers.
d) Paul's petition and God's rejection to remove the thorn from his side.
e) etc.

I'm so sure that all of us are in line with one another but nor am I sure that it even matters.

I felt the subject matter a bit too exhausting and complex to do via e-mails. To that end, please pray for guidance on our mutual behalf, if you would be so kind!

'Till then, sweet dreams, my dear sweet Susan! Only God's very, very best for you!

—Dave

Tuesday, April 23, 2013, at 9:33 p.m.
From: Dave
Subject: Wonderful Susan…

Susan, so very sorry that I did not call you earlier this evening, but it's pretty late now. I was a wee bit tired after work today and messed up by sitting down in the living room to talk to David. Next thing I knew, it was after nine o'clock in the evening! Bless his heart, he let me sleep and woke me up with dinner—his infamous gun-smoked burrito. I don't know if I ever told you but he is quite the Chef Boyardee!

In Indonesia, it is April 24 right now, as they are twelve hours ahead of us. I mention this because today (Wednesday) is David's wife's birthday. Speaking of birthdays, I know we had previously discussed mine, but I don't think I ever found out yours. Perhaps you would be willing to share that with me.

As always, I hope this finds you doing well, and I wish you God's very, very best!

—Dave

Wednesday, April 24, 2013, at 9:57 p.m.
From: Susan

Thanks, Dave, for letting me know what happened. I figured something like you fell asleep or that you did something with your son. No worries.

Ahh, so now you have a cook for you. Lol! When he is not there, do you do much cooking yourself? Because it is just Mom and me, and I am working all day. There are times we get things from the local deli and heat them up. It is as good as having homemade food. Sometimes I do things in a Crock-Pot. Sometimes it is just a good salad, or we may go out to eat. We don't go out that much, but it is nice to get out.

My birthday is February 20. I think we figured out you were about just a month older than I am.

Tonight started our missions' conference at the church. I enjoy the first meeting because they had a parade of nations this year with the kids. Once I get my pictures on my computer, I will send them to you. The thing is that they have meetings on Thursday and Friday nights, and because I teach at the school there, I am a paid staff and am required to go to the meetings. So we will not be able to talk on those two days. I am still going to my swimming because I *need* to for my health, and my joints need it. So by the time I get home, grab a bite to eat, and get out the door, there is no time left. So it is back to e-mails for a bit.

Well, it is late, and I need to head to bed. Take care.

—Susan

Thursday, April 25, 2013, at 7:07 p.m.
From: Dave
Subject: Wonderful Susan…

Susan, 'tis okay! just let me know when I can call again. I just miss talking to you! Now that you've given me phone privileges for a while, you have me spoiled!

Yep! Davey Boy is one of the few people on earth that I truly trust on eating. Essentially, I am a big chicken! When I find things that I like, I pretty much stick to them as I am not a very adventuresome diner. He is so artistically inclined that he comes up with some very strange yet wonderful concoctions. He got his artistic abilities solely from his mama, as I am in the negatives with that. In fact, I used to tease his mom and say, "Honey, if I knew how to cook, we never would have had to get married!" She knew I was just joking!

I'm just amazed how anyone on earth can get everything together all at once! If I were to cook, we'd have salad at five o'clock, vegetables at six o'clock, meat at seven o'clock, and desert at eight o'clock! Lots of time to talk though! I do, however, cook a good pancake!

Well, flip me an e-mail or give me a yelp on the phone as you are able with your new hectic schedule.

And, of course, may God provide you with his very, very best!

—Dave

Saturday, April 27, 2013, at 6:34 a.m.
From: Dave
Subject: Happy weekend to you!

Wonderful Susan, hope your church house activities are going well for you! My weekend started off *great*! Wonder of wonders…

Last night, my youngest son, Greg, came over to spend the night with us (unannounced)! 'Tis been a while since I've had both of my lads together with me! We went out to a new local Mexican eatery named Chuy's and had a great time together. Gotta love it, love it, love it!

I sincerely hope that you are doing even better than that!

I will be tied up this morning with my own church house activities (jobs-for-life mentoring), but if you have the time and desire, please send me an e-mail or give me a call, as I do miss you!

May God provide you only his very, very best! Take care!

—Dave

Monday, April 29, 2013, at 6:49 p.m.
From: Susan

Hi, Dave,

Here are the pictures from the opening night of the missions' conference. They had a parade of nations and announced each country. Then the missionaries that were there were introduced, and during the course of the conference, each missionary presented their field through

PowerPoint. They do the parade of nations every other year.

The conference was great but, wow, so tiring. I am glad that it is over though. The church is very missions' minded—foreign and home missions.

Hope you had a good day.

—Susan

Monday, April 29, 2013 at 10:02 p.m.
From: Dave
Subject: Nice!

Susan, wow, very nice! I'll bet it is quite a thrill for the kids! Are any of them from your class?

As always, I thoroughly enjoyed our phone time together this evening! Thank you so very much for allowing me those opportunities to be with you, albeit across hundreds of miles. To that end and to the point at which you are comfortable, please be considering an actual person-to-person meeting now that the weather is getting better. Again, please understand that I don't want to be pushy, and I am more than content to proceed at whatever pace you are comfortable with, but it does seem like the next logical step.

Meanwhile, have a lovely day off tomorrow!

I just now remembered I do have a dinner meeting with our mutual boss and two other department directors from work tomorrow night, so depending on how long it goes, I may or may not be able to call you. I will call if it gets done early enough.

Take care for now, and as always, I truly wish you only God's very, very *best*!

—Dave

Thursday, May 2, 2013 at 8:08 p.m.
From: Susan

Hi, Dave,

Sending you some more pictures of the house and some of the park that is only ten minutes away from me.

Yes, some of those children in the pictures were my students. They loved doing the parade.

I do agree with you that a meeting should soon take place. We can talk more about it when we talk on the phone.

—Susan

Thursday, May 2, 2013, at 9:59 p.m.
From: Dave
Subject: Bouquet for Susan!

Susan, thank you ever so much for such a great looong chat tonight and for sharing such intimate talks from your heart. I enjoy talking to you so very much time seems to just fly by! Just thought I'd take a moment before going off to bed to send you the attached bouquet. Sweet dreams and God's very best for you!

—Dave

Wednesday, May 8, 2013, at 7:57 p.m.
From: Dave
Subject: Wonderful Susan…

Susan, I know this is a church night for you, so I figured that I would send this e-mail to wish you well. But if you're feeling spunky, always feel free to call! Otherwise, take care! I'll try to give you a call tomorrow night!

—Dave

Sunday, May 12, 2013, at 6:07 p.m.
From: Dave
Subject: Happy, happy, happy Sunday to you!

Susan, just wanted to wish you well on this beautiful *happy Sunday*! And wish your mom, "Happy Mama's Day!" Hope you and your entire family are doing well! Take care for now!

—Dave

Sunday, May 12, 2013, at 7:28 p.m.
From: Susan

Awwww, thanks, Dave. I had a wonderful day! Church was very good. The pastor's message was on the measure of a woman taken from Proverbs 31.

Had a great lunch with my sister, Carol, and her two sons. Her son, Jesse, surprised her by driving up from Virginia, so he came along to the lunch. Of course, we were all happy to see him. We must have spent almost two hours talking after we ate catching up on everyone. So much fun! Carol also had to ask about the Indy guy who I am corresponding with. Her remark was "Wow, he sounds so nice, genuine, and a gentleman."

By the time I got home, relaxed, and then started some schoolwork, it was time for evening church. I didn't make it.

Sending you a few pictures of my class and classroom. I had a theme for this whole year, and it was called the Wild West. One of the days in the beginning of the school year, we dressed the part and had a ranch or farm lunch. My moms of the classroom were a great help. The last picture is from the beginning of the year when I had them do a scavenger hunt. They had to find the things in the classroom that were listed on the paper.

Also sending you the Valley Forge National Park website to look at: (http://www.nps.gov/vafo/index.htm). We don't have to do the tours as I can be your private tour guide. Lol! This site just gives you an idea what is there. This is within ten minutes of my house.

Hope you're having a great Sunday. It has been a beautiful sunny spring day, a little chilly in the shade, but I love this kind of weather!

—Susan

Sunday, May 12, 2013, at 9:06 p.m.
From: Dave
Subject: Measuring women west of Valley Forge in the Indiana Wild, Wild West on Mama's Day…

Susan, thank you for the kind response as the day closes out. So very happy to hear that you had such a great family day! As always, I wish you and your family only God's very, very best!

As I recall, the Proverbs 31 measure of a godly woman sets the bar rather high, but I'm confident that you measure up quite well! How thoughtful of your nephew to make the surprise visit! That is always such a thrill!

Bless Carol for her kind compliment! Will I have the pleasure of meeting her or any of the rest of the family members during my trip?

Nice photos! I enjoyed them! And love, love, love the scavenger hunt! Always have! I don't know if I ever told you but many was the time that I would give my wife a gift card for a special event, and inside would be the first of many clues scattered throughout the house, ending with her present. She and the two boys used to love it!

Also, thank you for the Valley Forge website. Sounds like fun! Of course, I'm sure the Susan private tour is *always* preferable to the ranger guided tour, but I am willing to go for whatever I get!

Next weekend, David and I are probably headed back to St. Louis, our homeland, after work on Friday evening for another whirlwind tour.

Saturday morning, our niece has a graduation ceremony at St. Louis University to get her diploma as a law student grad, followed by a family get-together at a local Mexican restaurant. She is the only child of the Florida brother, and all my brothers should be there, including the one from Colorado, so it should be a great time! Hopefully, the local brother will put on a Saturday night family game night at his house, but if not, David and I will probably host one at Mom and Dad's house. We will probably return to Indiana Sunday morning so I can catch my breath for Monday back at work.

I hope you have a great week ahead on one of your last couple of countdown weeks at Ye Ol' Schoolhouse!

I'll try to give you a call tomorrow evening. Until then, sweet dreams, my Sweet Susan!

—Dave

Wednesday, May 15, 2013, at 9:11 p.m.
From: Dave
Subject: Wonderful Susan…

Sweet Susan, couldn't go to bed without at least saying hi! So…hi!

Also, wanted to let you know that I've had a wee bit of a change of plans in the little life as of this afternoon. I'm about to pack my suitcase and take it to work in the morning for a ride tomorrow after work to south of Nashville, Tennessee. I'll spend the night at a motel, go to court with one of our drivers Friday, and return to work Friday afternoon, with the Friday evening departure for the previously arranged whirlwind weekend tour of St. Louis. Whew! I'm tired just thinking of it!

I'll try to call you somewhere in there but probably will not have Internet connections throughout the adventure.

Until then, hope you have a great end of this week and a better weekend.

Thinking of you! Take care!

—Dave

Wednesday, May 15, 2013, at 9:34 p.m.
From: Susan

Awwww, Dave, thanks for the hi! Yes, I am up late. Lol! Got home from church around nine o'clock in the evening 'cause I stayed longer and talked to people after church. So I had been going through e-mails and found your wonderful e-mail. So I thought I would return your e-mail and give you something in your inbox if you get a chance to open it in your busy schedule.

Thanks for letting me know of the change of plans. Wow, you are quite the jet-setter. Lol! Off to many different places in such a short time. I will be praying for you this weekend as I know it will be tough yet fun. Have a safe trip!

Yep, seven more school days! Yeah, and they can't get here fast enough. Lol! Then countdown for my vacation and countdown till the Indiana Dave comes to Pennsylvania.

Okay, I was thinking of our time together here. Once we get the reservation for Sight and Sound on that Friday, we will know what we can do until then. You might just want to take a leisurely drive into the Lancaster county area and see some sights. There is also a place that I just remembered that is in the same town as Sight and Sound. It is run by the Mennonites, and it is called the Tabernacle. You do take a tour, and they take you inside a room built just like the Tabernacle and explain the meaning of it. I know there is a cost but can't remember what it is. Just found the site: https://mennoinfocenter.org/tabernacle/.

Anyway, if we do that on Friday, then on Saturday, we might tour the Valley Forge National

Park and have a picnic lunch there in the park. It could be a more relaxed day—go out to dinner at a place called Bahama Breeze, then maybe spend the evening back at my house playing some board games, talking, etc. Then on Sunday, church and tour of the church and school. In the afternoon, we might go to my sister Carol's house, forty-five minutes away, if she will be home.

Now remember, I am very flexible, and this could all change. For example, if Carol won't be home, we might have to do that all on Saturday or do something else. These are just some of my thoughts. Getting excited about our adventure.

Praying for you.

—Susan

Saturday, May 18, 2013, at 11:25 p.m.
From: Dave
Subject: Wonderful Susan, my personal travel planner!

Susan, thank you ever so much for this e-mail. I just now got it, and sadly, it is no doubt a wee bit too late to phone you (10:00 p.m., EDST). Very sorry that I missed our usual nightly chat, but I've been a bit busy with the family, brothers, son, etc. while here.

To that end, we had a good time visiting Mom the other night. She was already in bed but not asleep yet, and needless to say, our sudden presence was quite the surprise for her.

Today David had a morning interview but did not get the job (chef at a restaurant). They don't know what they missed! He is not disappointed though, as he views it (as I would) that

God did not want him to have that job. I am so happy that he has learned how to trust and depend on God for his life!

I love your thoughts about our time together, and of course, I cannot wait! Yep! I would love to see or tour the Mennonite tabernacle. Bless your sweet heart for doing the research, etc. We can definitely explore this together early next week once I get situated back at my house and decompressed from my recent whirlwind tours.

My brothers are planning on coming over to Mom and Dad's old house to meet at ten o'clock in the morning, CDST, to meet and discuss plans for the house, etc. tomorrow (Sunday) morning. I'm not sure at this point if I will stay to wait on it as that would put me back in South Indiana early evening and not give me much time to do laundry, etc., so I might just have my son sit in as my proxy and/or have them call me while I drive.

Despite bringing my own pillows from home (which I usually do), I really haven't slept very well the last couple of nights, although I took an off-and-on nap of sorts this afternoon, so I'm a bit sleep-deprived at this point of the journey.

I do miss talking to you during these times, and I deeply appreciate your prayers in my behalf, probably more than you will ever know! Again, bless your ever-lovin' sweet heart for that! And *thank you*!

And so, my dear sweet Susan, though I know and hope you are sleeping snug and soundly at this time, still I wish you sweet dreams and, of course, only God's very, very best for you! Have a wonderful Sunday, and if you get a chance and feel the urge, please feel free to call me. I will have a long drive and would love your company, though there are many long stretches of not-very-good reception along the way.

God bless you, Wonderful Susan!

—Dave

Sunday, May 19, 2013, at 7:54 p.m.
From: Dave
Subject: Hello, Little Ms. Wonderful Susan!

Susan, thank you for holding my hand across the many miles this afternoon! It makes the long arduous trip seem like but a quick moment in time and means so very much to me! So… *thank you, thank you, thank you*! I full well realize that you could have chosen to do any of another million things.

Hopefully, we can get together around our normal eight-ish phone call and set up getting theater tickets and a basic game plan for our mid-July meeting. I simply cannot wait! And bless your heart for taking the time to help in setting it up!

So…until then, *sweet, sweet* dreams, my wonderful Susan! Take care! Talk to you tomorrow night!

—Dave

Sunday, May 19, 2013, at 9:56 p.m.
From: Susan

You're so very welcome, Dave! It was great talking with you, and I am glad that I made the many miles seem to fly past. Always more fun with another! Again, you have me laughing so hard at your long explanations A, B, C, D until you get to the answer. And to think, my family thinks I tell long stories. Well, they haven't met you yet. Lol!

Thanks again for letting me express my fears to you again. You have reassured me, which I seem to need right now about the relationship. I wanted you to be open enough to share about your wife because I know she is very dear to your heart, yet as we seem to be getting to know more about each other, I would hope that at some time our conversation would be more a we than of Val. Again, this is all new to me, especially with a widower that I don't want to—see, I don't even know how to express this—umm, like I don't ever want you to think that what you had in your first marriage is not important. She must have been a very special lady to grab your attention. I need to tell you about my pastor and his second wife. His first wife passed away with cancer, so I know he knows what you and many other widowers face. I will tell you tomorrow when we talk on the phone.

Church was good tonight. He talked about our conscience, more like a Bible study tonight.

Yep, only five more days. Whoo-hoo! Okay, I need to head to bed.

"Grace is the gift of God's riches…the peace of God…the love of God and the hope of God"—Max Lucado.

Night.

—Susan

Oh, my address is [redacted] Street, Philly Suburbs, Pennsylvania.

Monday, May 20, 2013, at 9:3 p.m.
From: Dave
Subject: Good night!

Susan, sweet dreams!

—Dave

Monday, May 21, 2013, at 6:24 p.m.
From: Susan

Aww, thanks, Dave. I didn't get this until now. I did have a good night's sleep, and I hope you did too.

We had a great time at the aquarium today. Going over to New Jersey, we were held up in traffic. Once we got to the bridge to cross into New Jersey (picture 1), we breezed through. Second picture: group photo with Philly in the background. Third picture: Mighty Mike the alligator. This is only a sampling of the pictures I took.

I was so tired that I came home, talked with Mom, then lay down on the bed and fell asleep for about forty minutes. It was a great day! Loved the parents going along. Talk soon.

—Susan

Tuesday, May 21, 2013, at 7:12 p.m.
From: Dave
Subject: Sounds pretty fishy to me!

Susan, wow! Thanks! Looks cool! I particularly like the bubble in the middle of the tank! Thank you for sharing.

I will call you a bit later. Right now I'm in the middle of a couple of loads of wash, and Gregory and I decided to have them deliver a pizza to us tonight, so it has been called in as well.

Great photos. Looks like an exciting adventure for all! Wish I could have been there with you!

Call you around eight o'clock tonight. Until then, take care!

—Dave

Wednesday, May 22, 2013, at 6:49 p.m.
From: Dave
Subject: Two days 'til…*freedom*!

Wonderful Susan o' mine, just wanted to send you a quick note on this church house Wednesday night. I do miss actually talking to you over the phone on these nights. It reminds me of the early days of e-mail-only communique. And of course, I can scarcely wait until we meet eyeball to eyeball in mid-July. We'll have a great time!

Nothing particularly new or exciting to tell you tonight. I did my work-house routine today. I think I told you that another company had a tractor trailer burned to the ground on my way to work yesterday. Late last night, I found out that the trailer contained US Mail, so that should be interesting if someone had incoming checks or outgoing bill on board!

Well, for now, sweet, sweet dreams, my sweet, sweet Susan! Take care, and I'll call you tomorrow night!

—Dave

PS: Of course, only God's very, very best for you for tonight and tomorrow!

Saturday, May 25, 2013, at 10:51 a.m.
From: Susan

Hi, Dave,

Just posted my pictures from the end of the year and wanted to put something in your inbox for today.

I again enjoyed our long talk last night, and you never cease to amaze me what you are going to say. Lol! Thanks so much for the laughter and the serious side of our talks.

Got to get ready for graduation. Talk to you later tonight.

—Susan

Saturday, May 25, 2013, at 2:48 p.m.
From: Dave
Subject: Nice!

Wonderful, smokin'-hot-chick Susan, nice photos! Hope you had a lovely high school graduation in your cap and gown.

We did our final jobs-for-life class this morning at our church. My student, Nick, wasn't there as he had to work. Next Saturday is their graduation, and the church makes a big production out of it: catered lunch, official ceremony, etc.

And yep, love, love, love our nightly lengthy chats! Until tonight then. May God bless you!

—Dave

Saturday, May 25, 2013, at 3:22 p.m.
From: Dave
Subject: Something to talk about…

Susan, I created the attached to help me attempt to help both couples dating as well as married couples. It, as with most of my creations, is a work in progress. Feel free to look it over, and we can talk about it at some point. Take care!

—Dave

Monday, May 27, 2013, at 7:21 a.m.
From: Dave
Subject: Good morning, Ms. Wonderful Pennsylvania Smokin'-Hot Chick!

Susan, just thought I'd say hi! Have a wonderful, happy Memorial Day at your sister's house with the mama today! Talk to you tonight. Please be careful on the trip over, and of course, only God's very *best* for *you*!

—Dave

Friday, May 31, 2013, at 10:28 a.m.
From: Susan

Hi, Dave,

Sending you this e-mail in place of our nightly chat. I know it isn't as good, but I wanted you to have something in your inbox to remind you of me. I hope you have had a good Friday and will have a wonderful Saturday! Can't wait to talk to you on Saturday night. Until then, be safe, and God bless you.

Oh, something to think about. I was thinking of making french toast casserole and using the lactose milk you use, but the one recipe I am looking at also calls for half and half. Are you okay with the half and half? I thought the french toast casserole would be better than one that calls for cheese. Let me know what you think.

Till Saturday night.

—Susan

PS: I can get e-mails on my phone.

Friday, May 31, 2013, at 3:49 p.m.
From: Susan

Wow, thank you, thank you! Another surprise from my Indy guy. I love it. You are so sweet. You know my likes already. Mom thought that was sweet of you to include her. We stopped at our mailbox on our way out of the driveway. I am so glad we stopped. TY again. You are full of surprises.

—Susan

Friday, May 31, 2013, at 7:06 p.m.
From: Dave
Subject: Sounds delicious…

Susan, thank you so very much for this e-mail. Yep! It's not as good as talking to you! Please keep in mind that my itinerary has me departing after work on Thursday, so I probably will not get to your land until Friday really early in the a.m. just after midnight.

Also, *bless you* for remembering the lactose free! Please don't be offended if I ask you often about the ingredients. It just would not be good for any of us if I'm not careful. And I'm not good with the half and half. Oddly enough, I am okay with butter. Have no clue why.

Hope you have a wonderful time. Can't wait to talk to you Saturday evening. May God watch over you and your family!

—Dave

Friday, May 31, 2013, at 7:13 p.m.
From: Dave
Subject: You're welcome!

Susan, I had high hopes that at least one of your boyfriends might send you something. (I can only imagine what it must be like to be a Pennsylvania smokin'-*hot* chick and have the fellows trying to woo you!) And I had higher hopes that you might actually receive it prior to departure! Also, never hurts to attempt to befriend the mom! At any rate, I love surprising my special lady, and I hope you enjoy it! Take care for now!

—Dave

PS: Happy Total Freedom Day!

Friday, June 7, 2013, at 4:22 p.m.
From: Susan

Hey there, Dave. Thought I'd send you a song to get you in the mood for the ball game tonight! Well, that is, if you get to your e-mail before leaving. Enjoy your time there tonight!

—Susan

Saturday, June 8, 2013, at 9:19 a.m.
From: Dave
Subject: Wonderful Pennsylvania smokin'-hot chick o' mine…

Wonderful Susan, ah, bless you! What a great surprise! I just now go to it: Saturday at nine five in the morning.

Missed our extended time together, but our short chat got me through, and I did have a good time with our great church house folks, as usual. That being said, our beloved hometown Bats did go down in defeat 1 against 2, but the ambiance was nice! So was the fun video you sent me! Thank you!

I hope and trust that the rest of your night went well.

Also, be ye warned that Ye' Ol' Church House crew is still trying their best to get me to go to Turkey with them this October, having now ramped it up a bit to: "Hey, here's an idea: you"—meaning me—"could take the Pennsylvania smokin'-hot chick with you!" This is coming because they know that you have previously gone on mission trips out of our homeland. So…be prepared for them!

Hope you have a great Saturday as well as Sunday. Of course, now they probably mean very little to you since you have the entire rest of the summer off to lounge around the pool and eat bonbons!

Talk to you tonight! Take care!

—Dave

Saturday, June 8, 2013, at 9:23 a.m.
From: Dave
Subject: Wonderful Pennsylvania smokin'-hot chick match o' mine…

Wonderful Susan, see, 'twas meant to be!

—Dave

------------ Forwarded Message ------------

From: HisMatchForMe
Date: Saturday, June 8, 2013, at 12:03 a.m.
Subject: New matches from His Match for Me.com
To: Dave

You have one match. See all matches.

Teachgems
Active within: 24 hours

Teachgems age: 59, female, I am a born-again Christian schoolteacher who lives Phoenixville, Pennsylvania, and teaches the most adorable third graders one could ever ask for. Friends and family have described me as very warm and friendly. I love to laugh (giggle), as my sister would say. I enjoy life and my students…

Ideal match: 98 percent

Compatibility: 93 percent

Sunday, June 23, 2013, at 9:32 p.m.
From: Susan

Had my phone with me as I went to the grocery store with my sister Carol. This was taken off the front porch [photo of the sunset]

—Your SMHC

Sunday, June 23, 2013, at 9:50 p.m.
From: Dave
Subject: Ah…

Susan, straight from the paintbrush of the Almighty! *Beautiful!* Granted, no doubt not as wonderful as a certain Pennsylvania smokin'-hot chick! But still beautiful!

Have a fun-filled, *great* vacation with the family and friends! And as you well know by now, I wish on God's very *best* for my very special Susan! Sweet dreams! Take care!

—Dave

Monday, June 24, 2013, at 5:28 p.m.
From: Dave
Subject: The early bird gets the fire…

Wonderful Pennsylvania smokin'-hot chick, got the beach picture! *Nice!* Hope you and the others are having a *great* time!

Hate to do this to you but…it is going to have to be an early night for me. I'm kinda running on empty. My day started off with a four-thirty-in-the-morning wake-up call to a tractor fire.

Feel free to call me if you want, but if not, don't fret it. Still, you *know* I would *love* to talk to you, even if for only a short time!

Take care for now, and may our dear Savior bless you and your family and friends!

—Dave

Monday, June 24, 2013, at 8:45 p.m.
From: Susan

My nephew, Ethan, and I outside the pizza place we ate at tonight. [photos attached]

—Susan

Tuesday, June 25, 2013, at 9:00 p.m.
From: Dave
Subject: Have you seen…

Pennsylvania smokin'-hot beach bunny o' mine? Well? Have you seen Sally yet? How about Waldo? At any rate, it sure looks like you are all having a great time! I'm so happy for all of you!

And...wonder of wonders, today I got not one but several e-mails from the Pennsylvania smokin'-hot beach bunny! They made my evening...and with photos! Thank you!

I did go to bed around seven o'clock last night, got up around ten o'clock in the evening, dozed in and out of sleep with the TV on in the living room, and gave up and went back to bed around one o'clock in the morning with *no* late-night or early-morning calls!

Well...have another great night, and as always, I pray for only God's very, very best for you and your family! Take care!

—Dave

Wednesday, June 26, 2013, at 7:53 p.m.
From: Dave
Subject: Pennsylvania smokin'-hot beach bunny at sunset...

Susan, love all of them! The sunset photo from yesterday was beautiful!

It rained something fierce a couple of times today. I started my day off in a different part of Louisville around six thirty in the morning investigating a collision in which a pickup truck hit a large puddle of water on the interstate, hydroplaned into the center wall, bounced off into the side of our trailer, bounced off it, and ended up perched on the same wall.

Hope you and your family continue to have a great time together!

As always, wish all y'll only God's very, very best! Call if you can, but if not, don't fret it. Take care for now!

—Dave

Friday, June 28, 2013, at 9:16 p.m.
From: Dave
Subject: Pennsylvania smokin'-hot beach bunny…

Susan, so sorry about not getting back with you quicker. Davey Boy came back last night, and I was pretty much beaten from work, so I didn't even open up my e-mail account last night. Tonight I'm up and at 'em and having to return a bunch of e-mails, including yours.

I'm about to get my butt blistered once again by my old high school teacher in chess. He is a pawn up on me near the end of the game. I will keep playing for a bit to see if he messes it up, but I doubt it.

I thoroughly enjoyed the photos! You're right! Fabulous sunsets…and creepy crawly critters! So did you get to drive the boat?

And *congratulations* on winning the Putt-Putt Crown!

And great to have the weekend start up again! And one week closer to my landing on Pennsylvania turf!

I'm so happy for you having such a great time with your family, et al!

Please call if you can, but if not, that's okay.

May our dear Lord continue to watch over all of you! Take care for now!

—Dave

Sunday, June 30, 2013, at 1:44 p.m.
From: Susan

Hi, Dave,

This picture is of my baby brother and me taken this morning.

Got a few questions for you. I know we discussed my favorite color, but what is your favorite color?

Also, what is your favorite book of the Bible and why?

Rainy and then some breaks here today.

It was good talking with you last night. ☺

—Your SHBB

Sunday, June 30, 2013, at 8:50 p.m.
From: Dave
Subject: Pennsylvania smokin'-hot beach bunny

Susan, sorry 'tis a bit late, but here I am!

The photo was pretty good, but a bit dark.

Favorite color: Bright but a deeper shade of green. A lot like the darker shades of green in a forest on a sunny day.

Favorite Bible book: Hmmmm…that would be hard to say as it would depend on so many variables—my mood for the moment, the circumstances surrounding my life at the moment, etc. Since they speak to so much of life, I don't think I can really select only one and be either fair or completely honest with any answer. With that as a backdrop, I suppose if I was boxed in and absolutely had to give an answer, I would go with the Gospel of John since, after all, all the Bible and life, for that matter, is pretty much about him [Jesus]!

And you?

Sweet dreams and take care for tonight! As always, I wish only God's very best for you and your family!

—Dave

Monday, July 1, 2013, at 12:25 p.m.
From: Susan

Dave, ah, no problem. I would ring you and see if you could talk. Yes, I realize the photo was a bit dark, but at the time, it was the best I could do. How was your day at work today?

Deep green is a very nice color. My colors are bright, vivid colors that pop. Like the bright blues, orange, green, purple, fuchsia, etc.

My favorite books are Esther or Ruth from the Old Testament and Philippians from the New Testament. I enjoy the story of Ruth because she became queen for such a time as this, and she was very brave and wise. I love telling the story of Esther to my students. I also love the book of Ruth because of the kinsman redeemer and because it is a sweet love story. I love the book of Philippians because it has many practical concepts in it. Of course, Psalms and Proverbs are right there in my list.

Late this afternoon, my nephew, Jesse, is coming. He is Carol's son who is a senior in college this next year. He took a week off work to come. My niece, Kaley, who is Carol's daughter and a nurse in Virginia, is coming tonight to surprise my mom. She will be staying for two or three days. Carol's friend from college and her husband will be here for a night and one day before heading up to visit their family in northern Pennsylvania. So all that to say, I might not be able to call you tonight, depending on what we are all doing, but you never know. ☺

I have been trying to take a morning walk each morning around nine-ish. I missed yesterday when my brother's family was here. Today, I took my walk, five blocks down, and was on my way back to the house when it started to rain. By the time I got back to the house, I was drenching wet. It actually felt refreshing because it was so muggy out.

Well, I guess that is all for now. It has now stopped raining but very cloudy out and still muggy.

Talk soon.

Your SHBB,
Susan

Monday, July 1, 2013, at 6:38 p.m.
From: Dave
Subject: Pennsylvania smokin'-hot beach bunny bearing sweet gifts

Hello, PASHBBBSG!

Yep! Your sweet present arrived today and was a *hit* with Davey Boy and me! Greg is not a fan of the saltwater [taffy] other than to fish! Both of us had a couple of pieces, and it was *delicious*! *Thank you* ever so much!

I'm so very happy for all of you to have such a good time together.

I'm sorry to tell you that we are unfortunately sending yet more rain your way. We tried getting out the *big* fans to blow it northwest but couldn't get the job done. Sorry about that!

So…get out the ol' yellow rubber galoshes and hooded raincoats and leave the umbrellas and golf clubs at home! I don't want to end up with a crispy fried PASHBBBSG! Whew! I don't know what I'm going to do if your name keeps growing looonger!

On the work front, my little college intern started today. He's all excited to have landed a "big-league job"! Of course, it's just temporary, but a great starting point for him!

Call if you can, but if not, 'tis okay! Have a great time!

And, 'til next time, as always, only God's very, very BEST for YOU and your family!

Take care for now!

—Dave

Tuesday, July 2, 2013, at 3:44 p.m.
From: Susan

Ohhhhh my, you did it again. Wow and wow! Apparently, the florist had called yesterday and left a message, but no one here at the house checked messages. I happened to be home alone for an hour today, and the florist called again. He also said the street Shore Drive was not on there, so he investigated and found the right street. The house number and phone number were correct.

They are so beautiful. Thank you! You are so thoughtful and sweet! Can't wait to hear everyone's reaction when they come back.

—Your SHBB

Tuesday, July 2, 2013, at 6:05 p.m.
From: Dave
Subject: Pennsylvania smokin'-hot flower child beach bunny bearing sweet gifts…

Susan, so glad you liked it! When I got the taffy, I had high hopes you would have gotten the flowers that day as well.

Hope you had a great day and a better tomorrow! Call if you can, but if not, 'tis okay. Enjoy your time with the family!

For now, take care, and may our dear Savior bless you *all*!

—Dave

Wednesday, July 3, 2013, at 9:50 p.m.
From: Susan

Nice fireworks

Thursday, July 4, 2013, at 1:12 p.m.
From: Dave

Susan, happy July 4 to you as well! Nice photo!

Last night, I got home later as I stopped off at Ye Ol' Church House where we held a sandwich and salad (which turned out to be sandwich and fruit) dinner for James and Jen who head up a Nashville, Tennessee, mission for the Kurds. They used to attend our church, and although I had heard about them, prayed for them, etc., I had never actually met them in person. It was great to actually meet them, and I was surprised that they were both quite young—I'd guess midtwenties—and James has a master's degree in theology and is a *fabulous* preacher! In short, it was *great*!

Please give me a yelp if you can, but if not, it's okay.

As always, here's to wishing God's very, very best to you and your family! Take care!

—Dave

Thursday, July 4, 2013, at 11:01 p.m.
From: Susan

Thanks, Dave! Lol! Ahh, I see you added more names in the subject line. I can't even keep up with them. ☺ But I love them!

The sandwich and fruit dinner sounds like it was a lot of fun. Glad you got to meet J and J. Yes, I see on the radar map that you all have the rain there, and it should be coming our way by Sunday or Monday. Our last few days here look rain free. ☺

We saw Kaley off on the ferry this afternoon. It was great having her here for two days. After she got off the ferry in Lewis, Delaware, she had to drive the five hours back to Virginia.

My sister, Janice, and her husband are leaving tomorrow. Carol's husband who has not been here yet is coming tomorrow after work and will stay till Sunday.

Have a great day tomorrow. But at least it is just one day then the weekend.

—Susan ☺

Friday, July 5, 2013, at 5:13 p.m.
From: Dave
Subject: Pennsylvania smokin'-hot beach bunny bearing gifts fire-crackin' flower child o' mine...

Susan, yep, work was nice today! With half the workforce taking off, there was very little traffic either morning or afternoon. In addition, my boss came around about two o'clock in the afternoon to proclaim that she was going home and anyone else was welcome to depart as well. I was in the middle of a project, so I left around four o'clock in the afternoon, which was lovely!

So glad that you have been having such a great time with the family!

Well, I guess the countdown has begun for the touchdown of Indiana Jones on Pennsylvania turf!

Once again, I'm sad to report that we are yet again sending you more rain! Otherwise, I do hope you and your family have a wonderful Fourth o' July and weekend as well.

Call if you can, but if not, have a tremendous vacation! Take care for now!

—Dave

Saturday, July 6, 2013, at 7:39 p.m.
From: Susan

Picture of the store at historical Cold Spring Village. At least they had air conditioner inside. Ninety-one degrees here today.

Saturday, July 7, 2013, at 3:50 p.m.
From: Dave
Subject: Country bumpkin fire-workin' Pennsylvania smokin'-hot beach bunny bearing gifts…

Susan, nice to know that y'all had a place to get some vitals and stay cool!

Hope you had a nice ride home!

Wish you all God's very best!

—Dave

Wednesday, August 14, 2013, at 1:57 p.m.
From: Susan

Hi, Dave,

This is the bookcase in my classroom.. Notice the ocean theme?

Hope you had a good day.

—SHC in Pennsylvania

Wednesday, August 14, 2013, at 8:04 p.m.
From: Dave

Nice!

Wednesday, August 14, 2013, at 8:06 p.m.
From: Dave
Subject: Deep down in the ocean…

Pennsylvania smokin'-hot chick, I assume, of course, that you will be wearing your mermaid outfit on opening day!

—Dave

Sunday, October 13, 2013, at 8:52 a.m.
From: Dave

♡ *I love you!* ♡

Sunday, October 13, 2013, at 12:19 p.m.
From: Susan

Awww, what a way to make a girl's heart swoon! Thank you!

I have been waiting a long time to tell my beloved this poem. Here it is for you.

I wrote your name on a piece of paper but by accident I threw it away.

I wrote your name on my hand but it washed away.

I wrote your name in the sky but it faded away.

I wrote your name in the sand but the waves whispered it away.

I wrote your name in my heart and forever it will stay!

I don't know who wrote the poem, but I have kept it on a piece of paper for just the right guy.

[by Ashley Kanapaux, October 20, 2006]

Sunday, October 13, 2013, at 12:34 p.m.
From: Dave
Subject: Happy Sunday!

Thank you! Talk to you later this afternoon!

Love,
Dave

Tuesday, October 15, 2013, at 8:53 a.m.
From: Susan

Hi, babe!

Fog this morning driving to school. Most mornings in October are foggy.

XOXO,
Your wife-to-be

Tuesday, October 15, 2013, at 7:27 p.m.
From: Dave
Subject: Wow! Please be careful!

Wonderful wife-to-be,
Please be careful! I worked far too hard to hook ya!

Love,
Dave

APPENDIX C

Recommended Reading List

Dave's List

Dobson, James. *Life on the Edge.* (Written for sixteen- to twenty-six-year-olds or older.)

Dobson, James. *When God Doesn't Make Sense.* (A great resource prior to experiencing a tragedy in life.)

Gonzalez, Guillermo and Jay Richards. *The Privileged Planet.* (Come and watch the authors demonstrate that of all the multitudes of planets in our universe, Earth alone is positioned in such a fashion to allow us to have a "window" through which to explore God's wonders of the universe.)

Hanegraaff, Hank. *The Face that Demonstrates the Farce of Evolution.* (See Hank Hanegraaff demonstrate how modern advances in science have demonstrated that the Darwinian evolutionary theory taught as fact in our public schools completely crumbles under the weight of the evidence to the contrary.)

Stein, Ben. *Expelled: No Intelligence Allowed.* (See Ben Stein expose the modern US school system, including colleges, for their active prevention of the free and open exchange of thoughts and ideas by both students and faculty in our schools.

Strobel, Lee. *The Case for a Creator.* (Accompany atheist reporter Lee Strobel on his global research to disprove the validity of Christianity.)

Strobel, Lee. *The Case for Christ.*

Strobel, Lee. *The Case for Faith.*

Susan's List

Chapman, Gary. *The Five Love Languages.*
Eldredge, John and Stasi. *Captivating.*
Elliott, Elizabeth. *Passion and Purity.*
Harper, Lisa. *What Every Girl Wants.*
Kent, Carol. *Secret Passions of the Christian Woman.*
Nelson, Tommy. *The Book of Romance.*

Websites

www.bible.org (The Bible)
www.christiancafe.com
www.christianmingle.com
www.eharmony.com
https://www.5lovelanguages.com/ *The Five Love Languages* by Gary Chapman
www.hismatchforme.com (Dating Site where Dave and Susan met.)
www.prageru.com (Prager University—five-minute videos teaching truths that are rarely taught.)

Movies

www.youtube.com/watch?v=99bbBKSrZfE *The Case for Christ* by Lee Strobel
https://www.youtube.com/watch?v=ajqH4y8G0MI *The Case for a Creator*
https://www.youtube.com/watch?v=vaQxCyoalJQ *The Case for Faith"*
https://www.youtube.com/watch?v=Y57VUN2TO5M *The Case for Miracles*
https://www.youtube.com/watch?v=V5EPymcWp-g *Expelled: No Intelligence Allowed* by Ben Stein
https://www.youtube.com/watch?v=QmIc42oRjm8 *The Privileged Planet* by Guillermo Gonzalez and Jay Richards

Radio Shows

The Salem Radio Network, featuring:
Mike Gallagher
Dennis Prager
Larry Evans
Sebastian Gorka
New Life Live

APPENDIX D

Bible Notes

Dave

I have found over the course of my life that the Bible truly is not only the very Word of God but also his instruction manual to guide us through our lives while on this earth so that we may have an eternity with him, which is his ultimate desire for us. However, one thing that has troubled me all my life is that some Christians have a tendency to quickly reference one verse of the Bible here and one there. Admittedly, sometimes that is just fine. However, in many cases, the quick-fix verse is often taken out of context and has little, if anything, to do with the subject matter. I also readily admit that I am very poor at rote memorization of almost anything. Frankly, I have never seen a need for it. I've always felt that was the reason most books have a handy glossary, index, table of contents, etc. As long as I knew what book something was in, I could always find it. Accordingly, in the following, we've provided Bible notes in which we've referenced key verses that have been helpful to us in our own lives. But we also wanted to encourage you to research further the full context in which it was written.

General key and topic verses brief description

Seek God:

> So I say to you: Ask and it will be given to you; seek and you will find; knock and the door will be opened to you. (Luke 11:9)

> You will seek me [God] and find me when you seek me with all your heart. (Jeremiah 29:13)

> The God who made the world and everything in it is the Lord of heaven and earth and does not live in temples built by human hands. And he is not served by human hands, as if he needed anything. Rather, he himself gives everyone life and breath and everything else. From one man he made all the nations, that they should inhabit the whole earth; and he marked out their appointed times in history and the boundaries of their lands. God did this so that they would seek him and perhaps reach out for him and find him, though he is not far from any one of us. (Acts 17:24–27)

God's plan for your life:

> "For I know the plans I have for you," declares the LORD, "plans to prosper you and not to harm you, plans to give you hope and a future." (Jeremiah 29:11)

Creation:

> God saw all that he had made, and it was very good. And there was evening, and there was morning—the sixth day. (Genesis 1:31)

Creation of man:

> Then the LORD God formed a man from the dust of the ground and breathed into his nostrils the breath of life, and the man became a living being. (Genesis 2:7)

The garden of Eden:

> Now the LORD God had planted a garden in the east, in Eden; and there he put the man he had formed. The LORD God made all kinds of trees grow out of the ground—trees that were pleasing to the eye and good for food. In the middle of the garden were the tree of life and the tree of the knowledge of good and evil. (Genesis 2:8–9)

First Commandment:

> The LORD God took the man and put him in the Garden of Eden to work it and take care of it. And the LORD God commanded the man, "You are free to eat from any tree in the garden; but you must not eat from the tree of the knowledge of good and evil, for when you eat from it you will certainly die." (Genesis 2:15–17)

Creation of woman:

> The LORD God said, "It is not good for the man to be alone. I will make a helper suitable for him." Now the LORD God had formed out of the ground all the wild animals and all the birds in the sky. He brought them to the man to see what he would name them; and whatever the man called each living creature, that was its name. So the man gave names to all the livestock, the birds in the sky and all the wild animals. But for Adam no suitable helper was found. So the LORD God caused the man to fall into a deep sleep; and while he was sleeping, he took one of the man's ribs and then closed up the place with flesh. Then the LORD God made a woman from the rib he had taken out of the man, and he brought her to the man. The man said, "This is now bone of my bones and flesh of my flesh; she shall be called 'woman,' for she was taken out of man." (Genesis 2:18–23)

First marriage:

> That is why a man leaves his father and mother and is united to his wife and they become one flesh. Adam and his wife were both naked, and they felt no shame. (Genesis 2:24–25)

First sin:

> Now the serpent was more crafty than any of the animals the LORD God had made. He said to the woman, "Did God really say, 'You must not eat from *any* tree in the garden'?" The woman said to the serpent, "We may eat fruit from the

> trees in the garden, but God did say, 'You must not eat fruit from the tree that is in the middle of the garden, and you must not touch it, or you will die.'" "You will *not* certainly die," the serpent said to the woman. "For God knows that when you eat from it your eyes will be opened, and you will be like God, knowing good and evil." When the woman saw that the fruit of the tree was good for food and pleasing to the eye, and also desirable for gaining wisdom, she took some and ate it. She also gave some to her husband, who was with her, and he ate it. Then the eyes of both of them were opened, and they realized they were naked; so they sewed fig leaves together and made coverings for themselves. Then the man and his wife heard the sound of the LORD God as was walking in the garden in the cool of the day, and they hid from the LORD God among the trees of the garden. But the LORD God called to the man, "Where are you?" He answered, "I heard you in the garden, and I was afraid because I was naked; so I hid." And he said, "Who told you that you were naked? Have you eaten from the tree that I commanded you not to eat from?" The man said, "The woman you put here with me—she gave me some fruit from the tree, and I ate it." (Genesis 3:1–12, emphasis added)

Wickedness on earth:

> The LORD saw how great the wickedness of the human race had become on the earth, and that every inclination of the thoughts of the human heart was only evil all the time. The LORD regretted that he had made human beings on the earth, and his heart was deeply troubled. So the

> Lord said, "I will wipe from the face of the earth the human race I have created—and with them the animals, the birds and the creatures that move along the ground—for I regret that I have made them." But Noah found favor in the eyes of the Lord. (Genesis 6:5–8)

No one is good:

> Man's evil heart from childhood…(Genesis 8:21)

> There is no one righteous, not even one; there is no one who understands; there is no one who seeks God. All have turned away, they have together become worthless; there is no one who does good, not even one. (Romans 3:11–12)

Animals on Noah's ark:

> The Lord then said to Noah, "Go into the ark, you and your whole family because I have found you righteous in this generation. Take with you seven pairs of every kind of clean animal, a male and its mate, and one pair of every kind of unclean animal, a male and its mate, and also seven pairs of every kind of bird, male and female, to keep their various kinds alive throughout the earth. Seven days from now I will send rain on the earth for forty days and forty nights, and I will wipe from the face of the earth every living creature I have made." And Noah did all that the Lord commanded him. (Genesis 7:1–5)

The Ten Commandments:

> And God spoke all these words: "I am the Lord your God, who brought you out of Egypt, out of the land of slavery. You shall have no other gods before me. You shall not make for yourself an image [of God] in the form of anything in heaven above or on the earth beneath or in the waters below. You shall not bow down to them or worship them; for I, the Lord your God, am a jealous God, punishing the children for the sin of the parents to the third and fourth generation of those who hate me, but showing love to a thousand generations of those who love me and keep my commandments. You shall not misuse the name of the Lord your God, for the Lord will not hold anyone guiltless who misuses his name. Remember the Sabbath day by keeping it holy. Six days you shall labor and do all your work, but the seventh day is a sabbath to the Lord your God. On it you shall not do any work, neither you, nor your son or daughter, nor your male or female servant, nor your animals, nor any foreigner residing in your towns. For in six days the Lord made the heavens and the earth, the sea, and all that is in them, but he rested on the seventh day. Therefore the Lord blessed the Sabbath day and made it holy. Honor your father and your mother, so that you may live long in the land the Lord your God is giving you. You shall not murder. You shall not commit adultery. You shall not steal. You shall not give false testimony [lie] against your neighbor. You shall not covet your neighbor's house. You shall not covet your neighbor's wife, or his male or female servant, his

> ox or donkey, or anything that belongs to your neighbor." (Exodus 20:1–17)

Jesus, our Lord and Savior:

> In the beginning was the Word [Jesus], and the Word was with God, and the Word was God. He was with God in the beginning. Through him all things were made; without him nothing was made that has been made. In him was life, and that life was the light [Jesus] of all mankind. The light shines in the darkness, and the darkness has not overcome it. There was a man sent from God whose name was John. He came as a witness to testify concerning that light, so that through him all might believe. He himself was not the light; he came only as a witness to the light. The true light that gives light to everyone was coming into the world. He was in the world, and though the world was made through him, the world did not recognize him. He came to that which was his own, but his own did not receive him. Yet to all who did receive him, to those who believed in his name, he gave the right to become children of God—children born not of natural descent, nor of human decision or a husband's will, but born of God. The Word became flesh and made his dwelling among us. We have seen his glory, the glory of the one and only Son, who came from the Father, full of grace and truth. (John testified concerning him. He cried out, saying, "This is the one I spoke about when I said, 'He who comes after me has surpassed me because he was before me.'") Out of his fullness we have all received grace in place of grace already given.

> For the law was given through Moses; grace and truth came through Jesus Christ. No one has ever seen God, but the one and only Son, who is himself God and is in closest relationship with the Father, has made him known…(John 1 entire chapter)

Salvation through faith:

> But now apart from the law the righteousness of God has been made known, to which the Law and the Prophets testify. This righteousness is given through faith in Jesus Christ to all who believe. There is no difference between Jew and Gentile, for all have sinned and fall short of the glory of God, and all are justified freely by his grace through the redemption that came by Christ Jesus. God presented Christ as a sacrifice of atonement, through the shedding of his blood—to be received by faith. (Romans 3:21–25)

> For God so loved the world that he gave his one and only Son, that whoever believes in him shall not perish but have eternal life. For God did not send his Son into the world to condemn the world, but to save the world through him. Whoever believes in him is not condemned, but whoever does not believe stands condemned already because they have not believed in the name of God's one and only Son… Whoever believes in the Son has eternal life, but whoever rejects the Son will not see life, for God's wrath remains on them. (John 3:16–18, 36)

Jesus alone is the *only* way to heaven:

> Jesus answered, "I am *the* way and *the* truth and *the* life. *No one* comes to the Father *except* through me." (John 14:6, emphasis added)

The eternal question:

> Jesus and his disciples went on to the villages around Caesarea Philippi. On the way he asked them, "*Who* do people say *I am*?" (Mark 8:27, emphasis added)

Persecution of Christians:

> In fact, everyone who wants to live a godly life in Christ Jesus will be persecuted...(2 Timothy 3:12)

Signs of the last days:

> But mark this: There will be terrible times in the last days. People will be lovers of themselves, lovers of money, boastful, proud, abusive, disobedient to their parents, ungrateful, unholy, without love, unforgiving, slanderous, without self-control, brutal, not lovers of the good, treacherous, rash, conceited, lovers of pleasure rather than lovers of God—having a form of godliness but denying its power. (2 Timothy 3:1–5)

Life is short:

> Your life is a mist that appears for a little while and then vanishes. (James 4:14)

> Man's days are determined; You [God] have decreed the number of his months and have set limits he cannot exceed. (Job 14:5)

> Show me, O Lord, my life's end and the number of my days; let me know how fleeting is my life. [Val's earthly days were numbered at 20,336. How many will you have?] (Psalm 39:4)

Second coming of Jesus:

> Then will appear the sign of the Son of Man [Jesus] in heaven. And then all the peoples of the earth will mourn when they see the Son of Man coming on the clouds of heaven, with power and great glory. And he will send his angels with a loud trumpet call, and they will gather his elect from the four winds, from one end of the heavens to the other. Now learn this lesson from the fig tree: As soon as its twigs get tender and its leaves come out, you know that summer is near. Even so, when you see all these things, you know that it is near, right at the door. Truly I tell you, this generation will certainly not pass away until all these things have happened. Heaven and earth will pass away, but my words will never pass away. But about that day or hour no one knows, not even the angels in heaven, nor the Son, but *only* the Father. As it was in the days of Noah, so it will be at the coming of the Son of Man. For in the days before the flood, people were eating and drinking, marrying and giving in marriage, up to the day Noah entered the ark; and they knew nothing about what would happen until the flood came and took them all away. That is how it will be at the coming of the Son

> of Man. Two men will be in the field; one will be taken and the other left. Two women will be grinding with a hand mill; one will be taken and the other left. Therefore keep watch because you do not know on what day your Lord will come. But understand this: If the owner of the house had known at what time of night the thief was coming, he would have kept watch and would not have let his house be broken into. So you also must be ready because the Son of Man will come at an hour when you do not expect him. (Matthew 24:30–44, emphasis added)

Pray persistently:

> Then Jesus told his disciples a parable to show them that they should always pray and not give up…(Luke 18:1–8)

Protection of God:

> Be strong and take heart, all you who hope in the LORD. (Psalm 31:24)

> I will say of the LORD, "He is my refuge and my fortress, my God, in whom I trust." (Psalm 91:2)

Wait patiently on the Lord God:

> I wait for the LORD, my whole being waits, and in his word I put my hope. I wait for the Lord more than watchmen wait for the morning…(Psalm 130:5–6)

Waiting with expectation:

> Hope deferred makes the heart sick, but a longing fulfilled is a tree of life. (Proverbs 13:12)

Love:

> Love is patient, love is kind. It does not envy, it does not boast, it is not proud. It does not dishonor others, it is not self-seeking, it is not easily angered, it keeps no record of wrongs. Love does not delight in evil but rejoices with the truth. It always protects, always trusts, always hopes, always perseveres… And now these three remain: faith, hope and love. But the greatest of these is love. (1 Corinthians 13:4–13)

Faith:

> Now faith is confidence in what we hope for and assurance about what we do not see… since God had planned something better for us so that only together with us would they be made perfect. (Hebrews 11)
>
> "Do you now believe?" Jesus replied. "A time is coming and in fact has come when you will be scattered, each to your own home. You will leave me all alone. Yet I am not alone, for my Father is with me. I have told you these things, so that in me you may have peace. In this world you will have trouble. But take heart! I have overcome the world." (John 16:31–33)

Hannah's prayer:

> Because the LORD had closed Hannah's womb, her rival kept provoking her in order to irritate her. This went on year after year… In her deep anguish Hannah prayed to the LORD, weeping bitterly. And she made a vow, saying, "LORD Almighty, if you will only look on your servant's misery and remember me, and not forget your servant but give her a son, then I will give him to the LORD for all the days of his life… So in the course of time Hannah became pregnant and gave birth to a son. She named him Samuel, saying, "Because I asked the LORD for him." (1 Samuel 1:6–19)

Eternal life:

> Then Jesus declared… "For my Father's will is that everyone who looks to the Son and believes in him shall have eternal life, and I will raise them up at the last day." (John 6:35–40)

> Jesus answered, "I am the way and the truth and the life. *No one* comes to the Father except through me. If you really know me, you will know my Father as well…" (John 14:6–7, emphasis added)

Judging others:

> Do not judge, or you too will be judged. For in the same way you judge others, you will be judged, and with the measure you use, it will be measured to you. Why do you look at the speck of sawdust in your brother's eye and pay

> no attention to the plank in your own eye? How can you say to your brother, "Let me take the speck out of your eye," when all the time there is a plank in your own eye? You hypocrite, first take the plank out of your own eye, and then you will see clearly to remove the speck from your brother's eye. (Matthew 7:1–5)

Seek Jesus:

> Ask and it will be given to you; seek and you will find; knock and the door will be opened to you… Enter through the narrow gate [Jesus]. For wide is the gate and broad is the road that leads to destruction, and many enter through it. But small is the gate and narrow the road that leads to life, and only a few find it. (Matthew 7:7–14)

> Whoever is not with me is against me, and whoever does not gather with me scatters. (Luke 11:23)

False preachers:

> Watch out for false prophets. They come to you in sheep's clothing, but inwardly they are ferocious wolves. By their fruit you will recognize them. Do people pick grapes from thorn bushes, or figs from thistles? Likewise, every good tree bears good fruit, but a bad tree bears bad fruit. A good tree cannot bear bad fruit, and a bad tree cannot bear good fruit. Every tree that does not bear good fruit is cut down and thrown into the fire. Thus, by their fruit you will recognize them. (Matthew 7:15–20)

Self-righteous people:

> Not everyone who says to me, "Lord, Lord," will enter the kingdom of heaven, but only the one who does the will of my Father who is in heaven. Many will say to me on that day, "Lord, Lord, did we not prophesy in your name and in your name drive out demons and in your name perform many miracles?" Then I will tell them plainly, "I never knew you. Away from me, you evildoers!" Therefore everyone who hears these words of mine and puts them into practice is like a wise man who built his house on the rock. The rain came down, the streams rose, and the winds blew and beat against that house; yet it did not fall because it had its foundation on the rock. But everyone who hears these words of mine and does not put them into practice is like a foolish man who built his house on sand. The rain came down, the streams rose, and the winds blew and beat against that house, and it fell with a great crash. (Matthew 7:21–27)

Speaking in tongues:

> Everything must be done so that the church may be built up. If anyone speaks in a tongue, two—or at the most three—should speak, one at a time, and someone must interpret. If there is no interpreter, the speaker should keep quiet in the church and speak to himself and to God. (1 Corinthians 14:26–28)

Traits of God defined

Omnificent—(adjective) unlimited in creative power

Omnipotent—(adjective) almighty: having complete or unlimited power

Omnipresent—(adjective) present in all places at all times

Omniscient—(adjective) knowing everything: having unlimited understanding or knowledge

ABOUT THE AUTHORS

Coauthors, Dave and Susan, met online and married in 2013.

Dave grew up in St. Louis, Missouri, and is the father of two grown and married sons. His oldest son met online and married his own wonderful wife from Indonesia. They gave Dave and Susan two grandsons. During Dave's career path as a long-term transportation safety professional, he has driven every type of vehicle from a motorcycle to a bus and tractor trailer.

Susan grew up in Harrisburg, Pennsylvania, and spent a couple of years during her early childhood in Texas before moving back to Pennsylvania. She graduated from Liberty University with a degree in elementary education and worked as a teacher of primarily third grade students in several schools for thirty-six years.

Dave and Susan are now retired and reside in Southern Indiana. This is the first book that either of them has written. They hope you enjoy walking with them through the pages of this book as they share with you some of the intimate memories that they have of this first part of their eternal grand adventure.

CPSIA information can be obtained
at www.ICGtesting.com
Printed in the USA
BVHW081133030121
596789BV00008B/27/J